Teacher-Student Relationships

Causes and Consequences

JERE E. BROPHY
The University of Texas at Austin

THOMAS L. GOOD
The University of Missouri

HOLT, RINEHART AND WINSTON, INC.
New York   Chicago   San Francisco   Atlanta
Dallas   Montreal   Toronto   London   Sydney

Library of Congress Cataloging in Publication Data

Brophy, Jere E.
   Teacher–Student Relationships:
      Causes and Consequences

1. Teacher-student relationships.   2. Interaction
analysis in education.   3. Child study.   I. Good,
Thomas L., joint author.   II. Title.
[DNLM: 1. Child development.   2. Psychology,
Educational.   3. Students.   LB1051 B873i 1974]
LB1033.B67   371.1'02   73-14740
ISBN 0-03-085749-X

To our wives, Arlene and Suzi.

Preface

This book is about the kinds of individual differences in students that make differential impressions upon teachers, the ways that such differential impressions lead teachers to form differential attitudes and expectations regarding different students, and the ways that these differential teacher attitudes and expectations begin to affect teacher–student interaction patterns. Attention will focus on several interrelated investigations by the authors and their colleagues, although the general literature relevant to these topics will be reviewed and discussed.

In the first chapter we will cite evidence showing that teachers behave quite differently toward different students in their classrooms, and that the treatment of some students is so consistently inappropriate as to erode their general confidence and aspirations. Also, we will argue that teachers hold different expectations for their students, and that these expectations influence the ways teachers and students interact. Further, it will be argued that to understand the psychological impact of schooling on individual students, it is necessary to observe teachers and students during their day-to-day activities in schools. In this preface, however, we will sketch in broad terms our reasons for writing this book and for why we think the information contained in it is important.

We, the authors, were motivated to embark on the series of investigations described in this book partly out of concern and partly out of interest. Before getting into the research itself, we wish to briefly describe this concern and interest. We do this partly as a service to readers, because we think information about our purpose and frame of reference in writing the book is important in reading and evaluating it. There is also a second, more personal reason, however: We hope to show that research conducted in ordinary classrooms and focused on the individual student is sorely needed, and therefore to motivate other educational researchers to do similar kinds of studies. Thus we see the book as an overview and impetus to expansion of a new field, as opposed to a text or review of well-established facts. The research to be described provides answers to many questions, but it raises far more questions than it answers.

We previously stated that we were motivated to get into this kind of research by both concern and interest. Our concern is the same one shared by many in our society, especially those involved in education. It is the knowledge that the schools are not doing the job they are supposed to be doing, at least with certain kinds of students. Too many students drop out of school as soon as they can do so legally, and many others are thrown out for truancy or for misbehavior in the classroom. Most of these students have found only continued failure and frustration in their school experience, so that school was a punishing environment to be escaped at the first opportunity. Hamachek (1972) provides an excellent analysis of school failure, reminding us that roughly one-third of the youngsters who enter first grade do not complete eleventh grade, even today.

Some information is available about who these students are. For example, they are more likely to be boys than girls, to be from lower class homes than middle or upper class homes, to be from broken homes rather than intact families, and to be low achievers rather than medium or high achievers. This is all common knowledge, and many other factors could have been added to the list. Yet, somehow, this information hasn't helped much in changing the situation.

There are also problems among those students who proceed smoothly through elementary and secondary school. Although these students conform to school demands sufficiently to stay out of serious trouble, relatively few appear to be truly happy, satisfied, or fulfilled in their school experience. They tend to see it as a negative experience to be endured, rather than as a positive experience providing opportunities and satisfactions. An especially common complaint is that the curriculum is not relevant to their needs or interests. Even students from middle and upper class homes have begun to drop out of secondary schools in increasing numbers, some for just a semester or two, and some for good.

What can be done to change this? Part of the answer, of course, lies in updating and otherwise improving curricula. Another part lies in improving teacher training, both at the preservice and inservice levels. We believe that the research to be described in this book is the kind of research that is needed for making improvements of the latter type. Books such as Jonathon Kozol's (1967) *Death at an Early Age*, as well as our own observations, have convinced us that, poor curricula notwithstanding, teachers themselves are frequently responsible for discouraging students by behaving in ways that cause student failure and frustration.

In observing and talking with teachers, however, we have become convinced that most instances of poor teaching, including most instances of grossly inappropriate behavior that might seem to stem from malice or callousness, are not done deliberately or even consciously by the teachers involved. They result from a combination of inadequate or inappropriate training, conditioning processes which cause bad teaching habits to become established and maintained, and the lack of adequate mechanisms for giving teachers feedback and helping them to change their behavior.

If it is true that much inappropriate teacher behavior results from inappropriate training and from lack of sufficient awareness, it follows that teachers will improve if given more appropriate training, and if mechanisms are developed to make them more aware of their classroom behavior. This is more easily said than done, however, for a variety of reasons. One major reason, in our opinion, is the lack of a data base sufficient to provide specific information in classrooms. Despite years of educational research, relatively little is known about the characteristics of effective teachers or the behaviors involved in effective teaching (Rosenshine, 1971; Dunkin and Biddle, 1974).

The problem becomes compounded when the need to individualize instruction to tailor it to individual students' needs and interests is taken into account. To do this, the teacher must know relevant facts about each individual student, and know how to adapt his general instructional style to meet each student's particular needs and interests. Research data to provide a basis for making recommendations about individualizing instruction are all but nonexistent, because, as we will explain more fully in Chapter 1, remarkably little research focusing on the individual student has been done. In fact, until very recently, there was practically no research focusing on the individual student in everyday, ordinary classrooms.

In addition to our belief that research on the individual student is needed to remedy school problems that are of concern to ourselves and others, we were also drawn to this area of research simply because we were interested in it. Much of this interest was sparked by the work of Dr. Philip Jackson of the University of Chicago, especially by his book *Life in Classrooms* (Jackson, 1968). This book, along with several other publications by Jackson and some of his students, demonstrates that "life in classrooms" is vastly different for different individuals in the same class. Works by Jackson and his colleagues have shown that some students interact very frequently with their teacher, while other students rarely do, and that some students are objects of their teacher's affection and interest, while others provoke mere indifference or even hostility. This led us to focus on the individual student as the object of analysis in our classroom research.

Jackson and his colleagues influenced us in another way, in that their research has been conducted largely in regular, ordinary classrooms at the elementary and secondary level. Too much educational research has been conducted in college classrooms or in microteaching or other special situations quite different from the ordinary elementary or secondary classroom. In addition, a large number of the studies that did involve ordinary classrooms were conducted in connection with special experimental programs (such as the introduction of a new curriculum), so that the teacher and student behavior being observed was probably not typical. Also, many of the teachers involved in previous educational research studies have been preservice student teachers, first year teachers, or teachers working in special experimental programs. In contrast, our research has been conducted in ordinary classrooms while teachers and students were engaged in typical, everyday activities.

Our initial research efforts in the classroom were in the area of teacher expectations and their communication to students. In the beginning we concentrated primarily upon attempting to identify the mechanisms by which teacher expectations for student performance could come to function as self-fulfilling prophecies. Our interests quickly broadened, however, because we began to see that teacher expectations are just one part of a much larger network of influences that shape teacher–child interaction. Our data and observations showed that the sex of the student and his behavioral characteristics were important predictors of teacher–student interaction patterns, and that teacher attitudes as well as teacher expectations often had predictable effects upon interaction patterns. Although certain aspects of classroom interaction are largely under the control of the teacher and affect all of the students (textbooks and teaching methods used, relative amount of lecture versus discussion, etc.), our classroom research led us to become increasingly impressed with and interested in the different patterns of interaction that teachers have with different students in their classrooms. These almost always show a wide range and many sharp contrasts, and many of them appear to be much more predictable from knowledge about the individual student than from knowledge about the teacher. Thus students shape teacher behavior at the same time that their own behavior is being influenced by the teacher.

There appear to be several reasons for this. First, we are continually impressed with the vast range of individual differences within classrooms, even those supposedly homogeneous because of *de facto* segregation and/or the use of tracking systems. Second, the complexity of the job demands that the teacher continually focus his attention on at least one thing while at the same time attempting to monitor events going on all over the classroom. As a result, few teachers are able to consciously monitor each individual student on a continuing basis and treat him in a deliberate, proactive manner. Instead, we find that most teachers are primarily reactive in their responses to students, often showing evidence that the students have shaped their behavior rather than vice versa. Thus, our original focus on teacher expectations has broadened to encompass the topics of group and individual differences among students which may cause teachers to form differential expectations or attitudes towards the students, and which then in turn might begin to function as self-fulfilling prophecies.

We believe that these group and individual differences among students are the key to understanding intra-classroom differences in teacher–student interaction patterns. Many patterns are understandable and predictable solely with knowledge of what the student is like, without complementary information about the teacher. However, teacher reactions to student individual differences are also important. Some teachers react more or less passively and predictably to whatever student behavior confronts them, so that their behavior is quite predictable from knowledge of student behavior. Other teachers find the time and methods needed to overcome the differential press presented to them by different students, so that their behavior is less conditioned by student behavior and they are more effective as change agents in working with the student. Still other teachers not only react but over-react to student differences, treating the students as even more different than they actually are. The expectations and attitudes of these teachers are most likely to function as self-fulfilling prophecies, since such teachers tend to develop simplistic and rigid stereotypes concerning students and are especially prone to react to stereotypes rather than to the students themselves, even when student behavior does not fit the stereotype.

This book is about some of the more important group and individual student differences that affect teachers. Much of our own research is included in it, but it has been integrated with the work of others dealing with related topics. In selecting topics for inclusion in the book, and in presenting our own research, we hope not only to provide information useful to teachers and classroom researchers, but also to stimulate fellow investigators to do more of the kind of research reviewed in this volume. In particular, we hope to see more research conducted in naturalistic, real-world classroom settings. Data presented here and elsewhere (Rosenshine, 1971; Dunkin and Biddle, 1974) have convinced us that the complexities of classroom life can be profitably investigated only in real-world settings. The simplicity and control achievable in simulation and laboratory settings come at too high a price: lack of generalizability to the classroom.

We also hope to see more research in which the investigator works cooperatively with the teacher, either by observing him naturalistically and then discussing classroom events with him, or by systematically trying out techniques and treatments for students and then evaluating their relative success. While this kind of research is difficult to conduct and does not allow for the kind of precise controls that are possible in the laboratory, we believe that ultimately it will prove to be the most viable method for accumulating information useful to teachers. Future teachers have long complained that the content of educational psychology is largely irrelevant to their needs. To the extent that this charge is valid, the problem is not in the quality of the information presented in these books; most of it is well substantiated by research. Instead, the problem is that most of this information is the wrong kind of information, information only indirectly relevant to the needs of teachers. Much of it is in the form of theoretical principles which are too general to be of use in particular cases or which have not been sufficiently tested outside of the laboratory for us to know whether or not they apply to the classroom.

The solution, obviously, lies in presenting information in a form that teachers can use. In many areas this is not possible at present, however, because the necessary underlying research has not been done. In our opinion, the greatest present need is for research carried out in classrooms similar or identical to those to which the researcher wishes to generalize his results. This means frequently using unorthodox designs and sacrificing experimental control for the sake of the generalizability (or "external validity," as it is sometimes called) of the results. This is no major sacrifice provided that the research is interrelated and programmatic, however, since replication over several studies rather than the elegance of the design of a single study is what ultimately determines the acceptability of scientific data.

Although the book reviews, analyzes, and integrates research findings, some of them of an intricate nature, we have made every effort to avoid jargon and to write with a readability that will appeal to a wide potential audience. Thus, although our primary audience is the graduate student interested in educational research, our hope and intention is that teachers and future teachers will read and benefit from the book also. We see it as a resource book and teaching vehicle for graduate courses in educational research, educational psychology, social psychology, school psychology, educational supervision, and related areas, and in undergraduate teacher preparation courses. It brings together much of the psychological research that has been conducted in classroom settings, and in particular almost all of the available research on intraclass group and individual differences among students as they affect classroom interaction patterns. In addition to the variety of information presented, the book contains examples of several different types of research designs, providing grist for the mill of those who wish to approach it from a more methodological orientation. In undergraduate teacher education courses, we believe that the book will be especially useful in educational psychology courses and student teaching courses or other courses in which the future teacher gets an opportunity to interact with students and to receive feedback from a supervisor.

Data from studies conducted by ourselves and our colleagues are scattered throughout the book and integrated with those of other investigators. Because of the topical organization, data originally collected by ourselves or our colleagues in a single study are sometimes presented in two or three different places in the book. Furthermore, in the interest of readability, the data presented in tables are simplified and selective, reflecting only statistically significant findings or findings of greatest relevance to the topic at hand. Thus conclusions from our studies are sometimes presented without the complete accompanying data to support them. For the convenience of our fellow investigators, however, we have taken care to insure that the original reports containing the full data are easily available. Each separate study has a separate reference, either to a published research article or to a research report appearing in the report series of either the Research and Development Center for Teacher Education at the University of Texas at Austin or the Center for Research in Social Behavior at the University of Missouri at Columbia. Readers interested in seeing the original studies could consult the published articles or write for copies of the report series reprints.

January 1974   J. E. B.
                                                                          T. L. G.

Acknowledgements

We could never have completed the series of research investigations described in this book, nor prepared the book itself, without the help and cooperation of others. Only when we looked back in the process of preparing this acknowledgement section, however, did we realize just how much cooperation and help we had received or how many "others" there are. The organizations and individuals listed below, numerous as they are, include only those that were directly involved in the research and/or the development of the book. Many teachers, colleagues, and students have contributed to our professional development or our research activities in some way, and we extend our gratitude to them.

Before citing individuals, we wish to extend our gratitude to an organization, the Research and Development Center for Teacher Education at the University of Texas at Austin (Oliver H. Bown and Robert F. Peck, co-directors). The Center provided direct support to Dr. Brophy from 1968 through the present and to Dr. Good from 1968 until 1971, while he was also on the faculty of the University of Texas at Austin. In addition to direct support to ourselves, the Center has provided indirect support in the form of secretarial assistance, supplies, programming, and data analysis. Dr. Bown and Dr. Peck have been continually supportive of our efforts, and Dr. Donald Veldman of the Center has been invaluable as a consultant in the areas of research design and data analysis.

In addition to support from the Center, specific research projects have been supported by NIMH small grant MH 19316–01, USPHS small grant MH 17907–01, and USOE contract OEC–6–71–0477–(509), Project No. 1F012.

Also, since he has been at the University of Missouri at Columbia, Dr. Good has received research support, secretarial assistance, and programming and data analysis assistance from the Center for Research in Social Behavior (Bruce J. Biddle, Director). The support of these research centers and funding agencies is gratefully acknowledged. However, points of view or opinions stated in the book do not necessarily represent the official positions of these centers or agencies.

Marshel Ashley, Coordinator of Research for the Austin Independent School District, was vitally instrumental in helping us initiate our series of investigations in the classroom, and he has been of invaluable help to us through the years in his role as a liaison person between ourselves and the school personnel involved in our research. We also wish to express our appreciation to Roger Williams, former Education Editor for Holt, Rinehart and Winston, whose support and encouragement provided the initial impetus for planning the book. We are equally grateful to Richard Owen, the present Education Editor for Holt, Rinehart and Winston, for his consistent support and helpful suggestions which were so instrumental in helping us move the book toward final form. Dr. Bruce Biddle and Dr. Philip Jackson were quite helpful in reviewing and responding to early drafts of the manuscript.

The following individuals have served as classroom observers and/or data analysts for one or more of our projects: Dr. Shyam Ahuja, Connie Anderson, Alice Bruce, Maria Buczynski, Dr. Jean Chandy, Candy Chazanow, John Crawford, Mary Elder, Dr. Carolyn Evertson, Susan Florence, Dr. Ruth Friedenberg, Suzi Good, Linda Graham, Dr. Teresa Harris Teck, Dr. Dwain Hearn, Sylvia Hearn, Dr. Peter Jennings, Sue Jones, Dr. Vern Jones, Carol King, John Kirkland, Dr. Douglas Kleiber, Dr. Luis Laosa, Dr. Mark Mays, Sonia Mendoza, Dr. Piara Pannu, Kathey Paredes, Brian Peck, Dr. Dennis Romig, Kellyn Rozier, Dr. Kathleen Senior, Dr. Jev Sikes, Dr. Michael Weissberg, Jo Ann Williamson, Robert Williamson, and Dr. Sherry Willis.

Programming assistance was provided by James Buchanan, Clint Schumacher, John Sheffield, James Sherrill, and Donald Witzke.

Assistance in preparing manuscripts for our earlier research articles or for the present volume was provided by: Marilyn Arnold, James Blackwell, Arlene Brophy, Bitsy Brumage, Toni Carter, Teresa DeLay, Sandi Farkas, Sue Gunn, Frances Head, Gail Hinkel, Janet Honea, Betty Johnson, Jean Jones, Anne Karlo, Linda Keough, Karen Mays, Becky Mendoza, Shirley O'Bryant, Jean Waltman, David Wilson, and Hazel Witzke. Sherry Kilgore assumed major responsibility for typing the final draft of the manuscript and we fully appreciate her capable assistance.

Special recognition and appreciation are extended to Dr. Carolyn Evertson, Dr. Teresa Harris Teck, Karen Mays, and John Sheffield, who made continuing and important contributions to our research program and to the preparation of the present volume.

Finally, although they are far too numerous to name, we deeply appreciate the cooperation extended us by the school administrators, teachers, and students involved in our various studies, particularly the personnel of the Austin Independent School District, where the bulk of our research has been conducted.

This book is fondly dedicated to our wives, Arlene and Suzi. They have provided many forms of direct help, such as classroom coding, proofreading, and constructive criticism of successive drafts of the manuscript. More importantly, however, both in their roles as wives and mothers, they have provided the love, support, security, and tolerance for constraints on our time which have enabled us to conduct the series of research investigations described in this volume and to prepare the volume itself. More than anyone else, they have made it all possible.

Contents

chapter 1

Individual Differences
in Teacher-Student
Interaction Patterns

IMPROVING EDUCATIONAL RESEARCH

Despite years of educational research, relatively few findings which can be usefully applied to the improvement of educational practice have been produced. This has been true even of classroom interaction analysis research, even though this area of investigation bears directly upon the teaching process. We believe that there are several reasons for this, but the two discussed below are probably the most important.

Need for Criteria to Judge Appropriate Teaching Methods

Although there may be a few teacher attributes or behaviors which are appropriate in all situations (showing respect for students as individuals, listening attentively to what students say, avoiding hostile personal criticism, and so on), most teacher behavior is appropriate in some contexts but not in others. Appropriateness of teacher behavior depends upon the educational objectives the teacher is pursuing and such factors as the age and level of background preparation of the students. For example, if the objective is to introduce facts which must be committed to memory (such as spelling words or arithmetic tables), activities such as drill exercises and spelling and math tests would be appropriate and activities such as class discussions

1

or essay assignments would not (except for an assignment such as asking students to write an essay using the spelling words that they are learning). In contrast, when the teacher's educational objectives involve such things as stimulating students to analyze or solve complex problems, to give opinions about or develop solutions to social or political problems, or to develop creativity in their writing, class discussions and essay assignments would be quite appropriate while drill exercises and tests for memory of factual material would not.

Similarly, a technique that would be appropriate for secondary students might be completely inappropriate for early elementary students. Failure to take this point into account has led some writers to extrapolate from educational research in an overgeneralized way. We believe that teaching in the early elementary grades is very different from teaching in secondary and college settings, so much so that research findings generated in a study at one of these settings should not be extrapolated to the other setting without replication. Yet, this is commonly done by textbook writers and by educational consultants giving advice to teachers.

One common example of this concerns the work of Flanders and his associates, who have produced evidence that indirect teaching is sometimes more effective than direct teaching (Flanders, 1970). Some writers have taken an oversimplified and overgeneralized view of this research so that they proclaim that "teacher talk is bad, student talk is good."

This is even found as a generalized, unqualified statement in many textbooks and other books written for teachers. It is not appropriate as an unqualified general statement in any case, and it is especially inappropriate for the early elementary schoolteacher. To put it simply, you cannot teach first graders to read, write, and learn elementary math tables by conducting class discussions. Instruction here must be heavily teacher dominated and will require frequent drill and repetition, because the educational objective is to get the children to master fundamental skills to the point of overlearning, where they become automatic. Since much of the teacher's time in the early grades is spent working toward such objectives, the "teacher talk is bad, student talk is good" dictum is grossly inappropriate for teachers at this level.

This is not to suggest, of course, that student talk is never appropriate in the early elementary grades. It is quite appropriate whenever the teacher is attempting to generate a discussion (regarding understanding of a story in the reader, "show and tell," and for curriculum areas such as social studies which lend themselves more easily to discussion even at this early age), or when teachers are helping children to express their feelings. Also, even in teaching basic reading, writing, and math skills, it is important for teachers to question children to help identify the particular nature of their difficulty if they are having trouble learning and to help establish and maintain the general habit of communicating with the teacher when they need help. However, the point remains that class discussion is not an appropriate teaching technique to meet many of the important objectives of the early grades.

In summary, we feel that if educational research is to become more productive in yielding knowledge that will be applicable to teaching, both educational research-ers and those who interpret research findings to teachers will have to learn to avoid the tendency to make oversimplified and overgeneralized statements about particular teaching behaviors; they will have to be more systematic and careful in stating the contextual variables that make a given behavior appropriate or inappropriate. Unless accompanied by statements concerning the criteria for judging when a given behavior is appropriate, extrapolation from educational research studies to give advice to the teacher is bound to be overgeneralized and oversimplified and may even do more harm than good.

Need for Research on Interaction between Individual Students and Teachers

Although the movement towards individually prescribed education represents recognition by practitioners that the individual student should be the focus of educational effort, relatively little educational research has focused on the individual student. We believe that this is a major reason why educational research has contributed relatively little knowledge that teachers can apply in the classroom. The need for such research is clear. Tyler (1969) reports that approximately 15 percent of children in the United States do not attain a level of literacy required for employment, and that 40 to 60 percent of the urban poor sixth graders studied did not function at better than the second-grade level in their school achievement.

Sperry (1972) also called for more attention to individual differences in learning and instructional style and in expectations. He notes that the kinds of applications of psychology and general research methodology to education which have been made to date not only have failed to provide much prescriptive help, but sometimes have backfired by providing rationalizations for failures. It has become typical for both school personnel and educational psychologists to "explain" school failure as a result of social class, personality problems, or some other (usually considered unchangeable) trait of the student, rather than to focus attention on the individual student's present status, his pattern of strengths and weaknesses, his methods of approaching problems, and his interests, in order to prescribe an educational experience which is likely to succeed for him where others have failed. To do this, of course, the classroom investigator must focus his attention upon the individual student.

One flaw in much of the research that has looked at naturalistic behavior in classrooms has been the stress upon teacher behavior directed toward the entire class rather than toward individual students. We see this strategy as too general and undifferentiated to be very useful for addressing most of the questions that we are interested in exploring. Students perform differently in the classroom. Some show consistent improvement; others fall further and further behind the longer they remain in school. Their decline in academic performance is frequently matched by a growing sense of personal inadequacy and an increasing apathy or hostility toward an environment that offers mostly frustration. Much of this differential performance can be explained by different biological factors and home environments. However, some can be explained by what happens to students in school, especially the treatment they receive from teachers. Do teachers compensate for differences in student performance, or do they behave so as to widen the performance gap between high and low achievement students? Do teachers expecting students to do poorly either consciously or subconsciously act to make their predictions come true? Do teachers demand and reinforce good academic performance from their good students, while accepting inadequate performance and failing to encourage poor students?

To answer such questions and to collect information that will help teachers understand and monitor their behavior toward different students, it is not feasible to use observational instruments that only record teacher behavior toward the class as a whole. Focus upon how teachers interact with individual students is needed.

Although individual differences have been discussed in education and psychology for a long time, studies analyzing classroom interaction have seldom focused upon the individual student. Some have focused almost solely on the teacher, recording information such as the number and kinds of questions he asks or the different teaching strategies he uses. Others have focused more clearly on teacher-student interaction, but even here the students are treated as a class or group rather than as a collection of different individuals. For example, the amount of verbalization by students ("student talk") is an important variable in several interaction analysis systems. The ratio of teacher talk to student talk is often used as an index of the degree to which a teacher dominates or directs the classroom interaction.

In such studies verbalization by the teacher is counted as "teacher talk," and verbalization by a student (any student) is counted as "student talk." Verbalizations by different students are lumped together into a single student talk index, so that individual differences among students in their rates of verbalizing are lost. This kind of index is useful in some types of studies, but in others it masks important differences between contrasting classrooms. For example, students may talk 40 percent of the time in each of two classrooms. In one, the student talk may be distributed rather equally among the twenty students. In the other, however, five students may do almost all of the talking while the other fifteen participate only rarely or perhaps not at all. The 40-percent student talk figure is deceptive here, because it implies that two very different classrooms are identical in student talk patterns.

Failure to take into account individual differences can affect the interpretation of measures of teacher behavior as well as measures of student behavior. For example, investigators are often interested in the degree to which a teacher praises his students or in the degree to which he shows warmth in his interactions with them. Again, a single index representing a teacher's general tendency can be deceptive. Two teachers can praise with equal frequency, but the implications are very different if one distributes his praise equally while the other heaps praise upon a few students but rarely or never praises the majority.

The use of general indexes of teacher behavior in the classroom can also be questioned on logical grounds. When such an index is used, it implies that the teacher's behavior was directed to the class as a group rather than toward individual students at different times. Sometimes this underlying assumption holds, as when the indexes concern the teacher's behavior when lecturing to the group or when giving the class a test. More often, though, the teacher behavior studied in interaction analysis research involves words and actions directed to individual students. Praise and warmth, for example, are much more often directed toward individuals than toward the class as a group.

This is also true of many of the other variables that have been stressed in interaction research (indirectness, use of student ideas, probing for improved response, acceptance of feelings). This presents no real problem if the teacher has a typical pattern of behavior that does not vary much from one student to another. Here the single index will accurately represent both the teacher's typical behavior and the way any particular student in his class is typically treated. Where large individual differences exist, however, use of a single index distorts both types of data. First, the teacher in this case has no "typical" pattern which can be represented in a single index. Second, different students receive very different treatment, so that the index does not accurately describe the treatment of some of the students. In the extreme case where the teacher acts one way toward one group of students and another way toward the rest of the students, a single index representing his "average" score would not be representative of his behavior toward *any* of his students (see Good and Brophy, 1971a, for a more extended discussion of this point).

Our focus on individual students does not deny the existence of meaningful variance between teachers in terms of their general style. Quite the contrary, we acknowledge the fact that different classrooms present different psychological environments. For example, Lightfoot (1972) compared two urban second-grade classrooms and noted that one teacher made approval statements twice as frequently as the other. These differences between classes are interesting and worthy of study. In fact, the investigator who chooses to study individual students can also obtain class profiles by averaging the scores of individuals. However, the converse is not true. Researchers studying teacher behavior toward the class can provide only indirect clues about the psychological environment of a particular student.

We also know that much teacher behavior is directed toward individual students. For example, teachers can interact with single pupils, groups of pupils, or the whole class. Power (1971) studied the interaction of four Australian high school science teachers and concluded that 92 percent of teacher interactions were with individual students! These figures may not be representative of teacher behavior in elementary classrooms where children spend most time in reading groups and where teachers sometimes direct questions to groups. Teachers at the elementary level show considerable variation in the extent to which they interact with the class per se, groups of students, and individual students. For example, Lightfoot (1972), contrasting the behavior of two teachers, reported that teacher A asked 75 percent of her questions to individual students, while teacher B asked only 35 percent of her questions to individuals.

In any case, the data suggest that classification of some information as teacher behavior toward "the class" is of dubious validity. Furthermore, given the increasing curricular emphasis upon mastery learning, individualized instruction, learning centers, modular instruction, and so on, we suspect that more and more teacher behavior in elementary classrooms will be directed toward individual students and subgroups of students rather than the entire class.

Given that teachers already direct much of their behavior toward individual students and subgroups of students, and that the frequency of such behavior is likely to increase, it is more important than ever to study this phase of classroom life if we are to understand it and improve upon current practice. Thus, to interpret the meaning and implications of classroom interaction analysis research we need to know the extent and importance of individual differences in teachers' interaction patterns with different students in their classrooms. Studies which have focused on the individual student or on separate subgroups of students within the same classroom are reviewed and discussed in the remainder of this chapter. Even before doing so, however, we can state the following generalization: within any class, group and individual differences of considerable importance are regularly found when the investigator looks for them.

INFLUENCE OF GROUP DIFFERENCES IN THE CLASSROOM

Many student attributes have been found to influence teachers' perceptions of students and their patterns of interaction with them in the classroom. Some of these include student membership in various identifiable groups (social class, race, sex), while others are individual differences in personal attributes or classroom behavior and achievement.

Social Class Differences

One important group variable is social class, or socioeconomic status (SES). A teacher interview study by Becker (1952) found that teachers took social status into account in making evaluations of students and in planning classroom strategies for teaching them. Davis and Dollard (1940) showed that higher status children get most of the teacher's praise and rewards, while lower class children get more criticism and punishment. Similarly, Smith (1965) noted that teachers interacted more positively with male students for whom they predicted high occupational attainment than males for whom they had predicted low occupational status.

Yee (1968) administered a teacher attitude inventory to 100 intermediate grade teachers in middle class schools and also measured students' attitudes toward teachers. The experiment was repeated the following year using 112 teachers and their students in lower class schools. Analyses of the data showed that middle class teachers and pupils were consistently more favorable in their attitudes than teachers and students in lower class schools. Furthermore, student SES was by far the most important variable determining teacher attitudes toward students. Teachers in the middle class schools had more favorable attitudes on every subscale of the teacher attitude inventory. These teachers appeared to be modernistic, tolerant, warm, trustful, and sympathetic, while teachers in lower class schools appeared to be traditionalistic, blaming, cold, fault finding, and punitive. Student attitudes toward the teachers in lower class schools were poorer to begin with, but nevertheless they dropped sharply as the year progressed. This sharp drop in favorableness of attitude toward the teacher was not noted among middle class pupils. Drop in student attitude was also related to teacher attitude in that the teachers who had the most negative and intolerant attitudes toward students were those teachers about whom students became most negative as the year progressed.

Goodwin and Sanders (1969) provided strong evidence of the importance of SES to teachers. They asked teachers to rank the importance of seven variables for predicting a child's school success. Teachers ranked the variables as predictors for first-grade and sixth-grade pupils. The teachers sampled felt that SES was most important for predicting success in a first-grade pupil, followed in order by IQ, standardized tests, age, sex, anecdotal notes, and grade-point average (GPA). When the same variables were ranked for predicting the performance of a hypothetical sixth grader, the order was: standardized tests, GPA, SES, sex, IQ, age, and anecdotal notes. Thus SES was considered most important at the first-grade level and was still considered more important than IQ even at the sixth-grade level.

Hoehn (1954) observed nineteen middle class female third-grade teachers interacting with their students during five hours of typical everyday interaction. There were no quantitative differences in teacher–student contact by social class, but there were qualitative differences. Lower class students received more dominative contacts from the teachers, while their middle class peers received more supportive and integrative contacts. These SES differences disappeared when the children's scores were controlled for achievement, and Hoehn interpreted the data to mean that teachers were responding primarily to achievement rather than to social class. Gabbert (1973) obtained identical results in a later study. Nevertheless, the data reviewed above suggest that social class was probably equally or more important, especially if one adopts the view that SES differences partially shape IQ in the first place.

Friedman and Friedman (1973) observed twenty-four fifth- and sixth-grade classrooms to see if teacher reinforcing behavior was related to student social class. They found that significantly more total reinforcements, and especially nonverbal reinforcements, were given to the middle class children than to lower class children.

Brown (1969) observed the classroom interactions of middle class teachers with either middle class or lower class students. The several significant differences which emerged all suggested a more positive and facilitative classroom environment in the middle class school. Relative to the lower class schools, interaction in the classrooms of middle class schools was characterized by more content orientation, more neutral, unemotional, and routine pupil responses, more lecturing, and less questioning. Despite the latter two findings, however, there was more pupil talk in the middle class schools. Apparently the teachers in these schools made a more extended effort to present content through lectures, but once they switched to a question-and-answer or discussion mode they allowed (or at least got) more pupil talk from their students than did teachers in the lower class schools. The talk of both the teachers and the pupils was more neutral in its emotional tone, suggesting that it was more concerned with curriculum content and less with interruptions due to disciplinary problems.

Low expectations for lower class relative to middle class students were observed by Leacock (1969). Two classrooms in each of three types of schools were observed for a total of three hours, and all instances in which the teachers engaged students in overt, specific goal setting were recorded. Such instances were observed 43 times and 46 times, respectively, in two middle income white classrooms. In contrast, goal setting was observed only twelve and thirteen times, respectively, in two low income black classrooms, and only fifteen and eighteen times, respectively, in two low income white classrooms. Although there was no attempt by the teachers to impose middle class goals on lower class children, there was a tacit assumption that the lower class children could not meet these goals, and thus a generally lowered expectation and level of concern about achievement in these schools.

The influence of social class is brought out very clearly in a fascinating but disturbing case study by Rist (1970). Rist periodically made classroom observations of ghetto children, starting when they began kindergarten and continuing through second grade. From the time they entered kindergarten, these students were divided into three groups, each seated at different tables and treated somewhat differently by the teacher. Initial placement into groups at kindergarten was done basically according to SES, using information from registration forms and from interviews with mothers and social workers. The higher-status children were seated closer to the teacher and were quickly labeled "fast learners." The teacher interacted more frequently and more positively with these students, who soon developed a feeling of superiority over the others.

These differences initiated in kindergarten were enhanced as the children went through the first and second grades. The higher status children stayed together as an elite group enjoying frequent and favorable interactions with teachers. Grouping tended to remain fixed and rigid, *regardless* of the children's performance. Thus, the initial grouping done in kindergarten determined the students' relative status in the room and their learning potential in the eyes of the teachers, even though it was based mostly on readiness and SES rather than on ability or potential. Teachers were concerned mostly about *instructing* the higher status children whom they saw as fast learners but were concerned more about *controlling and disciplining* the lower status students whom they saw as slow learners.

Similar findings were reported by Mackler (1969) in a case study of the effects of a tracking system used in a school in Harlem. Here again, tracking started in kindergarten, where teachers judged who was and was not "mature." Once placed in a track, few children moved out of it, and tracking affected the attitudes of both the teachers and the students.

Three large-scale studies of ability grouping (Douglas, 1964; Goldberg, Passow, and Justman, 1966; Husen and Svensson, 1960) showed that, when a tracking or ability grouping system is used, children of higher SES tend to be placed in higher tracks and children of lower status tend to be placed in lower tracks than their measured ability would predict. Furthermore, once placed in a given track, students tend to stay there. Relatively small percentages of children are recommended to move from one track to another at the end of each year (usually less than 5 percent), and most of these are slated to move down to lower tracks rather than up to higher ones. Thus, to put it baldly, in some school systems a student's career is somewhat determined as of the day he enters school simply on the basis of his clothing, appearance, and other factors related to the SES of his family but not necessarily to his ability or potential.

An experimental study by Miller et al. (1968) also showed the importance of social status in determining teachers' expectations for students. In this study future teachers were asked to read four "case history reports" concerning fictional students and then to rate the probable future academic success, classroom behavior, and post–high school achievement of these students. The case histories were matched for IQ, school grades, and history of behavior problems. However, economic information was included to suggest that two students were from middle class homes and two from lower class homes. Despite the matching on other more relevant factors, the middle class students were rated higher on ten of the twelve scales, while the lower class students were rated as more likely to get into fights and to have poorer grades in the future!

In another study, in which inservice teachers rated their like or dislike of children in their classes, middle income children were rated much more positively than lower income children (Leacock, 1969). This same tendency to view low income children less favorably than middle class children has also been noted in British teachers (Goodacre, 1967; Morrison and McIntyre, 1969).

Thus socioeconomic status predicts both teachers' perceptions of their children and their treatment of them in the classroom.

Race

Despite national concern about and interest in school integration, there has been relatively little research on teacher-student interaction as related to the race of the student. However, Rubovits and Maehr (1973) studied this in an experimental microteaching situation. In this study sixty-six "teachers" (white female undergraduates enrolled in a child development course for prospective elementary teachers) each taught a lesson to a group of four seventh- or eighth-grade students. Each group of four students contained two black and two white students.

Significant differences based on the race of the student were found on six of the eight measures of teacher-child interaction used in this study, and all six favored the white students. The teachers gave less attention to the blacks; they requested fewer statements from them; they encouraged blacks to continue with an idea less frequently; they ignored a greater percentage of their statements; and they praised them less and criticized them more.

These findings are disturbing, even though they come from an experimental situation rather than an actual classroom. The undergraduate teachers in this experiment are probably typical of the students going into teaching, so that one implication of this study is that white teachers probably have a tendency to behave inappropriately toward black students, at least in situations where they are teaching both blacks and whites.

This prediction is further suggested by studies showing that teachers have more negative attitudes toward black than white students (Datta, Schaefer, and Davis, 1968; Leacock, 1969). The Leacock study showed not only that black students were rated generally less favorably than white students, but also that teachers showed particular hostility and rejection toward the *brighter* black students. This is a reversal of the usual finding in studies involving white students. In the same research Leacock reported that teachers at a middle class white school favored students whose IQ's averaged ten points higher than the students they rejected. However, teachers working in a low income black school favored fifth-grade students whose average IQ was ten points *lower* than that of the students they rejected. Further, even though these rejected black children had an IQ almost ten points higher than that of their positively or neutrally viewed classmates, their reading achievement level was slightly lower. This may well have resulted from inappropriate treatment by teachers who disliked and rejected them.

Leacock also noticed other differences in teacher behavior in middle class white versus lower class black classrooms. In the middle class white school, student inattention was taken as an indication of teacher need to arouse student interest, but the same behavior in a lower class black school was rationalized as boredom due to limited student attention span. In general, the teachers in the lower class black school were characterized by low expectations for the children and low respect for their ability to learn.

The Datta, Schaefer, and Davis study concerned descriptions of seventh-grade students by forty teachers. In general, girls were described more favorably than boys and nonblacks more favorably than blacks. In contrast to the Leacock study, black students with low IQ's were seen in particularly bad light by the teachers in this research.

In general, blacks were described as low in task orientation and less likely to be helpful, cheerful, and gregarious. However, black students with high and low IQ's were seen quite differently. The blacks with high IQ's were described as task oriented, methodical, persevering, sociable, trustful, submissive, and not very rebellious or verbally aggressive. Thus they were seen as hard working, well-behaved, and studious. In contrast, black students with low IQ's were described as poorly adjusted, not task oriented, verbally aggressive, rebellious, asocial, and generally unruly.

The authors noted that some of the general race differences were confounded by SES differences, since the whites were generally of higher SES than the blacks. While this may have been a factor, other aspects of the data suggested that race as such partially explained the attitudes the teachers held toward the black students with low IQ's. For example, when IQ was controlled (and this has the effect of controlling SES also), certain differences still emerged. Blacks with high IQ's were described just as favorably as their classmates with high IQ's, but blacks with low IQ's were more likely than their classmates with low IQ's to be described as maladjusted, verbally aggressive, and not very task oriented.

Coates (1972) conducted an experimental study similar to that reported above by Rubovits and Maehr (1973). In this study adult subjects taught learning problems to one of four nine-year-old boys who were confederates of the experimenters. Two of the boys were black, and two were white. The adults could see the boy while working with him but could not see his responses; the children were actually pretending to respond while the adults received feedback suggesting that the child was slowly and gradually learning the problem. After each response, feedback was given to the adult to indicate whether the child had responded correctly or incorrectly. The same feedback was given to all adult subjects about each of the four children. The adult was instructed to give the child a feedback statement following each response, selected from among a list of five ranging from praise to criticism. Also, after the experiment each adult filled out a list of nineteen adjective description ratings of the child.

Analyses of the feedback statements made by the adults when teaching the children showed that the female adults did not differentiate between the two groups, but that the male adults were significantly more negative toward the black children. Worse yet, analyses of the nineteen trait-rating scales showed that the child's race was a significant factor on sixteen of them, and in each case the black boys were rated more negatively (dull, passive, unfriendly, and so on) than the white boys. This was true for female as well as male raters.

Katz (1973), in a study of 150 students in integrated schools, showed that race, sex, and SES were all significantly related to the frequency of verbal initiation in the classroom. With regard to race she concluded that integrated schools simply reinforced rather than mitigated the racial differences existing in society at large, at least according to the verbal initiation measure. Whites initiated interactions much more frequently than blacks, and teachers apparently either passively accepted or actively reinforced this trend rather than attempting to compensate for it.

Byers and Byers (1972) studied non-verbal communication between teachers and students and concluded that some of the differences which might at first appear to represent discrimination on the part of the teacher might actually result from differential familiarity with the habit patterns of white teachers, with white students gaining more successful interactions with teachers because of their greater familiarity. In this study, interaction between a white teacher and two black and two white girls in a nursery school were filmed. The films were then examined to analyze the behavior of the teacher and the children. Two of the girls, one black and one white, were notably more active and interested in initiating interactions with the teacher than were the other two. However, the white girl was notably more successful in getting interactions with the teacher. This girl looked at the teacher 14 times and managed to catch the teacher's eye 8 of these times, while the black girl looked at the teacher 35 times but caught the teacher's eye only 4 times. This at first suggests teacher bias. However, careful analysis of the films showed that the white child timed her glances at the teacher during those periods in which the teacher was pausing to scan the room, and thus was more likely to notice her, while most of the glances of the black child were timed at moments when the teacher's attention was directed at something else so that she did not realize that the black girl was looking at her. Other data suggested a similar difference in the affective area. The white girl often approached the teacher at times which "naturally" led the teacher to put her arm around her or otherwise express affection, and often followed this up by smoothly moving closer to the teacher, sitting on her lap, etc. In contrast, even though the teacher seemed equally willing to communicate affectively with the black girl, the the girl made inappropriate moves at crucial moments, pulling when she should have pushed or pushing when she should have pulled, as it were. Because the black girl did not share the implicit pattern of expectations and understanding of meaning of gestures that was implicitly understood and shared by both the white teacher and the white girl, many opportunities which would have resulted in expressions of affection for the white girl resulted instead only in frustration for both the teacher and the child in the case of the black girl.

This case study illustrates a point which will be made frequently in this book: teacher-student interaction is a two-way process, and often the student conditions teacher behavior as much or more than the teacher conditions student behavior. A related point is that much teacher discrimination in the sense of treating two individuals or groups of students differently is not necessarily due to any conscious differential treatment on the part of the teacher but instead is due to unconscious conditioning of the teacher by differential behavior of the students.

The problem of racial hostility toward students is not confined to blacks by any means. In a fascinating series of studies Kleinfeld (1972) described the plight of Indian and Eskimo students in Alaska who go to elementary schools in their own villages but then must enter urban high schools and become integrated with a predominately white student population. Some (not all) of the teachers and the students at the urban high schools showed overt hostility and negativism toward the Indian and Eskimo students. Most teachers reacted to them inappropriately; they either treated them with some combination of apathy and hostility or with a misguided sentimentalism featuring favorable attitudes but low expectations for performance. The teachers who were most successful with the Indian and Eskimo students were those who communicated warmth and acceptance to them but at the same time held high expectations and demanded good performance from them.

In Yee's (1968) teacher and student attitude study mentioned previously, student race and ethnicity as well as student SES affected teacher attitudes. The teachers were most favorable toward middle class Anglo students, next favorable toward lower class Anglo students, next favorable toward lower class Mexican-American students, and least favorable toward lower class black students. This was true even though most teachers of black students were themselves black. Thus even among equally low-SES students, Anglos were favored over Mexican-Americans, who were in turn favored over blacks.

The studies reviewed in this section show that teachers are likely to have negative attitudes toward minority group students and to treat these students inappropriately in the classroom.

Student's Sex

Many authors have suggested that elementary school is more meaningful for girls than boys. Some point out that the demands the school places on students are more easily accepted by girls, because the activities defined as appropriate for young girls in our society are less active and more verbally and intellectually oriented than those defined as appropriate for boys. In addition to this factor of sex role differentiation, however, many authors point to the fact that teachers in American elementary grades are almost always female. They suggest that female teachers may be differentially treating boys and girls in ways that favor girls, either because they prefer girls or because they simply are more familiar with and more effective in female-oriented situations.

The data available on these issues are mixed and confusing. Apparently, teachers view girls more favorably than boys (Arnold, 1968; Datta, Schaefer, and Davis, 1968). One behavioral finding that has emerged repeatedly is that boys get much more teacher disapproval and criticism than girls (Jackson and Lahaderne, 1967; Lippitt and Gold, 1959; Meyer and Thompson, 1956). Not only that, but teachers are more likely to use a harsh or angry tone when criticizing boys, while criticism directed toward girls is usually delivered in a more conversational tone (Spaulding, 1963; Waetjen, 1962).

A similar sex difference apparently exists in teachers' grading practices. Carter (1952) examined the measured achievement of boys and girls in six classrooms and compared their grades to their achievement scores. He concluded that the boys had been graded lower than their actual achievement dictated. Similar results were found by Hess, Shipman, Brophy, and Bear (1969). The data in this study also suggested that first- and second-grade children's marks in academic subject areas were partially affected by their grades in conduct.

Thus, it appears that (female) teachers criticize boys more frequently and grade them lower relative to their measured achievement in comparison to their treatment of girls. The influence of the student's sex will be taken up in detail in Chapter 7. Meanwhile, it should be noted that these differences do not necessarily indicate unfair discrimination on the part of (female) teachers. It may be that boys are criticized more frequently because they break classroom rules more frequently, and that they are graded lower because they do not perform so well as girls on teacher-made tests, although they may do as well on standardized achievement tests given at the end of the year.

In any case, probably for a combination of the above reasons, girls have more favorable attitudes toward school than boys (Antes, Andersen, and DeVault, 1965; Jackson, 1968), and they feel that their teachers hold more favorable attitudes toward them (Davidson and Lang, 1960).

INFLUENCE OF INDIVIDUAL DIFFERENCES IN THE CLASSROOM

Besides reacting to students on the basis of the group variables of social class, race, and sex, teachers respond to individual differences in students' personal attributes and behavior. Perhaps the most important individual difference is student achievement level.

Student Achievement

There is considerable evidence that students of different achievement levels have very different kinds of interactions with their teachers. Hoehn (1954) found that high achieving students enjoyed more promotive and supportive contacts from their teachers, while low achievers had a greater proportion of teacher contacts involving conflict with the teacher or domination and direction by the teacher. De Groat and Thompson (1949) found that high achievers received more praise, while lower achievers received a disproportionate share of disapproval.

Data collected on English school children confirmed this difference and showed that the children are aware of how teachers perceive them (Morrison and McIntyre, 1969). Self-report data from students showed that 73 percent of low achievers thought that their teachers thought poorly of them, while only 10 percent of high achievers had this belief.

Besides addressing more favorable comments to high achieving students and more critical comments to low achieving students, teachers have been found to differ in the number of opportunities for academic response that they provide high- and low achieving students. This was first noted long ago by Horn (1914) who examined the distribution of student recitation opportunities in 229 classrooms and noted large individual differences related to student achievement. Horn asked the teachers to divide their classes into quartiles according to general ability and then noted the distribution of recitation opportunities across these four groups of students within each class. For the sample as a whole, the students in the top quartile recited about 40 percent more than those in the bottom quartile.

Horn also noticed an age effect: the inequality favoring the high achieving students increased with grade level. The difference was relatively small in the early grades, but with advances in grade the percentage of reciting done by the lowest quartile of students decreased, so that by high school the top group was doing almost twice as much reciting as the bottom group. Jersild *et al.* (1941), studying sixteen classrooms (eight from control schools and eight from "activity" schools) noted that roughly 25 percent of the students in each classroom accounted for two-thirds of all classroom responses. Structured discussions yielded more equality than free discussions, because some students were much more willing to initiate contacts with teachers than others.

It is possible, of course, that things have changed considerably since Horn and Jersild did their research, so that it no longer accurately describes what goes on in schools. However, two recent studies support these findings and show that even now some teachers allow their "better" students to participate in classroom discussions more frequently.

Good (1970) found that first grade students whom teachers perceived as high achievers received more response opportunities and more positive feedback than classmates perceived as low achievers. He observed each of four classrooms for ten hours, noting each teacher's interactions with four high achievers, four average achievers, and four low achievers. His results are shown in Table 1.1. In each classroom the four high achievers received many more opportunities to respond to questions than did the four low achievers.

It should be noted that the figures in Table 1.1 reflect only those response opportunities in which the teacher deliberately called upon a student to respond. Response opportunities that occurred because a student called out an answer were not counted. If they had been, the discrepancy between high- and low-achieving students would have been even greater than that shown in the table.

Similar results were found by Kranz, Weber, and Fishell (1970), whose data are shown in Table 1.2. These investigators made observations for two hours in each of eleven elementary classrooms. They tallied the number of substantive interactions that teachers had with students whom they ranked as high, average, or low achievers. *Substantive* interactions were those that involved teaching and learning the curriculum. Interactions concerning procedural matters or control of behavior were not included.

TABLE 1.1   Response Opportunities Provided to High, Middle, and Low Achievers in Four First Grade Classrooms (from Good, 1970).*

RESPONSE OPPORTUNITY	HIGH	MIDDLE	LOW
Class I Mean Response Opportunity	40.5	26.3	15.5
Class II Mean Response Opportunity	23.3	10.5	3.3
Class III Mean Response Opportunity	33.3	11.0	12.0
Class IV Mean Response Opportunity	22.8	20.8	9.8
Total Mean Response Opportunity	29.9	17.1	10.1
Range of Pupil Response Opportunity	17–35	7–37	1–21
Total Number of Response Opportunities	479	274	162

* Copyright 1970 by the American Psychological Assn. Reprinted by permission.

TABLE 1.2.   Substantive Teacher-Student Interactions in Eleven Elementary School Classrooms (from Kranz, Weber, and Fishell, 1970).

TEACHER	HIGH	AVERAGE	LOW
01	149	147	106
02	158	151	41
03	164	78	137
04	142	81	45
05	99	92	27
06	206	78	112
07	178	168	117
08	176	160	212
09	108	59	88
10	107	74	29
11	227	87	39
Mean for all classes	155.8	106.8	86.6

The data in Table 1.2 show that teachers consistently had more substantive interactions with the top third of their class. All eleven teachers had more interactions with the high achievers than with the average students, and ten of the eleven had more interactions with the high achievers than with the low achievers.

Thus the data reviewed in this section indicate that teachers interact more frequently with high achieving than with low achieving students, and that their interactions with high achievers are more positive and facilitative than their interactions with low achievers.

The effects of student achievement differences on teachers are magnified when the school uses a tracking system. First, students in the high track are likely to be from high SES homes, which usually means preferential treatment in the teacher assignments and resource allocations made by school administrators. Second, teachers prefer teaching in high tracks and dislike teaching in low tracks, so that teachers in the high track are likely to have high morale and enthusiasm. Third, general stimulation and opportunities to learn from peers are greater in classes filled with bright, high achieving students than in homogenous low ability classes. Thus, the tracking system insures that the highest achieving children are likely to get the best education that the school system has to offer, while the low achievers are likely to get the worst. Over time this factor alone is liable to increase the differences between the two groups of children.

If Rist's observations are generalizable, it will also tend to induce feelings of failure and frustration in the low achievers and an unhealthy attitude of superiority in the high achievers. Many very capable children will not get a chance to reveal their talents or fulfill their potential, partly because they will be getting several years of less adequate education than their more well-heeled classmates, and partly because, as mentioned previously, tracking systems tend to produce their own inertia such that few students are transferred from one track to another and most of those who are transferred are moved to lower rather than higher tracks. High achieving students in low tracks will still be better off than their low track classmates, however. Although they may not get the best that the school has to offer, they at least will tend to enjoy more optimal interaction patterns with their teachers than their lower achieving classmates in the same track (this point will be expanded upon in subsequent chapters).

Student Personality

Teachers react differently to different students. Jackson, Silberman, and Wolfson (1969) asked teachers to name all their students from memory. They found that the teachers knew more about and showed more signs of personal involvement with students named first (salient students) than students remembered last (nonsalient students). They also showed more signs of personal involvement with boys than girls, although a greater proportion of the statements regarding boys were negative. Both these sex-difference findings are typical (see Chapter 7).

Individual differences make some students more salient to the teacher than others. They determine whether or not a teacher likes a student, and this affects how the student is treated. For example, Hadley (1954) investigated the relationship between grades and measured achievement in twenty classrooms and concluded that the teachers graded the students they liked higher, and the students that they disliked lower, than their measured achievement would dictate.

Silberman (1969) studied the interaction of ten third-grade teachers with students toward whom they held attitudes of attachment, concern, indifference, or rejection. Students about whom the teachers were indifferent received less teacher contact and less positive evaluation, while students about whom teachers were concerned received more teacher contact than their classmates. However, no special pattern was seen in the teachers' interactions with students toward whom they felt attachment or rejection (but see Chapter 5 for replications of this study which did show differential treatment of these groups).

These studies show that the attitudes teachers hold toward their individual students can influence the ways that they treat the students. Since no two teachers or students have the same personality, a given student will provoke somewhat different reactions in each of the different teachers he meets. We can also predict certain generalities, however: certain kinds of students will be liked by most teachers, and others will be disliked by most teachers. To the extent that a teacher experiences a strong emotional response to a student and forms clear-cut attitudes toward him, teacher-student interaction will be affected for better or worse.

A study by Feshbach (1969) provided some information about the kinds of student attributes that attract or repel teachers. Subjects were 240 female undergraduate student teachers. Each read sixteen stories about elementary school children in typical school situations and then rated each child in the story according to his probable popularity among peers, his generosity, his intelligence, his grades, and the degree to which the student teacher would prefer him as a student in her class.

Results showed that teachers most generally preferred rigid, conforming, and orderly students. The next most popular group were dependent, passive, and acquiescent students, followed by flexible, nonconforming, and untidy students. The least preferred group were the independent, active, and assertive students.

These data tie in neatly with several results already reported and many more to be discussed later in the book. In general, they show that teachers tend to prefer conforming and acquiescent students and to reject active, assertive ones. Note also that the preferred qualities are those usually associated with the female sex role as it is defined for young girls in our society, while the rejected qualities are usually associated with the male sex role. This suggests that the tendency of (female) teachers to prefer girls to boys is based more on their behavioral differences than on their sex as such. This and related points will be discussed more fully in Chapter 7.

The teachers not only preferred these qualities in describing the kind of student that they wanted in their classroom, but they also projected these same preferences to the students themselves in judging probable popularity with peers. That is, the student teachers who were the subjects of this study thought that the classmates of the children would show the same pattern of preferences that the teachers themselves showed (rigid, conforming, and orderly students would be most popular, and so on). They also expected that the students they preferred would be more generous in their interactions with classmates, would have higher intelligence, and would earn higher grades.

Feshbach's findings were replicated in a study by Good and Grouws (1972), on a sample of student teachers that included males as well as females. The males showed the same preference patterns as the females. This study shows that teacher preferences result from the role expectations harbored by adults in our society for teachers and children rather than from the sex of the respondents as such. This point was further demonstrated in a recent replication by Beigel and Feshbach (1970), who repeated the experiment with three different groups: preservice teachers, psychology majors, and teachers who had received special training for Peace Corps work. In this follow-up study the original results were replicated only for the preservice teachers in the traditional teacher-training program. Undergraduate psychology majors and teachers who had had special Peace Corps training did not place such a high value on passive, compliant, conforming behaviors as did future teachers in a traditional teacher-preparation program. The responses of the group of psychology majors are especially revealing, because they show that a high value on compliance is not shared by all young adults who grow up in our society, and who have not been exposed to some kind of specialized training such as that offered by the Peace Corps. These findings suggest that there is something about the kind of person who chooses to become a teacher in our society, and/or the kind of training he gets at our society's teacher-training institutions, that causes him to value compliance and conformity over independence and creativity (this point will be taken up at length in Chapter 6).

Kelly (1958) found that instructors gave higher grades to students characterized as conforming, compulsive, rigid, and insecure, despite the fact that these same students had lower aptitude and reading scores on end-of-course departmental tests than students who received lower grades. Thus children possessing personality attributes valued by teachers will be better liked by them, and one outcome of this will be higher grades than they deserve on the basis of objective performance. Note the similarity between the traits of the preferred children in this study and those preferred by teachers in the Feshbach (1969) and Good and Grouws (1972) studies.

Battle (1954) showed that congruence in values between teachers and pupils is associated with higher pupil grades. This is probably related to Hadley's finding that better liked students are graded higher than less liked students.

Medinnus (1962) found that students who were preferred by their teachers and received more praise from the teachers were more likely to be chosen by their peers in sociometric interviews. Thus being preferred by one's teacher apparently can affect one's peer status as well as one's grades.

Gronlund (1950) found that teachers tend to overjudge the peer popularity of pupils they most prefer and to underjudge the popularity of those that they least prefer. Here again, teachers tend to project their own values to the children they teach.

A study by Yarrow, Waxler, and Scott (1971) showed that, just as teacher treatment of students can affect their peer popularity, students' popularity with peers can affect their popularity with the teacher. In this study two adult caretakers were trained to act either highly nurturantly or nonnurturantly toward preschool children at different times. In the nurturant condition they were supposed to be nurturant toward all children, and in the nonnurturant they were supposed to be nonnurturant toward all children. Thus there should not have been any difference in nurturance toward different students. However, considerable individual differences appeared, and the investigators attribute these to the effects of peer group factors and child behavior in shaping the behavior of the teachers. The child's sex and other individual differences in nurturance seeking affected the teachers' behavior and, in the case of girls, so did peer relationships. Girls who were treated more aggressively by their classmates were also treated less nurturantly by the caretakers than were their female classmates, and girls who received more friendly overtures from their classmates also received more friendly overtures from the caretakers. Thus child behavior seemed to condition teacher behavior toward these girls. There were no similar differences among the boys, however.

The peer popularity variable was also shown to be important in a study by Schmuck (1963). He found that children who perceived themselves to be unpopular with their classmates (whether or not they actually were) tended to be underachievers, to have negative self-concepts, and to have generally negative attitudes toward school. This kind of self-concept and the behavior associated with it is likely to initiate a vicious circle, both provoking undesirable responses from teachers and classmates and causing the child himself to treat others in undesirable ways.

In summary, the research reviewed in this section shows that students' individual differences in personality characteristics will affect teachers for better or for worse, and that the attitude a teacher forms toward a student may affect how he treats him in the classroom and how he grades his performance.

Physical Attractiveness

Sheer physical attractiveness has been found to affect teacher's expectations about students. In one experiment (Dion, 1970) subjects were given fictitious reports about disturbances created by school children. Along with the student's name and age and the report of the supposed disturbance the experimenter attached a photograph, supposedly of the student involved. These photographs had earlier been judged to be either attractive or unattractive by adult judges.

Each subject was asked to read the report and then evaluate the seriousness of the disturbance and give general impressions of the student. Although physical attractiveness of the student did not affect the subjects' reaction when the supposed misconduct was mild, when the report mentioned a severe disturbance the subjects tended to assume that the unattractive boys and girls were chronically antisocial in their everyday behavior. In contrast, they did not usually make this kind of assumption when serious misconduct was reported in the folder of an attractive student. Here, they were more likely to see the student as an essentially normal child who was having a bad day.

The subjects in this study also showed a general tendency to believe that unattractive children were more characteristically dishonest than their attractive classmates were.

In a related study (Clifford and Walster, 1971) pictures previously judged to be attractive or unattractive by adults were attached to student report cards containing grades, attendance information, and ratings of personal development, work habits, and attitudes. The subjects for this study were 400 fifth-grade teachers. They were asked to examine a report card and evaluate the student's IQ, his parents' attitudes toward school, his future educational accomplishments, and his social status with the peer group. Each subject rated the identical report, but half the subjects read reports accompanied by a picture of an attractive child, while the other half read reports accompanied by a picture of an unattractive child. Again, physical attractiveness as seen in these photographs affected the judgments about the children.

The teachers in the study assumed that the more attractive boys and girls had higher IQ's, were more likely to go to college, and had parents who were more interested in their education. They also assumed that the attractive children adjusted better and interacted socially better with peers than the unattractive ones.

In a third study, Dion, Berscheid, and Walster (1972) again found strong evidence that physical attractiveness breeds positive expectations. In this study, male and female undergraduates looked at photographs previously judged to show attractive or unattractive people, and then rated their impressions of the people on a variety of personality traits. With the exception of the rating of probable success as a parent, which showed no significant difference, all other ratings showed significant differences favoring the physically attractive group. Physically attractive people were rated as more socially desirable, likely to secure more prestigious jobs, likely to experience happier marriages, likely to marry earlier, less likely to remain single, and more likely to enjoy fulfilling social and occupational lives than physically unattractive people. Furthermore, this finding was general across raters. There was no "jealousy" effect; raters who were judged to be physically unattractive were just as likely to show favoritism toward the physically attractive people shown in the pictures as raters judged to be physically attractive themselves.

Although none of these studies involves behavioral data on teacher-student interaction, they demonstrate that physical attractiveness is noticed and used as the basis for forming attitudes and expectations about students. Thus, at the very least, attractive children get a head start in forming a productive relationship with the teacher on the basis of their physical appearance alone.

Seating Location

Adams and Biddle (1970) discovered that most classrooms contain what they call an "action zone," an area of the classroom where the teacher spends most of his time and carries on a large proportion of his interactions. In most classrooms this action zone included the students who were seated along the first row and down the center aisle directly facing the teacher's desk. These students were much more active in the classroom than their classmates, in many cases almost completely dominating discussion and getting a large proportion of the teacher's individual attention. Students seated toward the back of the room, especially those toward the sides, tended to be less frequently noticed by the teacher because they were more in his peripheral than focal vision, and they were much less active in classroom discussion.

Delefes and Jackson (1972) attempted to replicate the Adams and Biddle finding by observing teacher-student interaction in one fifth-grade and one eighth-grade class in a middle class school. Although they did not replicate the exact "action zone" that Adams and Biddle had described, they did find that both students who contributed to discussion more often and students who were called on more often tended to be seated towards the front or at least the middle of the room (never the back of the room). Thus these two studies agree in finding that students seated towards the back of the room tend to be less involved in classroom interaction.

From these data alone it is difficult to tell the direction of the relationship involved. Does seating location determine classroom interaction patterns, or does the teacher's relationship with the student determine where he is seated? We suspect that the latter is probably more typically the case, at least in elementary school. Research by Rist (1970) and by Brophy and Good (1970a) showed that the highest achieving students tended to be seated closest to the teacher, while the lowest achievers tended to be seated the farthest away. Thus, in the early grades at least, where teachers typically assign permanent seats to students, seating patterns probably do not causally affect teacher-child interaction in any direct way.

Schwebel and Cherlin (1972) hypothesized that a teacher's physical distance from a student may affect the way the teacher perceives him, independent of the student's other characteristics. They collected behavioral data on students whom teachers had assigned to first-, middle-, or back-row seats. (Eleven classrooms were studied, ranging from kindergarten through fifth grade.) Following the collection of behavioral data and teaching ratings, students were randomly assigned to new seats. One-third of the students in each row remained there, while one-third were reassigned to each of the other two rows under investigation. During the first observation period it had been found that students in front rows were attentive and engaged in work-related activity much more frequently than back row students. However, after the students' seats were changed, this finding did not hold up, although those students who were moved to the front row showed the largest mean increase in time spent on school-related tasks. Furthermore, teacher ratings (before and after seating locations were manipulated) indicated that students who moved forward were perceived as becoming more attentive (which was confirmed by the behavioral data) and more likable. The investigators suggested that the "most attentive" students were assigned initially to front-row seats. When assignments were manipulated, however, students who moved forward became more attentive. Thus seating location alone may causally affect certain student behaviors and teacher perceptions. Similarly, in later grades where students select their own seating locations, a student may partially determine the degree of attention he gets from the teacher and the number of opportunities he gets to participate in question-and-answer sessions and discussions merely by choosing a seat which is either inside or outside of the action zone.

Two experiments by Daum (1972) also provide experimental data showing that the student's seating location will affect his classroom performance even if he does not choose the seat himself. This two-part experiment was conducted in a college psychology course with fifty-eight undergraduate students. The first part of the study was naturalistic. Students were scored for whether they were seated in the front, the middle, or the rear of the room, and their scores on two classroom tests were investigated. Analyses showed that students sitting towards the front scored higher than those sitting at the back (the students had selected their own seats at the beginning of the course).

The second phase of the study was experimental. Thirty-two of the original students were selected as subjects, divided into two groups of sixteen students each matched on grade point average. One day a special "pop quiz" was announced in the class, and, in addition, students were asked to take seats in specific areas of the room. Half of each of the experimental groups were asked to sit at the front of the room and half at the rear, with the remaining students seated in between. Once this was accomplished, a lecture was delivered and the students were then given a quiz on its content. Again, students seated in the front scored higher than students seated in the back. Also, high ability students scored better than low ability students. There was also interaction between seating location and student ability. High ability students did well on the test regardless of where they were seated (in other words, moving their seating location did not affect their performance). However, low ability students who had originally been seated in the rear of the room scored higher on the test if they were among the group that had been moved to the front of the room than did low ability students who remained in the rear of the room. Although the results of this experiment must be taken with caution because they are based upon a single test based upon a single lecture, they nevertheless suggest that the performance of low ability students can be improved by seating them closer to the teacher.

Writing Neatness

Several studies (for example, Chase, 1968) have shown that students who have neat handwriting are more likely to receive high grades on essay tests than students whose handwriting is messy, even when the content is exactly the same. This is not a general finding; it interacts with the handwriting neatness of the teacher grading the paper. Huck and Bounds (1972) found that paper graders who were themselves neat writers tended to penalize for messy writing when grading essays, while graders whose own writing was messy were not affected by the neatness of the essay they were grading.

Speech Characteristics

Several studies have shown that children who speak in nonstandard English tend to be negatively perceived by teachers.

Guskin (1970) tape-recorded two ten-year-old boys reading an identical story. The black boy was from a working class home, while the white boy was from a middle class home. Guskin then had a group of education majors listen to one of the two stories and rate the speaker on a variety of measures. Whenever significant differences appeared, the black speaker was rated more unfavorably than the white speaker. These ratings were not confined to ratings of language ability; they also included personality factors which apparently were associated in the minds of the raters with usage of black dialect. Williams, Whitehead, and Miller (1972) presented several studies showing that teachers tend to associate nonstandard English (especially "black dialect") with negative attitudes and to develop low expectations for achievement in students who speak in this manner. Thus teachers are especially likely to show negative attitudes, expectations, or behavior toward black children if they speak the form of nonstandard English often referred to as "black dialect."

Williams, Whitehead, and Miller noted this tendency in both black and white teachers, although it was much less pronounced among black teachers. A similar pattern of findings regarding generalizations from language samples was reported by Naremore (1970). Again, speakers of nonstandard English were rated less favorably, but this tendency was less pronounced among black teachers. On the basis of their responses Naremore divided the teachers in her sample into several groups according to their tendency to generalize from speech characteristics. The group that stood out as most hostile toward speakers of nonstandard English and most likely to harbor unfavorable attitudes toward speakers of nonstandard English were all whites.

Speech characteristics influence teachers independently of student race, since comparisons of good and poor English speakers within samples restricted to white students have shown the same kind of results as those which have compared white standard English speakers with speakers of black dialect. Frender, Brown, and Lambert (1970) studied the effects of speech differences in lower class students who had been matched for age and verbal and nonverbal intelligence. Among these matched students those who received better grades from their teachers had distinctly different speech styles from those who received lower grades. They used intonation more appropriately and spoke in softer voices, and their voice tone was not so low pitched as the students who received lower grades. In view of the matching procedures employed, it seems likely that the students' speech characteristics (and probably also SES factors associated with these characteristics) were responsible for the differential grades that they received from the teachers.

The effects of speech characteristics were demonstrated even more clearly in a study by Seligman, Tucker, and Lambert (1972). In this study photographs, speech samples, drawings, and compositions from third-grade boys were given to student teachers for evaluation. The boys were from either an upper-class or a working class school. The writing and art samples were obtained by having each boy write a composition and draw a picture concerning *Voyage to the Bottom of the Sea*. Speech samples were obtained by having each boy read aloud the same passage from a third-grade reader. These data along with a photograph of each boy were then given in various combinations to the student teachers to rate. The investigators corrected spelling errors in the compositions but left grammatical and punctuation errors.

After IQ data were used to match the children, and ratings of the "goodness" and "badness" of the various samples of the children's work were made, three types of data were assembled: appealing or unappealing photographs, good or poor voice, and combinations of a good drawing and composition or a poor drawing and composition. Various combinations of these three types of data were then given to nineteen student teachers to rate.

The importance of voice was shown again in that boys with good voices were always rated significantly better than those with poor voices (more intelligent, more privileged, better student, more enthusiastic, more self-confident, and more gentle). The other two factors also had effects. Boys who looked more intelligent in their photographs were rated as significantly better students, as more privileged, and as more self-confident. Similarly, boys who were presented as having written better compositions and made better drawings were rated as more intelligent, as better students, and as more enthusiastic. Interaction data showed that the photographs were less potent than either the voice data or the composition and art data in inducing impressions in the raters.

Taken together, studies in the present section show that students who speak in ways judged to be inferior to the speech of other students are rated more negatively on other characteristics also. This includes the speech commonly referred to as black dialect, as well as other speech characteristics which are independent of the race of the students.

INFLUENCE OF TEACHER EXPECTATIONS IN THE CLASSROOM

Given that teachers and individual students do interact differently, one wonders about the determinants of interaction patterns. As the preceding studies have shown, student characteristics do shape teacher behavior. Indeed, we believe that student characteristics are the most important determinants; however, we also think that teachers' expectations for the class as a whole and for specific students, as well as teachers' definitions of their role as a classroom teacher also influence their general classroom behavior and their treatment of specific students.

Teachers, all teachers, form diverse opinions about their students. The accuracy of these opinions varies widely from teacher to teacher. Some teachers are generally accurate in their perceptions of the abilities and personalities of their students; others have distorted perceptions regarding many of their students. Ultimately, teachers' perceptions about students influence their interactions with them. Inappropriate teacher behavior occurs when teacher perceptions are inaccurate and inflexible. Teachers also form quick judgments about their students. This will be demonstrated with hard facts later in the book, but first let us hear a group of teachers speak for themselves.

Mrs. A., a first-grade teacher, comments about three of her students.

MARY   Very, very babyish. She sits and daydreams, looks at other children and does anything she can to entertain herself. Anything except settle down and do her work. She plays with her crayons, plays with her little strap-on bag at the desk. She wants to talk to the other children. This child I think will be a problem all year. Very doubtful if she will settle down. She's very immature in all her activities. She doesn't seem to be interested in anything.

NANCY   Comes from a family in which all the other children in school have had many, many problems all during their school lives. But Nancy seems to be one of the better ones of all the others, because just now she is able to distinguish differences in pictures and also in word forms. She will be one of the best of this particular family but she will be a slow learner. I was real pleased to know that she will be one of the best of that family. I have taught all the others in her family that have been in this school. She listens well, follows directions to some extent. I believe she will be below average.

PETE   All the other children in his family have excelled—in dancing, music, school, academically. But I'm afraid Pete possibly may be a disappointment because I don't think he's going to excel. I think he's going to be a good student. He follows directions fairly well and works and plays well with other children. But I don't think he will be—shall we say, as good as some of the others in the family. Darling little boy.

Mrs. B., another first-grade teacher, has the following to say about three of her students.

ROBERT   Robert is very slow, tries to a certain extent. I'm afraid he's going to have to work real hard to get out of the first grade—as it appears now. He's overgrown for one thing. He's not a repeater.

LOUISE   Louise is going to be, I believe, one of the best students in the room. She's interested, does her work and gets through and very quiet. What I mean, she doesn't talk or cause much disturbance or anything.

WILLIAM   Can't think of anything on him.

Mrs. C. sees three of her first graders as follows.

JEAN   Tall, pretty little girl. Well behaved, seems to have such lovely manners. Very interested. I had her little cousin, who was one of my favorite pupils, so I'm expecting Jean to do real well this year.

JOHN   John is such a pretty boy with big old brown eyes, and he smiles all the time, even his eyes smile. Wants to please, well behaved. Really joins in with any activity that is going on, and his work has been nice. I'm expecting him to be one of the better boys.

MICHELE   Is a little black girl. She wanted to sit by Calvin—they're neighbors. She's from a large family. Her father is disabled, but yet she dresses very pretty. She said today—I told her her dress was very pretty—she said her cousin gave it to her. I think it's nice that she has the cousin. Michele really isn't responding at all. I'm trying to teach Michele to hold her pencil properly. I don't know if she has had the opportunity to use crayons before or a pencil. I am hoping she'll respond to work in the room better. On the playground the children seem to like her. She can run fast. It seems that she's going to be a popular girl.

These comments are verbatim quotes from teachers talking about some of the children in their classrooms. They were made during interviews in which the teachers were asked to go through their classroom roster, one child at a time, and give their impressions of each child as an individual (Willis, 1972). The quotes are typical of the comments made during these interviews, in that the teachers notice different things about different children and report a great many things about some children but have very little to say about others. Sometimes the teacher includes not only information about what the child has been doing or about his present behavior but also predictions about how he is going to do in the future. Some of these predictions are very specific and are made with great confidence, while others are merely vague hunches.

Teachers can make such statements, usually with general accuracy, because they observe and react to their students in their everyday interactions with them. Teaching means more than simply transmitting information and skills to nameless and faceless learners; it also involves personal, one-to-one relationships with each student as an individual. By continually observing and interacting with their students, teachers become very familiar with both their general personalities and their more specific characteristics as learners. Over time they develop an increasingly detailed impression of each student. This impression allows the teacher to describe the student as he is right now, and, by inference, to predict what he will be like in the future. Thus, if you ask a teacher about his students, you get comments like those quoted above.

The quoted comments are unusual in one sense, however: *they were made by first-grade teachers on the third day of the school year.* The children had not been to kindergarten, had not taken tests, and had not had prior contact with the teachers before they arrived for school on the first morning. Thus the teachers' impressions were based solely on a few days of contact with them in the classroom and, in some cases, on knowledge about the family or earlier contact with a relative.

With this knowledge in mind, look again at the teachers' comments. Notice in particular the great variety in the amount and kinds of information that they provide about different children and the differences in the kinds of predictions they make about the children's future behavior and academic success. After only three days of school some children had made strong and rich impressions on their teachers, while others had made little or no impression. Among those who did make an impression, some are seen so positively that the teachers already feel confident in predicting good things for them. Others have so discouraged the teachers in these few initial contacts that the teachers already are seriously concerned about their abilities to adjust to school or to succeed academically.

These examples help dramatize the point that the students in any teacher's class will show huge individual differences in their abilities, their readiness for school tasks, and their personal attributes and behavior. Teachers notice some of these individual differences and use them as the basis for making judgments about what a student is like, what kind of teaching he needs, and how well he is likely to do.

On the basis of their perceptions about individual students, then, teachers develop attitudes toward those students and expectations about what the students are going to be like in the future. They then begin to behave differently toward different students. With one student the teacher becomes increasingly relaxed and informal, while with another he becomes increasingly tense and impersonal. As time goes on and individual differences between students emerge more clearly and begin to take greater effect, the teacher's interactions with his students become more differentiated and individualized. To an extent his pattern of interactions with each individual student is unique and somewhat predictable. In the following chapters this process will be analyzed in detail and some of the factors connected with it will be investigated.

SUMMARY

So far, educational research has been relatively unproductive in coming up with information applicable to the improvement of educational practice. In our view, the two major reasons for this are the lack of criteria for specifying when teaching behavior is appropriate or inappropriate and the lack of attention to individual differences in students. The lack of appropriate criteria has led to the overgeneralization of research results. Data taken from one kind of classroom are often generalized to a very different kind of classroom, and data taken from laboratory situations are often generalized to the classroom, without replication and validation in these new settings. Also, teaching principles yielded by educational research are sometimes presented in an overgeneralized way which suggests that they are universally applicable, when in fact they may apply only to certain situations or to certain kinds of students. Thus, at times, giving teachers information "based on research" is worse than giving them no information at all.

Failure to take into account individual differences among students also leads to application problems. With a few exceptions most educational research until very recently focused on the teacher and treated the class as an undifferentiated group, ignoring and masking student differences. Yet much teacher behavior is directed to individuals rather than to the class, including many of the behaviors that interaction analysis research has focused on. By lumping together data from individual students to compute a class mean, investigators may mask rather than reveal important relationships between teachers and student behavior.

To illustrate that different students in the same classroom have very different interaction patterns with their teacher, studies of group and individual differences in students which are known to affect teachers were reviewed. Teachers tend to prefer students from higher social class homes, to overestimate their ability relative to the abilities of students from lower class homes, and to have more positive and facilitating patterns of interactions with them. Similar findings were found for student race, where several studies indicated teacher discrimination against black students, and, more generally, against minority groups in integrated situations. The sex of the student was also found to be an important group factor determining classroom interaction, although the findings from different studies are mixed and do not yield a clear-cut advantage to one sex over the other (this topic will be dealt with at length in Chapter 7).

Student individual differences have also been shown to influence teachers. High achievers, students with personalities that appeal to teachers, and students who are physically attractive, compared to their opposites, tend to be the objects of higher teacher expectations and more positive teacher attitudes, as well as more frequent and more appropriate classroom interaction. Seating location in the classroom is also an important variable, independent of other student characteristics. Teachers interact more frequently with and are more attentive toward students seated at the front and down the center aisles, and students seated at the front tend to be more attentive and work oriented and to be more positively perceived than their class-mates. How neatly a student writes can also influence his grades from teachers, at least from teachers who are themselves neat writers and who are predisposed to discriminate against students who are messy writers. Finally, students who do not speak standard English are likely to engender low expectations and negative attitudes in teachers.

All of these student characteristics, and others to be discussed later in the book, affect teachers' perceptions of students. In particular, they affect teacher expectations and attitudes regarding students, and this in turn affects the way the teachers deal with the students. To illustrate the speed and power with which these effects operate, comments about students made by first-grade teachers on the third day of school were presented. These comments illustrate how, after even such a short period of contact, different students had made strikingly different impressions upon their teachers, and how the teachers were already beginning to use these impressions to formulate expectations about student performance and behavior and to plan their treatment of the students involved.

The remainder of the book will deal with research on student differences that affect teacher expectations and attitudes, and how the latter can affect teacher-student interaction patterns and student performance.

chapter 2

Teacher Expectations

Jackson (1968) showed in his book *Life in Classrooms* that inequality is the rule rather than the exception for teacher-student interactions in the same classroom. Some students have a great many interactions with their teachers every day, while others see the teacher less than once a week. Some are frequently praised, others are frequently criticized or disciplined, and still others are mostly ignored. Jackson's observations about the uneven patterns of teacher-student contact in classrooms have been supported by the work of many other investigators (Garner and Bing, 1973b; Hudgins, 1971; Lightfoot, 1972; Power, 1971).

Jackson attributed this to a variety of factors. First, and perhaps most important, is the extremely rapid pace with which events move in the classroom. It is very difficult for teachers to monitor their own behavior and the behavior of their students and at the same time present information, ask questions, evaluate answers, and otherwise carry on an almost continuous stream of interactions with students. Other factors include the great variety of individual differences among students that is found in any classroom, and certain beliefs that are common in teachers which tend to make them relatively unlikely to try to change established behavior patterns. If a teacher believes that intelligence or personality traits are fixed and unchangeable, for example, or if he believes that the job of matching the difficulty and interest level of the curriculum to the individual needs of the students has already been done for him by the publishers, he is likely to be the kind of teacher who takes the students' individual differences as they come and responds to them passively without attempting to change them. If he does not believe these things, he is more likely to try to change, rather than merely adapt to, undesirable achievement or behavior patterns.

INITIAL RESEARCH ON EXPECTATION EFFECTS

Life in Classrooms in particular, and the work of Jackson and his students in general, stimulated research interest in the interactions between teachers and individual students in their classrooms (previously most studies had investigated teacher behavior toward the entire class as a group, without looking at dyadic interactions between teachers and individual students). However, even greater interest in this area was generated with the publication of Rosenthal and Jacobson's (1968) *Pygmalion in the Classroom,* one of the most interesting and controversial volumes to appear in the history of educational research.

In this book Rosenthal and Jacobson presented their famous "Oak School" experiment, designed to test the hypothesis that teachers' expectations for students' achievement would function as self-fulfilling prophecies, causing the teachers to behave in ways that would make their expectations more likely to come true. Subjects for this experiment were three teachers at each of the six grades of an elementary school serving an urban lower class community. Early in the year the experimenters administered a test of general intellectual abilities to each student in the school. The test was *not* described as a test of general abilities to the teachers, however, it was described as a specially constructed test capable of identifying students who were late intellectual bloomers and who could be expected to show unusually high achievement gains during the coming school year. A few students in each teacher's classroom were selected as treatment subjects. The teachers were told that the tests had shown that these students were "late bloomers" who were going to make very large gains that year compared to their past performance. Thus the teachers were led to believe that these students would do unexpectedly well during the coming school year.

This single feedback session about the late bloomers constituted the sole treatment; there was no further contact between experimenters and teachers and no attempts to remind the teachers about who the bloomers were or otherwise to reinforce higher expectations for these randomly selected students. At the end of the year, however, the investigators again administered the same test of general abilities that had been used earlier, so that they could compare the gains of the treatment subjects (the late bloomers) with those of their classmates. The data indicated that the treatment subjects had outgained their classmates on this test, although the general group difference was almost completely due to large differences in grades one and two (the classes in grades three to six showed only minor differences, and none reached statistical significance). Also, gains were more pronounced among girl bloomers than boy bloomers. These positive findings (at least for grades one and two) were taken as evidence supporting the hypothesis that teachers' expectations function as self-fulfilling prophecies. The bloomers also outgained their classmates in reading achievement and were described by their teachers as more likely to succeed in the future, more interesting, happier, and more intellectually curious. Again, however, these differences were most pronounced in the early grades.

This study captured the imagination of the media and the general public. It was well publicized and widely acclaimed in the popular press and was reviewed favorably in several educational journals. Accounts of the study were often overly enthusiastic and uncritical, however, and secondary sources describing it often made exaggerated claims going far beyond those made by its authors. Some writers even seemed to suggest that any kind of teacher expectation would somehow magically and automatically become self-fulfilling, although this obviously is not true.

Within educational circles a controversy arose surrounding this study which has continued unabated since. Several critical reviews appeared (Snow, 1969; Taylor, 1970; Thorndike, 1968), and a replication of the study by another investigator (Claiborn, 1969) failed to find any evidence that artificially elevated teacher expectations had functioned as self-fulfilling prophecies, since the achievement of the experimental children in this study was not affected by the treatment.

All in all, the attention focused on *Pygmalion in the Classroom*, which has continued through the present and includes a full scale book (Elashoff and Snow, 1971) devoted almost entirely to an analysis of the original study, has long since passed the point of diminishing returns and has tended to focus attention on this single study instead of on the more general teacher expectation literature. Regardless of where one stands concerning Rosenthal and Jacobson's original data, work by a large number of investigators using a variety of methods over the past several years has established unequivocally that teachers' expectations can and do function as self-fulfilling prophecies, although not always or automatically. The research literature which leads us to these conclusions will be reviewed in the following two chapters. To set the stage however, we will first define a few terms and present a model for guiding and evaluating teacher expectation research.

TEACHER EXPECTATIONS

By "teacher expectations" we mean inferences that teachers make about the present and future academic achievement and general classroom behavior of their students. Ordinarily, teacher expectations are based in part upon available data concerning students (intelligence and achievement test data, past grades, comments by previous teachers, or knowledge about the student's family) when such data are available. When the teacher takes them into account, he may develop a well-formed set of expectations regarding students before he even sees them. Regardless of the degree to which teachers form expectations on the basis of other data, however, their expectations are shaped and changed by contact with students in the classroom (work habits, apparent ability to meet the demands of the curriculum, apparent motivation, willingness to comply to school rules, interest patterns, and so on).

Teacher expectations may concern the entire class or specific individual students. General expectations applying to the entire class include such things as the teacher's beliefs about the changeability versus the rigidity of students' ability, about the students' potential for benefiting from instruction, about the difficulty level of the material for the students in general or for particular subgroups, and about whether the class should be taught as a group or whether individuals should be taught individually as much as possible. These general expectations interact with specific expectations about individual students, which are based upon the factors described above. The research in this book primarily deals with teachers' specific expectations regarding individual students, although their general expectations are no doubt also important and exert influences upon classroom interaction and instructional style. In fact, in extreme cases where teachers have well-formed and inflexible expectations regarding the class as a whole (such as where classes are tracked and the teacher perceives the class as an undifferentiated group of high achievers), teacher behavior may be more influenced by this general expectation than by specific expectations regarding individuals. The degree to which teachers are oriented toward the class as an undifferentiated group or toward individual students is itself an individual difference variable among teachers.

Teacher expectations regarding students are simply a special case of the more general phenomenon that we all make observations and inferences about people on the basis of what we hear about them and what we see of them in everyday interactions with them. Thus, many of the findings of social psychology (attribution theory, interpersonal attraction, and similar topics) are applicable to the classroom although the implications usually need to be investigated and spelled out. Much of the social psychology literature relevant to the self-fulfilling prophecy hypothesis was reviewed by Rosenthal and Jacobson (1968). Thus, several generalizations regarding the expectations of people in general and the expectations of teachers regarding students in particular can be made.

EXPECTATIONS AS NORMAL

First, expectations are not abnormal or unusual; they are common, everyday experiences. Nor are they typically illogical; usually they are quite reasonable and logical inferences based upon observations. The expectations of many people are generally accurate, and, if they are in error, they are corrected if and when the person encounters contradictory evidence. Thus it is common for us to change our first impressions of another person after we have gotten to know him better. However, people differ in the general accuracy of their interpersonal perceptions, and thus also in the accuracy of their expectations based on those perceptions. Some people persist indefinitely with strong and rigid but incorrect expectations regarding another person even after they have gotten to know that person quite well.

Usually there are overdetermined dynamic reasons for this, and the incorrect perceptions reflect the perceivers' own needs. Two common examples are lovers, who may find it difficult to see anything bad about each other, and bitter enemies, who may find it difficult to see anything good about each other.

To some degree everyone harbors certain incorrect expectations regarding other people, either because they have not yet encountered contradictory evidence that would make them change their expectations, or because they have failed to notice or have explained away such contradictory evidence. Why would a person fail to notice or explain away contradictory evidence rather than change an expectation? Usually the answer lies in the person's personality makeup. Changing his expectation, at least at the present time, would cause the person to experience ego devaluation and perhaps develop symptoms of psychological disorder such as anxiety or depression. To avoid the anxiety or pain associated with continually experiencing failure in meeting one's goals, the person resorts to defense mechanisms which allow him to avoid seeing his failures or to redefine them in ways that locate the problem in someone other than himself, thus avoiding personal responsibility and its attendant guilt. An example that has been observed in teachers is that they tend to take personal credit when students succeed ("I taught them") but to rationalize when students fail ("they can't learn") (Ehman, 1970; Johnson, Feigenbaum, and Weiby, 1964).

When expectations are not rigid and self-defeating, any inaccuracies that exist are eliminated as new or previously unnoticed information is noticed and taken into account. Thus, interpersonal expectations in general, and teacher expectations regarding pupils in particular, are neither good nor bad in themselves. Their effects depend on their accuracy and on how they are used. Accurate expectations which are continually adjusted to keep in step with changes in the student and which are used as devices to help individualize instruction to the student's needs can benefit both teacher and student. In contrast, inappropriate expectations, especially if they are inflexible and not adapted to keep in step with changes in the student, can impede teaching effectiveness. Inappropriately high expectations will cause the teacher to try continually to push the student beyond his present capacities, so that he continually experiences failure and discouragement. Inappropriately low expectations will cause the teacher to be satisfied with work that is below the student's potential, so that the student will not achieve what he is potentially capable of achieving.

Expectations usually *result* from observed performance rather than *cause* it. They are capable of causing performance, however, if they are inflexibly rigid and inappropriate. Thus expectations are much more likely to act as self-fulfilling prophecies in some teachers than in others, depending upon the degree to which their expectations match the actual characteristics of their students, the frequency with which they experience failure, and their pattern of defense mechanisms as described above. In addition, expectations appear to be formed very rapidly and to show a marked primacy, or first impression, effect. Sometimes, as in the case of teachers who scan the school records concerning their class before they meet new students in the fall, expectations about performance and behavior can be formed before the students are even seen. However, strong first impressions or expectations can be formed without using these data. As will be shown in Chapter 6, expectations which not only are strong but also are relatively stable are formed by teachers on the basis of nothing more than a few hours of observation of a student in their classroom.

The latter point shows the futility of attempting to avoid forming expectations in order to prevent them from becoming self-fulfilling prophecies. Certain writers have suggested to teachers that they should avoid looking at school records and exposing themselves to information about their incoming students in order to avoid forming expectations that might be inappropriate. This suggestion, although well meant, will not succeed, because it is clear that teachers quickly form expectations regarding their students whether or not they look at data available in the students' records. Apparently contact with students in the classroom leads inexorably to the formation of differential expectations, even if the teacher deliberately tries to avoid forming them. Thus, to repeat and summarize, it should be kept in mind that expectations are normal and ubiquitous and are neither good nor bad in themselves. Their potential for interfering with teaching goals is determined not by their presence or absence, since they are ubiquitously present, but instead by their general degree of accuracy and flexibility and their potential for adjustment in response to change in the behavior of the student.

TEACHER EXPECTATIONS AS
SELF-FULFILLING PROPHECIES

When a teacher's expectation acts as a self-fulfilling prophecy, it functions as an antecedent or cause of student behavior rather than as a result of observed student behavior as in the more typical situation. The potential for self-fulfilling prophecy effects of teacher expectations (or "teacher expectation effects," as we will frequently term them) exists when teacher expectations are inaccurate and inflexible, so that the teacher begins to treat a student consistently as if he were somewhat different from what he actually is. Expectations can also be self-defeating when accurate, if they are also inflexible. If a teacher accurately perceives a student to be a low achiever, *and if he sees this as permanent and unchangeable*, he will be relatively unsuccessful in teaching the student. Thus teacher expectations do not have to be inaccurate (as implied in the usual definition of self-fulfilling prophecies) to affect students. Their degree of flexibility, or openness to being changed in response to new data, is even more crucial than their initial accuracy.

The self-fulfilling prophecy idea was introduced by Merton (1948). A self-fulfilling prophecy is an expectation or prediction, *initially false*, which initiates a series of events that cause the original expectation or prediction to become true. Merton gave bank failures as one example. Suppose a false but persistent rumor circulates that a bank is about to fail. People with savings in the bank who hear and believe the rumor will go to the bank and withdraw their money, to deposit it in a "safer" bank. If enough of the bank's depositors hear and believe this rumor and withdraw their money from the bank, the bank will be unable to withstand the strain and actually will fail. In this case, the rumor would have acted as a self-fulfilling prophecy. If the rumor had not begun, the bank would not have failed. However, once begun, the rumor set in motion a rash of savings withdrawals that ultimately caused the bank to fail.

The same kind of process can occur in the classroom. If a teacher harbors an inappropriate but rigid expectation that a particular student is not capable of doing the work assigned to his class or group, the teacher is likely to "give up" psychologically on this student, perhaps going through the motions of teaching him but not doing so with serious determination and with the expectation that the student will learn. This initial teacher expectation can set off a series of circular and mutually reinforcing events. First, the teacher is likely to treat the student with less enthusiasm than he treats other students, to call on the student less frequently, to persist in seeking responses with him less often and with less determination, and, in general, to make only half-hearted attempts to teach the student and to be relatively unconcerned when the student fails. Furthermore, since our expectations affect our perceptions as well as our behavior, the teacher will have a general tendency to notice evidence of failure in the student and at the same time will be less likely to notice the student's successes (this is merely a special case of the more general finding that we are more likely to see something when we expect it and are looking for it than when we are not). This mechanism of selective perception which makes the teacher more likely to notice the student's failures than his successes will of course reinforce the teacher's low expectations regarding the student.

Even if student performance is accurately perceived, teachers with contrasting expectations may interpret it differently. Thus perception of success when it was expected may lead to feelings of accomplishment and satisfaction in the teacher, along with a probability that he will praise or reinforce positive expectations in reacting to the student. In contrast, perception of unexpected student success might raise in the teacher a suspicion of cheating or blind luck and lead to a reaction which reinforces negative expectations.

While the above experiences are occurring within the teacher, experiences are occurring within the student which also reinforce the vicious circle. First, to the extent that the student is being taught less, both in terms of quantity of material taught and quality of teaching (enthusiasm, determination, patience, and support), he will learn relatively less than his classmates. The longer this continues, the further behind he will fall, thus further confirming the teacher's low expectations. In addition, the student's motivation is likely to be eroded, partly because he will be continually falling further behind and finding the work more difficult, and partly because he is likely to diagnose correctly the teacher's treatment of him and to reach the conclusion that the teacher does not think that he is very bright or very likely to be able to handle the material. This in turn is likely to lead to an attitude of frustration, apathy, and defeatism, producing symptomatic behavior such as withdrawal from the classroom and a tendency to give up easily rather than persist when difficulties in learning are encountered. To the extent that any of these effects occur in the student, the quality of his work will further deteriorate and the teachers' low expectations for him will be further reinforced.

Continued over the course of a school year, a vicious circle of low expectations and failure responses will set in, and the end result will be that the student will achieve at a level somewhat below (perhaps considerably below) the level at which he might have achieved had the teacher begun with a more positive set of expectations regarding his abilities and potential. This would be a true case of a teacher expectation or self-fulfilling prophecy effect, in that student underachievement resulted directly from inappropriately low teacher expectations and would not have resulted at all had not the inappropriately low expectations existed in the first place. Students' self-concepts, career goals, and general day-to-day coping attitudes may also be eroded by the consistent communication of low expectations.

When we refer to the self-fulfilling prophecy effect of teacher expectations or to the teacher expectancy effect, we will be referring to situations such as that just outlined above. These are to be distinguished from certain other situations which are similiar in some ways but which do not involve expectancy effects by our definition. The latter are situations in which teachers have accurate and flexible but nevertheless low expectations for student achievement. In such situations teachers accurately assess the students' potential for handling the curriculum as low, but they do not let this expectation or assessment interfere with their attempt to teach the students. They work just as hard or perhaps even harder with these students than with their classmates; doing their best to adjust their teaching to the students' present level of readiness, and to move them along at a pace they can master. In short, although the teachers harbor low expectations for the students, they do not let these expectations impede their teaching and in fact may go out of their way to show patience, encouragement, persistence, and perhaps even make extra attempts to diagnose and remediate the students' weaknesses.

In many such situations, despite the teachers' best efforts, students will make only minimum gains compared to their classmates and will therefore bear out their teachers' original expectations that their potential for handling the material was low. However, it would be inappropriate to speak of expectations as self-fulfilling prophecies in these situations. There is no evidence to suggest that the teachers' expectations were inappropriate or rigidly inflexible, or that they led the teachers to teach the students in inappropriate and self-defeating ways. In the absence of evidence of some inappropriate behavior on the part of the person holding an expectation which somehow helps bring about the expectation, it is incorrect to speak of self-fulfilling prophecies or expectation effects. Thus the mere fact that an expectation has been confirmed is not sufficient evidence of a self-fulfilling prophecy effect; there must also be evidence that the original expectation was inappropriate to some degree and that the person holding this expectation engaged in some kind of behavior which caused the other person to respond in a way that made the originally inappropriate expectation come true.

A MODEL FOR TEACHER EXPECTATION EFFECTS

To tie together the preceding comments and to set the stage for the review and discussion of the teacher expectation literature that appears in the next two chapters, we propose the following model as a basis for conceptualizing and guiding research on expectation effects in the classroom. We feel that the model is useful because it identifies the steps that must be included in the process where a true expectation effect occurs, and because it focuses attention on the cause-and-effect mechanisms involved. Although this is an important step in any scientific area of inquiry, it is especially vital in respect to the teacher expectation effects literature because of the aura of magic or mystery that has surrounded it since the publication of *Pygmalion in the Classroom*. As mentioned previously, this book was initially well publicized and generally acclaimed in the popular press. Reviewers often seemed to suggest that any kind of teacher expectation would somehow magically and automatically become self-fulfilling, although this is obviously untrue.

This problem was magnified, at least indirectly, by certain aspects of the Rosenthal and Jacobson study itself. The study was confined to the expectation induction treatment and to the collection of *product* measures (pretest and posttest scores); no classroom observations designed to identify the underlying *processes* involved (differences between the ways that teachers treated the late bloomers and the ways that they treated their classmates, which might explain the relatively greater gains made by the bloomers) were included in the study. Rosenthal and Jacobson clearly stated that they believed that teacher expectation effects were communicated through differential teacher behavior toward the two groups of students, but they offered only a few general suggestions and no behavioral data concerning the mechanisms underlying expectation effects.

Thus in the minds of many, the self-fulfilling prophecy effects of teacher expectations were, and in some cases still are, vaguely understood phenomena shrouded in mystery. Just as initial acceptance of *Pygmalion in the Classroom* was overly enthusiastic and oversimplified, in our opinion the extreme negative reaction that set in once the study became controversial because of negative criticism and several replication failures was equally oversimplified and unjustified. It was quite understandable, however, given the above. Educators who were under the impression that teacher expectation effects boiled down to "just make a wish and it will come true," recognizing the absurdity of this statement, were more than ready to accept the idea that the teacher expectation effects findings had been a flash in the pan disproven by subsequent research.

Because of these overreactions to and oversimplifications of the *Pygmalion* findings, we believe that it is important to specify a model describing the processes underlying teacher expectation effects. The model outlines a series of steps, *all* of which must be present if a given series of events is to be considered a valid instance of expectation effects. Note that there is nothing mystical or magical in the model; it presents teacher expectation effects as outcomes of a series of cause-and-effect relationships, each one of which is observable and measurable.

1. Early in the school year, using the school records and/or observations of students during classroom interaction, all teachers form differential expectations regarding the achievement potential and personal characteristics of the students in their classrooms. Some of these initial expectations are inappropriate, and some are relatively rigid and resistant to change even in the face of contradictory student behavior.

2. Teachers begin to treat students differently in accordance with their differential expectations for them. Where teacher expectations are inappropriate and rigid, treatment of the students will be inappropriate.

3. Students treat teachers differently because of their different personalities, and they also respond differentially to the teacher because the teacher treats them differentially. Other things being equal, student response to teacher behavior will be reciprocal (teacher warmth and initiation will lead to student warmth and initiation; teacher coldness or hostility will lead to student withdrawal or hostility; and so on).

4. Thus, in general, each student will respond to the teacher with behavior that complements and reinforces the teacher's particular expectations for him. In the case of students toward whom the teacher holds inappropriate and rigid expectations, the students will tend to be conditioned to respond with behavior that more closely approximates and therefore helps reinforce the teacher's expectations.

5. If continued indefinitely, this process will cause the students toward whom the teachers hold inappropriate and rigid expectations gradually to approximate those expectations more and more closely. This results from a combination of the effects of the teachers' differential treatment of the students and the effects of this differential treatment on the students' opportunities to learn, general motivations, and self-concepts, and their general relationships with the teacher.

   This process will not occur with students toward whom teacher expectations were originally appropriate or were inappropriate but not rigid. In the former case the teachers will simply respond to student behavior as they see it, and in the latter case they will quickly adjust their expectations to make them conform to the behavior that the student shows. In neither case will the student be confronted with persistent inappropriate behavior from the teacher which pressures him to behave in ways unnatural to him (initially) and to begin to become a different kind of student than he actually is.

6. If continued over the course of the school year, differential teacher treatment of different students will show differential effects on both process and product measures. Where teacher expectations are appropriate, or where they are flexible so that any inappropriate aspects are quickly corrected, the teacher-student interaction pattern will be largely predictable from knowledge of the student's general personality and specific classroom habits, and his achievement relative to that of his classmates will be highly

predictable on the basis of his previous achievement. In other words the classroom behavior and academic achievement of such students will be "about as expected."

Where teacher expectations have been inappropriate and rigid, students' classroom behavior and achievement levels will deviate from predictions based on past performance. Where expectations are inappropriately and rigidly high, the student will probably have many more than his share of interactions with the teacher during the year and will receive a great deal of encouragement and cajoling from the teacher. However, the teacher will be continually pushing him beyond his capacities and consequently he will often experience feelings of failure. Depending on the relative frequency and strengths of the former and latter factors, this student might achieve at higher than expected levels (if teacher determination and high expectations outweigh the frustrations associated with failure) or lower than expected levels (if he becomes so frustrated and anxious that he performs below his capacity despite the extra attention from the teacher). Even if he does better than expected, however, it may be at the cost of higher anxiety or other undesirable side effects.

If the teacher's expectations are inappropriately and rigidly low, the student will have fewer interactions with the teacher, will get less praise and more criticism than his classmates receive in comparable situations, and will be likely to experience generally half-hearted teaching in which the teacher attempts to teach him less material and is less persistent in teaching him the material that he does teach. For his part the student will be likely to experience ego devaluation and a general sense of frustration and failure, leading him to withdraw increasingly from classroom participation and to begin to give up easily on his work assignments. End-of-the-year test results will likely show that this student achieved significantly less than would have been expected on the basis of his past performance.

This model should be borne in mind when reading the research presented in the next two chapters. It helps keep teacher expectancy effects in perspective as observable and measurable phenomena. At the same time it helps distinguish true expectancy effects (in which an inappropriate and rigid expectancy causes a teacher to condition a student to behave differently than he might have behaved otherwise) from less complex situations which may include low teacher expectations and differential teacher treatment of different students but not involve true expectancy effects as defined above.

SUMMARY

Publication of Rosenthal and Jacobson's (1968) *Pygmalion in the Classroom* initiated a continuing controversy over the hypothesis that teacher expectations for student achievement can function as self-fulfilling prophecies. It is the authors' contention that the research to be reviewed in the following two chapters clearly establishes the validity of this hypothesis (but only for certain teachers in certain situations). To set the stage for reading the research presented in these chapters, the present chapter introduced some key terms and presented a model depicting the steps which must be included in the process if a true case of teacher expectation effects exists.

It was pointed out that expectations are ubiquitous, and generally are inferences based upon and following observations of another person, and that they are neither good nor bad in themselves. More important than their particular content are their accuracy and especially their degree of flexibility (openness to adjustment to take into account new evidence). Self-fulfilling prophecy effects of teacher expectations are most likely when the teachers' expectations are inaccurate and inflexible. Such expectations cause a teacher to perceive mostly those student characteristics that confirm expectations and to fail to perceive student characteristics that do not confirm expectations. Also, they cause the teacher to persistently treat the student in inappropriate ways (treating him as if he were someone else, as it were). If continued indefinitely, such treatment constitutes a pressure on the student to begin to conform to the teacher's expectations by behaving in the ways that the teacher expects the student to behave. This in turn reinforces the teacher's expectations all the more, and a self-regenerating vicious circle is established. If the situation persists, a true expectation effect is likely to occur. This will show up both in process measures (the degree of appropriateness of teacher–student interaction patterns in the classroom) and product measures (student gain on achievement tests, student enjoyment of school, student self-concept and self-esteem as a learner, and so on).

The following two chapters will review research dealing with teacher expectation effects. In contemplating this research the reader should bear in mind some of the distinctions made in this chapter and in particular the model for expectation effects which identifies the aspects that must be present if a true expectation effect has occurred.

chapter 3

Studies of Experimentally
Induced Expectations

To date, over sixty studies have accumulated, mostly in the years since the publication of *Pygmalion in the Classroom,* which bear directly on the question of teacher expectancy effects. To help break down this large number of studies into more manageable units and to introduce some distinctions that we think are worthwhile in evaluating the literature, we have divided the experiments into those in which expectations were experimentally induced and those in which expectations were naturalistically formed. Within each of these two major distinctions we have subdivided the studies into those which include product data only, those which include process data only, and those which include both product and process data.

In the present chapter we review the studies in which expectations were experimentally induced through some kind of treatment or intervention. When the subjects were teachers, the typical inducement procedure was to provide the teachers with some kind of false information that would lead them to believe that certain students were either more capable or less capable than their measured abilities suggested. When students were the subjects of the experiment, expectations were usually induced by manipulating their success or failure on a task and/or by providing them with evaluative feedback suggesting that they had done well or poorly. These studies contrast with those reviewed in the next chapter in which expectations were formed naturalistically on the basis of normal experience in the situation, without any attempts by the experimenters to influence expectations through provision of false information or other artificial treatments.

Studies involving inducement of expectations have used both product and process outcome measures to assess whether or not their experimental manipulations had succeeded in producing expectancy effects. Product measures include IQ tests, achievement tests, sociometric popularity tests, measures of student personality traits or behavior, and other normative devices which measure the student on variables of interest and allow analyses of his progress on these variables during the course of the experiment in comparison with the progress of other students. Most experiments involving product measures include the administration of the same measures at both the beginning and the end of the experiment with the first set of data serving as the pretest and the second as the posttest. By comparing the relative gains of experimental and control students, investigators can check for expectancy effects and determine whether the induced teacher expectations had the predicted effects upon the experimental students.

Product measures are so called because they reflect the results (products) of expectation effects. They measure student abilities or characteristics at two points in time (before and after the experiment), to assess whether the experiment has produced a different "product" than would have been produced if the experiment had not been performed. In contrast to product measures, which concern only students, process measures involve the interactions between teachers and students during the course of the experiment. When process measures are used to assess experimental outcome, the investigator looks for predicted group differences in teacher-student interaction patterns. It is expected that teachers will interact in ways that are known or suspected to promote achievement with students for whom they hold high expectations but will interact in ways that are known or suspected to retard achievement with students from whom they expect low achievement.

Product and process measures are both important. They complement and reinforce each other by providing related but different kinds of information about teacher-expectancy effects. Product measures are crucial for establishing the reality and potency of such effects. Expectancy effects cannot be established through process measures alone; experimental intervention can produce differential teacher-student interaction processes without making any measurable differences in student achievement or other relevant student product measures. Thus, product measures are necessary to establish that teacher expectations can affect student achievement, personality, or other product outcomes of interest.

Process measures, on the other hand, are needed to gain an understanding of the causal mechanisms which underlie expectancy effects that are demonstrated through changes in product measures. This is pointed up clearly in Rosenthal and Jacobson's (1968) study, which included product but not process measures. Let us assume that the advantage of the experimental over the control subjects in the first two grades in this study represent a true instance of expectancy effects as defined in the previous chapter (as noted previously, some critics would not accept this assumption). If these findings represent true expectancy effects, two important questions immediately come to mind: (1) what produced the effects? (2) why were the effects produced in grades one and two but not in grades three through six?

Although they discussed various possible answers to both of these questions in some detail, Rosenthal and Jacobson were unable to provide data bearing directly on either question, because their study did not include process measures involving observation of teacher-student interaction during the experiment. Drawing on social psychology literature involving study of expectancy effects outside the classroom, they suggested that their experimental subjects may have gained more than controls because their teachers treated them more pleasantly and enthusiastically, observed them more closely and noted their successes more often, and rewarded them more frequently and more appropriately when they did achieve success. Thus they hypothesized that the treatment led the teachers to adopt a generally positive set toward the late bloomers, featuring a greater tendency to look for, notice, and reward success in these students. These suggestions are appealing and reasonable (they have "face validity"), but they remain conjecture by the authors because they are not backed by observational data of teacher behavior toward late bloomers and their classmates.

Rosenthal and Jacobson stressed the quality rather than the quantity of teacher-student interaction in seeking to explain expectation effects, because postexperimental teacher interviews revealed that the teachers did not think that they spent any more time with experimental students than with matched controls. The validity of these data is highly questionable, however, as Rosenthal and Jacobson themselves noted. First, the interview was conducted ten months after the end of the experiment, and thus was heavily dependent upon the teachers' memories. Second, as will be mentioned frequently throughout this volume, teachers usually are not very aware of their patterns of interaction with individual students in their classrooms, even the ones that they presently teach, let alone students that they taught ten months previously.

Rosenthal and Jacobson also offered several hypotheses about why expectation effects were observed in the first two grades but not in grades three through six. They suggested that the differential findings may have resulted from one or a combination of the following reasons: younger children are more malleable and susceptible to adult influence than older ones; younger children have less firmly established reputations in the schools; teachers believe the younger children to be more malleable; younger children may be more sensitive to and affected by teachers' communication of expectation; student sampling error (unknown differences between students in the first two grades and those in grades three through six); and teacher sampling error (unknown differences between teachers in the first two grades and teachers in grades three through six). Again, Rosenthal and Jacobson were confined to speculation because their study did not include process observation of teacher-student interaction. They did note that the school administrators considered the teachers in the first two grades to be generally more competent than those in grades three through six. This is a judgment, however, and not an established fact.

Furthermore, it appears inconsistent with the general tenor of the results of studies reviewed in this volume, in that susceptibility to expectation effects appears to be associated with low rather than high teacher competence. However, the latter conclusion stems mostly from studies showing inappropriate teacher behavior toward students in low-expectation groups, while the Rosenthal and Jacobson study involved induction of only positive, or high, expectations. Thus the two conclusions are not necessarily inconsistent.

To summarize, the Rosenthal and Jacobson study provided product data bearing on the teacher expectancy effect hypothesis but contained no process data to indicate the mechanisms underlying expectancy effects or the reasons why they were observed in some classrooms but not others. In the remainder of this chapter we will review the available research on experimentally induced teacher expectancy effects, beginning with studies involving product measures only, then discussing studies involving both product and process measures, and concluding with a review of studies involving process measures only. A selective review of studies involving the inducement of student expectations will follow. We will then conclude with a general discussion of the literature on induced expectancies.

INDUCED TEACHER EXPECTATIONS
AND PRODUCT MEASURES

Evans and Rosenthal (1969) conducted a study very similar to the original Rosenthal and Jacobson study, except that it involved two elementary schools rather than one and the students in these schools were primarily from middle class rather than lower class homes. This replication study produced mixed, mostly negative results. No expectancy advantage was found for either boys or girls on either total IQ or verbal IQ. The data for reasoning IQ showed a significant interaction: boys in the experimental group gained more than controls but girls in the control group gained more than experimentals. Thus this study, very similar in design to the original and conducted by one of the original authors, failed to replicate the Rosenthal and Jacobson findings. These findings are typical of the replication studies conducted by Rosenthal and his colleagues and, more generally, of studies involving induced teacher expectations, use of product measures, and inclusion of all or most of the school year as the time span of the experiment.

Pitt (1956), in one of the few studies in this area conducted before *Pygmalion in the Classroom,* induced expectations in teachers by falsifying the IQ scores of their students. This study involved 165 fifth-grade boys whose IQ's were 94 or higher. In reporting IQ's to the teacher Pitt randomly added ten points to the scores of one-third of the boys, reported another third accurately, and randomly deducted ten points from the scores of the remaining third. Achievement test data and school grades taken at the end of the year provided no support for the expectancy effect hypothesis. However, there were some effects on a self-report measure administered to the boys themselves at the end of the year. The boys whose IQ's had been lowered felt that they did not work so hard at their schoolwork as other boys, that schoolwork was more difficult for them, that the teachers were harder in grading them, and that in general school was less enjoyable for them. Thus the treatment affected the boys' feelings about themselves and about school, although this effect was not strong enough to affect the boys' achievement scores.

Fielder, Cohen, and Feeney (1971) conducted a quasi-replication of Rosenthal and Jacobson's study in thirty-six classrooms in three schools. Procedures and measurement techniques were essentially the same as Rosenthal and Jacobson's, except that the study did not begin until the second semester. Analyses of student gains showed no expectancy advantage to the late bloomers, either for the total group or within grade level, sex, or minority subgroups. Nor were there any suggestive trends. Thus this study produced totally negative results regarding the self-fulfilling prophecy hypothesis.

Goldsmith and Fry (1970) tried a variation of the Rosenthal and Jacobson study at the high school level. They used the same general abilities test that Rosenthal and Jacobson had used, along with an achievement test. Teacher expectancies regarding 112 experimental and 112 control students were induced in September, but postmeasures were taken only five months later instead of at the end of the school year. Since Rosenthal and Jacobson had found that some teachers had forgotten which of their students were supposed to be late bloomers, Goldsmith and Fry tried to strengthen their treatment by reminding each teacher three to five times during the semester about the identities of the high expectation students in their classes. Despite this effort postexperimental interviews indicated that only about half of the teachers acquired the expectations that the experimenters had tried to induce. Unsurprisingly the study failed to replicate Rosenthal and Jacobson's findings; there was no evidence that the experimental students made greater gains than the control students.

More recently Fleming and Anttonen (1971) attempted a similar but more extreme version of Pitt's (1956) study. This study involved about 900 second-grade students and their teachers. Within each classroom students were randomly assigned to one of four treatment conditions which determined the kind of information that their teachers were given about them in the fall: (1) their actual IQ inflated by sixteen points; (2) their actual IQ as measured; (3) their actual scores on a test of primary mental abilities; or (4) no information at all. The main expectancy effect hypothesis in this study was that the students whose IQ's had been inflated by sixteen points would show greater than expected gains on measures of IQ, school achievement, and self-concept. The latter product measures were administered twice, once in February and once again in the spring.

No evidence of expectancy effects appeared in either administration of the IQ or the self-concept measures. A single subtest of the abilities test did show an advantage to the high expectation group in the scores taken in February, but even this advantage had disappeared by the spring. Thus, in general, this study produced no evidence of teacher expectation effects.

Two interesting findings emerged from a postexperimental interview conducted in this study. First, most teachers simply did not believe the inflated IQ's and therefore discounted them and did not raise their expectations regarding the students involved. This points up an important weakness of studies which attempt to induce teacher expectations: there is no certainty that the teachers will acquire the expectations the experimenters desire them to acquire. If the experimenters' information is too discrepant from what the teacher already knows about the student or from what the teacher can see in his everyday interactions with the student, the teacher is likely to reject the experimenters' information rather than to reject the everyday evidence seen through his own eyes. Also, the very success and notoriety of *Pygmalion in the Classroom* has probably made it more difficult for subsequent studies, including those conducted by Rosenthal himself, to replicate Rosenthal and Jacobson's (1968) original findings. The study has been so widely publicized that most teachers have heard about it and are therefore likely to be suspicious of anyone giving them unusual information regarding student IQ or aptitude.

A second interesting point that emerged from the interview data was that teachers' opinions regarding the usefulness and validity of tests were related to their teaching effectiveness. Teachers holding a high opinion of tests were more successful in producing gains in IQ and achievement, and they gave higher grades. They also were less likely to discriminate between SES groups in assigning grades than teachers who had a lower opinion of tests. Thus test data as such had an effect on the teachers in this study, although falsified test data in the form of inflated IQ's did not.

So far, the studies reviewed in this section have been replications or near replications of the Rosenthal and Jacobson (1968) study. However, several studies have been conducted which differed from the preceding in many ways, although they all involved artificially induced teacher expectations and the collection of product data on the students.

Pellegrini and Hicks (1972) induced expectations in volunteer college tutors working with low income elementary school students. Within age, the forty-four students were randomly assigned to one of four treatment groups, designed to control the tutor's familiarity with the tests being used as well as his level of expectation for student performance. For three of the groups the tutors were given a typical expectation induction treatment. Each tutor was told that his child had been given two intelligence tests and was provided with a summary of the child's performance. Although the two tests actually had been administered, students had been randomly assigned to the treatment conditions so that the information presented to the tutors was not based on their actual test scores. The high expectation tutors were told that their children had very high intelligence (120–129 range), the middle expectation tutors were told that their children scored in the average range (95–105), and the low expectation tutors were told that their child was below average (85–95 range). A fourth group of tutors were given high expectations just like the other high expectation group, but they were also familiarized with the tests used and were aware that the children would be retested with the same tests at the end of the experiment.

Tutoring continued two hours a week for seventeen weeks, and the tests were then readministered. Among the three groups of children tutored by tutors who were unfamiliar with the tests used, the high expectation group gained over the other two groups on both tests. However, the differences were very small and not statistically significant. The group with high expectation tutors who had familiarity with the tests showed a sharp and significant gain on one test but a relatively modest gain (actually slightly less than that of the other high expectation group) on the other test. These two tests, while typical of IQ subtests, measure somewhat contrasting mental abilities. One test (the Peabody Picture Vocabulary Test) requires the child to listen to a word and then point to the correct one of a group of pictures that illustrates that word. This involves primarily associative learning, generally considered a relatively lower-order mental skill (Jensen, 1969). Tests of this type lend themselves particularly well to improvement through coaching. In contrast, the other test (the Similarities Subtest from the Wechsler Intelligence Scales for Children) requires the child to listen to two words and then state how they are similar or what they have in common. The ability to perceive similarities is generally considered to be a more abstract and difficult conceptual task than associative learning, and one that is less easily acquired or improved through coaching. Consequently, Pellegrini and Hicks concluded that teacher familiarity with the nature of the tests is an important factor to be considered and controlled in expectancy effect experiments, and they suggested that this factor may have accounted for some of the discrepancies in the research reviewed above. Experiments involving expectations induced by using test results may have been affected by the degree to which teachers felt motivated or in some way personally responsible for seeing that the test results came out as predicted and by their degree of familiarity with the tests (and thus their opportunity to do deliberate coaching). These conclusions follow reasonably from the data presented in the study, although they should remain tentative in view of the small numbers of subjects included in each group and the large number of variables that the experimenters were unable to control.

In addition to failing to replicate the expectancy effects data of Rosenthal and Jacobson (1968), the studies reviewed so far indicate that teacher acceptance of the experimenter's information is crucial, and that among the factors determining this acceptance is the face validity or believability of the information. One factor already mentioned is the possibility that the information might clash with the student's past record of achievement or with his present performance as observed by the teacher. Another potential problem, illustrated in a study by Opdyke and Williams (1972), is the lack of agreement between the information and the teacher's notions about how a given student or type of student should be expected to perform. This study involved thirty male and female mentally retarded pupils and three female student teachers. Each student teacher worked with ten subjects on sixteen learning trials with a pursuit rotor apparatus. One teacher was led to expect superior performance, one was led to expect poor performance, and the third was a control teacher given no particular expectation. The results showed no main effect for expectancy, but expectancy interacted significantly with student sex. This was because in the positive expectancy group, the performance of boys was facilitated and the performance of girls debilitated by the treatment. Consequently, the differences between the boys and the girls in this group increased over the sixteen trials. Although the findings are weak and mixed (parallel results did not occur in the low expectancy group), they can be interpreted as demonstrating the importance of sex role expectations on this male-oriented task. The teacher very probably found it easier to adopt high expectations for the boys than the girls in the high expectation group in this experiment, since the task is sex typed and boys are generally expected to do better on it than girls. Thus it is possible that the teacher accepted the high expectations for the boys but not the girls in her group. It is also possible that she adopted high expectations for both sexes but became frustrated and ineffective in teaching the girls when those expectations were not realized easily. In any case this study suggests that sex role expectations and other factors that might predispose teachers toward or against acceptance of the experimenter's information must be taken into account in studies involving induction of teacher expectations.

The importance of teacher acceptance of the experimenter's information is brought out especially clearly in two studies by Schrank (1968, 1970). Working with Air Force instructors and recruits enrolled in Air Force mathematics courses, Schrank manipulated teachers' expectations about whole classes rather than individual students. In his first study Schrank (1968) assigned recruits to one of five ability groups randomly, instead of assigning them according to measured ability as was usually done. These five groups were taught mathematics by several instructors who used standardized materials. Even though the students had been assigned to the ability groups randomly, students in the highest group achieved significantly more than students in the lowest group. Furthermore, group means on the achievement measures fell into position in the same order as the ability labels of the groups. Thus, the amount that each group learned was clearly affected by the expectations of the teachers.

Having obtained clear evidence of expectancy effects in his first study, Schrank (1970) then repeated the study, but with one important exception: this time the teachers were *told* that students were being assigned to groups randomly rather than by test scores. Thus they knew that the ability groups did not really differ by ability. However, they were asked to teach the group *as if* they had been formed according to measured ability. Despite this attempt to get the teachers deliberately to simulate differential teaching of high and low ability groups, Schrank's second experiment showed no evidence of expectancy effects. In combination Shrank's two studies show that teachers must really believe that students differ in the ways that experimenters say that they differ if expectancy effects are to occur.

Flowers (1966), in another study conducted before *Pygmalion in the Classroom,* induced teacher expectations through fictitious ability grouping data in two junior high schools serving lower class populations. In each school two seventh-grade classes whose students were average for the school and who were comparable to each other as classes were selected for study. However, teachers in each school were told that one of the two classes was a high ability class. Partially successful results confirming the teacher expectancy hypothesis were found in each school. In one school the students in the experimental group made significantly greater gains in reading and arithmetic achievement (but not IQ), while in the other school the experimental group made significantly greater gains in IQ (but not achievement). A postexperimental teacher interview revealed some of the effects that the treatment had had on the teachers. Teachers who had worked with the allegedly high-achieving group reacted the following ways: they referred more often to what the students were able to do rather than what they were not able to do; they reported far fewer discipline problems; they referred more often to efforts to motivate the students and mentioned less often any inadequacy of their teaching materials; and they said that they preferred to teach the higher-ability group.

Jacobs and Richard (1970) used sociometric peer popularity rather than IQ or achievement as their measure in a teacher expectation effects study. After collecting sociometric popularity data in fourteen elementary classrooms, they told each teacher that a few students in the class would emerge as sociometric "stars," becoming more and more popular with their classmates with time. Sociometric data were collected from the students again ten weeks later, and at this time the teachers were also asked to indicate which children they thought had gained or lost in peer popularity during the experiment. The data taken from the teachers generally matched the changes seen in the sociometric data taken from students, indicating that the teachers were able to perceive the peer popularity of their students fairly accurately. However, there was no evidence of expectation effects; students who had been identified as "stars" to the teachers did not make greater gains in sociometric popularity than their classmates had made.

Johnson (1970) reported expectation effects in an experiment involving a marble-dropping task. Twenty experimenters, who were actually the subjects of the study, were told that the rate of marble-dropping learning was related to IQ, so that brighter subjects would show quicker learning on the task. They each then worked with eight subjects, half presented as relatively high and half presented as relatively low in IQ. As predicted, the experimenters obtained more marble dropping from subjects whom they thought to be especially bright. The strong expectation effects obtained in this study are especially notable because the role of the experimenter was confined to providing reinforcement to the subjects following each trial; there was no actual instruction (in the usual sense of the word) by the experimenter.

Dusek (1972) also used a marble-dropping task, but with less clear-cut results. In this study adult female experimenters worked with nine- and ten-year-old boys who were either high or low on a measure of test anxiety. The experimenters were led to expect either that the boys would perform better than the girls or that the girls would perform better than the boys. Among experimenters led to expect better performance by boys, no expectancy effects were observed. Experimenters expecting better performance by girls did obtain it, but only for girls low in test anxiety. The high test-anxious girls did not show expectancy effects; they were more influenced by the social reinforcement of the experimenters than by the experimenters' expectancies. Thus only one of four groups in the experiment showed expectancy effects.

Other Studies

The final studies to be reviewed in this section involved instruction but did not take place in the usual classroom. One was conducted by Burnham (1968) and involved swimming instruction conducted with boys and girls age seven through fourteen attending a summer camp for the disadvantaged. None could swim at the beginning of the two-week experimental period. However, camp staff members were told that a battery of tests had shown that certain children had unusually high potential for learning to swim. Half of the children were given this high-potential label, while no particular expectations were induced concerning the remainder. All children then were given a standard two-week swimming instruction course and retested with the standard Red Cross Beginners Swimming Test. As predicted, children who had been labeled as having a higher potential for learning to swim actually did show greater improvement in swimming ability than the children in the control group.

King (1970) conducted five studies on expectation effects in job training. Three involved workers being trained to be press machine operators, welders, or auto mechanics in Manpower Training programs, one involved nurses' aides being trained by a nursing school in a hospital, and one involved women being trained for electronics assembly line skills in a factory. In each study supervisors were told that certain trainees (selected at random) appeared to have special potential for success on the job involved. Measures of performance data included standardized tests, peer ratings, absenteeism rates, and general over-all ratings of performance on criterion-referenced tests of the job skills being taught. Expectation effects were observed in four of the five experiments on most or all of these measures. Differences in the fifth study were in the predicted direction but did not reach statistical significance. Also, expectancy effects were stronger when the subjects were males than when they were females.

Although King did not collect process observation data, he did collect trainee comments showing that the experimental subjects felt that they were given more demanding assignments and were observed and supervised more intensely than controls. A follow-up study (King, 1971) provided indirect evidence that experimental subjects were observed more closely or at least felt that they were. For this study workers were shown two photographs of their supervisor and asked to indicate which photo most nearly reflected the way that the supervisor looked at them. The pictures were identical except that in one the supervisor's pupils were dilated. Although none of the subjects noticed this difference, all five of the subjects who had been in the experimental group picked the picture with the larger pupils, while only two of the seven control subjects picked this picture. Significant findings on such a subtle measure with such a small number of subjects would seem to provide strong evidence that the subjects were, or at least felt that they were, more closely observed by their supervisors during the experiment. These results should be taken with caution, however, since they might reflect experimenter bias effects! It is not clear from King's (1971) report whether or not the experimenter in the follow-up study knew which subjects had been experimentals and which had been controls in the previous study. If the experimenter did know, he could have influenced the subjects' selection of pictures. In this situation, where the subjects could not tell any difference between the two pictures, the possibility for experimenter bias effects was maximized.

In summarizing this section, it should be noted that most of the experiments which were similar to *Pygmalion in the Classroom,* in that they used induced teacher expectations and involved a product criterion for determining the presence or absence of expectation effects, provided negative or mixed results. However, the teachers' acceptance of the experimenters' expectations was either known to be poor or at least suspected in most of these studies. Thus they do not necessarily mean that teacher expectations do not function as self-fulfilling prophecies; an alternate, and usually more plausible, hypothesis is that the teachers in these studies did not acquire the expectations that the experimenters attempted to induce.

INDUCED TEACHER EXPECTATIONS, BOTH PRODUCT AND PROCESS MEASURES

The studies to be reviewed in this section include both product measures to relate the experimental treatment to student outcomes and process measures designed to reveal something about how the treatment worked when positive results were obtained. The first two were done by Rosenthal and his associates, following up on some of their earlier studies.

Conn, Edwards, Rosenthal, and Crowne (1968) performed a partial replication of the original Oak School experiment. The major differences were that the children in this experiment were from middle or upper-middle class homes, and the expectancy inducement treatment was not begun until the start of the second semester rather than right at the beginning of the year as in the earlier study. Thus the teachers had a full semester of experience with the students before the experimenters attempted to influence their expectations. Two sets of test data were taken in this experiment, one four months after the expectancy induction treatment and another three semesters after the treatment. The first set of data showed small but non-significant differences in favor of the experimental students; the second set showed that this initial advantage had dissipated and, in fact, at this point the experimental students had gained relatively *less* than the control students to a degree that approached statistical significance. Thus this study failed to produce data supporting a general expectancy effect.

Some additional data collected in this experiment suggest one of the mechanisms through which teacher expectation effects may be mediated, however. The children were administered a measure of their ability to determine the emotional component of an adult female's voice. Analyses relating this measure to gain data showed that children who could more accurately judge the voice tone of an adult female speaker showed a significantly greater advantage from positive teacher expectations than other children in the experimental group. Thus, although the study as a whole produced negative results regarding teacher expectation effects, it did identify an individual difference variable among students which may relate to student potential for benefitting from positive teacher expectations.

Anderson and Rosenthal (1968) identified randomly selected late bloomers to summer camp counselors in a camp for mentally retarded boys. Product measures for this study included the usual general ability test plus a self-help test of the boys' abilities to care for their own needs without assistance. Process measures focused on the amount of attention that counselors gave to the boys. The experiment lasted about two months.

The expectancy treatment failed to provide any IQ advantage to the late bloomers, but the experimental boys did gain over the controls on the measure of self-help. Process measures showed that the camp staff paid *less* attention to the experimental than the control boys. The latter two findings are congruent and mutually supportive although in a negative sense. It seems reasonable to suppose that the camp staff paid less attention to the late bloomers, because they felt that these boys needed less attention.

However, these data also suggest that the expectancy effect in this study, if it was real, was mediated indirectly rather than directly through positive behavior. In the absence of other data we must conclude that the late bloomers made greater gains on the self-help measure because they were allowed (or required, for lack of help from the staff) to learn to do things on their own, because the staff was busy helping the control group boys whom they felt were in need of more help. Thus it may be that the experimental boys gained largely because they were left alone and allowed (as well as expected) to learn through practice, while the staff may have been doing many unnecessary things for the control group boys and thus initiated or sustained a pattern of "learned helplessness" in these boys. In any case, although this study failed to show an expectancy effect on IQ, it did reveal an expectancy effect on the self-help measure.

Claiborn (1969) attempted to replicate the Rosenthal and Jacobson (1968) data. He used twelve first-grade classrooms, confining himself to this grade because Rosenthal and Jacobson data had shown that the first-grade students showed the strongest expectancy advantage. Although the expectancy induction procedures were the same as those used by Rosenthal and Jacobson and the same abilities test was used, the expectancy treatment did not begin until the second semester and the posttests were administered only two months later. Thus the treatment was considerably weaker. Perhaps unsurprisingly, Claiborn found no evidence of teacher expectancy effects on student IQ.

Postexperimental teacher interview data showed that the teachers as a group were able to remember which children had been identified as late bloomers in their classrooms better than the teachers in the *Pygmalion* study. However, their accuracy was not perfect. Furthermore, as Rosenthal and Rubin (1971) have subsequently pointed out, some of the teachers in this study were aware of the nature of the experiment. These considerations, in combination with the generally weak treatment mentioned above, suggest that the chances of obtaining positive results in this study were quite slim from the beginning. Nevertheless, this study, largely because it was the first replication to be widely publicized and to be conducted by someone unconnected with Rosenthal, was one important reason for the negative reaction to *Pygmalion in the Classroom* that set in once the initial enthusiasm had subsided. Critical reaction to the study was almost as oversimplified and overgeneralized as the critical reaction to the original *Pygmalion* study had been. Despite several crucial differences between the two studies the Claiborn study typically was reported as a replication of the Rosenthal and Jacobson study and typically was cited as evidence that Rosenthal and Jacobson's findings had been a flash in the pan.

Claiborn's study also included process observations of teacher-student contact frequency and of the quality of affect expressed by teachers toward students. Results from these process measures complemented the product data; there was no evidence to suggest that the teachers were treating the late bloomers more favorably or interacting with them more frequently than with the control students. Thus his study produced negative results on both the product and the process measures.

José and Cody (1971) conducted an experiment similar to Claiborn's. This study involved eighteen first- and second-grade classrooms. Again, expectancy induction did not occur until the beginning of the spring semester. IQ and achievement test data, as well as measures of teacher-student interaction, were collected about four months later. The process data involved the use of Bales's Observation System (Bales, 1950). No expectancy effects occurred in the IQ data, the achievement data, or the interaction data. Thus this study constitutes another general replication failure. However, postexperimental interview data revealed that eleven of the eighteen teachers involved did not change their expectations regarding late bloomers on the basis of the experimenters' information. Thus this study represents a fairly clear case in which negative findings were due to the failure of the expectation induction procedure to affect teacher expectations rather than to the failure of teacher expectations to affect students.

Beez (1968) obtained positive results in a study requiring graduate students in education to tutor children in a summer Head Start program. Tutors were given twenty signs, each containing a single word and were instructed to teach as many words as they could during a ten-minute teaching period, using whatever strategies they desired. Although the children had been assigned randomly to experimental and control groups, half the tutors were told that they were working with a low-ability child. Process data were obtained by observing each tutor as he worked with his child, and product data were obtained by testing the child on the twenty words after the tutoring session was completed. Also, tutors filled out a questionnaire concerning their opinions about the child they had worked with when they finished the tutoring session.

Product data showed that the experimental group showed a significant expectancy advantage; they learned about six words in comparison with the average of about three words learned by the control group. Observational data showed that the major cause of this difference was the number of words that tutors tried to teach. Tutors with high expectations attempted to teach an average of 10.4 words, while those with low expectations tried to teach an average of 5.7 words. Eighty-seven percent of the high expectation teachers tried to teach eight or more words, while only 13 percent of the low expectation teachers tried to teach this many.

Tutors with low expectations also explained the meaning of a given word significantly more often, gave more examples of the same word, and spent more time on nonteaching activities than tutors with high expectations. Thus the so-called high ability students learned more because their tutors spent more of the time teaching them and attempted to teach them more of the words.

Treatment effects were also shown in the questionnaire data obtained from the tutors. High expectation tutors rated their children higher on achievement, social competency, and intellectual ability than low expectation tutors. The most spectacular difference occurred on an item concerning the difficulty level of the task. Only one of the thirty high expectation tutors (3 percent) felt that the task was too difficult for his child, whereas 63 percent of the low expectation tutors felt that the task was too difficult. Thus this experiment had profound effects upon teacher expectations and teaching behavior and provided clear-cut positive evidence of teacher expectation effects upon student learning. It should be noted, however, that the tutors and children were unacquainted before the experiment, and that the experiment itself lasted only ten minutes. This minimized the tutors' opportunities to form their own impressions of the children and maximized their dependence upon, and therefore their likelihood of accepting, the experimenter's information concerning student ability.

A partial replication of the Beez study was conducted by Carter (1969). In this study female education majors tutored kindergarten students, using ten of the twenty word signs that Beez had used. Again, experimental subjects outperformed controls, essentially because the tutors taught them more. The tutors tried to teach all ten of the words to 73 percent of the "brighter" students but only to 53 percent of the "duller" students.

A study very similar to Carter's was performed by Panda and Guskin (1970), except that this time the results were negative. Tutors led to expect better performance did not succeed in teaching more words than tutors led to expect poor performance. The series of experiments by Beez (1968), Carter (1969), and Panda and Guskin (1970) all involved similar procedures and were conducted at Indiana University. Each succeeding study produced less positive results than the earlier studies (Guskin, 1971). It seems probable that word of mouth about the experiments affected their results, since it is likely that the tutors in the final study had heard about one or both of the earlier ones and thus probably did not believe the information that they were given in an attempt to induce positive or negative expectations.

Brown (1970) also performed a study similar to that of Beez but with different results. This study involved ten teacher trainees and eighty first-grade students. As in the Beez study, the trainees were given faked psychological reports intended to induce either high or low expectations regarding student ability and then were asked to tutor students, this time using a list of paired associates (states and their capital cities). Each teacher trainee tutored eight first graders. The product data from this study indicated that the experimental subjects showed no expectancy advantage; they did not learn more state capitals than the controls. However, process data confirmed the results reported by Beez, in that the teachers with high expectations attempted to teach more pairs than did the teachers with low expectations. Thus the treatment was strong enough to affect the teaching behavior of the tutors, even though this did not result in greater learning gains by the experimental group.

Similar results were reported by Kester and Letchworth (1972), in a study involving 23 teachers and 150 average ability seventh-grade students. At the beginning of the year, several students in each teacher's classroom were identified as being especially bright and as students who were going to be included in a special study of bright students. Teacher interaction with these students and their classmates was then observed for about two months, and an IQ test and an achievement test were then administered to provide product data. An attitude scale was also administered to the students before and after the experiment. Although the researchers observed that the experimental students did not show an expectancy advantage on any of the product measures (achievement tests, IQ tests, or pupil attitude tests), process observations revealed interesting differences in the teachers' behavior toward experimental and control students. The teachers spent more time with the "bright" students, talked with them more often, and were generally more supportive toward them. These teacher behaviors were especially noticeable with those bright students who responded reciprocally by being initiatory and supportive in their contacts with the teachers. Thus the process data in this study showed both a general effect that the teachers were more positive toward the bright students in their classroom interactions and a specific effect that such teacher behavior was especially likely if the students responded reciprocally. These process differences in teacher-student interactions were not powerful enough, however, to produce an expectancy advantage for the bright students on any of the product measures.

Meichenbaum, Bowers, and Ross (1969) induced expectancies in four teachers who were working with fourteen juvenile delinquent girls. Six of the girls were identified to the teachers as bloomers. Product measures in this study were achievement test data, while process measures included observation of teacher-student interaction during the two weeks that the experiment took place. Teacher behavior toward students was rated as positive, negative, or neutral, and student behavior was rated for whether or not it was class appropriate.

This study produced positive results on both product and process measures. The bloomers showed an expectancy advantage in the achievement test scores and in the ratings of appropriateness of classroom behavior. However, the bloomers showed no expectancy advantage in the grades that teachers assigned. Teacher observations showed that the teachers had more positive interactions and fewer negative interactions with bloomers than with their classmates.

An interesting additional aspect to this study was that, prior to expectancy induction, the teachers were asked to label the girls as good or poor students. The six girls later identified to the teachers as bloomers, presumably on the basis of psychological test data, deliberately included three whom the teachers previously agreed in seeing as good and three whom they agreed in seeing as poor. Thus in half the cases the expectancy induction confirmed teachers' already existing preconceptions, while in the other half, these preconceptions were contradicted. Nevertheless, the teachers all accepted the accuracy of the tests in identifying bloomers. The expectancy induction changed their attitudes so that they began seeing positive behaviors and indications of achievement potential in the three girls whom they had previously seen as poor. Here again, teacher attitudes toward test data and the credibility of the specific information given in the expectancy induction procedure loom as important variables in studies involving induced expectations.

The remaining study in this section involved both process and product measures but not typical classroom instruction. Page (1971) studied twenty-five male undergraduates working as experimenters attempting to condition female undergraduate subjects to construct sentences using certain pronouns. The experimenters reinforced the learners by saying *good* whenever they used the desired pronouns. Experimenters were given either positive, neutral, or negative expectations regarding learner aptitude for this task. Significant expectation effects were obtained for the twenty-five experimenters as a group, indicating that conditioning scores were higher under positive (21.8) or neutral (20.4) expectation conditions than under negative expectation conditions (12.4). Although the group effect was significant, there were large individual differences among the experimenters. Six showed no expectancy effects at all, while several others showed very large expectancy effects. The data also suggest, as do those in several other experiments, that negative expectations are more potent in influencing behavior than are positive expectations.

The conditioning sessions were videotaped and scored to provide process measures concerning the mediation of expectation effects. These data showed that conditioning scores were higher when the experimenter smiled frequently, spent more time reinforcing the learners, and spent more total time with the learners, giving them information and talking to them during pauses. Among the experimenters, those who did more of these kinds of things under high expectation conditions and less under low expectation conditions were the ones who showed the strongest expectation effects. These data fit in with those from several previous studies showing that high expectation learners are likely to receive closer attention and greater warmth than low expectation learners.

Spector (1973) conducted a study designed to discover whether experimenters communicate expectancies through subtle linguistic or bodily cues (Rosenthal and Jacobson's hypothesis), or whether they do it by reinforcing subject responses which conform to experimenter expectations. Both the experimenters and the subjects of this study were college students. A projective task was used in which the subjects were asked to look at a picture and then tell a story in response to the picture. Half of the experimenters were led to expect that subjects would tell adult-oriented stories in response to the pictures, while the others were led to expect that the subjects would tell child-oriented stories. Within each of these two groups of experimenters, one-third were instructed to reinforce subject responses that were consistent with their expectancies, one-third were told to reinforce responses that were inconsistent with their expectancies, and the remaining third received no special reinforcement instructions. The process data for this experiment were the experimenters' reinforcing behaviors; the product data were the stories told by the subjects (coded for whether they were adult-oriented or child-oriented).

The product data showed no expectation effect. The experimenters expecting adult-oriented stories did not receive more adult-oriented stories than did experimenters expecting child-oriented stories. However, the process data indicated that the induced expectancies did affect experimenter behavior. Experimenters found it much easier to reinforce accurately the subject responses which were consonant with their expectations than to reinforce responses which were dissonant with their expectations, even though they had been instructed to do so. Experimenters who expected adult-oriented responses reinforced with 94 percent accuracy, and experimenters who expected child-oriented responses reinforced with 62 percent accuracy, when they were in the groups instructed to reinforce responses that were consonant with their expectations. However, experimenters with these two contrasting expectations reinforced with only 29 percent accuracy and 38 percent accuracy, respectively, when they had been instructed to reinforce responses that countered their expectations. Thus reinforcement of responses which countered expectations proved to be a confusing and difficult assignment, despite its apparent simplicity.

Further analyses of reinforcement behavior showed that the great majority of errors were in *failure to reinforce* appropriate behavior rather than in inappropriately reinforcing behavior. That is, the experimenters rarely reinforced the wrong behavior, but they very often failed to take advantage of an opportunity to reinforce appropriate behavior (behavior that they had been told to reinforce). These experimental data illustrate the point made earlier that expectations tend to structure our perceptions so that we are less likely to notice events which are unexpected.

The studies reviewed in this section show generally mixed results. Those showing primarily or completely negative results are questionable on the basis that the treatment was weak and/or that the teachers did not accept the information given to them by the experimenters. At the same time, the studies showing the most clearly positive results tended to be ones in which the teachers and students were unfamiliar with each other and which lasted for only short time periods. Thus while they demonstrate the reality of teacher expectation effects under some conditions, they do not constitute replication or direct support for the original Rosenthal and Jacobson findings. Also, several studies reviewed in this section showed positive findings on process measures and negative findings on product measures, showing that teacher expectations can affect teachers' behavior without necessarily making a difference on student achievement, IQ, or other student product measures.

INDUCED TEACHER EXPECTATIONS
AND PROCESS MEASURES

The studies to be reviewed in this section all involved artificially induced teacher expectations related to process measures of teachers or teachers and students. Some involved measures of teacher-student interaction, while others related teacher expectations to grading practices or feelings about students.

Babad (1971) showed that induced expectations can affect teachers' attitudes towards their students. In this study, teachers working in eight classes for 58 mentally retarded students were given either appropriate or inappropriate feedback concerning student learning potential. It was found that, when students actually had very low potential and also were labeled as being of low potential, the teachers adopted very negative attitudes towards them. Also, when teachers had been led to expect a high level of performance but did not obtain it, they tended to change their perceptions of the students in the negative direction. Thus low expectations which are fulfilled or high expectations which are not fulfilled are likely to induce negative attitudes in teachers and/or to make them become defensive.

Measures of Teacher-Student Interaction

Rubovits and Maehr (1971) induced expectations in undergraduate volunteer teachers who were working with sixth and seventh graders in microteaching situations. Each teacher worked with a group of four students, two labeled as gifted and two as nongifted. It was found that the teachers initiated more interactions with the gifted students, requested more statements from them, and praised them more frequently. These results are similar to the findings of Kester and Letchworth (1972) reported previously.

Rothbart, Dalfen, and Barrett (1971) conducted a similar study. In this research undergraduate teachers worked with groups of four eighth and ninth graders, two described as having considerably greater academic ability, and two as lacking in intellectual potential. Interaction sessions involved a thirty-minute literature discussion. There were no group differences in teacher praise and criticism, but the teachers were more attentive toward the brighter students. Also, the bright students contributed to the discussions more frequently.

Following the discussions the teachers rated each of the four students with whom they had worked. These data showed that the teachers considered the brighter students to be more intelligent, to have greater potential for future school success, and to have less need for teacher approval. The latter may explain why bright students in this study did not receive more praise from the teachers, as had the bright students in the Rubovits and Maehr study.

Another similar study was conducted by Medinnus and Unruh (1971), using twenty Head Start teachers and two boys enrolled in each of their respective classes. Within each class two boys who had scored within the average range

(95–105) on an IQ test were selected for inclusion in the study. One was designated to his teacher as a high-ability child with an IQ above 105, while the other was designated as a low-ability child with an IQ below 95. The teachers then presented a block-sorting task to the boys, working with each individually. These tutoring sessions were tape-recorded, and the teachers were scored on the variables of contacting, giving praise, lending cooperation, criticizing, directing, and interfering. Analyses showed no differences on four of the scales, but the teachers directed more praise and less criticism toward the high ability students.

The above three studies were all generally similar in design and results. They all suggest that teachers are likely to interact more frequently and more positively with high expectation than with low-expectation students. As in the case of studies in the previous section that showed generally positive results, these experiments involved only short periods of contact between teachers and students. Two of them also had the additional feature that the teachers and students were previously unacquainted before the experiment. However, the Medinnus and Unruh study involved teachers working with students in their own classrooms. Like the Meichenbaum, Bowers, and Ross (1969) study reviewed above, it demonstrates that expectancy induction procedures will sometimes be successful even when teachers have had opportunities to interact with the students involved and form their own opinions regarding their capabilities.

Related studies have produced similar results. Davis and Levine (1970) showed that teacher expectations affected the frequencies of interaction with high and low expectation students. Classroom observations revealed that teachers called on students who had been presented as having unusual potential for intellectual development an average of 11.9 times, while their classmates were called on an average of only 7.3 times. This probably reflects greater attention toward high expectation students.

A study by Chaikin, Sigler, and Derlega (1972) revealed a variety of process differences. In this study, undergraduates were asked to teach a short unit on home and family safety to a twelve-year-old boy. Some were told that the boy was bright, with an IQ of 130, and that he did well in school. Others were told that the child was dull, had an IQ of 85, and did not do well in school. The third group was a control group who were told that IQ and school achievement data had been omitted from the child's folder inadvertently. All boys were described as getting along well with their teachers. Teacher-student interaction during the tutoring was videotaped and scored for process variables. Analyses showed that teachers working with high expectation students smiled at the students three times more often than teachers in the other two groups, nodded their heads up and down two and one-half times more often, and looked their students in the eye more often than teachers in the other two groups. Also, teachers believing their students to be bright leaned forward toward their students four times longer than teachers in the control group and almost eight times longer than teachers in the dull group. Here again, the bright students were treated more warmly and with closer attention than the other students.

An interaction between expectation regarding student ability and expectancy regarding task difficulty was revealed in a study by Lanzetta and Hannah (1969). In this study, undergraduates taught fellow students a concept formation task. Half of the learners were presented as having high potential for the task and half as having low potential. Within each of these conditions half of the teachers were led to believe that the task was easy and half to believe that it would be very difficult. After each learner response, the experimenter-subject was to give the learner one of five possible reinforcements: a strong shock, a mild shock, a neutral light, a small money reward, or a large money reward. Experimenters were instructed to provide the reinforcement that they thought most appropriate following a given response. Each experimenter taught the same learner (who was a confederate of the investigator), who provided the same pattern of correct and incorrect responses to each experimenter-subject (responses were arranged to suggest slow, gradual learning). Postexperimental interviews revealed that the experimenters believed what they had been told about the competency of the learner and did not suspect that the learner's responses were preplanned or deliberate. Analysis of the results showed that the experimenter-subjects gave stronger rewards and stronger punishments in the high expectation condition. When the student responded correctly, he was more likely to be given a large monetary reward than a small one. Conversely, when he made errors, he was more likely to be given a strong shock than a mild one. These data tie in with data from several experiments showing that high-expectation students are more salient than low expectation students in the eyes of the beholder. However, the interaction between expectations regarding student ability and expectations regarding task difficulty in this experiment suggest that high expectations regarding student ability are not necessarily an unmixed blessing. As long as the learner fulfills the high expectations, he is likely to be rewarded more often or more intensely than a classmate who does equally well when this is not expected of him. However, a high-expectation student who performs below expectations may suffer more severe negative consequences than a classmate of whom less is expected.

In addition to the preceding studies of teacher behavior in the process of teaching, there have been several studies of the behavior of teachers or examiners when administering or scoring tests.

Effects of Expectations on Administering or Grading Tests

Kleinfeld (1972), having previously established that Indian and Eskimo students responded favorably to teacher warmth and physical proximity, investigated the effects of these variables on students' test performance. Subjects were fifteen Indian and Eskimo high school students in Alaska who had previously been given the full Wechsler Adult Intelligence Scale by a school counselor. These tests were given neutrally, with the examiner seated sixty inches from the subject and giving the test in a businesslike manner. Three weeks later, the digit symbol and information subtests (believed to be the subtests most responsive to examiner warmth) were readministered to the fifteen experimental subjects. Seven were randomly assigned to a nonverbal warmth group and eight to a nonverbal cold group. In the warmth condition the examiner sat thirty inches away from the subjects, sat at their level, sat at right angles to them, and smiled frequently when giving the test. In the cold condition the examiner sat eighty inches from the subjects, stood up while the subjects remained seated, and did not smile. Analyses of change scores showed small but significant differences, with subjects in the warmth condition gaining a few points on the average and subjects in the cold condition remaining constant or losing a few points. Thus the warmth condition produced better test performance in these Indian and Eskimo high school students.

Jacobs and DeGraff (1973) had thirty-two practicing psychologists evaluate videotaped administrations of an intelligence test given to children. Before evaluating the tests, each psychologist was given a case history suggesting that the child being tested was either bright or dull. Analyses reveal that the psychologists' judgments of the children's test performance were significantly affected by these case histories. Even professionals trained to observe and administer tests objectively and exposed to exactly the same videotaped testing session were influenced by case histories containing other information about the children.

Weaker results were obtained in a similar experiment by Mason (1973). In this study, seventy-nine teachers or future teachers were given psychological reports containing favorable, neutral, or unfavorable information about a fictional child. After looking through the reports, they heard a lecture on either bias effects or test validation, and they then watched a videotape of a kindergarten child (presumably the child described in the report that had been given them) while he was being given a test of basic concepts. While watching the videotape, they recorded responses of the child as either correct or incorrect. After viewing the tape, they also filled out an expectation measure requiring them to state the grades that they expected the child to receive in first grade. In this study, the psychological reports did not affect the scoring of the child's responses on the videotaped test. Perhaps the responses on this test were easier to score correctly than the responses on the test used in the previous study, or perhaps the lectures that the subjects had been given were sufficient to eliminate their susceptibility to expectation effects in test scoring. In any case, subjects who had been led to expect good performance did not score the child more favorably than subjects who had been led to expect poor performance. However, expectation effects were noted in the expectations measure. Subjects who had been led to expect that the child was bright predicted higher marks in the first grade than did subjects who had been led to expect that the child was dull.

Hersh (1971) also showed the effects of expectations on the administration of "standardized" IQ tests. The subjects were twenty-eight graduate students in a testing course, who administered the Stanford-Binet to fifty-six Head Start children. The children were presented as being either high or low in intellectual, social, and academic abilities. Expectation was significantly related to IQ's, with testers obtaining higher scores when they expected higher scores. Also, in rating the test taking behavior of the children, the experimenters favored the high expectation children on thirteen of fifteen scales with no difference on the remaining scales. Differences were significant for the ratings of the children's confidence, assurance, and need for praise (with high expectation students perceived as needing less praise). The experimenters also favored the high expectation children on six of seven questions regarding recommendations, with the group difference for expected school achievement reaching statistical significance. Thus the induced expectations had led the experimenters to see the "brighter" students as being generally brighter than the "duller" students and led them to give higher scores on an IQ test which they were learning to administer in "standardized" fashion. Despite these differences, however, there were no significant differences on tester behavior such as smiling, encouraging, or leaning toward the child. Thus this study produced considerable evidence of expectation effects in the product measures but none in the process measures.

Larrabee and Kleinsasser (1967) had five examiners administer the Wechsler Intelligence Scales for Children to twelve sixth graders of average intelligence. Each student was tested by two different testers, one administering the even-numbered items and the other the odd-numbered items. Before testing a given child, examiners were told that the child was either above average or below average in general IQ. Analyses showed that, when experimenters expected better performance, total IQ was seven points higher on the average than when they expected poorer performance. Differences were especially noticeable on the verbal subtests, where the average difference was over ten points, than on the performance subtests, where the average difference was less than three points. Effects were strongest for the information subtests. This could have been due to differential behavior by the testers when administering the tests or to more lenient scoring by testers when they held high expectations for performance. The latter interpretation is suggested by the findings of the studies reviewed below.

Wartenberg-Ekren (1962) related examiner expectancy to IQ scores and self-report data in a college student sample. Although she did not find that examiner expectancy affected the IQ scores earned by the college students, the students reported differential treatment by examiners which was related to examiner expectancy. This is another example of a study showing process findings without product findings. The students were somehow aware of the examiners' expectations for their performance, but this awareness did not affect their performance significantly.

Several studies have shown that expectations can affect test grading. Simon (1969) had college students score items from the vocabulary subtests of the Wechsler Intelligence Scales for Children. Higher scores were assigned when the scorers believed that the student who took the test was of above average intelligence than when they believed that the student was not above average. Cahen (1966) gave 256 future teachers fictitious information about the IQ's and reading-group placements of fictional students and then asked them to grade examples of the students' work. Higher grades were assigned to the allegedly brighter students than to the allegedly duller ones.

Finn (1972) found similar but more complex results. He asked 300 fifth-grade teachers (187 from suburban schools and 113 from urban schools) to complete rating forms on two typed essays presumably written by fifth-grade students. The essays were accompanied by fictitious information concerning the student's sex and race, as well as IQ data suggesting that he was either of high ability (115–120) or low ability (87–90), and a teacher ability rating suggesting that the child was generally bright or dull. This fictitious information did not affect the ratings made by the teachers from suburban schools, but it did affect the teachers from urban schools. The urban teachers rated the essays higher when they had high expectations and lower when they had low expectations. Finn attributed these differential results to better morale and higher expectations among suburban teachers. This may have been the case, although it is also possible that the suburban teachers were more aware of the intent of the experiment and less taken in by the expectation induction procedure. This study did not include a postexperimental interview to determine whether or not the induction was successful, so the question cannot be decided from the available data. There were also no significant main effects for sex or race of student, but again there were some interactions. Suburban teachers assigned higher scores to blacks than whites (again suggesting that perhaps the suburban teachers were on to the true intent of the study), while the urban teachers gave particularly low grades to essays depicted as written by white girls (perhaps because they had high expectations for these girls and tended to downgrade them because they did not fulfill these expectations). In general, female teachers graded girls' essays more harshly than boys' essays in comparison with male teachers.

Heapy and Siess (1970) showed that provision of information can produce a halo impression of a student which will affect grading of his papers even when the information does not concern student attributes relevant to the abilities involved in the test being graded. In this study, teachers were asked to grade an essay. Some teachers were given an essay that had been previously judged to be highly creative, while the others were given an essay that had been judged to be notably uncreative. In addition to the essay to be graded, teachers were given information depicting the writer of the essay as either a very aggressive or a nonaggressive boy. Although aggressiveness should be unrelated or perhaps even positively related to creativity, noncreative essays allegedly written by an aggressive boy were given lower grades than noncreative essays allegedly written by nonaggressive boys. These findings are reminiscent of those reported in Chapter 1, showing that children who were liked by teachers or who possessed traits valued by teachers tended to receive higher grades than other children.

These studies show that teachers' expectations can influence their grading practices. In most cases, the direction of influence is likely to be congruent with the type of expectation, so that high expectations will tend to influence the grader to give the test taker the benefit of the doubt, while low expectations will tend to influence the grader to grade more strictly or harshly. However, the possibility of a reverse effect exists under some circumstances and with some graders. If a grader feels that a particular student "should have done better than that," he may grade unduly harshly. If he feels that the student "really worked hard and did surprisingly well," he may be excessively lenient in his grading.

Taken together, the studies of testers' expectations suggest that effects are easier to obtain on grading behavior than on student test performance, although effects on the latter have also been demonstrated.

CHANGING STUDENT EXPECTATIONS

So far in all of the studies reviewed in this chapter the researchers have attempted to induce expectations in teachers as an indirect means of affecting student performance. A few studies have attempted to affect student performance more directly by affecting student expectations directly.

A series of studies have been conducted by Entwisle and Webster (1972), using similar tasks and paradigms. Typically, subjects were told that the experimenters were looking for children who could tell good stories, and the children were then divided into teams of four (all of the same sex and grade). Each team was taken to a room where an experimenter read sentence stems to them. They were asked to listen to each of twelve sentence stems and construct a story by supplying the missing word in each sentence. Teams were encouraged to think of the best words that they could in order to make the story as good and interesting as possible. After reading a sentence stem, the experimenter allowed thirty seconds for the children to think of an answer and then called on a child who raised his hand seeking a response opportunity.

During the initial, or baseline, phase, the experimenter noted the rate of volunteering for each child and made sure that each child was called upon an equal number of times. During the second, or treatment, phase, the experimenter identified one of the four children, selected because his volunteering rate had been close to the group median, and kept this child with him for a special session designed to raise the child's expectations. Meanwhile, other members of the team were taken to a large room where they heard a story read to them. While this was going on, the treatment child underwent an individual session with the experimenter in which he again supplied the missing words to twelve sentences to make a story. This time, however, the experimenter enthusiastically praised or otherwise indicated approval of the child's responses, in contrast to the team session in the first phase when he merely wrote down the answers without comment. Thus this second phase, by providing heavy doses of praise and other reinforcement, was designed to produce high expectations in the child regarding the quality of his responses and his general aptitude for this task.

During phase three, the original teams were brought back together for a repeat of phase one, except that experimenters rotated so that they would not know who the treatment child in each team is. The experimenters again recorded hand raising frequency, which constituted the process measure used in this research paradigm.

Several different studies by Entwisle and Webster have shown that treatment subjects tended to increase their hand raising frequencies from phase one to phase three, suggesting that the treatment does effectively raise expectations and increase the confidence and rates of participation of the treatment students. Replication studies using the same basic paradigm have provided answers to some interesting questions raised in earlier studies.

First, one study showed that the treatment was considerably more successful with white than with black subjects. One obvious possible explanation was that all of the experimenters were white, so that one replication study involved the use of black experimenters with black subjects. This study produced results similar to those involving white experimenters and white subjects, indicating that the race of the examiners and students was a variable which would affect the results.

Another study (Entwisle, 1973) produced somewhat more complex results. In this experiment white adults were effective in raising the expectations of both white and black children in mixed racial groups, but black adults were effective only with black children. These studies suggest that adults can raise children's expectations more effectively if the children are more familiar with them or if they identify with them easily.

Another replication study was designed to show that the results are in fact due to the praise and other reinforcing behavior shown by the examiners during the second phase of the experiments and not simply to a practice effect because the treatment child gets an extra trial at the task. In this study some treatment subjects were given the usual treatment, while others were simply given an extra trial without any praise or other reinforcing behavior from the examiner. This study showed that only the treatment subjects who had experienced praise and reinforcement from the examiner showed significant increases in participation from phase one to phase three. Thus the increased participation rates the treatment subjects show in the Entwisle and Webster studies cannot be attributed simply to practice effects; the supportive and reinforcing behavior that the examiners show in the treatment phase appears to be the causal mechanism involved.

Meichenbaum and Smart (1971) performed an expectation experiment with twenty-four borderline freshmen engineering students following the first semester of a three-semester sequence in mathematics, physics, and chemistry. Twelve of twenty-four subjects were led to believe the test data had shown them to be academic bloomers who would do well in the following semester, while the twelve in the control group were told that the test data were inconclusive and that no prediction could be made about their future performance. Following this feedback all subjects were given pointers about good study habits. Later a letter was sent to all subjects, reminding them both about good study habits and about the group to which they were assigned. The experimenters then collected product data consisting of student achievement scores and student self-report data. The results showed that the high-expectancy subjects did significantly better in the two math courses but no better in the physics or chemistry courses. Thus the treatment had led to improved performance in two of the four courses, although, even after improvement, these borderline students still remained below the mean for their classes. Questionnaire data showed that all subjects remembered the expectancy or prediction that had been assigned to them, but there were no significant group differences in self-reported study habits, use of guide notes, amount of supplementary reading, class attendance, contact with teachers, or evaluations of teachers, course content, or textbooks. Thus the improvement in achievement was accomplished even though students' self-report data indicated no parallel improvement in study habits.

The questionnaire data also revealed, however, that high expectancy subjects felt more confident, believed that the testing program had helped them realize that they could do better, became more interested in their course work, and felt the course to be more relevant to their future careers, in comparison with the low expectancy subjects. Thus, the treatment in this study apparently worked primarily by altering the subjects' self-confidence and expectations for success.

A study by Bradley and Gaa (1973) showed that goal setting conferences could increase the degree of internal locus of control of students (that is, the degree to which students perceive their performance as due to their own efforts rather than to chance or luck). Tenth graders were divided into three treatment groups: a group that held a goal setting conference each week to review progress and set specific goals for the following week; a group that held a weekly conference but did not do specific goal setting; and a control group that did not have a weekly conference. As predicted, only the group that met weekly and set specific goals for the following week showed significant gains in locus of control. These students learned to take more specific and individual responsibilities for their academic achievement, and their achievement expectations became more realistically in line with their actual probable success in meeting explicitly stated goals.

A series of studies by Moore and his associates has shown that the effectiveness of expectancy statements from adults on child performance is influenced by the degree to which the child believes or accepts the adult's statement. In one study (Biddle and Moore, 1973) children were conditioned either to believe or not to believe the expectancy statements of adults concerning their probable success on a task. Following this training the children conditioned to believe the adults' predictions showed impaired performance following low expectation statements from the adults, while children conditioned not to believe these statements showed no impairment of performance under negative expectation conditions. A related study (Gagné and Biddle 1973) involved conditioning the children to believe expectation statements by providing success feedback to their responses only when they had been preceded by an expectation of success and when the response itself was good. This procedure not only paired success feedback with attainment of actual success; it also conditioned the children to believe that successful performance would result when the experimenter predicted it. Over time children exposed to this training paradigm learned to increase their efforts on trials in which the experimenter gave a prediction of good performance. These data suggest that if direct communication of expectancies are to function as self-fulfilling prophecies they must be credible to the children, and that credibility is established primarily with a record of accuracy and success in predicting the student's achievement.

Subsequent work involving manipulation of both expectation and feedback showed that these factors interact with student achievement level and motivational patterns. Moore, Gagné, and Hauck (1973) manipulated teacher expectancy statements and teacher feedback regarding performance with seventy-two fourth graders at three levels of IQ. All of the students were overachievers in the sense that their school performance was higher than their IQ's would predict. Thus all were relatively highly motivated towards school tasks, although they differed in general intelligence. Students individually performed a task in the company of an adult experimenter who delivered expectancy statements before each response and feedback statements afterwards. Expectancy statements were high, low, or no-expectancy, and feedback statements were positive, negative, or intermittent. The results of this interesting experiment showed some findings consonant with the expectation effects hypothesis and some which contradicted it. First, in this group of overachievers, students in the negative feedback condition outperformed those in the positive feedback condition, with intermittent feedback groups in between. For these overachievers, negative feedback (being told that they had made a mistake) was positively motivating and stimulated greater effort.

There were also some interactions with IQ. The best performance among the high IQ subjects was obtained from those where high expectation statements and negative feedback statements were combined. In other words, these students did best when teachers told them that they expected them to do well but then gave them feedback suggesting that they were not doing so well. In contrast, optimal performance in low IQ subjects was obtained when low expectation statements were combined with negative feedback statements. Apparently the low expectation statements functioned as challenges to these students, and they were so highly motivated that the negative feedback did not deter them from persisting in their efforts to succeed. In any case, these data run counter to the expectation effects hypothesis, and suggest that very highly motivated students may actually be more motivated or challenged by low expectation statements than by high expectation statements.

Subjects who were given intermittent feedback regarding their performance conformed to the self-fulfilling prophecy hypothesis, in that those exposed to high expectation statements outperformed those exposed to low expectation statements. Low expectation statements were especially debilitating to the high IQ subjects in this group, while high expectation statements were especially rewarding and motivating to the low IQ subjects in this group. In general, high expectancy statements produced more positive attitudes in the students than low expectancy or no expectancy statements, across groups. However, expectancy did not produce a significant main effect on performance, and in general was less potent in affecting performance than feedback regarding success or failure.

Moore, Means, and Gagné (1973) performed a follow-up study at the senior high school level. This study included an attention-only group to check for the effects of attention as opposed to attention combined with verbalization of expectations. Subjects were forty-three eleventh graders with records as low achievers. The students received either high, neutral, or low expectancy statements for performance, and either positive or negative feedback regarding their performance. Each subject received one expectancy statement and one feedback statement per day over each of the ten days of the experiment. In this study, neither expectancy nor feedback produced a significant main effect on performance. However, a significant interaction between the two factors was obtained. The students exposed to low expectancy statements but then given positive feedback scored better than the remaining groups. The students who received high expectancies followed by negative feedback scored next best. These were the two groups who had the most incentive to exert effort and the most reinforcement for their efforts. The first group, who received low expectancy and high feedback, were receiving unexpectedly positive reinforcement, which was probably doubly reinforcing because of the low expectancies that had been verbalized to them. In contrast, the students receiving high expectancy statements and negative feedback were receiving high incentives for performance and also for renewed effort, because the high expectancy statements constituted a challenge that they were failing to meet (at least according to the negative feedback that they were receiving).

The neutral expectancy group were least responsive to feedback conditions, showing that verbalization of expectancy was an important causal factor affecting performance. Taken together, the work of Moore and his associates shows that in addition to the usual expectancy effects that occur because high expectations produce confidence and expectations of success, verbalization of low expectations can sometimes produce good performance by making the task seem difficult or challenging and motivating the student to try to prove himself by doing better than he is expected to do. Thus the student's expectations will interact with his motivational structure and with his success or failure on the task to determine whether or not his expectations are positively motivating. This series of experiments also indicates that teacher attention by itself is unlikely to affect student effort or performance, but that teacher approval or other evidence of positive feedback are likely to increase both expectations and effort in the student, at least among students whose expectations are initially low. These effects can occur even without an explicit statement by the teacher that he expects good performance from the student. Other data indicating that the expectations of others or the degree of success achieved on a task can differentially affect one's motivation depending upon one's self-concept are reviewed by Hamachek (1973).

Kelley (1950) manipulated student behavior toward the teacher by manipulating student expectations regarding the teacher. In this study college classes were led to expect a guest lecturer to be either a warm or a cold person. Although the guest lecturer was the same person in each instance and made every effort to act the same way in each class, students expecting the lecturer to be warm interacted with him more frequently than those expecting him to be cold.

In addition to the studies reviewed previously showing the effects of direct manipulation of student expectations, several studies have shaped student expectations and/or behavior by exposing them to contrasting treatments. Flanders and Havumaki (1960) assembled two groups of students who did not know one another for special group discussions. In one group, the adult leader recognized for participation and praise only one-half of the students (randomly selected). No such discrimination was made in the control group, and praise was given to the group rather than to individuals. Sociometric data collected following the group discussions revealed that the students singled out for participation and praise in the experimental group were evaluated more positively than other members of the group. This constitutes an experimental demonstration of the same phenomenon noted in some of the studies mentioned in Chapter 1: students who are favored by teachers tend to be ranked higher in sociometric popularity rankings than their less favored classmates.

Sarbin and Allen (1968) influenced verbal participation in an on-going seminar through positive and negative reinforcement. The first four meetings of the group were used to collect baseline data concerning the participation rates of each member. Then, for the next four sessions, contributions by the two lowest participators were positively reinforced and contributions by the two highest participators were negatively reinforced by the two professors. Positive reinforcement included close attention, head nodding, and expression of agreement with the student's contribution, while negative reinforcement involved ignoring the student's contribution or expressing boredom when listening to it. After this systematic reinforcement for four meetings, no systematic reinforcement was given for the final four meetings. Analyses of participation rates showed that the low participators increased their participation during the four reinforcement sessions and retained these rates during the last four sessions, while the high participators showed a sharp decrease in participation during the negative reinforcement sessions. However, once the negative reinforcement ceased, the participation rates of the two high participators rose almost to their original level during the final four sessions. The positive results with the low participators in this study show that indication of interest and attention on the part of the teacher can increase participation rates in students who are low participators.

A similar experiment by Hughes (1973) even produced significant results on product measures. The study involved seventh-grade science lessons. Teachers systematically reacted in supportive fashion to some students, frequently praising their correct answers and supporting them when they answered incorrectly. They sometimes urged them on or mildly reproved them when necessary, but negative reactions never went beyond this. Students in the control group did not receive these indicators of support. When they gave correct answers, they received no praise, although their answers were acknowledged as correct. Student learning data from this study indicated that the group who received consistent teacher support outgained the controls in science knowledge.

Tyler (1958) manipulated the subjective probability of success in problem solving tasks in four groups of students. Each group had an initial warm-up in which their success in problem solving tasks was controlled so that each group had an average amount of success. Then, the groups began receiving differential treatment in the form of positive or negative verbal reinforcement from the experimenter. One group received consistent encouragement, another consistent discouragement, and a third inconsistency (both encouragement and discouragement).

A fourth group was a control group that received no verbal reinforcement at all. As expected, the encouragement group outperformed the discouragement group. However, the control group did almost as well as the encouragement group, and the inconsistency group almost as poorly as the discouragement group. This suggests that discouragement is more potent as a negative factor in hampering student performance than encouragement is as a positive factor facilitating performance. Both the encouragement and the control group were superior to the discouragement group and the inconsistency group.

Further analyses revealed some interesting insights on how low expectations hamper student performance. First, students in the low expectancy or discouragement group tended to try to memorize solutions to problems rather than to work them out logically. Thus they approached problem solving with a more primitive and generally less successful process. Also, there was an inverse relationship between positive expectations and decision time needed for making a response. The encouragement group made quicker responses than the discouragement group. This was true even though the encouragement group used logical strategies whereas the discouragement group tended to try to memorize the answers.

This inverse relationship between positive expectations and response latency had been predicted on the basis of earlier studies showing that decision times are longer in unpleasant situations involving possible or actual negative reinforcement (Lotzoff, 1956; Marquart, 1948). Thus failure expectations can hamper student performance by eroding student confidence and concentration, so that the student takes longer to respond, and by making the student more likely to use primitive response strategies in approaching the problem. If these results can be generalized to ordinary elementary and secondary classrooms, we might expect low expectation students to remain silent or take a long time to respond when asked a question, to guess rather than attempt to reason out solutions, and/or to perseverate with primitive or inappropriate response strategies rather than recognize that these are not working and seek more appropriate strategies. Any such behavior would be likely to hamper student performance on product measures and would also be likely to induce or reinforce negative expectations in the teachers.

A series of studies dealing with inducement of student expectations has also been conducted by Means and Means and their colleagues. Means and Means (1971) attempted to affect achievement by college students in three sections of an adolescent psychology class through manipulation of student expectations. Students were first divided into high and low GPA groups and then, within these two groups, were randomly assigned to one of three treatments. In one treatment, the students were told that aptitude test results suggested that they had high aptitude for mastery of the concepts taught in the course. A second group were told that their test scores revealed little aptitude for the course. A third group was given no information. The results showed that although grade point average was related to achievement in the course, expectation induction was not. There was a significant interaction between grade point average and expectation, however: high GPA students performed better when given negative information, while low GPA students performed better when given positive information. This is not an isolated finding; similar findings have been observed previously by other investigators. Many (not all) successful students may be spurred to better performance by challenging remarks or even criticism, but generally unsuccessful students tend to respond especially favorably to encouragement and especially unfavorably to discouragement.

In another aspect of the same study Means, Means, Castleman, and Elsom (1971) investigated the effects of expectancy induction upon students' verbal participation in classes. Here again, although there was no main effect for expectancy induction, an interaction between expectancy and grade point average emerged. Subjects with low grade point averages who had been given low expectations showed notably low rates of participation in the classes. This illustrates the statement made just above that generally unsuccessful students are especially prone to become discouraged and withdrawn or apathetic if faced with teacher treatment that communicates low expectations.

In a follow-up study Alexander, Elsom, Means, and Means (1971) arranged for differential treatment of forty of the fifty-three students enrolled in two sections of an undergraduate education course taught by the same instructor. On the basis of grade point average the forty subjects were divided into twenty high and twenty low achievers, and within each of these two groups ten matched pairs were formed. One member of each pair was then randomly assigned to each of the two treatment groups. Students in the first treatment group were not addressed before or after class, and their names were not used in class or during any out-of-class exchanges. Their questions were answered politely but briefly during class. In contrast, the teacher made a point of learning and using the names of the subjects in the treatment group and initiated conversations with each of them before or after class at least three times a week. Achievement in the course was assessed at the end of the semester with a ninety-item multiple-choice test. Analyses showed significant main effects for both grade point average and treatments. The subjects with high grade-point averages outperformed the subjects with low grade point averages, and the subjects given personalized attention by the teachers outperformed the subjects ignored by the teachers. This student achievement effect appeared despite the fact that desensitization interviews revealed that no students were aware that any kind of treatment was going on. Also, although no formal process data were taken, the instructor reported that the students with whom he interacted frequently reciprocated this treatment by gradually initiating more and more interactions with him as the course progressed. Thus this study demonstrated effects on student achievement, and possibly also effects on student behavior, even though expectation induction involved no explicit provision of information and, in fact, students were unaware of the systematic teacher differences in behavior toward different students. Thus student performance can be conditioned without any awareness on the part of students that they are being systematically conditioned. This is probably true also of student expectations, although expectation data were not included in this research.

This study also revealed an interaction between grade point average and treatment groups which almost but did not quite reach significance. This interaction trend was similar to the significant interaction reported in the two previous studies in suggesting that the treatment was particularly effective with students with low grade-point averages. Although the favored students outperformed the ignored students at both grade point average levels, the relative difference was much greater among the students with low grade point averages. This again illustrates that encouragement is especially important and facilitating for high achievers and that discouragement is especially important and debilitating for low achievers.

DISCUSSION

In this chapter we have reviewed a large number of studies involving inducement of expectations in teachers and several involving inducement of expectations in students. The studies involving teachers as subjects have produced mixed and somewhat confusing results. Most studies using product measures found no expectancy advantage for the experimental group, but most studies using process measures did show teachers to be treating the experimental group more favorably or appropriately than they were treating the control group. None of the long-term studies designed to replicate the Rosenthal and Jacobson (1968) findings succeeded in doing so, so that these controversial findings remain unreplicated. However, the replication studies tended to involve weaker treatments because expectations were induced in midyear or posttests were given in midyear, because the teachers did not adopt the expectations that the experimenters were attempting to induce, and/or because the teachers were aware of the nature of the experiment. This points up the major weakness of paradigms involving inducement of teacher expectations through provision of false information. When negative results are produced in studies using this paradigm, it is often unclear whether the teachers did not adopt the expectations that the experimenters were trying to induce, or whether the teachers adopted these expectations but their expectations did not affect the students. Any future experiments conducted with this paradigm should include postexperimental interviews to determine which teachers adopted the desired expectations, and data should be analyzed separately for those teachers who did adopt the expectations and those who did not.

For studies conducted in naturalistic school settings, it seems most appropriate that in the future teachers be given genuine information about their students rather than phony information designed to make them view the students as something other than what they actually are. This will insure that the information is credible and will avoid some of the ethical problems mentioned above, and it will also provide a basis for examining the effects of causing teachers to articulate consciously their expectations regarding their students. This question is of some importance because many writers maintain that such articulation of expectations only leads to labeling of students, which does no good and may do considerable harm. Thus they advocate avoiding doing anything that will lead a teacher to label a student or to articulate explicit expectations regarding him. We doubt that this is so, partly because we know that expectations exist and can affect the teacher whether or not he has explicitly articulated them in his mind, and partly because we think that specific expectations can potentially become helpful teacher tools if they are linked with prescriptive behavior and if they are flexible so that they change to keep in step with changes in the student. In fact, accurate perceptions and expectations regarding students are probably essential for truly effective individualization of instruction. Thus we think that attempts to get teachers to avoid forming expectations about students will not succeed. Nevertheless, at this point the question remains an empirical one; it remains to be seen what effects, if any, will result if a deliberate attempt is made to make teacher expectations sharper and more accurate.

As will be argued more fully in the following chapter, we believe that, at this point, there is little reason to conduct additional research involving inducement of teacher expectations and that, instead, future teacher expectation research should use teachers' naturalistically formed expectations. In addition to the inference problems caused by the factor discussed above, there is the ethical question raised in inducement studies. It is beginning to become clear that, although it is important to understand the dynamics involved in communication of both high and low expectations, teacher communication of low expectations and its effect upon students appears to be most pressingly in need of further research. In view of the already demonstrated undesirable outcomes that can occur when low expectations are successfully induced in teachers, it is difficult ethically to justify research involving inducement of low expectations toward certain students.

Even the inducement of high expectations toward certain students seems to be of limited value for the future. The major reason is that, at this point, it seems clear that expectation effects occur in some teachers and not in others. Thus further attempts to replicate *Pygmalion in the Classroom* or otherwise simply demonstrate the *existence* of expectation effects is unnecessary. Instead, we now need research designed to identify the causal mechanisms which explain such effects when they exist and explain why they exist in some teachers but not others. A second reason for dropping this paradigm is the very popularity of *Pygmalion in the Classroom* and of the research paradigm itself. It has been used so often and has received so much publicity, that it may be difficult if not impossible these days to find a teacher who will accept information at face value and adopt the expectations that the experimenter hopes to induce!

All in all, however, the studies reviewed in this chapter have been valuable. Some of those including product measures have been important in establishing the reality of teacher expectation effects. Those including process measures have added to our understanding of how teacher expectations are communicated to students and of the effects that they have on students when they are communicated. Perhaps the most important contribution of the studies involving induction of teacher expectations (compared with studies involving naturalistically formed teacher expectations discussed in the next chapter), however, has been their role in establishing that positive results involve true expectation effects and cannot be explained through more simple conditioning and learning concepts that do not involve teacher expectations. Some of the data in the studies reviewed in the next chapter can be explained via simple conditioning and reinforcement paradigms without getting into teacher or student expectations. That is, differential teacher behavior toward different students may simply reflect conditioned teacher responsiveness to differential student behavior, as patterns of teacher-student interaction are established over time. However, in several of the induction studies reviewed in this chapter, the teachers were completely unfamiliar with the students before the experiments began, and the experiment itself was too short for conditioning and reinforcement mechanisms, which work slowly and gradually, to have been a very large factor. These studies seem to compel a teacher expectation explanation, to demonstrate that true expectation effects exist, and to provide evidence of some of the kinds of effects that can be observed.

The studies regarding improvement of student expectations for their own performance seem to be quite worthwhile and worthy of continued interest from researchers. The available evidence suggests that students will try harder to succeed when they have high expectations or when their low expectations are raised, and this increased effort is likely to result in increased performance. Thus studies like those of Entwisle and Webster and of Moore and his colleagues seem likely to produce information useful for improving or maximizing student expectations. Again, however, we would strongly stress the importance of credibility and accuracy in giving information to students. Providing the student with unrealistically positive information might have a short-run effect in raising his expectations temporarily, but the long-run effect is likely to be a deepened sense of frustration and failure and a tendency to disregard or distrust future teacher statements about ability or performance. Teacher expectations can act as self-fulfilling prophecies in raising student performance levels above what they might have been otherwise, but only if the expectations are realistic.

SUMMARY

A variety of studies involving experimental induction of expectations in teachers or students were reviewed in this chapter. Rather than repeat the specific findings of individual studies, we will list what we believe to be some of the major conclusions to be drawn from this body of research. These include the following:

1. The controversial findings of *Pygmalion in the Classroom* have yet to be replicated unambiguously, in that no other investigators have succeeded in showing significant expectancy effects on achievement tests or IQ tests when expectations were induced through experimental manipulations and when the experiment spanned the entire school year. However, most of the replication attempts involved weaker treatments than the original because the treatment was initiated later in the school year, because the posttests were administered earlier in the school year, because some or all of the teachers involved failed to acquire the desired expectations, or because some or all of the teachers were aware of the nature of the

experiment. Thus it would be inappropriate to dismiss the *Pygmalion* findings because of these replication failures, especially since many other studies by many different investigators have unequivocally established the reality of expectation effects even though the original *Pygmalion* findings remain unreplicated.

2. Data showing that the degree to which the teacher believes and accepts the information given to him by the experimenter will affect the likelihood of expectation effects, as well as data to be presented in the following chapter showing that susceptibility to expectation effects is in itself an individual difference variable across teachers, strongly suggest that neither the *Pygmalion* findings nor any other findings in this area should be evaluated solely on the basis of group data. At this point it seems clear that expectation effects occur in some teachers and not in others. Thus, the negative findings for the teachers in grades three through six in the *Pygmalion* study cannot be used to argue that the positive findings for the first two grades are invalid. The findings for the first two grades should be judged on their own merits.

3. The publicity that *Pygmalion in the Classroom* has received, and the popularity of the research paradigm it represents, make it increasingly difficult to replicate the original results. As more and more teachers become familiar with the study, it will become increasingly difficult to find teachers who will accept phony information at face value.

4. In any case, we question the value of continuing to do research involving induction of expectations in teachers. The reality of the phenomenon is an established fact at this point, whether or not the *Pygmalion* results are ever replicated. Furthermore, induction of negative expectations regarding students raises serious ethical problems, and even studies involving induction of positive expectations appear to have reached the point of diminishing returns. On the other hand, more studies using teachers' naturalistically formed expectations, especially when conducted in the naturalistic classroom setting, are needed to establish the frequency and impact of expectation effects in everyday schools.

5. The probability of obtaining expectancy effects varies not only with the teacher but also with situational factors and with the type of measure used. Positive effects are more likely when the teacher and students have not met before the experiment and when the time of the experiment is short than when teachers and students are well acquainted and the experiment spans a long time period. Also, it seems to be very difficult to achieve positive effects on IQ tests, less difficult on achievement tests, somewhat easier on tests of self-concept or attitudes, and easiest on process measures of teacher and student behavior during interaction. Several researchers reported positive findings on process measures that were not strong enough to produce congruent positive findings on product measures. A few studies also showed the reverse pattern, however.

6. Process data have revealed that, when expectation effects are operating, teachers are likely to interact more frequently and more warmly with high expectation students, to observe them more carefully, to attempt to teach them more material, and to reinforce their successes more frequently and/or more intensely.

In studies where the latter finding was not observed, teacher interview data sometimes suggested that the high expectation students were perceived as needing less praise, so that individual differences among teachers on this variable probably explain the conflicting findings regarding praise and general warmth toward high expectation students.

7. Independent of whether or not teachers are familiar with *Pygmalion in the Classroom* or with this area of research in general, it seems clear that information provided by the experimenters must be credible to the teachers if it is going to be believed and if it is going to lead to adoption of the desired expectations. Information which is too discrepant from the evidence that teachers get in their everyday interactions with students will not be accepted, and the desired expectations will not be adopted.

8. The positive results obtained in several of the studies cannot be satisfactorily explained without a teacher expectation paradigm such as that outlined in Chapter 2. Simpler explanations based on reinforcement and other more purely behavioristic concepts are adequate to handle the data from some studies but not others. The data seem to compel a theory postulating an intervening cognitive variable, whether it is called "expectation" or something else. Some studies can be quite adequately explained via conditioning and reinforcement concepts, however, especially those which did not involve any explicit provision of information or statement of expectations and which did not appear to involve any conscious awareness of expectations on the part of the subjects. In fact, investigation of the possible differential implications when teachers do or do not consciously articulate their expectations regarding particular students would seem to be a potentially fruitful line of inquiry.

9. Several studies have shown that student expectations and/or behavior can be affected by direct expression of teacher expectancy or, more indirectly, by exposing them to differential experiences. This line of research seems quite promising, and applicable strategies for dealing with students who have low expectations and/or self-defeating behavior patterns in the classroom should result from it.

10. At this point the idea that teacher expectations can function as self-fulfilling prophecies appears to be an established fact rather than a mere hypothesis. At the same time the data indicate that expectation effects do not appear in all teachers or in all situations. Thus, we conclude that there is no further need for studies designed solely to establish the existence of expectation effects, but there is considerable need for research on situational factors, design factors, and individual difference variables in teachers and students that may be related to expectancy effects. This point will be elaborated on in the following chapter.

chapter 4

Naturalistic Studies
of Teacher Expectation
Effects

In contrast to the studies reviewed in Chapter 3, in which teacher expectations were induced through provision of phony information or some other experimental treatment, all of the studies in the present chapter involved the use of expectations which teachers formed naturalistically as they interacted with their students. Naturalistic studies have contrasting strengths and weaknesses in comparison with induced expectation studies. First, they do not present the same kind of inference problems, since there is no question about the reality of the teachers' expectations (unless for some reason a teacher has been untruthful in reporting his expectations). Neither do they raise the ethical issues involved in inducing negative expectations in particular students. An additional advantage, at least for those studies conducted in ordinary classrooms, is that such studies have greater generalizability or external validity than studies involving induced expectations. They take place in the naturalistic setting, and they do not involve experimental manipulations that may cause teachers or students to think or act differently than they would have under more normal conditions. Thus positive results obtained in ordinary classrooms can more safely be generalized to other similar classrooms than results obtained in laboratory situations or in classrooms involved in a manipulative experiment. In short, such studies show that teacher expectation effects exist in real-world classrooms as well as in the laboratory. In contrast, one never knows whether the results of laboratory studies or even classroom studies involving experimental manipulation will generalize to the naturalistic classroom setting unless one conducts a naturalistic study. All too often this step is skipped, so that experimental data frequently are inappropriately extrapolated to the classroom.

Naturalistic studies involve two major weaknesses, however. First, there is the trade-off between external validity, or generalizability, and degree of experimental control. The naturalistic setting allows greater generalizability of results, but the researcher cannot institute the kinds of controls that are possible in the laboratory. Thus, naturalistic studies are more easily affected by unknown and/or uncontrolled sources of variation in teacher or student behavior (although some investigators have instituted partial control in naturalistic studies by using interview data to preselect teachers who meet relevant criteria). Second, naturalistic studies provide inference problems of their own. Since the interaction to be studied is neither controlled nor predictable, data collection becomes much more difficult. Coding systems capable of appropriately describing and recording the behavior of interest must be devised, and they must be planned so that the data can be collected without disrupting the naturalistic process. Furthermore, since teacher-student interaction involves a series of actions and reactions, none of which are controlled in naturalistic studies, coding systems must be designed so that they are capable not only of identifying correlations between teacher and student behavior, but also of allowing inferences regarding the direction of causality underlying such correlations. For example, if there are relationships among teacher praise, teacher expectations for student achievement, and actual student achievement, does differential teacher praise toward different students merely reflect their differential achievement, or is the teacher going beyond these objective differences by praising high achievers even more frequently than their achievement would dictate and by praising low achievers correspondingly less frequently? Devising coding schemes and other measurement devices capable of answering such questions is a major challenge facing investigators who choose to do naturalistic research.

Despite such difficulties a considerable number of naturalistic studies relevant to the teacher expectation hypothesis have been completed. These will be reviewed below. Again, studies will be divided according to whether they included product data, process data, or both.

NATURALISTIC STUDIES AND PRODUCT DATA

Teacher Expectations and Student Achievement

Most of the studies in this category involve study of the effects of tracking in school systems which use this procedure. However, there are also two studies which elicited teachers' naturalistically formed expectations and then related them to student achievement in those teachers' classrooms. The first of these was conducted by Palardy (1969), who studied the effects of teachers' beliefs about sex differences in potential for first-grade reading achievement. Palardy asked first-grade teachers whether or not they thought boys could learn to read as well as girls. This question was merely one item in a much longer questionnaire, so the teachers did not realize that it had any special importance or would be used as the basis for a later study. However, this was precisely its purpose. Based on responses to this item, Palardy identified five teachers who did not believe that boys could learn to read as well as girls and paired these five with five others who expected no sex difference. Teachers were paired according to sex, race, teaching experience, type of school in which they taught, and textbook used for teaching beginning reading. Thus the two groups were closely matched except for their beliefs regarding male and female reading achievement in the first grade.

Having identified these ten teachers for special study, Palardy then obtained the reading achievement scores for students in their classrooms during the following school year. The reading scores first were adjusted to control for differences in the children's abilities, using IQ as a covariate, and then were analyzed for teacher expectation effects. These analyses revealed a significant interaction between students' sex and teachers' beliefs about sex differences in first-grade reading potential. The adjusted reading achievement scores were almost exactly equal for boys and girls in classrooms taught by teachers who expected no sex difference. In the classrooms of the teachers who expected a sex difference, however, the scores for girls were very similar to those for both boys and girls in the other classrooms, but the scores for boys were notably lower. Thus boys taught beginning reading by teachers who expected them to do as well as girls actually did do as well as girls, while boys taught by teachers who did not expect them to do so well as girls actually failed to do as well as girls. These data provide striking evidence of a teacher expectation effect, especially since no interactions with the researcher were involved and the teachers did not know that an investigation was going on.

A related set of findings was reported by Doyle, Hancock, and Kifer (1972). These investigators asked a group of first-grade teachers to estimate their children's IQ's shortly before an IQ test was routinely administered. They found that teachers systematically overestimated the IQ's of girls and underestimated those of boys. Further, the IQ estimates were found to be related to reading achievement scores from tests given at the end of the school year. Students who had been overestimated by the teachers showed higher reading achievement than their measured IQ would predict, while students underestimated by the teachers showed less achievement than their measured IQ would predict. Thus, when teachers had higher expectations for students, they actually produced higher achievement in those students than in students for whom they had lower expectations.

In addition to demonstrating this expectation effect within classrooms, this study also showed a more general expectation effect across classrooms. When teachers were divided into high and low groups according to whether they tended to generally overestimate or generally underestimate their students' IQ's, it was found that the overestimators produced higher achievement than expected in their classes than the underestimators produced in their classes. Thus teacher expectations not only can affect the achievement of individual students; they can affect the achievement of the class as a whole.

Teacher Expectations and Tracking Systems

The latter conclusion is supported by several studies, to be reviewed below, showing that tracking tends to influence student achievement. Part of the reason for this lies in the peer segregation that tracking produces; students placed in a higher track will receive more stimulation and help from their classmates than students placed in lower tracks. However, teacher expectations are also involved. It is abundantly clear at this point that tracking influences teacher expectations, so that teachers adjust their level of instruction to what they believe to be appropriate for the ability level of the students in the track in which they teach. On an a priori basis, this appears to be a logical and appropriate procedure; however, empirical data suggest that teachers usually overreact to tracking labels, so that their teaching is not always appropriately matched to student ability levels. In particular, teachers working with low ability level students in tracked schools tend to have inappropriately low expectations.

Mackler (1969), in a case study of a school in Harlem, noted that formal tracking began in first grade and was based primarily on the reports of kindergarten teachers. Tracking began informally in kindergarten, when teachers judged who was and was not mature, basing their judgments primarily on valued traits such as politeness, passivity, and listening to and following directions. Students with these traits were placed in high groups and were recommended for higher tracks in the first grade. Other students were recommended for lower tracks. The lowest first-grade tracks contained children who had not gone to kindergarten at all and who, therefore, were starting behind their peers. Thus, initial tracking was based largely on teacher impressions and on preschool experience rather than on objective assessment of student ability or potential. This might have been only a temporary problem if the children had been regularly moved back and forth between tracks on the basis of their performance, but Mackler reported that mobility between tracks was very slight. At the end of the first grade the difference in achievement (grade-level equivalent score) between the highest and lowest tracks was seven months. By the third grade this gap had increased to twenty months. Although no formal data are presented, Mackler reports that the tracking procedure influenced the expectations and attitudes of teachers, parents, and students. Thus a rigid tracking system was used to define (and in many cases limit) student potential, even though many students had initially been tracked for inappropriate reasons.

Consider the case of a potential high achiever who is placed in the bottom section in first grade because he has not attended kindergarten. Because the class is filled with inexperienced students, much teacher time will be spent instilling classroom rules and engaging in other noninstructional activities. Thus the student will get less opportunity to learn than students in higher tracks. If he does especially well, however, he might make it to the next highest track for the second grade. If he does especially well here, he might make it to the highest track by the third grade. This is very unlikely, however, in view of the very low rates of movement between tracks. It is much more likely that the student will stay in the lowest track and will fall increasingly behind students of equal ability who have been placed in higher tracks. If he does move up he must do so quickly, because Mackler found that no student made it into the top track after the third grade.

Husén and Svensson (1960), in a large-scale study of the effects of tracking, reached general conclusions similar to those reached by Mackler in his case study. They found that students from lower class homes did not move into higher tracks as early or as frequently as students from higher social class homes, even when their achievement merited it. Here again, tracking was based in part on factors other than the students' measured achievement.

Several studies conducted in Britain have shown that tracking systems tend to lower teacher expectations and retard the academic achievement of low SES and/or low achieving students. Barker Lunn (1970), as part of a larger study of ability grouping, compared teacher ratings of student ability with actual student performance on an English test. Sixty-five percent of the teacher ratings were classified as accurate. However, analysis of the 35 percent classified as inaccurate showed that low SES children were generally underrated and high SES children were generally overrated. Although this discrepancy was observable both in schools that practiced tracking and in schools which did not, there was evidence that ability grouping exaggerated the effect. This evidence came from 288 comparisons between streamed and unstreamed schools on variability in student test scores. Seventy-eight of these 288 comparisons were statistically significant, and all 78 showed larger variability in the streamed schools. Thus it appears that streaming maximizes the achievement of students placed in the high tracks and minimizes the achievement of those placed in the low tracks. This effect also has been noted in Sweden by Dahlöff (1971).

Evidence of a similar sort appeared in cross-national research by Pidgeon (1970). In two separate studies comparisons of achievement from thirteen- and fourteen-year-old students in twelve countries showed that variability was highest in the British schools, which at the time were the most rigidly streamed of those included in the sample. Further, streaming was generally associated with high variance in the test scores. This research also suggests that streaming maximizes variability in student achievement, probably because of teacher expectation effects.

Additional evidence was in a study by Burstall (1968). Among 1711 low ability British students who were taking French, Burstall identified a subsample of 308 whose scores in listening comprehension in French were significantly above the means for the stream that they were in. These data were then related to data from the schools' head teachers concerning their opinions about teaching French to low ability students. Burstall found that a significantly high percentage of these 308 students who were demonstrating better achievement in French than their general ability scores would suggest were attending schools in which the head teacher had favorable opinions regarding the teaching of French to low ability students. That is, in schools where the head teacher favored teaching French to low ability students, low ability students tended to do better in French than in schools where the head teacher did not favor this. Though less direct than the similar findings of Palardy (1969) and Doyle, Hancock, and Kifer (1972), Burstall's data suggested that French achievement in these low ability students was affected by teacher expectations.

Of all the British studies dealing with the effects of tracking on teacher expectation and student achievement, the data of Douglas (1964) were perhaps the most definitive and compelling. Douglas reported a three-year follow-up study of British students who were assigned to ability tracks at age eight. He discovered that although most students had been assigned accurately, many had been misplaced into higher or lower tracks than their measured ability dictated. This occurred because teachers were influenced by socioeconomic status and by student personality traits and behavior which were unrelated to measured performance. In general, high SES students and students who pleased the teachers were misplaced upwards, and lower SES students and students who displeased the teachers were misplaced downwards. This occurred both among high ability and low ability students.

Douglas then compared the students' relative achievement three years later, at age eleven, with their relative achievement at age eight. The results were strikingly clear and were exactly the same for both high and low ability students: students who had been placed into higher sections improved and students who had been placed into lower sections deteriorated.

The preceding studies demonstrate quite clearly that tracking tends to increase variability in student performance, maximizing the achievement of students placed in high tracks but minimizing that of students placed in low tracks. The data are also consistent with a teacher expectancy effect explanation, although the evidence is only indirect because none of the studies involved formal collection of data on teacher expectations. Furthermore, all are open to the criticism that tracking might have been more accurate than the investigators suggest. That is, perhaps the teachers were not merely prejudiced or misled when they placed students into tracks higher or lower than their measured abilities would dictate. Perhaps they had knowledge of these students that was more complete or more correct than the students' test scores, so that students really did belong in the tracks into which they were placed rather than in the tracks into which they would have been placed if test scores alone had been used as the criterion. Although this seems unlikely, it remains a real possibility. However, the following study did involve collection of teacher expectation data, and it provides strong evidence that teacher expectations are an important factor in the data on the effects of tracking practices.

Tuckman and Bierman (1971) conducted a naturalistic experiment involving 805 black junior and senior high school students and their teachers. The students first were divided into high and low groups on the basis of measured ability and then were randomly assigned to experimental or control conditions. Control students were assigned to tracks on the basis of their measured abilities. However, experimental students were deliberately assigned to higher tracks. Low ability students were placed into medium groups, and medium ability students into high groups. The data collected included grades, standardized test scores, measures of student satisfaction, attendance data, and teacher recommendations for tracking the following year.

Although the achievement test scores were mixed and did not show a significant overall difference, the general trend was for students who had been placed into higher groups to outperform students who remained in their original assignment groups. Low ability experimental students got somewhat lower grades from teachers than low ability control students, but they nevertheless showed better attendance and greater satisfaction with school. Thus, in general, this experiment benefitted many of the experimental students and did not appear to harm the others.

Perhaps the most striking data from this research are the teachers' recommendations about assigning students to ability groups for the following year. For sheer magnitude of effects they are rivaled only by the comments of the tutors in the Beez (1968) study concerning the difficulty of the words that they were attempting to teach Head Start children. Tuckman and Bierman report that 64 percent of the students who had been arbitrarily placed into a higher group for the experiment were recommended for retention in that group by their teachers at the end of the school year. In stark contrast, teachers nominated only 1 percent of the control students to move up to a higher track for the following year. This demonstrates the powerful effects that tracking or labeling of classes of students by ability level can have on teacher expectations, and, indirectly, upon student expectations and student performance. Note that the treatment affected the students as well as the teachers. Even though their grades suffered somewhat, the experimental students had better attendance records and expressed greater satisfaction with school after they had been placed into the higher track. Also, when student achievement was affected, placement into a higher track typically increased measured achievement.

Seaver (1971), in an ingenious study using records from a middle class suburban school system, investigated the influence of prior experience with an older sibling upon teacher expectations and student achievement by younger siblings. Seaver identified seventy-nine pairs of siblings in two elementary schools and divided them into two groups according to whether the same teacher taught both siblings or whether the siblings were taught by different teachers. He then used IQ, achievement, and grade point average data to classify the older siblings as "good" or "bad." Reasoning that experience with the older sibling would induce teachers to expect similar performance from the younger sibling, he predicted that evidence of teacher expectation effects would show up in the group whose older siblings had been taught by the same teacher. This prediction was confirmed. Sibling performance made no difference for the students who were taught by a different teacher, but students taught by teachers who had taught their older siblings were affected by teacher expectations. Although differences in IQ and grade point averages were not significant, younger siblings of good students got higher scores on four of the six subtests of the Stanford Achievement Tests than younger siblings of bad students, if they were assigned to the same teacher who taught their older siblings. In contrast, younger siblings of poor students did better when assigned to another teacher. This study confirms the findings of several studies reported previously showing that teachers take into account socioeconomic status or general knowledge about a student's family in judging his achievement potential, and it also provides product data showing that these teacher expectations can affect student achievement. One rather direct implication from this study is that school principals could help minimize undesirable expectation effects by making sure that younger siblings of poor students are assigned to different teachers than the ones who taught the older siblings.

NATURALISTIC STUDIES OF BOTH PROCESS AND PRODUCT MEASURES

No studies were located which included both product measures and process observations of teacher-student interaction in the classroom. It is not clear why no such studies have been done, although our own experience suggests that expense is probably the major, if not the only, reason. Data from process observations using the individual student as the unit of analysis are expensive to collect, especially in naturalistic settings. However, there is need for such a study if and when financial resources make it possible. The studies reviewed above confirm that teacher expectation effects exist in naturalistic settings and not just in contrived experiments, but they do not provide information about the cause and effect mechanisms mediating these effects. On the other hand, the studies involving only process measures, to be reviewed below, are quite instructive regarding some of the behavioral interaction mechanisms by which teacher expectation effects are mediated. None of these studies, however, included product measures, so that they cannot show that teacher expectations affected student performance as well as teacher behavior. Further, they show that differential teacher expectations do not always or necessarily lead to differential treatment of different students.

Thus there is need for a large scale study (fifty or more teachers) in naturalistic settings which would include both process and product measures. Such a study would allow for the division of teachers into two or more groups according to the degree to which their teaching behavior (as indicated in the process observation measures) was affected by their differential expectations for different students, and, among those teachers who did show expectation effects in their teaching behavior, it would allow investigation of the degree to which differential teacher treatment affects student performance over the course of a school year. The various studies already reviewed and those to be reviewed below all bear on separate aspects of the teacher expectation phenomenon, but only a large scale, year long, process-product study such as that described above could provide answers to the following three major questions surrounding the hypothesis that teacher expectations can act as self-fulfilling prophecies: (1) What kinds of teachers are most likely to allow their expectations for a student's performance to affect their teaching behavior? (2) When teaching behavior is affected by expectations, what aspects of teacher–student interaction are affected (how does the teacher differentially treat high and low expectation students)? (3) If teacher behavior is affected, so that teachers differentially treat high and low expectation students consistently over the course of the school year, how will this affect product measures of student achievement, self-concept, or attitudes toward school? The latter question particularly needs to be carefully researched, because at the moment there are no direct data bearing upon it. Studies conducted in naturalistic classroom settings have had mixed, mostly negative results regarding teacher expectation effects on product measures of student performance, especially when the experiment spanned the entire school year. Thus, although teacher expectation effects have been rather clearly demonstrated in short term studies, their frequency and importance in naturalistic settings remains open to question. Process data from several long term studies have demonstrated that teacher behavior is often affected by teacher expectations, even over the course of the school year, and these data would seem to provide strong arguments for the existence and importance of expectation effects in the naturalistic setting. However, the results of several studies reviewed in the previous chapter which reported positive effects on process measures but negative effects on product measures remind us that changes in teacher behavior do not necessarily affect student IQ, achievement, or attitudes toward self or school. Only a well-planned, large scale study containing all of the features mentioned above can produce definitive answers to these questions.

NATURALISTIC STUDIES AND PROCESS MEASURES

Many studies, including several by ourselves and by our colleagues, have attempted to link differential teacher expectations toward particular students with teacher treatment of those students in naturalistic classroom settings. As you will see, the vast majority of these have produced positive results. However, many are open to the criticism that the differential teacher treatment may simply be reaction to differential student behavior rather than evidence of expectation effects, and all are open to the criticism that, lacking product measures, they do not demonstrate that differential teacher treatment produced differential student performance.

Although his report is largely impressionistic and contains little formal data, the previously described case study by Rist (1970), involving periodic observation of teacher-student interaction with the same group of students as they progressed from kindergarten through second grade, is a richly descriptive source of hypotheses about how differential teacher expectations will affect the behavior of teachers and students. Rist noted that the kindergarten teacher's first impressions of the children were quickly formalized as the class was divided into three groups and seated at different distances from the teacher. The teacher began to interact increasingly more frequently and more positively with the high group, and these children began to see themselves as special and to show disdain for their less "worthy" peers. This pattern continued as the children moved through first and second grade. Furthermore, as noted in several of the studies of tracking, there was little movement between groups, so that the kindergarten teacher's original grouping was in fact a permanent grouping in most cases. Rist's report is worthwhile reading because of the rich detail it contains about teacher behavior toward high and low achievers, especially the many gripping anecdotes showing strikingly inappropriate behavior toward low achievers.

Dalton (1969) asked a fourth-grade teacher to rank her students according to the achievement she expected of them. The rankings were then used to identify a high, a medium, and a low expectation group among the students in the room. Observation of teacher-student interaction revealed that the teacher was more direct and critical when interacting with the lows but more indirect when interacting with the highs. This can be interpreted as more appropriate teaching of highs than lows, although it may also be explained by differences in the behavior of the two groups of children.

Similar findings were reported by Kranz and Tyo (1973), who studied teachers' interactions with students whom they perceived as high, average, or low achievers. Significantly different treatment of these groups consistent with the teacher expectancy hypothesis was found for the teaching behaviors of positive appraisal, negative appraisal, and managerial behaviors.

Good (1970) and Kranz, Weber, and Fishell (1970) conducted similar studies of the interaction of first-grade teachers with students whom they perceived as high or low achievers. Both studies found that teachers had more frequent interactions with highs than lows. Similar findings were reported by Tyo and Kranz (1973), who studied teacher-student verbal interaction in classrooms containing migrant and nonmigrant students. In general, the teachers had lower expectations for the migrant students. Teacher behavior toward students was classified as positive, neutral, or negative. Analyses showed that the teachers had significantly more positive and neutral contacts, and thus significantly more total contacts, with the nonmigrant students. These studies indicate that teachers are likely to have more frequent and more positive interactions with students for whom they hold high expectations than with students for whom they hold low expectations.

Several studies concerned with teacher expectations in special education classes have been conducted. Babad (1971) showed that induced teacher expectations can affect teacher attitudes towards special education students. Veldman (1973) provides data showing that the students are likely to become aware of such attitudes. This study concerned students in Project Prime, an experimental project involving the removal of mentally retarded and learning disability students from special classes and placing them in classes with normal students. Questionnaire data from the students revealed that they saw that their teachers made less cognitive demands on them and that, in general, the teachers expected less of them than they expected of their classmates.

Teacher-student interaction in five special education classrooms was studied by Willis (1970). The five teachers were asked to rank their eight students from most to least efficient as learners. Each teacher's interaction with the top and bottom student in his class was then observed in simulated classroom sessions for thirty minutes a day for eight days. Analyses of these data indicated that the teachers provided more verbal responses to the comments of the students rated most efficient and were more likely to ignore the students rated as least efficient. These data confirm Rosenthal and Jacobson's (1968) suggestions that teachers may attend more closely to high expectation students and provide them with more appropriate reinforcement.

The process studies reviewed so far suggest that teachers may interact more frequently and/or more positively with high expectation students, pay closer attention to their responses, and reinforce these responses more appropriately. Another process variable apparently related to the communication of expectations has been identified by Rowe (1972), in a series of studies of the length of time teachers are willing to wait for a student response before prompting, giving the answer, or calling on someone else. In one study Rowe asked elementary social science teachers to name the five best and the five worst students in their classrooms. She then observed teacher-student interaction in these classrooms and timed the teachers as they waited for responses after they asked questions. She found that the teachers would wait an average of more than twice as long for a response from a high expectation student than a low expectation student. Thus, the students most able to respond correctly were given more time to answer, while the students least able to respond correctly had to respond more quickly or lose their turn!

Rowe also reported that students in the bottom group were both praised and criticized more frequently than those in the top group. However, the praise given to the students in the bottom group was less specific and generally less appropriate than the praise given to the students in the top group. Top students were praised for correct responses, while bottom group students were sometimes praised for incorrect responses. Apparently the teachers were at least trying to encourage these students, but they were not seriously working to get them to master the material. Thus, low expectation students were being reinforced, but not appropriately.

Rowe also conducted a treatment study in which teachers were asked to try deliberately to increase their waiting times. This proved to be very difficult for many of them, but when they succeeded in doing so, the length and quality of student responses and the frequency of unsolicited student suggestions and comments increased. Furthermore, student contributions to discussions began to be spread more evenly and widely across the classroom. This was because students in the bottom group began to speak up more frequently, sometimes enough to come to the teachers' attention and change their expectations. This study provides a glimpse of several phenomena that will be documented and discussed in more detail in Chapter 9: differential treatment of different students in the same classroom is usually done unconsciously by the teacher; teachers usually change their behavior when made aware of it; and if they do change their behavior, the change usually results in complementary changes in student behavior.

With the exception of the study by Good (1970), the studies reviewed so far in this section were conducted by investigators unconnected with the present authors. The nine studies to be reviewed below were all conducted by the authors, their colleagues, or others who collected their process data using the Brophy-Good Dyadic Interaction Observation System (Brophy and Good, 1970b). Although it has several other uses, this system was originally constructed for the explicit purposes of studying the quantity and quality of interactions that teachers have with individual students in their classrooms and relating these data to naturalistically formed teacher expectations for student performance.

At the time that our involvement in teacher expectation research began (1969), we were (and are) convinced that expectation effects were real despite the criticisms of Rosenthal and Jacobson's (1968) study. Thus we were less interested in research using product measures to establish the reality of teacher expectation effects and more interested in research using process measures designed to reveal how teacher expectations affect teacher and student behavior. By this means we could indicate the cause-and-effect mechanisms underlying the processes by which teacher expectations become self-fulfilling. Guided by an earlier version of the model for teacher expectancy effects presented in Chapter 2, we developed the original version of the Dyadic Interaction Observation System for use in our original teacher expectation study (Brophy and Good, 1970a). This original version has been expanded and modified since, although all of the essential features that make it uniquely useful for teacher expectation research have been retained. All nine of the studies reviewed below used a version of this basic system, although there were minor differences from study to study due to differences in the grade levels being investigated.

Observation System

Since one object of this series of studies was to see if teachers treated students differently when they held different expectations for them, an observation system was needed for classifying teacher and student behavior in situations where the teacher was dealing with individual students. Observation systems already available (Simon and Boyer, 1967) were not appropriate for this purpose, since they used the class rather than the individual student as the unit of analysis. Consequently, we constructed our own system (Brophy and Good, 1970b; Good and Brophy, 1970), guided by the following specifications: (1) the system should be geared to *dyadic* teacher-student interactions, in which the teacher is interacting with individual students; (2) it should retain the *sequence* of action and reaction in each interchange, so that effects due to the behavior of the teachers can be separated from those due to the behavior of the students; (3) it should be designed so that interactions can be coded by classroom observers as they occur, without requiring audio or video tapes; (4) it should be sensitive to teacher behavior which might be related to the teachers' communication of their *expectations* for student performance.

The first three specifications were accomplished by combining and expanding measurement techniques developed in earlier work on the distribution of response opportunities in the classroom (Good, 1970) and on the teaching behavior of mothers in dyadic interaction with their own children (Brophy, 1970; Hess, Shipman, Brophy, and Bear 1969). Meeting the fourth specification was more difficult, since there were few directly relevant previous data to build upon (although *Pygmalion in the Classroom* and the data cited in Chapter 1 on the treatment of children differing in achievement and social status provided valuable clues).

The system is designed so that all dyadic contacts between a teacher and an individual student are recorded. Special emphasis is given to contacts involving school-related work, since these seem most relevant to the communication of achievement expectations. Five types of dyadic contacts are distinguished: *public response opportunities*, in which the student tries to answer a question posed by the teacher; *reading turns*, in which he reads aloud from a primer or reader; *private work-related contacts*, which concern the student's seatwork or homework; *private procedural interactions*, which concern supplies, food or drink, washroom trips, errands for the teacher, or other matters not directly related to classwork; and *behavioral evaluations*, in which the teacher singles out a student for praise or criticism of his classroom behavior. Each type of interaction is coded as it occurs, with contacts initiated by the teacher being recorded separately from those initiated by the student. Teacher praise and criticism in each type of contact are also coded whenever they occur.

The sequence of events is preserved in coding public response opportunities that occur when a student is called on to respond to a question or when a student calls out an answer and receives feedback from the teacher. Called out answers which are ignored by the teacher are not coded. Thus public response opportunities are classified into three types: *open questions*, in which the teacher poses the question, waits for students to raise their hands, and then calls on a student with his hand up; *direct questions*, in which the teacher calls on a student who has not indicated a desire to respond (the teacher names the student before asking the question or calls on a student who does not have his hand up); and *call outs*, in which a student calls out an answer before the teacher has a chance to call on someone. Direct questions are the most clearly teacher-initiated response opportunities; open questions involve initiative by both the teacher and the student; and call outs are determined almost completely by the student (although the teacher must give a feedback response rather than ignore the student).

The level of response demand built into teacher questions is also coded. Five types of questions are identified: *process* questions, which require the student to give a detailed explanation or to explain the thinking and problem solving that underlies an answer; *product* questions, which require the student to provide a short factual answer or bit of information from memory; *choice* questions, which require the student to select from among response alternatives provided by the teacher or by a workbook; *opinion* questions, which require the student to make a prediction or give an opinion regarding some curriculum-relevant matter; and *self-reference questions*, which concern the student's personal experiences, likes and dislikes, or other personal matters. From the viewpoint of the level of demand made upon the student, process questions are usually the most difficult, followed in order by the other types of questions as listed above.

In addition to coding the type and difficulty level of response opportunities, observers also code the *quality of the student's response* (coded as correct, part correct, incorrect, or no response) and the types of *feedback reactions given by the teachers*. Teacher feedback reactions include praising, criticizing, giving the answer, giving more extensive process feedback, calling on someone else to give the answer, repeating the question, rephrasing the question or giving a clue, asking a new question, and failing to give any feedback at all.

These question-answer-feedback sequences of response opportunities are recorded in the order in which they occur, so that their sequence as well as their frequency can be determined from the coding sheets. This feature of the system makes possible the derivation of percentage scores which allows us to control for differences in frequency of different kinds of teacher-student interactions and therefore to make more direct comparisons between students than the more typically used frequency counts allow.

In addition to praise, criticism, and failure to give feedback, the process-product distinction is also used in coding teacher responses during private work-related interactions. If a teacher merely tells the student that his work is correct or incorrect, or if he merely gives the student an answer, he is coded for simple *product* feedback. However, if he takes time to explain the process by which the student can arrive at the correct answer or to explain the nature of an error that the student has made, he is coded for *process* feedback. This distinction is useful in assessing the degree to which teachers work with individual students when they are having difficulties. High rates of process feedback indicate that the teacher is working with the student, trying to help him learn the material. In contrast, low rates of process feedback imply that the teacher is simply giving the student answers rather than taking time to work with him until he clearly understands the concept or task.

Basic Methodological Procedures

With only minor variations from one study to the next, the same basic procedures for obtaining and analyzing data were used in all of the studies involving the Dyadic System. First, decisions were made about which variables should be included in a particular study. Variables pertaining to the reading group, for example, were not needed at later grades where no reading groups occur. Once the coding categories to be used in a given study were agreed upon, an appropriate coding sheet was designed, and observers practiced using the system in classrooms similar to those in which the study was to be conducted. Observer practice continued until acceptable levels of reliability (80 percent agreement) were achieved (see Brophy and Good, 1970b, for details). Then observers worked individually, each being responsible for coding one or more classrooms.

Unless hand raising is included in the study (as in Brophy and Good, 1970a), there never is more than one codable dyadic teacher-student interaction going on at any one time. Thus a single observer can code *all* dyadic interactions involving the teacher, so that only one coder is required per classroom once the coder's reliability is established.

So that data on individual students can be retrieved from the coding sheets, each student in a class is assigned a number. This number is recorded (along with other information), whenever he has a dyadic interaction with the teacher. Data are later tabulated separately for each student, and the student is assigned mean scores reflecting the *quantity* of his contacts with the teacher and percentage scores reflecting the *quality* of these contacts. The mean scores are determined by dividing the total number of contacts in a category by the number of times the student was present for observation.

Percentage scores are computed according to formulas designed to reflect the percentage of times that a teacher responds in a given way to a given situation. For example, the percentage of times a student is praised for a correct answer is computed by dividing his total number of correct answers into the number of those correct answers which were followed by teacher praise. Thus, if a student had a total of twenty correct answers and was praised after two of those answers, the praise rate would be two divided by twenty, or 10 percent.

For some studies the means and percentage scores derived in this way were used as the basic data in analyzing the results. Frequently, however, the data were standardized within each class before being further analyzed. The standardization procedure converts the data to a common scale, so that each class has a mean of zero and a standard deviation of one. These standard scores do not change the variability or form of the distribution *within* a given class, so that, for example, the student who had the highest mean number of response opportunities in a given class before standardization also has the highest standardized score. He also has the same position relative to his classmates on this variable, because the standardization procedure merely adjusts scores to set the class mean equal to zero—it does not affect the range of variability or the form of the distribution within the class. Thus, on each variable a given student has the same position relative to his classmates in both the unstandardized and the standardized scores.

Scores are sometimes standardized because there are very large differences between classrooms on certain variables, making comparison across classes difficult. These differences mostly reflect contrasting teaching styles, and are irrelevant to the within-class teacher-student interaction patterns which are of interest in assessing expectation effects. For example, one classroom might feature many question-and-answer periods and other verbal interaction sequences, with very little time spent in silent seatwork. Another classroom might have the opposite pattern. As a result, students in the first classroom would have high rates of response opportunities and low rates of individual work-related contacts with their teacher, relative to the students in the second classroom. Conversion to standardized scores sets all classes on a common scale (mean = 0, standard deviation = 1), so that comparisons between high and low expectation students can be made more easily when data from different classrooms are combined.

Once the means and percentage scores are computed (and after they are standardized, when this is part of the procedure), analyses of variance are used to test for group differences, and correlational analyses are performed to assess the relationships among the variables. Students' sex and expectancy group status are regularly used as fixed independent variables in the analyses of variance. Expectancy groups are formed by dividing the teachers' rankings into high, middle, and low groups. When a class does not divide evenly into three groups, surplus students are placed into the middle group.

In addition to the fixed variables of sex and expectancy group status, teacher (or class) is usually entered as a random independent variable. Other independent variables, such as teacher sex and teacher personality type, were used in certain studies.

Findings reported as significant in the following studies are confined to those in which the main effect or interaction from analyses of variance (or the correlation coefficient from correlational analyses) reached the .05 level of significance or better. Nonsignificant trends are labeled as such.

Initial Study

Our initial study (Brophy and Good, 1970a) was conducted in four of the nine first-grade classrooms in a school serving a predominantly lower class population. The first grade was selected for study because Rosenthal and Jacobson had reported the strongest expectation effects at this grade level. The four classes were chosen because no student teachers were present, as they were in the other classes. Since we were mainly interested in studying typical interactions in everyday classrooms rather than in classrooms affected by special experimental treatments, we decided to use the teachers' own naturalistically formed expectations rather than try to induce expectations, as Rosenthal and Jacobson had done. Consequently, each teacher was asked to rank the children in her classroom in order of expected achievement. The instructions for ranking were kept deliberately vague to encourage the teachers to use their own complex subjective criteria in making judgments.

The teachers' rankings were then used to select children for special study. In each case three boys and three girls high on the teacher's list (highs) and three boys and three girls low on the teacher's list (lows) were selected for observation. Substitutes for each type of child (high boys, high girls, low boys, and low girls) were also identified. Whenever a sample student was absent during a scheduled observation, a substitute was observed in his place. Thus equal numbers of each type of child were observed during each observation period.

The teachers knew that the study was concerned with the classroom behavior of children of various achievement levels, but they did not realize that their own behavior as well as that of the children was being specifically observed. In addition, they thought that observations were being taken on every child in the classroom and did not know that specific subgroups had been selected for study. These cautions were necessary to insure that teachers would not possess knowledge that would allow them deliberately to affect the outcome of the study. More specific information about the research was given to the teachers later, after the observational data had been collected.

By selecting only students who were high or low on the teachers' rankings, we increased the chances of discovering differential teacher treatment related to teacher expectations. However, the school district had tracked students according to abilities, using readiness and achievement test data. Our observations were taken in the spring, after the children already had been grouped on the basis of readiness tests given in the fall and then regrouped between semesters on the basis of achievement test scores. *Therefore, at least in terms of test scores, ability differences among the children in a given room were minimal, and there was little objective support for the teachers' expectation rankings.*

Thus, although we were observing children who were placed at the extremes within the rooms, according to the teachers' subjective judgments, the tracking procedure and test data suggest that actual ability differences between children at the extremes within rooms were relatively small compared to the differences between rooms. The rooms in which we observed were ranked third, sixth, seventh, and eighth among the nine first-grade classrooms.

Observations lasting an entire morning or afternoon (two of each for each class) were made on four separate days in each classroom. Data were recorded for all periods of academic activity, using one coding sheet for reading groups and another for all other situations. During nonacademic procedural activities (cleaning up, getting in line, pledging to the flag, and so on), only behavioral evaluations were coded.

In each class, one observer coded the interactions involving the six highs and the other coded the six lows. Assignments were balanced so that each observer spent half his time watching highs and the other half watching lows. Originally, observer assignments were to be made according to convenience, with one observer watching children in the left side of the room and the other watching the children in the right side. We had expected that this plan would randomize the highs and lows across observers (the Adams and Biddle study described in Chapter 1 had not been published at the time). However, in three of the four classrooms, dividing the children according to seating location resulted in the assignment of the six highs to one coder and the six lows to the other!

The children were seated around movable rectangular tables, with one at each end and six or eight along the sides. First-grade classrooms usually have three reading groups, and frequently there are three tables in the class. Teachers often find it convenient to assign each reading group to its own table. This facilitates giving assignments, monitoring seatwork, and other teaching activities which require different teacher behavior towards the different reading groups.

One effect of this practice, however, is to segregate the children according to achievement level. In three of the four classrooms in which we observed, the seating order, progressing from the head of one table through the middle table and back up the other table, was almost perfectly parallel to the teacher's achievement rankings! Over time this in itself would tend to polarize the classroom (increase the differences between highs and lows), because it minimizes the potential benefits that the less able students can derive from contact with the brighter students. In addition, as Rist (1970) also noted, the top group was usually seated closest to the teacher's desk, where they had easier access to her and were more likely to be noticed by her.

It is worth noting here that, although all four teachers were observed to treat children in the high and low groups differentially in ways that favored the highs, there was less favoritism by the teacher who dispersed her children randomly rather than seating them by reading groups. We suspect that teachers who seat their children randomly are more likely to treat them as individuals rather than as stereotyped group members.

Results

Raw data for each of the forty-eight children were tabulated and analyzed for group differences. The major findings will be presented in two sections (see Brophy and Good, 1970a, for details). The first section was concerned with group differences in interaction patterns which cannot be ascribed clearly to the teachers. Many of these are strictly child behavior measures, such as hand raising counts and frequencies of child-initiated private contacts. Others are teacher-child patterns which may result from behavioral differences between the groups of children, from teacher discrimination between the groups, or from a combination of these two factors. Examples here include teacher-initiated response opportunities, praise and criticism frequencies, and behavioral evaluations. These data appear in Table 4.1.

The data in Table 4.1 show large and consistent differences between the expectancy groups. The highs initiated more public response opportunities and work-related private contacts with the teacher, raised their hands more often, gave more correct and fewer incorrect answers, had fewer problems per reading turn, and received more praise and less criticism than the lows. This pattern of differences in classroom behavior was paralleled by differences favoring the highs on the Stanford Achievement Tests taken at the end of the year.

The large group differences on hand raising and on initiation of work contacts are consistent with what our model would predict for data collected late in the school year. Since no earlier data were collected, it is impossible to tell whether these

TABLE 4.1. Expectancy Group Differences in Child Behavior and Teacher-Child Interaction in the Initial Study (from Brophy and Good, 1970a)

MEASURES	LOWS	HIGHS
Number of times called on to answer an open question	1.71	1.96
Number of times called on to answer a direct question	1.83	2.50
Number of times called on by teacher during reading groups	4.79	3.29*
Number of times child called out answer during reading group	2.96	3.54
Procedural contacts initiated by child	3.17	5.13**
Work-related contacts initiated by child	1.79	7.38***
Procedural contacts initiated by teacher	2.58	2.04
Work-related contacts initiated by teacher	6.00	3.79
Number of behavioral criticisms from teacher	4.92	2.04***
Total teacher-initiated response opportunities	10.96	10.29
Total child-initiated response opportunities	7.92	16.04***
Total dyadic contacts with teacher	33.67	35.17
Number of times child raises hand to seek response opportunity	8.88	16.67***
Number of times called on/number of times raises hand	0.20	0.12**
Total correct answers	6.67	8.92*
Total incomplete, incorrect and "don't know" answers	4.63	2.38***
Average number of reading problems per reading turn	4.67	2.23***
Percent of total contacts involving praise from the teacher	3.88	11.00***
Percent of total contacts involving criticism from the teacher	24.33	10.75***

* $p < .10$ ** $p < .05$ *** $p < .001$

differences had been present all year long or had increased as the school year progressed. In any case, it is clear that late in the school year the highs were much more active in seeking response opportunities and in going to the teacher to discuss their seatwork.

The data concerning student-initiated contacts with the teachers are particularly revealing. Lows sought out the teachers less frequently than highs even for procedural matters, suggesting that they were less teacher oriented than highs and perhaps even alienated from their teachers. Differences were even greater for work-related contacts. The lows were notably reluctant to come to the teacher to discuss their work, even though they presumably needed more help and instruction. The teacher evaluation data suggest a possible reason for this reluctance: praise and criticism are closely balanced for the highs, but the lows averaged more than six critical comments for every favorable one. Such heavy rates of criticism probably discouraged lows from seeking help from the teachers, even though they needed it more.

Differences between highs and lows were mostly in *quality* rather than *quantity* of contacts with teachers. There was little difference in the total number of contacts with teachers, but more of the contacts involving highs were response opportunities or private work-related contacts, and more were initiated by the children themselves. The differences seem clearly attributable to the behavior of the children rather than to a teacher tendency to give more response opportunities to highs or to initiate more interactions with them. In fact, measures of teacher-initiated contacts usually favored the lows, although the differences usually were not significant.

These data might mean that the teachers were attempting to compensate for the differences in child-initiated contacts by seeking out lows more frequently for individual attention. However, the evidence suggests only a slight tendency at best. Although the teachers did initiate more procedural contacts, more work-related contacts, and more total response opportunities with the lows, none of these group differences were significant. Furthermore, the difference on the measure of direct questions favored the highs, even though teachers could have compensated here for the greater tendency of the highs to call out answers and seek response opportunities through hand raising.

The only frequency measure suggesting teacher compensation which reached statistical significance was the ratio of the number of times the child was called on to answer open questions over the number of times he raised his hand. Lows were called on an average of 20 percent of the times they raised their hands, while the average for the highs was 12 percent. However, these figures were not adjusted for the group difference in hand raising frequency. When hand raising rates are adjusted the results still favor the lows, but the difference no longer approaches statistical significance. Taken together, then, the data suggest that there was a small tendency at best for teachers to compensate for the lows' lower rates of initiation of interaction by taking it upon themselves to initiate contacts with lows.

In general, the findings on quantity of contacts were somewhat at variance with those of Good (1970) and Kranz, Weber, and Fishell (1970), who reported that first-grade teachers give significantly more response opportunities to highs. Perhaps the teachers in this study were more aware of the differences in the rates of child-initiated contacts and made a clear effort to counteract these differences through their own actions. However, it seems more likely that the discrepancy was due to the tracking system used in the school. That is, it is likely that there were smaller differences in abilities and behavior between the highs and the lows in this study than in the research reported by Good (1970) and Kranz, Weber, and Fishell (1970).

Teachers' Expectations as Self-fulfilling Prophecies

Most of the differences between highs and lows reviewed in the preceding section are consistent with the notion that the teachers were treating the two groups differently because they held different expectations for them. However, these group differences do not really provide direct evidence that teachers' expectations were functioning as self-fulfilling prophecies. Since the children differed in their behavior, the group differences discussed above would appear even if the teachers were merely reacting consistently. That is, the group differences could be due solely to differences in the children and not to any direct discrimination or favoritism by the teachers. More direct evidence to support the self-fulfilling prophecy hypothesis would require data to show that the teachers were treating the groups differently in equivalent situations. The data from five such measures are presented in Table 4.2.

The measures in Table 4.2 provide direct evidence that the teachers' differential expectations for student performance were affecting their classroom behavior. The measures all involve the teachers' reactions to student attempts to answer questions or to read in the reading groups. They are all percentage measures which take into account absolute differences in the frequencies of the various behaviors involved, allowing for a direct comparison of the teachers' behavior toward the two groups in *equivalent situations*.

The teachers consistently favored the highs in demanding and reinforcing quality performance. Despite the fact that highs gave more correct answers and fewer incorrect answers, they were *more* frequently praised when correct and *less* frequently criticized when incorrect or unable to respond. We were quite surprised by these findings, in view of the stress that teacher trainers place on the need to encourage children and to promote learning through praise and rewards.

In view of the highs' greater success in reading and answering questions, we were not surprised by the data in Table 4.1 showing that highs received more total praise and less total criticism than lows. However, in view of the advice given prospective teachers in educational psychology books and of our common sense predictions about teachers' reactions to successes and failures by these two contrasting groups, we had expected that the percentage measures for praise of success and criticism of failure in Table 4.2 would favor the lows.

Because the lows are successful less frequently, we assumed that a correct response from one of these children would be more significant to the teacher and more likely to elicit praise than a correct answer from one of the highs. Similarly, we expected that teachers would be less likely to criticize the lows for failure to

TABLE 4.2.   Group Differences from the Initial Study on Variables Related to the Communication of Teacher Expectations (from Brophy and Good, 1970a)

MEASURES	LOWS	HIGHS
Percent of correct answers followed by praise	5.88	12.08**
Percent of wrong answers followed by criticism	18.77	6.46***
Percent of wrong answers followed by repetition or rephrasing the question or by giving a clue	11.52	27.04*
Percent of reading problems followed by repetition or rephrasing the question or by giving a clue	38.37	67.05***
Percent of answers (correct or incorrect) not followed by any feedback from the teacher	14.75	3.33***

$* p < .10$ $** p < .05$ $*** p < .01$

respond correctly, because of their greater learning difficulty. However, the results were precisely the opposite. The lows were only half as likely as the highs to be praised following a correct response, and they were three times as likely to be criticized following failures. The teachers were encouraging and supportive toward the children who needed it least, but were cool and critical toward the children who most needed encouragement!

The next two measures in Table 4.2 show that the teachers were more persistent in eliciting responses from highs than lows. When highs responded incorrectly or were unable to respond, the teachers were more likely to provide a second response opportunity by repeating or rephrasing the question or by giving a clue. Conversely, they were more likely to give the answer or call on another child when reacting to lows in similar situations.

The final measure in Table 4.2 gives the percentages of instances in which the teachers gave no feedback reaction whatever following a student response. Teachers neglected to give feedback only 3.33 percent of the time when reacting to highs, while the corresponding figure for lows was 14.75 percent, a highly significant difference.

Taken together, the data in Table 4.2 show that the teachers took more appropriate action to elicit a good performance from the highs, and that they tended to reinforce it appropriately when it was elicited. In contrast, they tended to accept poor performance from lows, and they failed to reinforce good performance properly even when it did occur.

This differential treatment goes beyond the differences in performance between the two groups, and is the type of teacher behavior that would polarize the class over time by enhancing the motivation and performance of the highs and depressing that of the lows. In view of the data of Table 4.2, the contrasting patterns of student-initiated contacts with the teachers that were summarized in Table 4.1 are not surprising. The teachers were treating the highs in ways that would encourage these students to seek them out, while their treatment of the lows was more likely to induce alienation.

The data of Table 4.2 provide a glimpse of another phenomenon that appears frequently in our observations: teachers sometimes overvalue correct answers and those students who give correct answers frequently. From an objective standpoint, incorrect answers and failures are at least as useful as correct answers and successes. While the latter confirm that learning has occurred, the former are useful both as evidence of deficiencies in learning and as indicators of the nature of the difficulty. However, many teachers do not respond so objectively to right and wrong answers. Like anyone else, they want to have a sense of accomplishment and success in their work. In practice this means that correct answers and successful reading are experienced as rewards by some teachers, while failures to respond or to read correctly are experienced as punishments. This is probably one of the factors involved in making teachers more willing to stick with the highs by asking them another question when they have not been able to respond to the first one. Highs are

90758

more likely to "reward" the teacher with a correct response when given a second chance. This is less likely to occur with lows, so the teacher terminates the interaction and moves away from them.

Serious deterioration of classroom climate and effectiveness can occur if the teacher is strongly oriented toward hearing only correct answers. As the year progresses, such teachers spend more and more of their time and energy with only a select few children who receive the majority of the response opportunities and get more than their share of individual contacts with the teacher. When carried to extremes, this produces a classroom situation in which very little new learning goes on because the teacher confines questions and assignments to material she knows the children can handle. Much of the verbal interaction in such a classroom boils down to the recitation of overlearned material by high expectation students, with the teacher spending her time eliciting responses and labeling them as correct or incorrect but doing very little teaching in the normal sense of the word.

Data Limitations and Unanswered Questions

Although the results of our initial study were encouraging, certain limitations in the data and certain unanswered questions led us to initiate a series of follow-up studies. One important limitation was the small and restricted sample. Only four teachers were observed, and all were working in the same grade at the same school. How could we be sure they were typical?

In addition, the data were collected in the spring, near the end of the school year. Perhaps teachers give up on their low achieving students only after a long and determined effort to improve their performance. Perhaps at the beginning of the year there are no differences between expectancy groups. Data on this question were needed to evaluate the next step in our model. The model not only predicted that teachers would treat high and low achieving students differently, it also implied that polarization would occur as the school year progressed. That is, if teachers' classroom behavior is related to student achievement, and if teachers do in fact treat high achieving students more favorably than they treat low achieving students, the relative difference between high and low students should increase as the school year progresses.

The children should begin to respond to this differential teacher treatment with complementary behavior, reinforcing the teachers' tendency to differentiate. For example, if teachers more frequently give up on low achieving students when they make no response, and more often criticize them when they make errors, these students might learn in time that remaining silent when in doubt is the best way to "get off the hook." Such increasing silence might reinforce the teachers' suspicions that the students were falling hopelessly behind; it also might make the teachers more likely to call quickly on someone else to spare them further embarrassment. Systematic study of this idea required data from the beginning of the school year.

Also, the data in our original study were consistent with two earlier studies (Good, 1970; Kranz, Weber, and Fishell, 1970) in that teachers were found to be more positively responsive to high achieving students, but there was one major difference. In the earlier studies teachers were found to interact much more frequently with their highs than their lows. However, the frequency (*quantity*) of teacher interaction with high and low achieving students did not differ greatly in this study. Instead, the *quality* of interaction, *how* the teacher responded to the child, was the major indicant of differential teacher behavior.

In earlier studies classes had been grouped heterogeneously; however, in our study the children were homogeneously grouped. Perhaps when children are ability grouped so that differences between highs and lows within each classroom are smaller, the frequency of teacher contacts with different achievement groups is more similar. Additional data taken in classes which use heterogeneous grouping practices were needed to test this hypothesis.

An additional unanswered question concerned intervention. We had studied the teachers in their naturalistic state, without trying to change them in any way. What would happen if we informed the teachers about their behavior and made suggestions for change? Can teachers change undesirable interaction patterns with particular students after they have become firmly established? How would the students be affected if the teachers did improve?

Our model predicted that if the teachers changed their patterns the students would also change accordingly. That is, the vicious circle of undesirable effects set in motion by inappropriate teacher behavior would work in reverse to create positive changes if teacher behavior improved. The child who is treated more favorably would begin to respond more favorably (perhaps by gaining confidence, participating more in discussions, initiating more contacts with the teacher, and so on). This, in turn, should encourage the teacher and make it easier and more likely for him to treat the student still more favorably in the future.

Systematic study of these predictions required that we first collect data on how teachers interact with their students, then give them feedback about their interactions with particular students, including suggestions for change, and finally that we continue to collect data after giving this advice to see if the teachers and children changed their classroom interaction patterns in predictable fashion.

Follow-ups to the Initial Study

Our desire to get answers to some of these questions led us to undertake a series of studies related in one way or another to the original study. These included several replications of the study in other elementary grades and in junior high and high schools, three attempts to examine later steps of the model by searching for evidence of systematic polarization over time (increases in the relative difference between highs and lows), and a treatment study in which feedback was given to the teachers to see if they could change their already established interaction patterns with particular students (see Chapter 9).

To answer some of the research questions our initial study had raised, we replicated and extended it the following year (Evertson, Brophy, and Good, 1972). This follow-up study involved different kinds of students from those in the initial study, and they were grouped heterogeneously rather than homogeneously. Naturalistic classroom observations were collected over the entire fall semester to see if differential teacher expectations would lead to a gradual polarization of the class.

Data were collected in three classrooms in each of three different types of schools. In one school most of the teachers and all of the students were black, and the great majority of the students came from homes of lower socioeconomic status. The teaching staffs and student populations of the other two schools were overwhelmingly white. However, they differed in the socioeconomic status of their student population. One was similar to the black school in this regard, with the great majority of families being supported by an unskilled bread winner or by public assistance. In contrast, the students at the other white school came from middle and upper-middle class homes. Thus the three schools selected for study were different from one another in the student populations they served. This selection allowed us to see if the findings from the previous research would generalize to schools that differed from the one studied originally.

Resources were limited, so we had to choose between making a few observations in a large number of classrooms or making many observations in a few classrooms. Part of our solution to this dilemma was a decision to work only with the first grade. This was to maximize the comparability of data from all classrooms both with one another and with those in the original study. This was important because, at the time, the data from our initial study were still unique. We had developed a new observation system to do a new kind of research, and there was no body of data with which some of our findings could be compared. Replication at the first-grade level would enable us to get this kind of comparison data.

We also opted in favor of making extensive observations in a small number of classrooms. We anticipated that replications of the Rosenthal and Jacobson study and research similar to our own would begin to appear in the research literature more frequently, and that they would establish more firmly the finding that teachers' expectations sometimes act as self-fulfilling prophecies. Consequently, our interests focused on research designed to reveal more about how the process works. In particular, we wanted to test our model further, especially the hypothesis that a class will become polarized over time if the teacher consistently encourages the highs and discourages the lows.

Procedures

The first follow-up research was conducted over the entire school year but was divided into a naturalistic observation study done in the first semester and a treatment study done in the second semester (see Chapter 9). The naturalistic study began in late September and continued through mid-December. It was essentially a replication of our initial study, except that adjustments were made in the coding system so that a single observer could code the entire class rather than only a few children at the extremes of the teachers' rankings. The first-grade classes in each of the three schools were involved. In September teachers were given an orientation similar to the one used the previous year and were asked to rank their children according to the achievement they expected from them. At this point in the research the teachers did not know the full intent of the study.

Each of the nine classrooms was then observed sixteen times during the semester, eight mornings and eight afternoons, with observations spread across the days of the week and the weeks of the semester. A total of about forty hours of interaction data were collected from each classroom. The data were analyzed with two main questions in mind. Would the findings of the initial study be replicated? If so, would there be evidence that the differences between the low and high groups increased with time (that is, would the classes become more polarized)?

Results

Results related to the first question are reviewed in detail below. However, they can be simply summarized here. Few of the findings regarding communication of teachers' expectations were replicated across the whole sample of teachers. As a group, these nine teachers were not treating highs favorably and lows unfavorably. Three of the nine teachers did show this pattern, however.

There were considerable differences among the students ranked high, middle, and low in the teachers' rankings. Highs had a higher percentage of correct answers and fewer errors per reading turn than lows, with middles in between (middles were between highs and lows on almost all measures; exceptions to this general finding will be noted). Also, highs were more likely to make an incorrect response than to make no response at all when they did fail to respond correctly. This may be simply a knowledge or ability difference; perhaps the lows are more often stumped so completely that they cannot even offer a guess. However, it also may indicate a personality difference: perhaps highs are generally more secure and confident and lows generally more anxious and inhibited when "put on the spot" in public response opportunity situations.

Quantitative differences in the frequency of teacher-student interactions were mixed. Highs got more public response opportunities and more reading turns than lows. Similar nonsignificant trends also were seen in the data on self-reference questions and student-initiated work and procedural contacts. However, the measures for response opportunities in reading groups and for teacher-initiated work contacts showed the opposite trend (significant in the latter case). Thus, as a group, these teachers showed evidence of attempts to compensate for the highs' tendency to be more active in seeking response opportunities and initiating contacts. Behavioral contacts were most frequent with the low group and least frequent with the middle group.

In sum, the quantitative data suggest that highs were creating extra response opportunities for themselves, but that, in general, the teachers were attempting to compensate by calling on lows more frequently and especially by frequently initiating work-related contacts with them. The only really large difference favoring the highs is on the measure of reading turns, and this may be due to what was going on in the reading groups at the time rather than to teacher favoritism. That is, early in the semester, the high groups were already reading and therefore getting reading turns, while the low groups were still on readiness work and had not yet begun to read. Thus the reading group data probably reflect appropriate teaching rather than favoritism toward highs.

The data on teacher versus student initiation of individual private contacts show a clear pattern: highs initiated more contacts with the teachers, and teachers compensated by initiating more contacts with lows. Here again is evidence that teachers were actively trying to reach the lows rather than giving up on them or allowing themselves to be continually occupied with the highs.

Data on the difficulty level of questions, on teacher praise following correct answers, and on teacher criticism following incorrect answers showed no clear trends. Highs did get more total praise from the teachers, because of a large difference in praise given during teacher-initiated private work contacts. Again, this is probably due to differences in the quality of the students' work rather than to teacher favoritism. Students in the middle groups were rarely criticized for classroom misbehavior, while the lows were most frequently criticized for this reason. A similar pattern occurred on the measure of warning over warning plus criticism, indicating that teachers were likely merely to warn the middles when they misbehaved but were more likely to criticize the lows when they misbehaved. This ties in with the finding on behavioral contacts noted earlier and reflects a more general finding seen in several of our studies: the middle group is usually less salient in the classroom than the high and low groups, and teachers are usually more detached and unemotional when dealing with them. Middles tend not to make so strong an impression on teachers as highs and lows, and they do not provoke so much emotional response from the teachers.

The findings on measures of teacher persistence in seeking responses were mixed. There were no clear trends in teacher behavior following failure to answer an initial question. Thus, the tendency of the teachers in the initial study to give up on lows but stay with highs in these situations was not replicated in this study.

When the teachers did stay with students following their failure to respond correctly, they were more likely simply to repeat the question to highs but more likely to give a clue or some kind of help to lows. Thus they were more demanding in dealing with highs in these situations. This is one finding that can be interpreted as evidence of communication of expectations, although most observers would probably see it as an appropriate teaching strategy, given the differences in the children's abilities and other evidence in the study showing that these teachers seemed to be working to involve lows and help them master the material.

Measures of the teachers' frequencies of asking a second question following a correct answer to the first question actually favored the lows, and the group effect was significant on one measure. Thus, the teachers tended to stay with the lows when they were responding successfully.

Measures of process feedback given by teachers in responding to student answers or in working with them at their desks all show that lows got more process feedback. This again indicates a tendency for the teachers to work with the lows rather than give up on them. However, one difference was significant. This was on the measure of process feedback in teacher-initiated work contacts, and it can be interpreted in tandem with the findings reported earlier that teachers gave more praise to the highs in teacher-initiated work contacts. Taken together, these findings show that the teachers were praising the students when they had done the work correctly but were stopping to give explanation and instruction when they had not. Most observers would agree that this is appropriate teaching, even though it does result in the highs getting somewhat more praise than the other students.

The findings of teacher failure to give feedback were mixed. The one significant difference showed that the teachers more frequently failed to give feedback to the highs after they had responded to questions during reading groups. This is a reversal of the findings of the initial study. However, a trend that approached significance suggested more frequent failure to give feedback to the lows following reading turns, and a third measure (failure to give feedback during general class discussions) showed no important group differences. Thus it would not be appropriate to conclude that these teachers more frequently failed to give feedback to highs than lows. It is true, however, that the finding from the initial study that teachers more frequently failed to give feedback to lows was not replicated in this study.

To summarize, few of the key findings from the initial study were replicated in the follow-up. As a group, the teachers in the follow-up study showed no evidence of favoring highs or of treating them more appropriately than lows. If anything, the opposite was true. There was considerable evidence that the teachers were consistently compensating for the tendency of highs to demand more of their attention by seeking out lows for contacts and by persistently explaining the work to lows when they needed help. Furthermore, they did this even though lows apparently created more frequent control and discipline problems by misbehaving more often than their classmates. The measures that did favor highs over lows are most likely attributable to differences in the work and behavior of the groups of students rather than to teacher favoritism.

These findings are for the teachers as a group, however, and they gloss over individual differences among them. When data for each teacher were examined individually, it was found that three teachers tended to favor the highs (behaving similarly to the teachers in the initial study), three showed no particular pattern of group differences at all, and three showed evidence of special concern and effort directed toward the lows (in general, the opposite of the kinds of patterns seen in the initial study). The data for the three teachers who did favor highs were examined for evidence of polarization of their classes. One class did show polarization over time, while the other two showed no trend at all. Thus the findings regarding the polarization hypothesis were ambiguous.

Contrasts Between the Two Studies

The results of the two studies contrast sharply. In the first study all four teachers showed a tendency to treat the highs more appropriately than the lows in working for and reinforcing good responses (although the tendency was less noticeable in one teacher). In the second study only three of nine teachers showed that pattern, while three showed no group difference and the other three showed a contrasting pattern suggesting extra efforts to work with the lows. There were several differences between the two studies which might explain these contrasting findings.

First, the student populations were different. This apparently was not a factor, however. None of the three teachers in the lower class white school in the follow-up study, which was most similar to the school used in the initial study, showed the pattern that the teachers in the initial study had shown.

A second difference was that students in the follow-up study were grouped heterogeneously. Again, this is a possible but unlikely explanation for the difference in findings. If anything, heterogeneous grouping should increase rather than decrease the likelihood that a teacher will show differences in treating the highs and lows. Since the differences between these groups are greater in heterogeneously grouped than in homogeneously grouped classes, teachers' differential expectations for achievement will be more closely fulfilled in heterogeneously grouped classrooms. Thus a teacher who found work with highs rewarding and work with lows unrewarding should be especially disposed to favor highs in a heterogeneously grouped classroom.

A counter argument can be constructed, however, based on cognitive consistency notions. It may be that teachers in homogeneously grouped classrooms expect equal performance from everyone. If so, such teachers may become especially frustrated or angered by the relatively poor performance of their lows. This, in turn, may lead them to reject the lows and favor the highs. In contrast, teachers in heterogeneously grouped classrooms may not be disturbed or frustrated by the relatively poor performance of lows because they expect it, so that they may be emotionally freer to work with lows at their individual levels without letting anger or rejection get in the way.

Carrying this argument further, it could be predicted that teachers' treatment of individual students is influenced not so much by the nature of the particular expectations they have for the students as by the discrepancy between those expectations and what the student is actually doing. Students failing to meet expectations may provoke frustration and rejection, while students exceeding expectations may provoke pleasure and good will. However, although the first part of this prediction may prove true, the second part does not square with the praise and criticism findings from the initial study, or with data from other investigators suggesting that unexpected good performance may even be negatively perceived (Leacock, 1969; Rosenthal and Jacobson, 1968). If student performance that exceeds expectation really produces pleasure and good will in teachers, it seems reasonable to hypothesize that teachers should more frequently praise lows than highs in parallel situations and should react more positively and intensely to success from lows. This does not typically occur.

Obviously, more research is needed here. It may be that some teachers are more affected by their general expectancy than by student performance, that other teachers are more affected by discrepancy between expectancy and performance, and that still other teachers are relatively unaffected by either factor.

Another difference between the studies was the time of year in which the data were taken. The observations in the first study were made late in the spring, while the follow-up was done in the first semester. There are at least two reasons to believe that expectancy group differences will be larger later in the year. The first is the polarization hypothesis already discussed. The second is a developmental progression that may exist in teachers' attempts to work with low achievers. It may be that at the beginning of the year teachers suspend judgment or take into account readiness and maturity differences while trying to bring all students up to the same criteria (he will do all right once he settles down; he has ability but he has not had any preparation, and so on). Then, when certain students consistently show relatively poor achievement, the teachers may respond with redoubled effort and determination (he is going to need a lot of extra work and individual attention). During this second phase, research would turn up no differences or perhaps even differences favoring lows on measures related to teachers' attempts to work for response.

There may come a third phase, however, if redoubled efforts still have not succeeded with certain students. The teacher may reach a point where he gives up, consciously or unconsciously, feeling that his time and efforts have not succeeded and will not succeed. Once such resignation and acceptance of failure occurs, findings like those seen in the initial study would begin to appear.

This may explain the praise and criticism findings in the initial study. If teachers had given up serious attempts to teach lows, they would have been strongly motivated in their beliefs that lows could not handle the material. As long as this belief could be retained, their failure to persist in trying to teach lows could be justified (they cannot learn), and, more generally, their self-concept as teachers could be protected and preserved (their failure is not my failure; no one could teach these students any better than I have).

Dynamics of this sort would tend to reverse "normal" reactions. Instead of responding with satisfaction to the success of the lows, the teachers might respond with irritation. They might even fail to notice their success. Similar dynamics could reverse the "usual" response to failure by lows. Instead of responding with patience and compassion, the teacher who had given up might well respond with criticism and rejection, not in an attempt to motivate the student, but out of a need to reassure himself that the student indeed was not making it (and, implicitly, will not make it and therefore does not merit greater teaching efforts).

In any case homogeneous versus heterogeneous grouping and first versus second semester data are likely explanations for the differences in findings between the two studies. It is also possible that the teachers' achievement rankings in the second study, collected early in the school year, reflected merely fleeting first impressions. Perhaps our teacher expectation data were obsolete and did not accurately reflect the teachers' expectations during the time that data were collected. This was not a factor, however. As the data in Chapter 6 will show, the teachers' expectations remained remarkably stable across the school year.

Finally, the teachers in the follow-up may have been more skillful or competent than the teachers in the initial study. In this connection it should be noted that we have frequently used the term "failure to replicate," and have implied in other ways that the follow-up results were unfortunate or undesirable. Actually, they provoked mixed feelings in us, depending upon whether we viewed them from the perspective of research and theory or from the perspective of the quality of education in the schools. When viewed from the first perspective, the follow-up data were distressing, since they showed that the situation was more complex than we had realized and that our theorizing about teacher expectation effects and our ability to generalize from our initial study would have to be modified. In short, we were confronted with an occupational hazard faced by all scientific investigators: "the rape of a beautiful theory by a gang of brutal facts."

Our distress here was mitigated, of course, by the fact that the follow-up findings were not completely negative. Three of the nine teachers did show the same pattern that had been observed in all four of the teachers studied in the initial research. Thus the follow-up did not so much completely contradict the initial findings as it complicated the interpretation of them by showing that not all teachers are affected by their expectations (the expectations we had measured, at least; unknown and unmeasured expectation effects are always a possibility).

We were pleased and impressed with the follow-up findings when we viewed them from the perspective of the quality of education in schools studied. It is encouraging that six of the nine teachers showed no evidence of giving up on the lows or otherwise treating them inappropriately, and three apparently were going out of their way to give them special help and attention. We had found the results of our initial study discouraging from this perspective, since they suggested that inappropriate teaching was typical, perhaps even universal. The follow-up data helped us to correct this overly pessimistic perspective. They showed that undesirable teacher expectation effects were not necessary or universal, and that teachers will differ in the degree to which they show these effects in their classroom behavior. This was the first naturalistic study in which undesirable expectation effects were not observed.

Other Follow-up Studies

Almost identical results were obtained in two other follow-up studies involving attempts to replicate the original findings and to provide evidence for the polarization hypothesis. The first of these (Evertson, Brophy, and Good, 1973) was conducted in the second grade and was a partial follow-up of some of the same students that we had studied in the first grade (Evertson, Brophy, and Good, 1972). The same students were followed a second year to see if they provoked similar teacher expectations and attitudes (see Chapter 5) in two different sets of teachers. The collection of teacher expectation rankings and of teacher-student interaction data was very similar to the first-grade study, except that the second-grade data were collected during the spring semester. Two classrooms at the lower class black school and four at the middle class white school were included.

Analyses of quantitative measures revealed remarkably even frequencies of teacher interaction with the three achievement groups, except that the highs had more reading turns than the other two groups (as in the first grade). Similarly, analyses of qualitative measures showed only one significant expectancy group effect, and this is difficult to interpret with regard to expectation effects. During reading groups teachers tended to repeat the question rather than to give help when dealing with lows, but they showed the opposite pattern when dealing with middles. The highs were in between on this measure. Nonsignificant group trends suggested that highs got more response opportunities and more and better feedback from the teachers during these public interactions, but that lows were given more frequent work-related feedback by the teachers and received more process feedback during private interactions. In short, teachers were allowing highs to dominate public interactions but were compensating for this during private interactions, so that no general expectation effects were observed in this study. Examination of the individual teachers' data showed that one clearly favored the highs over the lows, three showed no clear-cut pattern, and two tended to favor lows.

A second replication study (Brophy, Evertson, Harris, and Good, 1973) was conducted at the fifth-grade level and included two teachers in a lower class, predominantly white school and three teachers in an upper-middle class white school. Teacher expectation data and teacher-student observation data were collected in the fall semester and the beginning of the spring semester. Teachers were exchanging children for different lessons, so they were observed during particular subject matter instruction (language arts, math, social studies), when they had the same groups of children every day, instead of being observed for an entire morning or afternoon. Four of the five teachers were observed teaching two different groups, allowing investigation of the hypothesis that the teacher would show the same pattern across groups. As in the previous study, few expectancy group differences were statistically significant, and in general the study failed to replicate the Brophy and Good (1970a) findings.

Investigation of each teacher's individual data showed that two teachers tended to favor highs over lows (mostly on quantitative measures) in both of their classes, even though, in each case, one was a high ability class and one was a low ability class. Of the remaining teachers, one showed no group difference pattern at all, one favored the highs in one class and the lows in the other class, and the third showed a very slight tendency to favor the lows in both classes.

Taken together, the three replication studies reviewed so far show that the pattern of teacher communication of expectations observed in the Brophy and Good (1970a) study is not universal across teachers, although it appears in many. Each of the replication studies, although they did not provide support for the original findings in the data for the main effects across teachers, did include a minority of teachers who showed the same pattern of favoritism of highs and inappropriate teaching of lows that was observed in the original study. *This indicates that susceptibility to teacher-expectation effects is an individual difference variable, and data are needed to identify the teacher characteristics which make teachers more or less susceptible to such effects.* Another implication is that data from each teacher or class should be analyzed separately, so that teachers who show expectation effects can be identified and separated from those who show no pattern or who give evidence of a deliberate effort to work especially hard with low expectation students. Differential predictions would be made regarding group differences on product and process measures taken from these three contrasting types of classrooms.

The polarization hypothesis remains untested to date, because the studies designed to test it did not include enough teachers who showed a pattern of expectation effects. It appears that only a large-scale study, including a large number of teachers and spanning the entire school year, is capable of adequately testing this hypothesis.

Quantitative and Qualitative Effects of Expectations

Although its overall results regarding expectancy effects were negative, the Brophy, Evertson, Harris, and Good (1973) study conducted at the fifth-grade level did confirm one hypothesis: as students get older, expectation effects are more likely to show up in quantitative than in qualitative measures. This hypothesis was based on our observations of the nature of teacher-student interaction at different grade levels. In the early grades, reading groups tend to equalize the quantity of contacts that students have with their teachers (although several studies reviewed earlier show that this equalizing tendency is sometimes overcome by the behavior of high achievers in seeking response opportunities during discussions and in coming to the teacher to discuss their work). Without the equalizing effects of small group instruction, high achievers in the later grades are especially likely to dominate the teacher's time and attention, unless the teachers deliberately try to compensate.

Also, teaching at the later grades is more departmentalized, with teachers often seeing five different classes of students for five fifty-minute periods rather than seeing the same students all day long. They do not get to know the students individually so well as early elementary schoolteachers, and student differences in rates of initiation of contact with teachers are likely to have even greater effects on quantitative interaction measures.

A third reason that quantitative measures become more important than qualitative measures in the later grades is that classroom interaction with older students tends to be more organized and businesslike, centering around the presentation of curricular material and review or discussion of assignments. There are fewer dyadic interactions per unit of time in the later grades, and the interactions that do occur rarely involve teacher praise or criticism (in fact, in several of our studies teacher praise and criticism at the higher grades were so infrequent that the data could not even be analyzed for group differences).

For several reasons, then, we hypothesize that, when teacher expectation effects are operating in a classroom at the higher grades, they are likely to be mediated primarily through quantitative · rather than qualitative aspects of teacher-student interaction. That is, the primary group differences will be that the teachers will have many more interactions with highs than with lows. This was observed in a study by Mendoza, Good, and Brophy (1972) involving four seventh-grade junior high classrooms in a school serving an urban lower class population. Observations were made in the spring in two low level classes, one combination of low and medium level students, and one combination of medium and high level students.

Most significant expectation group differences in this study were quantitative. Lows regularly had fewer response opportunities than students in the middle and high groups. Highs initiated more work-related contacts with the teachers, but teachers compensated by initiating more such contacts with the lows and middles. Thus the largest overall differences were in public response opportunities rather than in private contacts with the teachers. Over all, students in the middle group had the most contacts with teachers in this study (44 percent, as compared to 33 percent for highs and 23 percent for lows).

Qualitative differences appeared only in the difficulty level of the questions that teachers asked. Highs were asked more of the difficult process questions and fewer of the easier choice questions. There were no significant group differences on the measures of praise, criticism, level of feedback, or persistence with students following errors.

In summary, there was little evidence of actively inappropriate treatment of lows. However, the lows were avoiding contacts with the teachers, who showed some attempts to compensate but not nearly enough to balance the differences in quantity of contacts caused by differences in the students' behavior. Thus lows had many fewer contacts with teachers than their classmates.

Good, Sikes, and Brophy (1972) studied teacher-student interaction in sixteen seventh- and eighth-grade classrooms in four junior high schools. Because the primary focus of this study was on the sex of the teacher (see Chapter 7), the sample included four male and four female math teachers, and four male and four female social studies teachers. All were whites teaching average classes in schools serving predominately white, urban, middle-to-upper class students. Classes were coded one hour a day for ten days, beginning in the seventh week of the fall semester. Both quantitative and qualitative group differences were observed, although again the quantitative differences were especially striking.

Highs initiated more comments and questions, received more response opportunities, called out more answers, and generally initiated more contacts of all kinds with the teachers. Also, the teachers did little or nothing to compensate for this. If anything, they were increasing the group differences by allowing the highs to dominate their attention and the classroom discussions.

Qualitative findings were mixed. Teachers more often failed to give feedback following responses by lows, but they did stay with these students more often after they failed to answer an initial question. When they failed to stay with lows, however, they were more likely to call on another student than to give the answer. These data, along with the large quantitative differences described above, suggest that the teachers' behavior was controlled largely by the students. Although a few data suggest that the teachers were trying to retain the initiative and compensate for differences in group behavior, for the most part they failed to take charge and were swayed by the tendency of the highs to call out answers and seek contacts and the tendency of the lows to avoid contacts.

Highs also got considerably more praise and less criticism than lows. Much of this difference, of course, is attributable to group differences in success and failure. However, when such differences were taken into account by computing a measure of the percentage of correct answers which were followed by teacher praise, the highs still showed a higher percentage than the lows (although the group effect was not significant). A parallel analysis for teacher criticism following failure could not be done because the teachers did not criticize often enough to allow group comparisons.

In summary, most of the qualitative group differences seen in our original first-grade study were replicated in this research at the junior high level. However, these findings were overshadowed by much larger and more consistent group differences on quantitative measures, as in the two previous studies.

Jones (1971) studied the interaction of sixteen student teachers with selected students in seventh- through tenth-grade classrooms. The teachers were all whites, and the students were all whites from urban middle class homes. Both the student teachers and the classroom students selected for inclusion in the study had been chosen because they were high or low on measures of achievement orientation and introversion-extroversion (see Chapter 8). Beginning in the sixth week of student teaching, each student teacher was observed for a total of 500 minutes of active interaction with her students. Measures of classroom interaction were then correlated with student achievement rankings to assess the relationship between these variables.

None of the qualitative measures correlated significantly with student achievement rankings. However, most quantitative measures did correlate significantly. Highs initiated more response opportunities and contacts of all kinds, and they also received both more direct and more open questions. The teachers did initiate more private contacts with the lows, but they also criticized them more frequently for poor work or misbehavior.

Cornbleth, Davis, and Button (1972) studied teacher interaction with high and low expectation students in seven social studies classrooms located in four urban high schools serving student populations of varying social class and ethnic composition. The students were heterogeneously grouped within schools. Three male and four female teachers were involved. Each was observed early in the fall semester for a total of four hours of interaction. Observers coded each teacher's interactions with four highs and four lows (the four highest and lowest, when these were all present, or the closest available substitute when one or more was absent). The highs included greater percentages of whites compared to Mexican-Americans and blacks and greater percentages of girls compared to boys, but neither of these differences was statistically significant.

Significant group differences were obtained on both quantitative and qualitative measures. The highs had more of every type of academic-related interaction, both public and private. Of these, the group difference was significant for teacher-initiated response opportunities, public-response opportunities, direct questions, and pupil-created contacts. Thus, in this study the teachers not only failed to try to compensate for the tendency of highs to seek out more contacts than lows; they were exaggerating the group difference by reciprocation, seeking out highs more often than lows.

There were group differences in the quality as well as the quantity of response opportunities. Highs responded to opinion, product, and process questions in roughly equal proportions, but lows responded to a higher percentage of opinion questions and a lower percentage of process questions. Other qualitative group differences were all in the direction found in our initial study, although none reached statistical significance. The trends were for highs to receive more praise and less criticism, for teachers to stay with highs more often to probe for better responses, for teachers to give highs process feedback more often, and for teachers to fail to give them any feedback less often. The differences on measures of staying with the student and of providing process feedback were due largely to differences in student-initiated interactions. Teachers treated highs and lows equivalently when the teachers asked the questions, but they were more likely to follow up with additional questions or to provide process feedback to highs when the student initiated the interaction. This, along with the large quantitative differences, suggests that the teachers felt much more comfortable in dealing with highs than lows.

Jeter and Davis (1973) studied ten fourth-grade social studies classes in three suburban schools. Teachers and students were from white middle class backgrounds, and the classes were heterogeneously grouped. Teachers were asked to rank their students on expected achievement in the usual way, and then the three highest and the three lowest ranking boys and girls were selected for study, with substitutes identified for use when the other students were absent (thus this was a quasi-replication of the Brophy and Good, 1970a, study). Six forty-five-minute observations were made in each class, spread over a week period in the spring.

Of fourteen interaction variables studied, nine showed a significant main effect for expectation level, and three more approached significance. The highs received more response opportunities, more total contacts, more process questions, more product questions, and more choice questions. They also initiated more work related interactions with the teachers. Qualitative findings showed that the highs got more feedback to their answers (teachers less often failed to give them feedback), that teachers stayed with highs more frequently after they failed to answer initial questions, and that highs were less frequently criticized following failure to answer a question correctly. Nonsignificant trends suggested that the teachers initiated more work related interactions with lows, asked highs more questions following right answers, and praised lows after right answers more frequently than they praised highs. With the exception of the last finding, these results all replicate the group differences reported in the Brophy and Good (1970a) study, although the data were taken in heterogeneously grouped fourth-grade classes in middle class schools. Its main commonalities with the Brophy and Good (1970a) study are that the data were collected in the spring and that only students at the extremes of the distribution of the teachers' rankings were included in the analyses. In any case, this study came closest to fully replicating our original findings, showing several ways in which teachers were acting so as to exacerbate the differences between highs and lows.

The mixed results of the studies reviewed above using the Brophy-Good Dyadic Interaction Observation System reflect the mixed results obtained in this field of research as a whole. Taken together, they provide evidence that the kinds of differences observed in our original study (and others discovered since) are parts of the process by which teacher expectation effects operate, but at the time the mixed pattern of findings shows that expectation effects are not universal across teachers and that susceptibility to such effects is an individual difference variable.

Our attempts to apply our model systematically by replicating our original study and testing the polarization hypothesis were frustrating, particularly since, at the time, these were the only studies we could locate which used both naturalistically formed teacher expectations and process outcome measures and failed to obtain a significant expectancy effect! This "exclusive" club has recently been joined by Garner and Bing (1973b), however, who conducted a naturalistic study in England using process variables very similar to those in the dyadic system. These investigators studied seven first-grade classrooms and related interaction data to factor scores representing the teachers' general perception of the goodness of their students. They found striking variability across the seven teachers rather than general expectation effects. Some did show such effects, but most did not.

As in our studies, the higher-rated students sought out response opportunities more vigorously and initiated more contacts with teachers than their classmates. The data were analyzed to see if teachers attempted to compensate for this student difference, and no evidence of compensation attempts was noted. Some teachers simply reacted to the differential student behavior patterns, while others exacerbated them by initiating more interactions themselves with the higher-rated students. Student personality differences which affected teacher-student interaction patterns were also noted (see Chapter 5).

CONCLUSIONS AND RESEARCH IMPLICATIONS

At first glance, the flurry of research set off by Rosenthal and Jacobson seems to have produced only more confusion rather than clarification. Both experimental and naturalistic studies have yielded conflicting findings which cannot be easily summarized and integrated. If we simply add up successes and failures and compute a "box score," the studies reporting expectation effects come out ahead, especially the naturalistic studies. This explains nothing, however.

Obviously the matter is complex, and further research along several lines is needed. Some findings seem clearly established, while others are suggestive at best. Depending upon which data they choose to stress and which they choose to minimize, different observers will reach different conclusions concerning the present state of research in this area. Our own interpretation of the available literature reviewed in the preceding two chapters follows.

Are Expectation Effects Real?

We believe that genuine expectation effects conforming to the conditions outlined in the model in Chapter 2 have been convincingly demonstrated and are an established fact at this point, but that they occur only in certain teachers. The model that guided our original study (Brophy and Good, 1970a) assumed that teacher expectation effects were universal across teachers and students, and thus did not take into account these individual difference variables.

Taking into account teacher individual differences, we now distinguish among three general types of teachers with regard to their susceptibility to expectation effects: *proactive* teachers, passive or *reactive* teachers, and *overreactive* teachers. *Proactive* teachers establish and maintain the initiative in structuring interactions with their classes as groups and with their students as individuals. Their expectations for students are used in planning treatment designed to individualize and optimize treatment of their students, but expectations are generally accurate and kept flexible to keep in touch with changes in the students. Thus, the proactive teacher uses his expectations, among other things, as tools in planning individualized instruction. He knows what he wants to do with the students and does not let student behavior or his own expectations for student behavior interfere with his progress toward his formulated goals.

The passive or *reactive* teacher has generally accurate and flexible expectations, so that he adjusts his reactions to students according to their behavior. Data from his classroom will show large expectancy group differences on measures related to student initiation but few differences on measures related to teacher initiation. Thus, in contrast to the more proactive teacher, the reactive teacher in effect allows the students to control or condition the patterns of teacher-student interaction in the classroom. He shows little evidence of an attempt to compensate for the differences in student behavior, but neither does he show an overreaction to these student differences that leads to undesirable teacher expectation effects.

The third type of teacher, the *overreactor,* provides the most evidence of expectation effects interfering with his teaching progress. He not only allows himself to be conditioned by student differences; he exacerbates these differences by treating the students as even more different than they really are, thus engaging in the kinds of behavior that produce self-fulfilling-prophecy effects. It is this type of teacher who will be most prone to favor students who show good performance and/or desirable classroom behavior, and to reject or to give up easily on students who show poor performance and/or undesirable classroom behavior. The overreactor is more likely than the other kinds of teachers to think of students as stereotypes (troublemaker, good student, slow learner) rather than as unique individuals.

As will be explained below, we believe that overreactors in general are likely to be less competent than other teachers and also to show certain patterns of defense mechanisms which make them especially prone to undesirable expectation effects. In suggesting the preceding three general types of teachers, we mean to provide a convenient and relatively loose categorization and not to imply that every teacher is clearly one of these three types in all of his interactions with students. Thus, for example, a teacher who is generally reactive may show evidence of attempts to compensate for student differences by working hard with one or two of his low achievers (but not the others) and may also show a tendency to overreact and show some expectation effects with regard to one or two other students (but not the others), while his general pattern might be one of passive reactive behavior to student differences. Similarly, a proactive teacher will probably be somewhat conditioned by some of his students, and an overreactive teacher will not necessarily show evidence of undesirable expectation effects in his interactions with all of his students. However, our observations suggest that most teachers fit under one of these three general labels, and we find them useful in thinking about and working with teachers and in identifying the reasons for the large differences from one classroom to the next in which there is evidence of the operation of expectation effects.

Teacher individual differences notwithstanding, evidence from many different sources shows that teacher expectation effects are a fact, not a fluke. At this point we must ask not whether they exist, but why they exist and how they operate.

What Explains Expectation Effects?

To the extent that a teacher's expectations cause him to treat highs more appropriately than lows, the effect of the teacher's behavior will operate to produce self-fulfilling prophecy effects. The effects will be produced in at least two ways, which will mutually support and reinforce each other.

First, there will be a direct effect on students' opportunities to learn the material. If a teacher attempts to teach more material to the highs, spends more time with them, calls on them more often, is more encouraging toward them, and persists in trying to teach them when they do not learn the first time, these students are virtually certain to learn more than low expectation students who do not get this kind of teacher treatment. This direct effect can be seen most obviously in the Beez (1968) study: high expectation students learned more than low expectation students simply because the teachers taught them more.

In addition to their direct effects on student opportunity to learn, teacher expectations also have indirect effects on student achievement via their effects on student motivation, level of aspiration, and self-concept. To the extent that a student perceives his teacher's expectations for him, his own expectations are going to be affected. Sometimes the teachers will communicate expectations directly. For example, we have observed teachers flatly tell students that certain work was too difficult for them (even though other students in the room were doing it and these students were voluntarily preparing to begin to do it themselves) or predict that one group would be able to solve a problem and another would not. Rist (1970) cites several gripping examples of this, and the work of Moore and his associates has shown experimentally that such direct communications of expectation affect the student.

More typically, however, teacher expectations are communicated in indirect ways. The teacher waits patiently for a response from one student but gives up easily with another; he expresses encouragement and confidence to one but says, "well, at least try" to another; he calls on one for hard and challenging questions but calls on another for only easy questions; he encourages one to "think" but tells another to "take a guess."

How these teacher differences will interact with individual differences among the students is based on how accurately the students perceive teacher behavior and the kinds of reactions they make to particular teacher behaviors. Expectation effects are likely to be greater when the student accurately perceives the teacher behavior and understands the implications regarding teacher expectations for him. A student who perceives that he is expected to do well is likely to develop confidence and high standards. Another will perceive that he is expected to do poorly and will be likely to develop failure expectations and low aspirations and persistence in working on assignments. Personal reactions of this sort will lead the first student to do his best but will tend to prevent the second student from achieving his full potential.

Some indirect effects can occur even without any conscious awareness on the student's part that the teacher has low expectations for him. This can occur through simple conditioning and reinforcement, independent of student perception. If a student does not get called on very often when he raises his hand, or if the interaction is unrewarding when he does get called on, he is likely to begin raising his hand less often. This, in turn, is likely to make the teacher less aware of him and less likely to call on him in the future.

Similarly, if a teacher demands quick responses and is impatient when waiting for an answer, his students are likely to become conditioned to raise their hands only when they are sure of the answer. Further, they also are likely to become conditioned to be anxious when they are not sure of the answer. To the degree that they are anxious and concerned about the teacher calling on someone else before they can come up with the answer, their ability to focus on the question and think about it will be impaired. This in turn will reduce the likelihood that they will be able to answer before the teacher loses patience.

Continued repetition of this vicious circle will mire both the teacher and the student into an unproductive rut. The more the student fails to answer, the more he will become anxious and less able to answer in the future; as this occurs, the teacher will become more impatient and more certain that this student will not be able to answer.

Thus, to summarize, teacher expectations have the potential for affecting student achievement both directly, by affecting the amount that the student learns, and indirectly, by affecting his motivation to learn. Some of the mechanisms involved in producing these effects are seen in the studies that involved observation of teacher-student interactions. In the early grades the important differences are usually in the quality of the interactions, since grouping for small group instruction tends to equalize the quantity of interactions that different students in the class have with the teacher. At higher levels, quantitative differences become increasingly noticeable, especially in measures of public interaction. By high school, the distribution of public response opportunities and contributions to discussions becomes extremely unbalanced. Most classrooms contain a small group of high achieving students who dominate the public interactions with the teacher and another group of low achieving students who seldom or even never participate.

Most teachers try to compensate for these differences in public interaction participation by seeking out low achievers more frequently for individual conferences at their desks.

To an extent these group differences in interaction patterns are probably necessary and appropriate; however, to an extent they also represent inappropriate communication of teacher expectations. We will return to this point in our discussion of implications for teachers in Chapter 9.

In addition to the above mentioned mechanisms by which teacher expectation effects can be mediated through the teacher's interactions with his individual students, there are also several mechanisms which can affect entire classes or schools of students. First, independent of their individual expectations for individual students, teachers tend to have a general level of expectation regarding what they expect their class as a group to accomplish during the school year (see Chapter 6). Bloom (1968) has pointed out that teachers tend to couch their expectations in terms of group and national norms rather than in terms of individual progress, so that, regardless of the amount of individual progress, they will tend to see a certain percentage of their students as "failing" during a given year. A teacher who overreacts to this perception is prone to show negative expectation effects.

Furthermore, the performance of the class as a whole will be affected by the general level of expectation that the teacher adopts. As studies comparing the curricula used at different grade levels in different countries and studies on the effects of tracking systems have shown, teachers tend to use the curricular materials with which they are provided as a norm for judging the expected progress of their students during the school year. A teacher who believes that his fourth graders cannot handle certain mathematical concepts because "that's sixth-grade level work," will not even attempt to teach the concepts. Meanwhile, another teacher working with a different curriculum, which defines these very same concepts as being appropriate for the fourth grade, will expect most of his pupils to master them during the fourth grade. In certain cases, most especially in schools serving predominantly economically disadvantaged students, this source of undesirable teacher expectation effects might be of considerably greater consequence than the intraclass individual-difference variables which have been studied in most teacher expectancy research.

Another important general variable is the level at which the teacher decides to aim his instruction. While some teachers attempt truly to individualize their instruction, moving each individual student along as rapidly as he can proceed, most teachers use a focal group of students or "steering group" as the basis for determining the level of their general instructions and expectations (Lundgren, 1972). Teachers with otherwise equal groups of students will probably get differential results, if one tends to gear his instruction primarily toward the high achievers in the classroom, and the other tends to gear his instruction primarily toward the low achievers. The first teacher might stimulate his high achievers to do very well but perhaps fail to instruct his low achievers adequately, while the second teacher might show the opposite pattern.

Thus, in addition to the factors of student individual differences which affect teacher expectations for individual students, teacher expectations can also be shaped by the curriculum materials used and the grade-level expectations associated with them and, within these, by the nature of the steering group toward which the teacher aims his level of instruction.

Why Do Expectation Effects Appear in Some Studies but Not in Others?

This is the crucial problem for researchers, and much work will likely be required before it can be resolved satisfactorily. A partial explanation can be constructed even now, however, on the basis of the available evidence.

As was mentioned earlier in discussing experimental manipulation studies, negative results in this kind of research may simply reflect the fact that the experimental treatment did not succeed in inducing the expectations that the experimenter wanted the teachers to have. Even if this were the explanation for *all* negative results in experimental studies, however, it could not explain the negative results in naturalistic observation studies. Negative results in these latter studies show that the mere existence of differential teacher expectations does not necessarily lead to differential treatment of different students or to self-fulfilling prophecy effects. Some teachers do not allow their expectations to interfere with their ability to treat students appropriately. If viewed in terms of a box-score approach, however, it seems clear that naturalistic studies have more frequently shown evidence of teacher expectation effects than have experimental studies involving manipulation or inducement of teacher expectations. Studies involving inducement of teacher expectations have shown mixed, mostly negative results, while naturalistic studies have shown mostly positive results.

We conclude from this, among other things, that unless a particular hypothesis is being tested which requires particular experimental manipulations, the naturalistic approach is more fruitful in studying teacher expectation effects. First, it is more direct, since the investigator can use the teachers' own naturalistically formed expectations and does not have to worry about whether his treatment has succeeded in inducing the expectations he wishes to induce. Second, naturalistic studies will usually have more generalizability or external validity with regard to classroom implications. Experimental manipulation studies usually involve treatment aspects that cause the entire experiment to create conditions that make the classroom unusual in one or more respects, and, therefore, experimental findings are of limited or unknown generalizability to other classrooms. Third, the naturalistic approach allows the study of low expectations without requiring the investigator to use the ethically questionable method of inducing low expectations for some students.

Two variables that do seem to make a big difference in teacher expectation research are the degree to which the teacher is already familiar with the students before the study begins and the amount of time that the teacher spends with the students during the study itself. The most extreme expectation effects have been found in studies in which the teachers and students did not know one another prior to the study and in which teacher-student interaction was confined to a brief period. Both factors can be explained on a common sense basis.

When the teacher knows nothing about the student except what the experimenter has told him, and when he spends only a short time with the student so that he does not get much of a chance to build up his own view of the student's capabilities, he is most likely to be swayed by the experimenter's treatment. The effect is magnified when a one-to-one tutoring relationship is involved, partly because detailed expectations about the single student can be given to the tutor, and partly because the continuous one-to-one interaction focuses the tutor's attention on the one student and makes it more likely that his expectations will affect his teaching of the student than if the student were part of a class so that the teacher saw him less often and had less clear-cut expectations about him.

In contrast, extended contact with students, such as over the course of an entire school year, allows the teacher time to build up his own expectations about them. Further, he sees the individual student in the context of the class as a whole. This gives him a better perspective, so that he is less likely to have an extreme and oversimplified stereotyped view than, for example, one of the tutors in the Beez (1968) study. Only certain teachers maintain rigid and inaccurate expectations over the course of a school year in naturalistic settings.

Also, in dealing with the whole class rather than in tutoring an individual, much of the teacher's attention is directed to the curriculum rather than to the learner. To this extent he will be more oriented toward his instructional activities than his concept of the learner's capabilities and personal qualities. This in turn will reduce the likelihood that expectations regarding students will affect his teaching.

One implication of the above is that expectation effects should be less frequent in the classrooms of teachers who are more preoccupied with the material they are trying to get across and with finding ways to put it across successfully than they are with the individual differences in their students' abilities. This is one characteristic that has been noticed in studies of teachers who have been judged to be especially successful (Bereiter et al. 1969; Jackson, 1968). It may also tie in with another inference that can be drawn from the various studies on expectation effects: there appears to be good reason to believe that successful master teachers do not show expectation effects, or, at least, that such effects are minimal in their classrooms. The most spectacular expectation effects have been shown in studies in which the teachers were untrained volunteers or student teachers without much experience. Studies that have used inservice teachers working with their regular students have found expectation effects less often, and the effects that did turn up were usually relatively weak compared to those in other studies.

To put it another way, expectation effects are an index of ineffective teaching. When they do show up in a teacher's classroom, they indicate that the teacher is systematically failing to teach low expectation students appropriately. The teacher does not know how to instruct these students appropriately, has not tried, or has given up. He is going through the motions of teaching them but without seriously and systematically doing so.

The teacher's manner of expressing expectations and the general quantity and quality of affect he expresses toward the students would also seem to be important in mediating expectation effects. D. Johnson (1970), along with several other studies reviewed previously, suggested that positive expectation effects are most likely to be mediated by teachers who are warm, friendly, and confident in dealing with their students. The obverse would also appear to be true: teachers who are notably hostile or rejecting would seem to be especially likely to produce undesirable negative expectancy effects. In contrast to both of the above, behaviorally restricted teachers who do not show much affect toward students seem likely to be primarily passive or reactive teachers unlikely to show either positive or negative expectation effects. Thus, generally more emotive teachers are probably more likely to show expectation effects, with the desirability of those effects being dependent upon the appropriateness of their teaching. Teachers who have appropriate teaching experiences and develop effective techniques are likely, among other things, to develop effective ways to communicate positive expectations to students, while teachers who have less favorable experiences are likely to begin to communicate consistently negative expectations to some or all of their students.

Combining the preceding considerations, we can classify our three types of teachers according to their probable responses to individual differences in students. The overreactive teacher is the one most susceptible to negative expectation effects. He not only allows himself to be conditioned by individual differences in students;

he exacerbates these differences by developing extreme and stereotyped expectations and by treating the students as even more different than they really are, thus increasing the differences from what they were originally. The passive or reactive teacher does not form inappropriately rigid and extreme expectations or engage in behavior that would exacerbate student differences in a direct way, but neither does he compensate for such differences. Instead, he merely reacts to the different behavior that different students present. Over time the effect of this depends upon differences in student behavior rather than upon inappropriate teacher expectations leading to inappropriate teaching behavior, and thus does not constitute a true expectation effect. The proactive teacher does not react to student differences merely passively, but instead attempts to actively compensate for them so that teacher-student interaction patterns are not determined by students. This type of teacher is least likely to show undesirable expectation effects stemming from inappropriate and rigid low expectations. He is likely to show positive expectation effects, however, if his teaching-role definition allows him to view learning difficulties as mere obstacles to be overcome, and if he adopts the general attitude that any student will learn if you can find the right way to approach him. Such teachers are capable of having *Pygmalion* effects on students with high anxiety and/or low self-confidence, because their patience, encouragement, and general positive expectations will help break down student fears and enable them to achieve more success than they would have if taught with less determination.

Certain methodological differences also appear relevant. For example, some studies have focused only on the teacher's interaction with a few students at the high and low extremes, while others have focused on the entire class. Not surprisingly, expectation effects have been more obvious in the former type of study. Perhaps expectation effects are important factors only at the high and low extremes of the student achievement distribution, where students are more salient and easily stereotyped.

Also, studies conducted in the spring have generally been more successful in showing expectation effects than studies conducted in the fall. It seems probable that the later in the school year that the research is done, the more likely the teacher is to have given up on some students (if he gives up on any). If a particular teacher had consciously or unconsciously given up and decided to coast along, group differences in the quality and quantity of classroom interaction would be enhanced from that point on.

Needed Research

The many studies dealing with expectation effects in the classroom have answered many questions, but further research in several areas is needed. In general, it appears that the reality of expectation effects is now established, and that future research should concentrate on identifying the individual differences in teachers and students that are related to these effects.

We have speculated about such differences, but few of them, especially the teacher differences, have been studied directly. Several likely hypotheses can be offered, however. First, it seems probable that more competent teachers are less susceptible to expectation effects than less competent teachers, at least to the kinds of negative expectation effects that occur when a teacher gives up on a student. This is because the highly competent teacher will be able to draw upon a rich repertoire of diagnostic and teaching skills when he encounters difficulty in teaching a student and will be more likely to succeed in solving the problem. His richer teaching repertoire will allow him to succeed in overcoming difficulties more regularly and therefore also allow him to be undisturbed by such difficulties and to view them as mere obstacles to be overcome. In contrast, the less competent teacher with a more limited repertoire will much more frequently try everything he knows and still fail to overcome a problem, so that the student does not learn what the teacher is trying to teach. Repeated frustrations of this sort will cause such a teacher to experience failure and will threaten his ego, making him more likely to begin to rationalize failure by adopting inflexible low expectations (this student cannot learn; nobody can teach him). The successful teacher will not need to do this because his attitudes and skills allow him to succeed regularly, minimizing the temptation to give up on a student. He is susceptible to the same dynamics and defense mechanisms as the less competent teacher, but his adaptive skills minimize failure so that defense mechanisms are not needed and expectations do not interfere with teaching performance.

Independent of general teaching competence, the teacher's pattern of coping styles and defense mechanisms would also seem to be important. Teachers who generally perceive reality accurately and are unthreatened by it, and therefore are relatively free of anxiety and the defense mechanisms that accompany it, would keep their expectations more open and flexible and would be less threatened by failure than more rigid, anxious, or dogmatic teachers.

The teacher's role definition is also important. Teachers who try to begin with each student at his own level and then to maximize his progress are unlikely to show negative expectation effects, although they may produce some of the positive expectation effects that occur when positive teacher treatment shows a student that he is more capable than he realized. In contrast, teachers who treat their class as an undifferentiated group and expect equal achievement from all are likely to work harder with lower achievers than with high achievers, with their general success being determined in large part by how high they set their sights. The former two types of teachers have in common the fact that they take personal responsibility for their students' learning.

This is in contrast with teachers who do not take such responsibility, who feel that their job is confined to presenting material and testing student knowledge, with the job of learning being the student's primary responsibility. Teachers who define their role in this way will be most susceptible to teacher expectation effects, especially effects of the negative kind that are present when a teacher gives up on students. Such teachers will not attempt to work toward particular goals with particular students. Instead, they will simply present the material and be relatively unconcerned about individual differences in achievement. They will be most prone to rationalize the failures of low achieving students and least likely to attempt to do anything about them. In schools using tracking systems, for example, teachers with this kind of role definition who are assigned to low ability classes often are primarily concerned with running an orderly and relatively problem-free classroom and relatively unconcerned with student learning (these students cannot learn anyway, so why teach them?).

Teachers' beliefs about the potential for change in student achievement are also important. Teachers who believe that IQ or achievement data represent accurate and unchanging characteristics of the student are likely to adapt their teaching to what they believe the student can handle and are unlikely to experiment with methods to get him to do better, on the grounds that such attempts would be fruitless. In contrast, teachers who see IQ and achievement tests as indications of the student's present performance, which are subject to change, rather than as measures of permanent characteristics, are more likely to experiment with different methods and to persist in trying to get the student to master the material.

Another factor is the teacher's usual method of resolving cognitive dissonance resulting from conflict between expectations and performance. Teachers who typically respond to such dissonance by quickly changing their expectations to conform to performance seem more likely to be susceptible to undesirable expectation effects, while teachers who first try to change performance in the direction of their expectations are more likely to produce positive expectation effects. Thus teachers higher in psychological differentiation (Dyk and Witkin, 1965), internal locus of control (Rotter, 1966), or cognitive level (Harvey, Hunt, and Schroder, 1961) are more likely to produce positive expectation effects and less likely to be susceptible to negative expectation effects.

Individual differences in students are also important in determining whether or not a particular student is affected by teacher expectations, and, if he is, whether the effect is desirable or undesirable. The more salient students in the classroom are likely to be perceived more accurately by their teachers (although not necessarily to be perceived positively). In contrast, the less salient students make it easier for teachers to continue having inappropriate expectations concerning them, because they give the teachers less frequent and less striking evidence about what they are like. Thus the former type of student is more likely to condition the teacher to respond to him with particular behavior, while the latter type of student is more likely to be conditioned by teacher expectation effects. In particular, the latter type of student is highly likely to underachieve because he gets less attention from the teacher and is not encouraged to do his best or is not given individualized help so much as his classmates.

Student coping styles and work habits are also involved. Students who regularly try their best (or give the teacher the impression that they do) are likely to be perceived as working up to their capacity, while students who give up easily, copy from neighbors, show little interest in the work, or are easily distractible are likely to be perceived as underachievers who could do better if their motivation were improved. Thus, in theory at least, the latter types of students should be more open to improvement through positive teacher expectations. However, in practice, teachers typically resent or are threatened by such student behavior, or they see it as permanent (he just does not care), so that negative rather than positive expectations develop.

Johnson (1970), extrapolating from research by Frank (1963) concerning the personality traits of patients who were most responsive to placebo treatments in medical research, suggests that students who are dependent, adult oriented, and generally "other directed" should be maximally susceptible to expectation effects. Such students would seem to be most likely to perceive and to be affected by teachers' expectations. In contrast, less teacher-oriented students would be less likely to perceive or care about the teachers' expectations, and students with more inner direction and self-confidence would be more likely to resist being affected by these expectations, even if they were accurately perceived.

In general, students liked by the teachers are more likely to benefit from positive expectation effects, while students disliked by the teachers are more likely to suffer from negative expectation effects. Some of the student traits that cause teachers to like or dislike students are described in the following chapters, but much research needs to be done in this area.

A fair amount is known at present (see Table 4.3) about the processes which underlie teacher expectation effects once expectations and attitudes regarding students are formed, but relatively little is known about student traits that are involved in initiating and changing such attitudes and expectations. More research is needed in this field.

Expectation effects appear to be less important and powerful than some enthusiasts have suggested. Studies using process measures or involving only a short time period make them seem quite impressive, but studies which have included long time periods have produced less spectacular results. Even where expectation effects were observed, their relative magnitude was rather small. Furthermore, it appears that expectation effects sometimes affect process without affecting product, and that they affect various product variables differentially. IQ's and scores from norm-referenced achievement tests are highly resistant to expectation effects when the study spans an entire semester or school year. Criterion-referenced tests from short-term experiments are much easier to affect (however, in many ways criterion-referenced tests are more appropriate than norm-referenced tests as product measures, and positive results from long-term study of criterion-referenced measures would provide strong evidence of expectation effects). Also, measures of student classroom behavior and of student attitudes toward teachers and schools are easier to affect than measures of student achievement or ability.

Data are needed concerning the question of why changes in process variables do not necessarily lead to changes in product variables. The idea that students given greater opportunity to learn and a generally more positive treatment by their teachers will learn more than students who do not have these benefits has strong face validity and appeal. However, several studies which reported expectation

TABLE 4.3. Teacher Process Variables Related to the Communication of Positive Expectations for Student Performance[a]

VARIABLE	STUDIES SHOWING A POSITIVE RELATIONSHIP[b]	STUDIES SHOWING NO RELATIONSHIP[b]	STUDIES SHOWING[a] NEGATIVE RELATIONSHIP[b]
1) Extent of Helping the Student (Fostering Dependency)		Medinnus and Unruh (1971)	Anderson and Rosenthal (1968) Beez (1968) Dalton (1969)
2) Frequency of Contact with the Student	Kester and Letchworth (1972) Page (1971) Rubovits and Maehr (1971) Davis and Levine (1970) Rist (1970) Good (1970) Kranz, Weber, and Fishell (1970) Tyo and Kranz (1973) Mendoza, Good, and Brophy (1972) Good, Sikes, and Brophy (1972) Jones (1971) Cornbleth, Davis, and Button (1972)	Claiborn (1969) Jose and Cody (1971) Medinnus and Unruh (1971) Brophy and Good (1970a) Evertson, Brophy, and Good (1972) Evertson, Brophy, and Good (1973) Brophy, Evertson, Harris, and Good (1973)	
3) Positive Affect (Warmth)	Jeter and Davis (1973) Kester and Letchworth (1972) Meichenbaum, Bowers, and Ross (1969) Page (1971) Rubovits and Maehr (1971) Medinnus and Unruh (1971) Chaikin, Sigler, and Derlega (1972) Rist (1970) Dalton (1969) Kranz and Tyo (1973) Tyo and Kranz (1973)	Claiborn (1969) Jose and Cody (1971) Rothbart, Dalfen, and Barrett (1971) Lanzetta and Hannah (1969) Evertson, Brophy, and Good (1972) Evertson, Brophy, and Good (1973) Brophy, Evertson, Harris, and Good (1973) Mendoza, Good and Brophy (1972)	

126

Variable		
4) Difficulty Level of Material Taught	Brophy and Good (1970a) Good, Sikes, and Brophy (1972) Jones 1971 Jeter and Davis (1973) Beez (1968) Carter (1969) Brown (1970) Mendoza, Good, and Brophy (1972) Cornbleth, Davis, and Button (1972) Jeter and Davis (1973)	
5) Time spent in Nonteaching Interaction		Beez (1968) Kranz and Tyo (1973) Brophy and Good (1970a) Evertson, Brophy, and Good (1972)
6) Closer Attentiveness	Page (1971) Rothbart, Dalfen, and Barrett (1971) Chaikin, Sigler, and Derlega (1972) Willis (1970)	
7) Persistence in Seeking Responses	Rowe (1971) Brophy and Good (1970a) Jeter and Davis (1973)	Evertson, Brophy, and Good (1972) Evertson, Brophy, and Good (1973) Brophy, Evertson, Harris, and Good (1973) Jones (1971) Jones (1971)
8) Inappropriate Reinforcement		Lanzetta and Hannah (1969) Rowe (1971) Brophy and Good (1970a) Good, Sikes, and Brophy (1972) Jeter and Davis (1973)

a Studies have been included on this table only when significant expectancy group findings were obtained for the sample as a whole. Studies reporting nonsignificant trends and/or mixed findings have been omitted.

b "Relationship" here refers to the relationship between the variable involved and *high* teacher expectations for student performance.

effects on such process variables failed to find evidence that student product measures had been affected. It may be that the differences simply were not great enough to make a difference, but other factors could also be involved.

Although many of the process mechanisms by which teacher expectation effects are mediated have been identified (see Table 4.3), additional studies in this area would be useful. In addition to the typical studies that use coding systems involving preset categories of teacher and student behavior, more case studies such as that by Rist (1970) would be useful. The rich descriptive detail and anecdotal incidents generated in such research provide deeper insights into the teacher-expectation phenomena than more quantitative studies using coding systems can provide. Another example is Kozol's (1967) *Death at an Early Age,* which, especially in its portrayal of the reading teacher at the school, provided rich clinical insights into the rationalizations and other defense mechanisms that some teachers use to evade responsibility for student learning and to adapt to student failure.

So far the polarization-over-time hypothesis has not been adequately tested. This is of some theoretical and also practical importance, in view of the generally negative results when teacher expectations have been studied over a long period of time. Although it seems almost certain that this process occurs among individual teachers and students, it has not yet been demonstrated as a group effect in a group of teachers who all showed expectation effects. However, only a very large and expensive study could adequately test this hypothesis, and it seems questionable at this point whether the payoff would be worth the effort and expense. Research designed to identify the individual differences that make teachers more or less susceptible to expectation effects and the individual differences in students that affect their teachers' expectations and attitudes toward them would seem to be more important and more promising at present.

Research is also needed regarding intervention and treatment. The authors have carried out one such study (see Chapter 9), but many more are needed. Since expectation effects tend to occur without the teachers' conscious awareness, mechanisms for getting feedback to teachers which will make them more aware of their patterns of interaction with their students need to be identified and used. In many cases simple provision of feedback will be enough to allow the teacher to correct the situation on his own. However, some teachers or some situations may require a more powerful treatment than simple provision of feedback, and research and development activities which will identify these situations and provide treatments that work are needed. Such activities would involve cooperation between teachers and researchers and would be quite different from the kinds of situations that have been typical in the past when researchers manipulated teacher behavior and gave teachers phony information or only partial information about the experiment. In contrast, the teachers would be cooperative partners in such research and development activities, participating with full awareness of the purpose of the activity and, ideally, helping to plan it.

chapter 5

The Influence of
Teachers' Attitudes
Toward Students
on Classroom Behavior

In the previous chapters we have shown how teachers' interactions with students can be affected by their expectations for student achievement and behavior. Expectations are primarily cognitive phenomena, inferential judgments about probable future achievement and behavior based upon the student's past record and his present achievement and behavior. In addition to these primarily cognitive *expectations* regarding students, teachers form primarily affective *attitudes* about the students they teach.

Attitudes and expectations are closely interrelated, and it is probably more correct to say that they lie on the same continuum of reactions to students than to attempt to draw a sharp distinction between them. The cognitive judgments involved in forming expectations often have strong affective components, as when a teacher not only decides that a student is a low achiever but also becomes angry or frustrated in response to this realization. Similarly, attitudes may be accompanied by conscious cognitive components. At first the teacher may be only vaguely aware (or even unaware) of his reaction of attraction or repulsion toward a particular student. Over time, however, teachers experiencing strong affective reactions are likely to become more and more aware of them and eventually to articulate them verbally and to analyze them to some degree. Thus, although we refer to a primarily cognitively derived prediction when we use the term "expectation," and to a primarily affective reaction when we use the term "attitude," we see the two as closely related and typically in interaction with each other.

As with expectations, teachers can have general attitudes toward students as such or toward a particular class as well as specific attitudes toward individuals. General attitudes stem from the teacher's personality and his definition of his role as a teacher. Person-oriented teachers are likely to enjoy their contacts with students and to hold generally favorable attitudes toward them. In contrast, introverted and withdrawn teachers may prefer to minimize social contacts with students and are more likely to develop neutral or relatively negative attitudes toward them. As examples of the effect of the teacher's role definitions, consider teachers who see their primary (or sole) responsibility as the transmission of information and consider teachers who are more person-oriented and feel that establishing a close relationship with students and helping them develop positive self-concepts is an important part of their job. The first type of teacher is unlikely to develop strong affective responses to students (except perhaps strong negative responses to students who interfere with his goals), and he is likely to respond to them primarily in terms of their role as learners rather than as individual personalities. The second type of teacher is much more likely to develop strong affective responses to his students and to concern himself with their general personalities rather than only with the more narrow range of their characteristics as learners.

In addition to these general orientations toward students, teachers will respond differentially to each different individual. No two students are alike, and their individual differences cause teachers to respond differentially to them. Some student attributes, like friendliness and an interest in learning, seem to affect almost all teachers favorably. Similarly, attributes such as laziness and hostility affect most teachers unfavorably.

With other kinds of student attributes, the effect on the teacher will depend in part upon the teacher's own needs and values. Some teachers will dislike a dependent, clinging child, while others will respond positively to the child and take a special interest in him.

We believe that teachers' attitudes can affect teacher-student interaction in much the same way that teachers' expectations can. That is, once a teacher forms a particular attitude toward an individual student, the teacher is likely to begin to treat this student in individualized ways. Attitudes, like expectations, will be communicated. A student whom the teacher particularly likes will probably know it, and so will his classmates. The same goes for a student whom the teacher dislikes. This knowledge is likely to affect the responses of the students to the teacher, probably causing them to behave in ways that will reinforce the teacher's attitudes. Thus, students that teachers like will probably begin to behave in ways that will make the teacher like them even more, while rejected students will probably begin to respond in ways that will increase the teacher's degree of rejection.

In short, our model for the effects of teacher attitudes on teacher-student interaction is similar to our model for the effects of teacher expectations. Once the teacher forms differential attitudes, the students may begin to respond differentially and in ways that will tend to complement and reinforce the teacher's attitudes. In some cases the results should be an increase in achievement and school satisfaction for some students and a decrease in achievement and school satisfaction for others. Thus attitudes, like expectations, have the potential for affecting students and for functioning as self-fulfilling prophecies.

As the quotations presented at the end of Chapter 1 show, it does not take long for teachers to form specific attitudes toward different students in their classes. In this chapter we will show, by citing research by ourselves and by other investigators, that four basic differential teacher attitudes toward different students in the same classroom (attachment, indifference, concern, and rejection) affected the patterns of teacher-student interaction observable in that classroom. In Chapter 6 we will summarize the results of several questionnaire studies that provided additional information about the implications of these attitudes on students' self-concepts, school interests, and achievement.

TEACHER ATTITUDES AND TEACHER–STUDENT INTERACTION IN THE CLASSROOM

Two Initial Studies

The teacher–student interaction studies to be described in this chapter all involve four basic teacher attitudes toward students: attachment, indifference, concern, and rejection. Systematic study of the influence of these four teacher attitudes on teacher–student interaction was begun by Silberman (1969), who was following up an earlier study by Jackson, Silberman, and Wolfson (1969). In the latter study thirty-two elementary schoolteachers were asked to name all their students from memory. They were then questioned about their attitudes and opinions concerning four students: the first boy and first girl and the last boy and last girl that they named. These teacher reactions were tape-reporded and later analyzed for "signs of emotional involvement" with the students. These signs included both positive and negative reactions to the students and referred to both their school-related academic performance and their more general personal qualities.

As expected, the teachers' remarks about the students named first (the salient students) contained more signs of personal involvement than their remarks about the students named last (the nonsalient students). There were also sex differences: the teachers showed more signs of personal involvement with boys than girls, and more of their signs of involvement with boys were negative ones. These results are consistent with findings from many studies showing that boys are more salient in the classroom and receive more teacher criticism than girls (see Chapter 7).

Silberman (1969), having noted that the attitudes of attachment, indifference, concern, and rejection were particularly frequent in the teachers' remarks about salient and nonsalient students, followed up by studying the effects of these four attitudes on teacher-student interaction in the classroom. His study involved ten female third-grade teachers who had taught in upper-middle class suburban schools for at least three years. Teachers were asked to respond to the following interview items:

1. *Attachment:* If you could keep one student another year for the sheer joy of it, whom would you pick?
2. *Indifference:* If a parent were to drop in unannounced for a conference, whose child would you be least prepared to talk about?
3. *Concern:* If you could devote all your attention to a child who concerned you a great deal, whom would you pick?
4. *Rejection:* If your class was to be reduced by one child, whom would you be relieved to have removed?

The teachers nominated one student in their class in answering each question. Silberman then collected twenty hours of observational data in each class to see how teachers interacted with these four students and to see what the students were like.

Silberman saw the students in the *attachment* group as conforming to and fulfilling the personal needs of the teachers. These children more frequently volunteered to answer questions, more frequently answered correctly, and made few demands on the teachers' energies, compared to their classmates. Thus, not only had the teachers expressed favoritism toward these students, classroom observation showed them to be "model" students. Nevertheless, there was relatively little evidence that they were treated preferentially. The teachers did not call on them more frequently, despite their more frequent hand raising. They did praise them more frequently, although this was probably due to their better general performance.

In a later discussion of his data, Silberman (1971) stated that he felt that the teachers were favoring these students in more subtle ways, through the quality of their interaction with the students rather than through the more quantitative aspects that he had measured. He noted, for example, that when attachment students were praised, they tended to be praised publicly, as if they were being held up as models to their classmates. He also felt that these students were more frequently asked to share their ideas with the class (implicitly suggesting that their ideas were especially good), and that they were less often and less harshly admonished when they broke classroom rules. Silberman also felt that part of the reason he did not find much evidence of favoritism toward attachment students was a deliberate effort on the teachers' part to avoid showing favoritism to these students. Remarks by some of the teachers suggested that they were quite aware of their tendency to favor these students and therefore deliberately exerted self-control to see that they avoided doing so.

Silberman saw the students in the *concern* group as making extensive but appropriate demands upon the teachers. Of the groups studied, these children received the most teacher attention. Teachers initiated frequent contacts with them and placed few restrictions on them, so that they could approach the teachers freely in most circumstances. The teachers also praised their work frequently and were careful to reward their efforts. However, at times the teachers did express their concern directly and openly, "I don't know what to do with you next." In general, the teachers saw these children as students who needed a lot of help, but they were quite willing to give this help.

The students in the *indifference* group were notable only for their very low frequencies of contacts with the teachers. Silberman (1971) later added that teacher contacts with indifference students not only were less frequent; they also tended to be briefer and less emotionally involving. These students were not rejected or disliked by the teachers; they were simply ignored or not noticed.

Silberman saw the students in the *rejection* group as making demands on the teachers that the teachers saw as illegitimate or overwhelming. Most of them were behavior problems, and Silberman reported that they were under almost continual surveillance, with the teachers ready to intervene quickly and reprimand them for misbehavior. Teachers had a large number of contacts with these students, a great proportion of which involved attempts to control their misbehavior. Yet, these students also received a lot of praise from the teachers. It was Silberman's impression that both praise and criticism directed at rejection students was often done publicly in front of the class, as if the teacher were making a point of it. The more frequent and intense criticism is understandable if these students presented more frequent and intense misbehavior problems. The frequent and intense praise is less readily understandable, although as noted in Chapter 1, boys frequently receive more praise as well as more criticism than girls. Spontaneous comments by some of the teachers suggested that they went out of their way to find things to praise their rejection students for in an attempt to compensate for their tendency to criticize them continually for misbehavior.

Differences in teacher treatment of concern and rejection students in parallel situations were particularly instructive. As noted previously, concern students were ordinarily free to approach the teacher for help whenever they needed it and were usually given this help upon request. In contrast, rejection students who approached the teacher for help were often refused when the teacher was busy or when she felt that they had not worked sufficiently long or hard. Often they not only were refused help when they came for it but also were criticized for having done so.

Obviously, in the eyes of the teachers, the concern and rejection students were two different groups. Yet, their classroom behavior on variables picked up in the coding system did not show such large differences. This theme will be repeated again in the studies to be described below. More intensive study of children in these two groups is needed to discover the attributes that trigger teacher concern versus rejection.

A modification of the Silberman study was conducted by Jenkins (1972). This research involved ten elementary teachers in middle class schools. All were women with at least three years of teaching experience. Jenkins used Silberman's interview questions and general procedures to identify one student in each class to represent each of the four teacher attitudes. She then collected at least ten hours of observational data in each classroom and later interviewed each teacher concerning her perception of the four children's behavior during observation periods. The observations included several aspects of the students' behavior and their interactions with the teachers, and the poststudy interview also included a twenty-nine-item rating scale in which teachers expressed their views of the students' classroom behavior and general characteristics.

There was great variation in the degree to which the teachers' perceptions of student behavior during observation periods agreed with the classroom observation data. Significant correlations (indicating agreement between teachers' perceptions and observers' codings) were obtained for the variables of tendency to waste time, amount of attention, amount of smiling at the teacher, occasions of neutral expression toward the teacher, correct and incorrect answers, failure to correct mistakes, initiation of work and personal conversations with the teacher, requests for assistance from the teacher or evaluation of work, and amount of hand raising.

Correlations did not reach significance (indicating poor agreement between teachers' perceptions and observers' scores) for student behaviors such as time on task, amount of frowning at the teacher, failure to respond to teacher questions, amount of correct answers after another student has given a wrong answer, failure to give correct answers after another student has also failed to give the correct answer, requests for permission, and typical reactions to work assignments (pleasure, displeasure, or neutral).

Thus teachers were most accurate in describing the students' general work habits, general level of achievement, tendency to seek response opportunities through hand raising, frequency of seeking help or evaluation regarding work assignments, and positive facial expressions directed at the teacher. Jenkins noted that most of these are behaviors that required some response from the teacher, while the student behaviors judged less accurately mostly did not require a response.

In general, the teachers were reasonably accurate in their perceptions of the students, although their inaccuracy regarding requests for permission, failure to respond to questions, and general attitude toward schoolwork seems somewhat puzzling. Even a moderate degree of accuracy in teacher perception data is noteworthy, however, since some previous studies have shown teachers to be remarkably inaccurate in observing and judging student behavior in the classroom (Ehman, 1970; Wolfson and Nash, 1968; Jecker, Maccoby, Breitrose, and Rose, 1964).

Jenkins also noted that although teacher perception of a particular behavior often correlated significantly with classroom observation of that same behavior, teacher perception of other behaviors sometimes correlated more highly with the observation scores for different behaviors than with teacher perception of that same behavior. For example, although teacher perception of students' attention correlated $r = .40$ with students' attention scores from the observation data, teacher perception of other variables, such as the students' frequency of hand raising or of giving correct answers, correlated even higher with the observation measure of student attention.

Findings like these exemplify the so-called "halo effect" that is found when people make ratings of others. It is difficult to rate people specifically on a number of different variables. Instead, ratings tend to be colored by a general impression or "halo" representing our general attitude toward the person. If we think highly of him, we tend to rate him positively on most or all scales; if we think poorly of him we tend to rate him generally negatively. This halo effect operates in teachers' ratings of students just as in any interpersonal ratings.

Thus, although Jenkins' teachers showed a fair amount of accuracy in terms of significant correlations between their perceptions and the observers' scores, some of this accuracy was due to halo effect. Inspection of Jenkins's data shows that the teachers were using a small number of criteria as key indicators in making their ratings, particularly the frequency of student hand raising, the frequency of correct answers, and the tendency to waste time. These three factors apparently were good predictors of the students' general motivation and achievement levels, and consequently good predictors of many of the more specific behaviors that Jenkins questioned the teachers about.

Having analyzed the relationship between teachers' perceptions of student behavior and observers' measures of this behavior, Jenkins went on to analyze the relationship between these data and membership in the four attitude groups. The results for the observations of students' classroom behavior were disappointing. Only two of twenty-two student behaviors, hand raising and student initiated work conversations, indicated significant discriminations based on attitude groups. These two behaviors in combination indicated significant discrimination among all pairs of attitude groups except for the concern and rejection groups, which were not significantly different from each other. Here again, despite the very different teacher reactions to students in these two groups, their classroom behavior as recorded by observers did not appear very different.

In contrast to the data from the recorded classroom observations, where only two of twenty-two scores indicated discrimination among the groups, eighteen of the twenty-two teacher perception scores indicated significant discrimination among the groups. Here again, however, the scores showed discrimination only among three groups; they did not separate the concern from the rejection students. Most important discriminations among the groups were the teachers' perceptions of the degree to which students wasted time and the frequency with which they initiated work or personal conversations. One implication here is that teachers' perceptions of the differences among these four kinds of students are much greater than the students' actual behavioral differences. We will return to this point again in discussing later research.

Jenkins's data also included seven items measuring teachers' general attitudes toward students. These cover the teachers' beliefs about the students' motivation, brightness, attitude toward the teacher, need for encouragement, and general performance; they also cover the amount of teacher effort needed to get the student to learn and the degree to which it was worthwhile for the teachers to spend extra time and energy trying to get the student to learn. All but the last of these seven general teacher attitude measures indicated discrimination among the groups, with the teachers' assessment of the students' general performance and attitude toward the teacher being the two most important predictors. This time the predictors only discriminated the attachment group from the other three, which were not discriminated from one another. That is, the teachers saw the attachment students as differing from the others in having higher achievement and in having warm rather than neutral or hostile attitudes toward the teachers. This ties in nicely with Silberman's description of attachment students as children who reward teachers or fulfill their personal needs.

The studies by Silberman and by Jenkins were in agreement in showing that teachers felt quite differently toward these four attitude groups and attributed different attributes and behavior to them. However, the behavioral data in both studies were relatively disappointing in view of the small percentage of significant results. Only two of twenty-two measures in the Jenkins study showed significant discrimination among the four groups, and her observations included only student behavior and not teacher-student interaction. The Silberman study did include measures of teacher-student interaction, but few differences were significant. The clearest differences were between the concern and indifference groups, and these related largely to the difference in the quantity of contacts that these two groups of students had with the teachers.

Although Silberman made many interesting impressionistic observations and reported many interesting teacher comments about the students, relatively few of his measures of classroom interaction showed significant differences among his groups. There was little evidence of favoritism toward attachment students, and the findings for rejection students showed a mixed pattern rather than clear-cut rejection.

In discussing his findings Silberman (1969) suggested that the teacher role may interact with teacher attitudes either to foster or to prevent the expression of different attitudes. In particular, he suggested that the attitudes of attachment and rejection conflict with the teacher role (treat everyone equally, play no favorites), making it difficult for teachers to show favoritism or rejection even when they feel it. He suggested that indifference and concern are less in conflict with the teacher role and therefore more likely to show up in the teacher's interaction with students.

Two Replication Studies

A puzzling finding from both the Silberman and Jenkins studies was that the concern and rejection students appeared quite similar on most indexes of classroom behavior yet were seen as quite different by the teachers. This, plus an interest in exploring teacher-student interaction with students of these four attitude groups, led us to replicate and extend this line of research in two studies to be reported in the following sections.

The first study (Good and Brophy, 1972a) replicated Silberman's original procedures except for three major changes. First, Silberman conducted his attitude interview *before* the observational measures were taken, so that the teachers knew the relevant variables being studied. This may have led them to distort their behavior during observational periods, such as by masking favoritism toward attachment students, demonstrating concern for concern students, and so on. To prevent this possible contamination of teachers' classroom behavior by knowledge of the relevant teacher attitudes, the teacher attitude data in the Good and Brophy (1972a) study were not collected until *after* the behavioral data had been collected.

Second, Silberman (and Jenkins) used only one student per classroom to represent each attitude group. While this insures that attention is focused on the student who is most extreme on each attitude, it reduces the possibility of discovering common student characteristics which trigger these attitudes in teachers. Thus, in our replication studies, teachers were asked to nominate at least three students to each attitude group.

Third, Silberman's study (and Jenkins's) had been done in upper middle class suburban schools. This left open the possibility that the results might be affected by something unique to this type of school. Thus, our replication studies involved classrooms in contrasting kinds of schools to see if the earlier findings would replicate in different types of schools.

Data for the Good and Brophy (1972a) study were collected in the nine first-grade classrooms which were already involved in the Evertson, Brophy, and Good (1972) study of the relationships between teachers' performance expectations and their behavior toward individual students. Thus, the sample included three first-grade classes in an upper-middle class white school, three in a lower class white school, and three in a lower class black school. Teachers were told that we were interested in observing differences in the classroom behavior of students who varied in achievement level, and were asked to supply lists ranking the students in order according to expected achievement.

Other than collection of achievement rankings in September and again in November and procurement of seating charts for each classroom, no information was requested from the teachers until all behavioral-observation data for the first semester were collected. This eliminated the possibility that knowledge of the relevant attitude variables might influence the behavioral data. Classroom observers knew that achievement rankings were being collected (although they did not see them), but they did not know that attitude data were going to be collected. Thus the observers also could not have been influenced by knowledge of the attitude groups.

After forty hours of behavioral observation data were collected in each classroom during the first semester, attitude information was collected through a questionnaire mailed to the teachers. The questions were the same as those used by Silberman, except that "if your class was to be reduced by a few children, which would you have removed?" was substituted for ". . . whom would you be relieved to have removed?" for the rejection item. This was done at the request of the school-district administration.

The behavioral data were standardized within each class, and then a series of analyses of variance were performed, in which scores for each attitude group were compared with the scores for all other students. These data were analyzed to investigate the ways and degrees to which the classroom behavior and teacher-student interaction patterns of the students in the four respective attitude groups differed from those of their classmates.

The data were also subjected to a series of two-way analyses of variance, in which school as well as attitude was used as a classifying variable. These analyses allowed us to investigate whether there were differences among the three different schools on the ways that teacher–student interactions were affected by the four teacher attitudes studied. The number of significant interactions that appeared in these two-way analyses was below that expected by chance, and no interpretable pattern was noticed in the ones that did occur. Furthermore, differences across schools were in degree rather than direction of effects; there were no reversals of main effects in individual schools. Thus the attitude effects were similar across the three schools despite their contrasting populations. Differences in social class and race in the student populations of the schools did not affect the findings related to the effects of teacher attitudes on teacher-student interaction. The findings concerning the four attitude groups follow.

As expected, *attachment* students showed qualities likely to endear them to teachers. Compared to their classmates, they more actively sought out the teachers, and they typically initiated contacts about work assignments rather than merely procedural matters. Although they were active in the classroom, they did not call out answers significantly more often than their classmates. Thus they appeared to be bright and active but able to control themselves and to avoid violating classroom norms by calling out answers.

The attachment students were also higher achievers. They had substantially more correct answers per response opportunity, fewer reading errors per reading turn, and more correct answers in reading group question–answer periods. In addition, when the attachment students did not know the answer they were more likely to try to make a response than to remain silent. Thus, compared to their classmates, they were more likely to succeed when they responded and more likely to make some kind of a response when confused or uncertain. They were also well-behaved, having considerably fewer behavioral contacts with their teachers relative to their work-related contacts.

In many ways these findings parallel those of Silberman and Jenkins. The attachment students appeared to be bright, hard working, and obedient, the kind of students that would appeal to most teachers. Nevertheless, as Silberman (1969) found, there was relatively little evidence of teacher favoritism toward them.

The attachment students did receive much more total praise for their academic work and also less criticism and more praise in teacher-initiated work contacts. However, this is explainable as a result of their higher achievement rather than as teacher favoritism. Attachment students were not praised significantly more often per correct answer than their classmates.

Again, as Silberman (1969) also reported, there was evidence that the teachers tried to minimize their contacts with attachment students. They sought out these students less often to discuss their work and less frequently directly called on them to answer questions. The teachers were compensating, in other words, for the attachment students' greater frequencies of initiating contacts and seeking response opportunities.

There were a few differences in teacher-student interaction patterns with attachment students which could be interpreted as subtle favoritism toward them (although other interpretations are possible). Attachment students received more reading turns than their classmates and also a greater percentage of the more difficult process questions. These data are reminiscent of Silberman's impression that the teachers were holding up attachment students as models to their classmates.

Lastly, the attachment students received less process feedback, apparently because the teachers felt that they understood the work and did not need this kind of detailed explanation. In summary, the data for the attachment group parallel Silberman's quite well. Although there were some minor differences suggesting favoritism toward this group, there certainly was no gross favoritism toward attachment students by the teachers.

The *concern* students, although not so active as the attachment students, also initiated more contacts with teachers than their classmates. However, their scores on indicators of performance quality were much lower. They had fewer correct answers per response opportunity and made more errors per reading turn, indicating generally lower achievement and greater learning difficulty. However, like the attachment students, when they did not know the answer they were more likely to take a guess than to remain silent.

As in Silberman's study, the interaction data clearly showed that concern students received considerably different teacher treatment than their classmates. They got many more opportunities to answer questions, both in general class activities and in reading groups, and the teachers sought them out much more frequently for private contacts regarding both work and procedural matters.

In addition to seeking out the concern students more frequently, the teachers responded to their failures more favorably than they responded to the failures of other students. For example, concern students received more process feedback in teacher-initiated work contacts, indicating efforts by the teachers to work with these students and help them learn material they were having difficulty with. Also, the teachers were more likely to stay with these students when they committed reading errors, and they showed nonsignificant but notable trends toward more frequently asking them new questions in the reading group after they failed to answer an initial question correctly and toward less frequently failing to give them feedback after an answer. In addition, when concern students failed to answer a question in the reading group correctly, the teachers were more likely to simply repeat the question than to give help in the form of clues. Thus, in summary, the teachers seemed to be more carefully monitoring the performance of concern students during reading groups and were pushing them to do their best. The same trends seen in the reading group data also appeared in the data for general class activities, but they were weaker and usually not statistically significant.

Even though the teachers sought out concern students for more contacts and stayed with them longer following both success and failure, they did not praise or criticize these students significantly more than their classmates. In general, then, the teachers' treatment of concern students reflected concern over their learning progress (not their behavior). This concern was expressed in frequent attempts to get the most out of concern students during discussion and recitation and to work with them to remediate their deficiencies during individual contacts.

These behavioral data bear out most of Silberman's (1971) impressions regarding teacher treatment of concern students, especially their much higher frequencies of interaction with these students and their willingness to help them and work with them. Two of Silberman's other impressions, however, were not borne out by the data. First, he felt that the teachers in his study were overpraising, or at least taking every opportunity to praise, concern students. Our data suggest no difference in teachers' praise or criticism of concern students as compared to their classmates. Second, Silberman (1971) implied that teachers were quick to give concern students help or to give them the answer rather than push them to work harder to solve problems on their own. Our behavioral data suggest otherwise; if anything, the teachers appeared to be pushing these students to do as much as they could on their own through such behaviors as staying with them after reading errors and repeating questions rather than giving help after an initial failure to answer. In any case the behavioral data show that teachers did appear to be highly concerned about the achievement of concern students, and they spent much time and effort working with them.

The only distinguishing characteristic Silberman (1969) discovered about *indifference* students was a low rate of interaction with the teachers. This finding was replicated in our study and is elaborated with several other findings. As a group, the indifference students were quite passive in the classroom. They initiated fewer work and procedural contacts with their teachers, and they seldom called out responses in either general class activities or reading groups. When they did not know an answer, they were more likely to remain silent than to offer a guess.

Indifference students responded adequately when they did answer a question, however, being correct about as frequently as their classmates. They also were about average in their frequency of discipline contacts. Thus, passivity was their primary observable trait.

The interaction data revealed some differences in teacher treatment of indifference students. These students received fewer response opportunities than their classmates. Much of this was due to the students' own unwillingness to seek response opportunities. However, the teachers also asked these students fewer direct questions than they asked their classmates, indicating that the low rates of response opportunities were at least partially due to a teacher tendency not to call on these students.

Also, the teachers initiated fewer individual contacts with indifference students. Their tendency to avoid these students was not so great as the students' tendency to avoid them, but it was nevertheless observable in the data. This was especially true for procedural contacts, although a trend also appeared for work contacts. The difference on the measure of teacher-initiated procedural contacts means that in-difference students were less often selected to run errands or perform classroom management and maintenance tasks for the teachers than were their classmates.

In summary, the indifference students as a group were generally passive, avoiding contact with the teachers. Moreover, the teachers responded to them in much the same way. They did not pursue these students in compensation for their tendency to avoid contacts with them. In fact, the teachers called on them and sought them out for personal contact less often than their classmates, and when they did have contacts with them they showed less emotional involvement with them. In many ways the teachers' treatment of indifference students sharply contrasted with their treatment of concern students, underscoring the accuracy of the teachers' perception of their feelings about both of these groups of students.

Thus our behavioral data on teacher-child interaction with indifference students bear out Silberman's (1971) claim that teachers not only had fewer interactions with these students but also had briefer and less affectively toned interactions with them. Also, the data again bear out the fact that the relationship here was one of indifference or lack of emotional involvement rather than one of rejection. The teachers were not critical or rejective toward indifference students; they were merely indifferent toward them. Their tendencies not to call on these students often and not to seek out as many contacts with them as with their classmates appeared to result from a failure to think about or perhaps even to notice these students rather than from a tendency to avoid them because of feelings of rejection or hostility.

Our behavioral data on *rejection* students bear out Silberman's claim that these students tended to make demands that teachers perceived as illegitimate or over-whelming. Rejection students were very active in the classroom, creating many more procedure and work contacts with the teachers and calling out answers without permission more frequently.

They were similar to their classmates in rates of reading errors and percentage of questions answered correctly in general class discussion, although there was a trend for them to have more frequent incorrect answers in reading group question-and-answer periods.

The fact that these students presented frequent behavior problems was shown in the extremely high number of behavioral criticism contacts that they had with their teachers. Thus, these students frequently presented discipline problems through misbehavior and, even when engaged in academic activities, tended to be hyperactive and aggressive compared to their classmates.

Analysis of the interaction data for rejection group students shows that the teachers did indeed reject these students. First, rejection students had many fewer public response opportunities than their classmates, even though they called out more answers than the others and the teachers asked them just as many direct questions. Thus the difference in total response opportunities was due to the low frequencies of open questions answered by rejection students. This could be due either to the students (they did not raise their hands and volunteer) or to the teachers (they did not call on these students when they did volunteer). Unfortunately, the data do not tell us how often either or both of these conditions were occurring.

However, evidence from other measures shows that the teachers tended to avoid rejection children in public situations. These children received fewer reading turns, and the teachers frequently failed to give them feedback after their reading turns and after they responded to questions. Thus the teachers avoided public interactions with these students and tended to move away from them quickly and go to someone else when they did have public interactions with them.

The teachers did not avoid rejection students in private situations, however. In fact, they initiated more individual work contacts with rejection students than with their classmates. Perhaps they preferred to deal with rejection students in private as much as possible. However, data on the quality of these private work-related interactions suggest that they were not so positive or helpful to the rejection students as similar private contacts with their classmates were. In particular, rejection students were more likely than their classmates to be criticized when they sought out the teachers for private work contacts and were more generally criticized for their classroom behavior and work.

The latter finding supports Silberman's (1971) impression about the difference between teacher treatment of concern and rejection students. He noted that in his study teachers tended to respond favorably to the overtures of concern students seeking help but to respond less favorably, sometimes even with criticism, to the overtures of rejection students. Our behavioral data bear out this impression. Rejection students who sought out the teacher for help with their work were more likely to be criticized than were their classmates in similar situations. In summary, data from several measures show that the teachers rejected and avoided this group of students.

In general, the findings of the Good and Brophy (1972a) study confirm most of the previous findings of Silberman (1969, 1971) and Jenkins (1972) and extend these findings by adding new ones concerning the nature of teacher-student interaction with children in these four attitude groups.

Findings regarding attachment students are similar across studies, showing slight tendencies but no clear evidence of teacher favoritism toward these students. The students themselves appeared to be bright, high-achieving, conforming students.

Findings across studies also suggest that the concern students were having difficulty and needed help from the teachers, who in turn were willing to give this help. However, our behavioral data do not bear out Silberman's impression that the teachers were "babying" the concern students and taking every opportunity to praise them. In our study the teachers were inclined to push these students as far as they could be pushed, and they showed no tendency to praise them any more frequently than they praised their classmates.

Our findings regarding indifference students confirm Silberman's report that they had considerably less interactions with the teachers than their classmates. However, our interaction data also show that the teachers tended to avoid calling on these students and to avoid seeking them out for individual contacts, and they confirm Silberman's impressions that the interactions they did have with them tend to be briefer and less emotionally involving.

Findings regarding rejection students agree in describing the students as active, assertive students who present frequent behavioral problems and make other difficult demands upon the teachers. However, while Silberman found a mixed pattern of results suggesting a teacher tendency to compensate for their recognized tendencies to reject these students, our data suggest a more general and clear-cut pattern of rejection.

The Second Replication Study

A second replication of this same basic study was carried out the following year in six second-grade classrooms in connection with the Evertson, Brophy, and Good (1973) study. These classrooms, four in an upper-middle class white school and two in a lower class black school, contained many of the children who had been studied the previous year in the first grade. The collection of data relating teacher attitudes toward these four types of students to teacher-student interaction in the classroom in the second grade was undertaken for two basic reasons. First, such data were important for their replication value alone. The findings of the three previous studies did not agree in all respects, and further data were needed to help separate generalizable findings from those which apparently were due to special conditions operating within a given study. Second, since many of the children involved in this second-grade study had also been studied the previous year in the first grade, we had an opportunity to investigate whether a given child would trigger the same attitudes in two different teachers and to investigate further the personal attributes of the children that were related to these teacher attitudes.

As in the first-grade study, the investigation was presented to teachers as a study of the differential classroom behavior of children differing in achievement level. Only a seating chart and achievement rankings were obtained from teachers before behavioral data were collected; attitude data were collected only after the completion of the behavioral observations. Except for the minor adaptation mentioned earlier on the rejection item, Silberman's four questions were used in collecting attitude data. Again, teachers were asked to nominate at least three students in each category. These teachers usually nominated five in each category, except for the indifference item, where they felt that there were fewer children with whom they were unfamiliar.

Observational data were collected during the second semester of the second grade. As in the first-grade study, teacher–student interaction scores were standardized within classrooms, and analyses of variance were performed to see how students in each of the four respective attitude groups differed from their classmates.

These analyses produced relatively few significant group differences. As was the case with the three teacher expectation groups in this study (see Chapter 4), teacher nomination of a student into one of the four attitude groups did not greatly affect his pattern of teacher-student interaction. This may have been because these teachers usually nominated five students for each group rather than only three, as in the Good and Brophy (1972a) study, or one, as in the Silberman (1969) and Jenkins (1972) studies. Thus, the teachers' lists for each of the four groups included not only the student who represented the teacher's strongest attitude but also (usually) four others about whom the teacher did not have such strong attitudes.

It is also possible that the teachers had some idea of the relevant variables involved in this study, since we had conducted a similar study in the same schools the previous year. Our treatment study (see Chapter 9) was also conducted in these same schools, so that the first-grade teachers had been given feedback about some of the variables included in the observation system used in all of the studies. Thus, it is possible that the second-grade teachers had learned something about the relevant attitudes and/or classroom behavior being studied through conversations with the first-grade teachers studied the previous year.

Also, it may be that the six teachers involved were more skillful teachers and/or better at controlling their attitudes to the extent of preventing them from influencing their interactions with students. In any case, the attitude groups were less important as determinants of teacher-student interaction than they were the previous year in the first-grade study. The results were as follows.

Differences between the attachment students and their classmates reached or approached statistical significance on only five of thirty-seven observational measures. These students created more work contacts, more procedural contacts, and more total contacts with their teachers; they received more reading turns; and their percentage of created work contacts over total work contacts was higher than that of their classmates. Thus these students again appeared to be students who frequently come to the teacher to create work-related contacts. The teachers did not respond by calling on them more often or seeking them out more often for contacts, except that they did give them more reading turns.

Other differences between attachment students and their classmates, while not statistically significant, were in the same direction as those seen earlier. They suggest somewhat higher achievement, more frequent praise, less frequent criticism, and less frequent behavioral contacts. Thus, again, the attachment students appeared to be bright, cooperative, and conforming. Again, too, the teachers showed little evidence of grossly favoring these students despite their liking for them. Only the higher frequency of reading turns suggests favoritism, and this may be due to their higher achievement level (and, therefore, membership in a high reading group that had somewhat different kinds of activities than lower reading groups) rather than to teacher favoritism.

In summary, the findings from all four studies agree in showing attachment students to be conforming, cooperative high achievers. Yet despite these qualities and despite the fact that the teachers nominated these students as the students that they particularly liked, none of the studies found any evidence of gross favoritism toward them in teacher–student interaction measures.

A Fifth Study

Similar findings were obtained in a dissertation study by McDonald (1972), which was designed specifically to explore this point. This study involved fourteen elementary school student teachers and their students. Information was obtained from each student teacher about her degree of liking for each of her students, and information was obtained from the students about their degree of liking of the teacher. It was predicted that the teachers would behave more warmly toward the students they liked, but this prediction was not confirmed. Results were in the predicted direction on seven of ten measures, but none reached statistical significance. Nor was there any evidence that teachers responded more warmly toward students whom they felt liked them. The same pattern of findings also was obtained for the students: students did not respond more warmly to teachers that they liked better or to teachers whom they thought liked them better. Thus this study showed that neither teacher liking for students nor teacher perception of being liked by students, nor student liking for the teacher, nor student perception of being liked by the teacher, affected the degree of warmth of the teacher-student relationship as observed in the classroom.

Comparisons and Conclusions

Thus, five separate studies agree that, despite the common sense importance attached to such variables as liking and feelings of attachment, these affective responses apparently do not make a notable difference in observable teacher-student interaction patterns in the classroom. Apparently attachment is communicated through subtle behaviors that are not picked up in the typical classroom observation system or through grades and comments on papers. It definitely does not show up in frequency measures of overt acts such as praise or criticism. The development of a classroom observation instrument capable of picking up teacher behavior involved in the communication of attachment to favored students would be a valuable methodological contribution.

Differences between *concern* students and their classmates reached or approached statistical significance on eight of thirty-seven behavioral measures. The teachers initiated more procedural contacts and more total contacts with these students. They initiated more work-related contacts, too, but the difference was not significant.

Concern students called out more answers to questions in the reading groups, and they initiated more work-related and procedural contacts than their classmates. Thus, again, both in terms of teacher-initiated interactions and student-initiated interactions, concern students had higher rates of interaction with their teachers than their classmates.

The other significant differences concerned teacher praise and criticism. The teachers more frequently praised the classroom behavior of concern students, but they also more frequently criticized their classroom misbehavior and therefore had a greater frequency of behavior contacts with these students than with their classmates. The praise finding ties in with the data of the studies described earlier, suggesting that teachers particularly encourage and praise concern students. However, the evidence of frequent behavior problems with concern students and frequent criticism of concern students for misbehavior that appeared in this second-grade study represents an unusual finding. This pattern is typical of that reported for rejection students in the earlier studies. The probable reason for this can be seen in Table 5.1. This table shows that the grade-two teachers nominated a higher percentage of boys for the concern group than did the grade-one teachers. In view of the consistent finding that boys more often misbehave and are more frequently criticized for misbehavior than girls (see Chapter 7), the higher rates of misbehavior and of teacher criticism of misbehavior by concern students in the second-grade data become understandable. This sex difference finding also helps explain the higher frequency of calling out during reading groups by concern students in the second-grade data. The latter finding is also at variance with earlier studies that portrayed concern students as hard working but as having difficulty due to limited ability and therefore less likely or able to call out answers.

In summary, the findings for concern students confirm the earlier findings that teacher concern is shown primarily in high frequencies of contact with these students. Some of the differences between the second-grade study and the earlier research by Silberman, Jenkins, and ourselves appear to be due to the fact that these second-grade teachers nominated more boys to the concern group than earlier teachers had.

Some of the nonsignificant trends in teachers' interaction with concern students relate to some of Silberman's (1971) impressions. The teachers showed a tendency to give the answer or move on to someone else when concern students did not answer an initial question correctly, and when they did stay with them they

TABLE 5.1. Sex and Achievement Status of Children in the Four Attitude Groups in the First-Grade and Second-Grade Studies (all Figures Are Percentages)

SEX:	ATTACHMENT		INDIFFERENCE		CONCERN		REJECTION	
	Grade One	Grade Two	Grade One	Grade Two	Grade One	Grade Two	Grade One	Grade Two
Boys	44	44	58	46	46	67	68	76
ACHIEVEMENT RANK:								
Top Third	75	52	0	0	11	10	8	16
Middle Third	21	36	50	67	14	23	29	32
Bottom Third	4	12	50	33	75	67	63	52

tended to give a clue or some form of help rather than simply repeat the question. The teachers were also less likely to criticize them for misbehavior.

Thus, in general the data fit the picture drawn by Silberman (1971). Teachers seemed to see concern students as in need of special help and to try to give them that help. They not only had more frequent contacts with them, but they appeared to be less critical and demanding in responding to their work and apparently tried to praise more frequently and to be more encouraging when possible. It is of special interest that these trends showed up in the second-grade data when many of the concern students were boys who presented behavioral problems. This particular aspect of the findings deepened our own puzzlement about why teachers respond with concern and generally favorable behavior toward certain students and yet reject certain other students who appear to be similar in many ways.

Only one of the differences between the *indifference* students and their class-mates reached statistical significance: these students had fewer behavioral contacts with their teachers (presumably because they misbehaved less often or misbehaved in minor, less noticeable ways). Patterns observable in the nonsignificant differences were generally consistent with previous data. Again, indifference students appeared to be passive and relatively inactive in the classroom and relatively unnoticed by the teachers. Measures of frequency of contact with teachers showed indifference students to have generally lower means, and measures of quality of contact showed little difference. There was little evidence in the second-grade data that the in-difference students were treated with less emotion or less favorable emotion than their classmates, as the first-grade data had suggested. In the second-grade data there simply were no differences between indifference students and their classmates on these variables.

Interaction measures involving *rejection* students showed significant differences on only two measures. The teachers initiated more procedural contacts and more total contacts with these students. Nonsignificant differences fell into the same pattern seen earlier: the rejection students had high frequencies of all kinds of interactions with their teachers but especially behavioral contacts due to misbehavior. They also tended to provoke stronger emotional reactions, getting both more praise and more criticism.

All in all, the data from the second-grade study coincide more closely with the data from Silberman's (1969) original study than with our own (Good and Brophy, 1972a) first-grade study involving many of these same students. The three studies agree in showing attachment students to be bright, conforming, and generally re-warding to the teachers and also in showing no gross teacher favoritism toward these students (although hints of subtle favoritism appeared in each study). In-difference students were distinguished primarily only by low rates of interaction with their teachers in the Silberman study and in our second-grade data, but our first-grade data (Good and Brophy, 1972a) showed a much more clear and extreme pattern involving mutual avoidance by the teachers and these students.

The three studies agree in showing that teachers perceive concern students as having great difficulties and being in need of help, and that one way they respond to this perceived need is to have many more interactions with them than with other students. There is less agreement on some of the qualitative measures of teacher-student interaction. Both Silberman's (1969) data and our own findings from the second-grade study suggest a tendency for the teachers to make things easy for these students, to give them the answer rather than push them, and to praise them more frequently. However, the Good and Brophy (1972a) first-grade data suggest a somewhat different pattern, in which the teachers apparently were pushing these students a little bit harder rather than making things easy for them. The second-grade data also showed high rates of misbehavior and criticism of misbehavior for concern students, but this most likely was due to the high percentage of boys in these concern groups.

Findings for the rejection students were similar across studies in showing them to be behavior problems and to be generally active in the classroom (and to be primarily boys). Thus all three studies agree in finding these students to be active, to misbehave frequently, and to be criticized frequently for misbehavior. However, the findings differ in certain other respects. Both Silberman's (1969) data and our own second-grade data do not show a clear-cut pattern of rejection of these students by the teachers. Both sets of data show these students to receive more than the average amount of praise as well as criticism. We did not conduct a poststudy interview with our second-grade teachers, but it is possible that they, like Silberman's (1969) teachers, were aware of their negative feelings toward such students and made deliberate attempts to compensate by attempting to treat them fairly and perhaps even to single them out for praise whenever opportunities arose. In any case the second-grade data showed a mixed pattern rather than a clear-cut pattern of rejection. In contrast, the Good and Brophy (1972a) first-grade data showed a much more clear-cut pattern of teacher rejection of these students.

After our first-grade study (Good and Brophy, 1972a), we thought that the discrepancies between our results and those of Silberman (1969) and Jenkins (1972) were due to the fact that we did not ask the teachers to nominate students to attitude groups until after the data had been collected, whereas Silberman and Jenkins had done so before classroom observations began. Thus we thought that awareness of the relevant variables under study might have affected the behavior of Silberman's and Jenkins's teachers in ways that would make them be less extreme in their treatment of the four attitude groups. However, although our second-grade study also involved delaying questioning teachers about the attitude groups until after the behavioral data had been collected, the data from this study fit more closely with Silberman's (1969) study than they do with our own first-grade data (Good and Brophy, 1972a). Thus the differences are obviously not simply due to the question of whether the teachers were asked to nominate attitude groups before or after observational data collection began (although, as noted above, the second-grade teachers may have received some information from the first-grade teachers). Other factors, such as differences in the students and/or in the teachers, must have been involved.

Thus one of our conclusions about teacher attitudes is similar to one of our major conclusions about teacher expectations: the effects of teacher attitudes on teacher-student interaction are not simple and universal. The degree to which teacher attitudes affect teacher-student interaction, and the particular ways that they do affect it when such effects are observed, will differ from teacher to teacher. As with teacher expectations, it seems to us that the more competent the teacher is, the more secure and confident he is, the better his personal adjustment is, and the more aware he is of his attitudes and their possible effects on his behavior, the less likely his teaching is to be influenced by his attitudes toward individual students.

A related conclusion also seems reasonable: it is unlikely that particular student attributes have simple and universal effects in triggering specific teacher attitudes. Although it is likely that the great majority of teachers will react to a given student attribute positively or negatively, there is much room for interaction between particular teachers' personality traits and particular students' personality traits, so that a given student might be liked by one teacher but disliked by another.

This factor was seen in the data from our two studies reported above. Since the studies were conducted in the first grade one year and in the second grade the next year at the same schools, it was possible to analyze the data to see the degree to which different teachers nominated the same children to the four attitude categories. These data show relatively low stability, suggesting that a given teacher's attitude toward a given student will depend greatly upon the particulars of the relationship between that student and that teacher. A fair degree of stability was shown for the attachment and concern groups (perhaps unsurprisingly, since these seem to be the best defined in terms of their personal characteristics). Thirteen of the nineteen first-grade attachment students were present in second grade, and four of these were nominated to the attachment group by their second-grade teachers. Ten of the nineteen first-grade concern students were present in second grade, and four of these were also again nominated to the concern group in second grade. This probably represents a moderately high degree of stability, since teachers were asked only to nominate a few children at the extremes. If we had asked them to rank their entire classes and computed correlations, it is likely that the correlations would have been moderately high for these two groups.

Only four of the first-grade indifference students were present for second grade, and none of these were nominated for the indifference groups by the second-grade teachers. These figures reflect two major facts: first, large numbers of the indifference students had moved, so that they were no longer in the school by the second grade; and second, indifference students apparently do not possess common qualities that make different teachers equally likely to respond to them with indifference.

Perhaps the most ironic and striking data concern the rejection students. Only four of the eighteen first-grade rejection students were in second-grade classrooms. In this case it was not because they had moved out of the district, but because they had been retained in the first grade. Ironically, the very students who had been nominated as the ones that the teachers would most like to see removed from their rooms were the students who were most likely to be retained for another year in the first grade. Apparently the teachers' concern about the academic failings of these students outweighed any tendency that they might have had to promote the students just to get rid of them, because rejection students made up the bulk of the retainers among children who started first grade together. Of the four rejection students who did go on to second grade, three were nominated for the rejection group by their second-grade teachers. This suggests that the rejection students have common qualities that affect different teachers in similar fashion, causing them to respond to them with rejection rather than with concern.

Taken together, these longitudinal data suggest that attachment, concern, and rejection students have somewhat stable and general traits which make them likely to strike different teachers similarly, but that indifference students do not. However, the effects of these general traits are not so strong as to create very high stability in teacher ratings from one year to the next; a teacher's attitudinal response to a particular student cannot be predicted with great confidence simply on the basis of the information about the student.

SEX AND ACHIEVEMENT AS DETERMINANTS OF TEACHER ATTITUDES

To the extent that teacher-student interaction is affected by and predictable from knowledge about the teachers' attitudes toward particular students, it is of obvious importance to find out what student attributes tend to trigger off particular attitudes in teachers. This question will be taken up in the present section, which deals with attributes of students that teachers nominate to four attitude groups, and will be continued in the following chapter.

Before turning to more personal attributes and behavior, let us examine the role of the general variables of sex and achievement in affecting teacher attitudes toward students. Table 5.1 shows the percentages of boys and the percentages of high, middle, and low achievers that teachers assigned to the four attitude groups in our first- and second-grade studies. These data help explain some of the findings concerning teacher-student interaction with the four attitude groups, as well as the behavior typically shown by students in these groups.

Regarding sex, note that boys are particularly likely to be nominated to the rejection group, and slightly less likely than girls to be nominated to the attachment group. These findings were constant across the two studies. Note also that more boys were nominated to the concern group in the grade-two study (we interpret this to be the reason for some of the unusual findings concerning teacher interaction with concern students in this study).

The sex data become more meaningful when examined in combination with the achievement data. Note that students in the attachment group tend to be high achievers, as would be expected from the studies reviewed previously. They are also slightly more likely to be girls than boys, although the difference here is nowhere near so large as might be expected by those who feel that female teachers favor girls over boys.

The indifference groups contain no high achievers in either study; they are concentrated in the middle and bottom thirds. Thus teachers get to know high achievers better than other students, on the average, and are not indifferent toward them. For the most part they are quite favorable toward them; although, as can be seen in the data for the concern and rejection groups, they do become concerned about a few high-achieving students and also reject a few of them.

For the most part, however, high achievers come to the teachers' attention and are perceived favorably by them. The data for concern and rejection students further deepen the mystery about why these two groups of students are differentially perceived by the teachers, since the data of Table 5.1 show them to be generally similar. They are mostly low achievers, and, at least in the second-grade study, boys. We had thought after the first-grade study that the difference was heavily tied up with sex and were reminded of Lippitt and Gold's (1959) observation that teachers tended to respond to low status girls with concern and support but to respond to low status boys with rejection and criticism. However, the second-grade data showed that this simple explanation does not hold up (at least not in general, but it might explain the first-grade data). Even if sex is involved, it is not the only factor. There is something else, something about the personal attributes or behavior of the students, that makes teachers become concerned and positively oriented toward one group but hostile and rejective toward the other group.

OTHER PERSONALITY ATTRIBUTES AS DETERMINANTS OF TEACHER ATTITUDES

In an attempt to explore this further, we asked the second-grade teachers to rate their children on a number of personality and behavioral attributes. Table 5.2 shows how the students in the four attitude groups were rated on personal attributes and classroom behavior. The sex of the student is also included in the table to show how the teachers saw the girls as opposed to the boys.

Children in the group variables (sex, attachment, indifference, concern, rejection) were classified as either present or absent. The student attribute and behavior measures came from rank order scales in which teachers were asked to rank their students, starting with the one who was most extreme on the variable and going through the class until they reached the one that was least extreme on the variable. If teachers felt that they could not distinguish between two or more students, these students were given the same score. Thus the ranking procedure did not force teachers to rank students differentially when they did not feel that they could do so with any confidence.

Quick inspection of Table 5.2 shows that the boys and the rejection students had most of the significant correlations with the ranking variables. The correlations involving boys are striking in that, without exception, every significant correlation

TABLE 5.2.   Correlations of Sex and Attitude Groups with Teachers' Ratings of Student Attributes and Behavior[a]
(N = 151 except for Indifference Group where N = 124)

	SEX[b]	ATTACHMENT	INDIFFERENCE	CONCERN	REJECTION
Restless	—.32*	—.10	—.02	.15*	.31*
Cheats	—.07	—.19*	.08	.19*	.26*
Independent	—.09	.04	—.10	—.10	.06
Embarrassed	—.01	—.15*	.11	.09	.10
Comfortable	.07	.30*	—.08	.02	—.19*
Sassy	—.20*	.06	—.06	.03	.25*
Defiant	—.15*	—.07	.02	—.06	.26*
Not Noticeable	.03	—.05	.34*	.03	.02
Lazy	—.16*	—.12	.06	.12	.25*
Makes Funny or Irrelevant Comments	—.21*	.09	—.08	—.02	.23*
Daydreams	—.28*	—.17*	.03	.13	.25*
Lacks Confidence	—.16*	—.10	.09	.34*	.14
Poor Speech	.04	—.09	—.08	.13	.02
Imaginative	.19*	.08	—.22*	—.20*	—.17*
Butts in with Answers	—.22*	—.02	—.11	—.07	.21*
Helpful	.11	.37*	—.12	—.10	—.13
Fights	—.29*	.04	—.07	.04	.21*
Defensive	—.15*	.00	—.06	—.11	.25*
Large	—.04	.05	—.02	—.08	.14
Unhappy	—.10	—.37*	.20*	.01	.28*
Neat	.07	.23*	.01	—.00	—.18*
Unattractive	—.01	—.28*	.15*	—.00	.13
Needs Encouragement (Rather than Needs Push)	.19*	.06	—.04	—.21*	—.04
Whispers	.12	—.26*	.25*	—.11	—.06
Healthy	.01	.11	.01	—.08	—.00
Immature	—.16*	—.29*	.13	.26*	.25*
Averts Eyes	—.11	—.32*	.20*	.07	.21*
Impulsive	—.17*	—.04	—.02	.08	.17*

[a] Coefficients are biserial r's between classifying variables scored as present-absent and teacher ranking scores for the student attributes and behavior.
[b] Sex was coded Boys = 1, Girls = 2, so that positive correlations indicate that the behavior or trait was associated with girls more than with boys.
* $p < .05$

pictures the boys on the negative side of the variable being measured. Compared to girls, these six teachers saw boys as being more restless, more sassy, more defiant, lazier, more likely to disrupt the class with a funny or irrelevant comment, more likely to daydream, more lacking in confidence, more likely to butt into classroom conversations, more likely to fight, more defensive, less mature, and more impulsive. They also saw more boys as needing to be pushed (presumably because more were lazy) rather than brought along slowly with encouragement. These data show once again, perhaps even more clearly than in some past studies, that teachers tend to view boys negatively in comparison with girls. Nevertheless, as noted in Chapter 7, these feelings usually do not cause grossly discriminatory or inappropriate treatment of boys as such, at least so far as can be detected on measures of classroom interaction. (Certain boys, especially assertive low achievers, do usually receive negative teacher treatment; however, high achieving boys are usually favored.)

Correlations involving attachment students reinforce and fill out the picture of them already drawn from Silberman's (1971) observations and our own previously described data. The teachers saw these students as unlikely to be daydreaming, as helpful, happy, neat, attractive, and mature, compared to their classmates. They also saw them as unlikely to whisper rather than speak up clearly and as unlikely to avert their eyes rather than look the teacher in the eye. None of these data are surprising, given the previously reviewed findings. Perhaps the most notable addition is the suggestion on several of these measures that such students were unusually well-adjusted in addition to being the kind of bright and conforming children that please and reinforce teachers. In the eyes of the teachers, anyway, these students were alert, happy, attractive, mature, and, in short, generally well-adjusted.

The data for the indifference students are also unsurprising, although they do add to the picture drawn already in previous findings. The trait most strongly associated with this group was that they were not noticeable in the classroom. This is obvious from both the teachers' nomination of the students into this group and from the data on their classroom behavior. Other significant correlations involving this group help fill out the picture, though, showing some of the reasons why they were not noticeable to the teachers. In the teachers' eyes these students were unhappy, unimaginative, and unattractive. Thus, they lack many of the positive qualities that would draw the teachers' attention toward them and make them salient and positive. Furthermore, they were seen as more likely to whisper than to speak up in interactions with the teachers and more likely to avert their gaze rather than look the teacher in the eye during such direct interaction. Thus, the teachers saw them as shy, introverted, and somewhat troubled students. Yet, despite this perception, the teachers' main response to these students was indifference rather than concern. Some of the reasons for this will be discussed in the following section, after we look at the correlations involving concern students.

The teachers saw the concern students as lacking in confidence, unimaginative, and immature. They also saw them as more restless and more likely to cheat than their classmates. Perhaps in connection with the latter trait (and also because two-thirds were boys), they saw the concern students as needing to be pushed to achieve, rather than to be brought along slowly and carefully with encouragement. These teacher perceptions tie in nicely with the teacher–student interaction data for the first-grade study described earlier, but not with the behavioral data for these second-grade teachers.

Comparisons between the correlations for the indifference and the concern students are interesting and instructive. Teachers agreed in seeing both groups as unimaginative, but otherwise the patterns of attributes and behaviors were quite different. The data suggest that the teachers' over-all personal reactions to these students were based on their behavior during face-to-face interaction, but that their degree of concern about the students' need for help was based more upon the students' behavior in working on and completing seatwork assignments. Notice that even though the indifference students were perceived to whisper rather than to speak up and to avert their eyes rather than look at the teacher, and also to be seen as generally unhappy, the teachers' responded to them with indifference rather than concern. Perhaps this type of nervous, shy student makes the teacher uncomfortable, and he is more likely to avoid rather than to spend much time with them. Perhaps this is also why the indifference students were the only group to be perceived as unattractive.

One would think, given the teacher perception of indifference students as unhappy, unattractive, and shy or nervous in interaction situations, that they would also perceive them as lacking in confidence, immature, and in need of encouragement. Yet, this was not the case. Apparently the qualities that these students possess tend to make teachers either truly indifferent or nervous and avoid them rather than become concerned about them.

The data for the concern group generally fit previous findings except for the teachers' perception that they need to be pushed rather than brought along slowly through encouragement. As mentioned previously, this finding is probably related to the fact that two-thirds of the concern students were boys in this second-grade sample.

The rejection students showed more significant correlations with teachers' ratings of personal attributes and behavior than any of the other groups. Unsurprisingly, the teachers' views of these students were quite consistently negative. They were seen as restless, likely to cheat, uncomfortable in the classroom, sassy and defiant, lazy, likely to interrupt with funny or irrelevant comments, likely to daydream, unimaginative, likely to butt in and interrupt interaction, likely to fight, defensive, unhappy, messy, immature, impulsive, and likely to avert their eyes rather than look the teacher in the eye.

As was the case with boys as compared to girls, every significant correlation involving the rejection students pictured them negatively. This set of data again exemplifies the halo effect spoken of previously. Apparently, when teachers develop strong feelings of rejection toward certain students, they tend to see them as bad on almost any measure that you use, so that a completely negative picture such as that seen in Table 5.2 emerges. While it is possible that the rejection students as a group differed systematically from their classmates in all of the ways that the teachers said that they did, this seems unlikely.

For example, the general picture that emerges is one of hyperactivity, aggression, defiance, and general acting out behavior. If rejection students have all these traits, it seems unlikely, at least on a common sense basis, that they also would tend to be daydreamers or to be less imaginative than their classmates. Yet the teachers attributed these two qualities to the rejection students, also. In any case, the data clearly show that the teachers see these rejection sudents as completely undesirable without any redeeming positive qualities.

The data in Table 5.2 help answer the question about why concern and rejection students, who are similar in some ways, provoke such different reactions from teachers. This is especially true because the proportions of boys and girls in the two groups are about the same, so that the findings regarding the personal attributes and behavior of the two groups are not contaminated by a sex difference.

In general, the data bear out Silberman's (1971) impression that concern students make considerable but "legitimate" demands on the teachers, while rejection students make "illegitimate" or overwhelming demands. The concern students are seen as immature and in need of help but not as hyperactive or hostile. These latter attributes uniquely characterize the students in the rejection group and are probably the major reason for the teachers' negativistic feelings toward them. Rejection students are described as sassy and defiant, as lazy, as likely to butt into a conversation or interrupt with a funny or irrelevant statement, and as more likely to become involved in fights. Thus they present major management problems to the teacher because of their hyperactivity and aggressiveness. Worse yet, from the teachers' viewpoint, they threaten the teachers' authority more directly through sassiness and defiance. Thus the rejection relationship goes both ways. Not only do the teachers reject these students; in the eyes of the teachers at least, the students reciprocate by rejecting the teachers also.

Since these data were taken in the spring after the patterns of teacher-student relationships were well-developed, it is not possible to state how the relationships developed, or to discover who started them. In any case, by spring there was no love lost between the teachers and the rejection students. Although we do not have data to show it, it is likely that the rejection students had negative attitudes toward their teachers.

Yet, as noted earlier in describing the interaction data from the second-grade study, the teachers showed a mixed pattern rather than clear-cut rejection in their classroom interactions with these students. There are at least two probable reasons for this. The first is halo effect. Studies comparing attitudes and behavior in a variety of contexts have shown that questionnaire responses or other data concerning attitudes toward two contrasting groups are almost always more internally consistent and more extreme in differentiating the groups than are measures of behavior toward the same groups. That is, our perceptions tend to exaggerate the commonness within groups and exaggerate the difference between groups compared to what exists in reality. Thus, it is not surprising that the teacher-attitude data in Table 5.2 are more consistent and extreme in many ways than the teacher behavior toward the students involved.

The responses of teachers about rejection students reported by Silberman (1971) provide another possible explanation for the mixed rather than generally negative pattern of behavior shown by the teachers in their interactions with rejection students. It is possible that, to the degree that they were aware of their own negative feelings toward these students, the teachers tried to compensate for them by going out of their way to treat these students fairly or by seeking out and taking advantage of opportunities to have positive interactions with them.

Other Studies

Four additional studies which had no connection with those reviewed above should be mentioned at this point, since they are related to the teacher attitudes of attachment, indifference, concern, or rejection, even though they were not designed to study these teacher attitudes as such.

Garner and Bing (1973b) studied teacher-student interaction in five first-grade classes in England after the teachers had filled out eleven ranking scales on student personality traits. They found that the highest frequencies of teacher-student contact were with two types of students. One type was described as bright and initiatory high achievers, corresponding roughly to the attachment group. The others, who were mostly boys, were described as naughty, sociable, imaginative, and as average achievers. This group got most of the disciplinary contacts, and in many ways sounds like the rejection group, except that they were average rather than low achievers. Another group was identified which looks even more like the rejection group. These students, again mostly boys, were described as indifferent and frequently disobedient students with high rates of discipline contacts.

Garner and Bing also identified two clusters of students who fit into the indifference category. One group was described as generally dull and lifeless, characterized primarily by low rates of interaction with the teacher. Another group was identified as bright and well-behaved children who had low contact frequencies with the teacher because they appeared to be independent learners who did not want or need such contact (in general, Garner and Bing found that teacher-student contact frequencies were determined almost entirely by the students; there was little evidence of teacher attempts to compensate for student individual differences).

Power (1971) studied the interaction of four male science teachers with 150 eighth graders. He found that generally bright and successful students were more frequently chosen to respond by the teacher and received more positive reinforcements than their classmates. Power also noted what he called a "social alienation syndrome" among students who had low general ability, were individualistic, and were sensitive to threat. These students tended to be seated at the rear of classrooms and were rarely called upon. When interactions did occur, they were usually initiated by the students. Data from these students suggested that they disliked school and were generally alienated from it, that they neither valued nor achieved success, and that they generally rejected others and consequently were rejected themselves. These seem similar to the traits seen in the rejection students described earlier. Interestingly, as was found by Silberman and by ourselves in our second study, Power noted that these rejection students frequently received teacher praise when they did have an interaction with the teacher. This fits in with Silberman's interpretation that the teachers may be compensating for guilt feelings involved in rejecting such students.

Power also identified what he called a "rejection-dependency syndrome" which looks similar to the concern group described above. These students were dependent and sensitive, had low abilities, and generally answered questions incorrectly, but they nevertheless had positive attitudes toward science (suggesting indirectly that the teachers were rewarding them somehow). Power noted that these students were rarely encouraged to initiate interactions or to attempt to tackle tasks at the threshold of their ability, suggesting that the teachers were "treating them with kid gloves."

Power's "success syndrome" students were quite similar to the high achievement and/or high expectancy group students discussed in the previous chapter. They scored well on measures of knowledge and ability, had high success expectations, participated successfully and actively in class, had positive attitudes toward the class, and enjoyed high status among their peers. Not only were they more likely to interact with the teachers more frequently; they were also the only group to avoid simple factual questions and take "calculated cognitive risks" by tackling the more difficult and higher-level questions that teachers asked and by initiating frequent interactions with the teachers.

Lundgren (1972) conducted a study which, among other things, involved requesting nine secondary mathematics teachers to name and describe their students at the end of the school year. He found that, with a single exception, the teachers regularly were unable to remember six or seven of their students, even though they had taught them for an entire school year. These "forgettable" students very probably had qualities similar to those nominated to the indifference groups in the study described previously.

An experimental study by Yarrow, Waxler, and Scott (1971) yielded findings relevant to several of the points raised in this chapter. This experiment involved two female adult caretakers and sixty boys and fifty-eight girls in preschool. To assess the effects of children's pressure on adult behavior, the two adults were trained to create either high or low nurturant conditions at various times of the day. They were to respond with warmth and reinforcement in the high nurturant condition but respond minimally or negatively during nonnurturant conditions. The underlying assumption of the experiment was that if children did not affect adult behavior, the adults would be equally nurturant toward all children under nurturant conditions and equally nonnurturant toward all children under the nonnurturant conditions. This assumption was not borne out by the data, however.

It was found that the teachers were heavily reactive to the children and unable to compensate for student differences in initiating contacts with them. Thus they were far from equally nurturant to all children in the nurturance condition or equally nonnurturant to all children in the nonnurturance condition. Instead, their reactions to individual children were heavily conditioned by the behavior of the children.

For example, boys drew out much more nonnurturant behavior than girls under both conditions, and they were generally more salient and had stronger modifying effects on the adults than the girls. During the nurturant condition, boys who sought help from the adults or who clowned more often received negative responses than positive ones, even though negative responses were not supposed to occur during this condition. Furthermore, boys who frequently clowned were more often singled out for criticism than other children, whether or not they were clowning at the time.

Comparative data on teacher behavior in the two conditions brought out some findings that appear relevant to the contrast in teacher treatment of concern and rejection students. In the high nurturant condition student bids for approval drew positive teacher attention 71 percent of the time, their bids for help 79 percent of the time, and their clowning 45 percent of the time. The more bids a child made, the more nurturant contacts he received during the high nurturant condition. In the low nurturant condition, however, bids for help drew an explicit negative response 70 percent of the time, while bids for approval drew a negative response only 47 percent of the time and clowning only 31 percent of the time (the remaining bids elicited nonresponse rather than an explicit negative response). Among other things, these findings suggest that when a teacher is nonnurturant toward a student, bids for help and other bids involving dependency pressure upon the teacher are especially likely to elicit a negative response, compared to other conditions or to other kinds of bids within the same condition. This is reminiscent of Silberman's note that concern students were perceived as making frequent but *legitimate* demands upon teachers, while rejection students were perceived as making frequent and *illegitimate* demands upon teachers. It may be that when a teacher's major attitude toward a student is one of concern he responds nurturantly and provides help when the student comes to seek it, but when his attitude is one of rejection he perceives this request negatively and responds with rejection.

In general, children who were persistent attention seekers, especially boys, bore the brunt of the adults' initiated negative contacts. On the other hand, children who frequently sought help (as opposed to approval or attention) tended to receive more positive teacher initiation.

There were no important differences between the two adult experimenters in the ways that they responded to different kinds of children, and neither showed a tendency or ability to compensate for student individual differences. In fact, some observational data in this study showed clearly that the adults were being conditioned by the students rather than vice versa. This was true not only for individual differences across students, but even for differences in behavior by the same student at different times.

The latter was shown in some ingenious data developed by observing the responses of a selected subsample of children to adult-initiated contacts during the high-nurturance condition. When adults initiated contacts with these children, the responses of the children were coded either as nonresponsive or as positively reinforcing (showing interest, attention, enjoyment, or compliance). The adults were then observed to see how soon they returned to the children to initiate another contact with them. For both adults the data were strikingly clear in showing that the adults were much quicker to return to initiate another contact with a student who had been positively reinforcing the last time than they were to return to a student who had been nonresponsive the last time. Thus the teachers were clearly reacting to the children's behavior and were generally conditioned by it, even though the children were preschoolers.

Although the authors do not mention the point themselves, data provided in their article suggest an interaction effect: it appears that the adults were especially likely to return sooner to students who gave them positive reinforcement when the student was one who was generally less likely to give positive reinforcement. That is, there appeared to be a "strike while the iron is hot" effect operating in the teachers. These data bring to mind Silberman's discussions with teachers, in which they noted that they were especially alert to find times and places in which they could praise the boys in the rejection group.

These data are probably a special case of the more general finding of a "recency effect" as a modulator of expectations and impressions. Although the first impression or primacy effect is generally the most important and potent predictor of impressions, there is also a recency effect in which the most recent behavior observed or experienced tends to influence the way we perceive and respond to situations. It seems likely that students who break a previously established pattern and begin to behave in unusual ways that come to the attention of the teacher are likely to change the teacher's established patterns of behavior toward them.

SUMMARY

In addition to expectations, which are primarily cognitive, contact with students causes teachers to form primarily affective attitudinal responses toward them. In the same general manner outlined in the model for expectation effects in Chapter 2, teacher attitudes toward students, once formed, can begin to act as self-fulfilling prophecies if the teacher begins rigidly and inflexibly to treat the student as more extreme or stereotyped than he actually is.

In the present chapter we summarize four studies dealing with teacher attitudes of attachment, indifference, concern, and rejection toward students, describing the contrasting patterns of interactions that teachers have with students toward whom they hold these contrasting attitudes. Other studies in which one or more of these attitude groups appeared were also reviewed.

In general, attachment students are high achieving, conforming students who reward the teachers by showing desirable classroom behavior. Despite these qualities, however, and despite the fact that the teachers name these students as individuals that they particularly like, five different studies agree in finding little evidence of overt teacher favoritism toward these students in process measures of teacher-student interaction. Some studies suggest that the teachers may have been favoring these students in subtle ways, but none show clear evidence of gross and significant favoritism.

Indifference students are characterized largely by their passivity and low salience in the classroom. The teachers seldom call on them or deal with them individually, and these students tend to reciprocate by avoiding the teachers. One study suggests that these students tend to be perceived as unhappy, shy, or nervous, and yet they do not provoke teacher concern. Apparently they possess some qualities that teachers dislike, or they lack qualities that would generate greater teacher interest in and concern about them. In any case, for whatever reason, teachers appear to be truly indifferent toward such students even when they perceive that the students are unhappy or in need of help.

Studies agree in seeing concern students as low achievers who require considerable teacher help and make considerable but legitimate demands upon the teachers, with the result that teachers have high rates of interaction with concern students. Although some conflicting findings emerge in the precise ways in which this teacher concern is manifested in interaction with concern students, all studies agree in showing the teachers to be concerned about the academic achievement of these students and to spend much time and effort with them in attempting to improve it.

Although the rejection students appear to be similar to the concern students in many ways, the teachers respond to them with rejection rather than concern. Sometimes the rejection is clear-cut and unambiguous, and sometimes criticism and other indicators of rejection are mixed in with high rates of praise and other indicators of attempts to balance or compensate for the feeling of rejection felt toward these students. In any case, the studies agree that teachers tend to develop strong affective responses toward rejection students and to be primarily concerned with controlling their classroom behavior, whereas they are more concerned with the academic achievement of students in the concern group.

Teacher ranking data collected in one study suggest that although the concern and rejection students are similar in many ways, the concern students are seen more as immature and in need of help while the rejection students are seen more as hyperactive or hostile. These data were taken toward the end of the school year, however, so that it is not clear whether they represent accurate teacher perceptions of the two groups or rationalizations used to support and justify the teachers' attitudes. In other words it is not yet clear whether these two groups are actually different in their classroom behavior and treatment of the teacher or whether they are essentially similar but are labeled differently once the teacher formulates a rigid attitude toward them.

The points raised in the preceding paragraphs are specific examples of the more general questions to be dealt with in the following chapter: what are the characteristics of students who provoke contrasting attitudes in teachers, and what variables do teachers use in forming impressions about students? These questions have been studied in a number of questionnaire and interview studies, which will be reviewed in the following chapter.

chapter 6

Teacher Interview
and Questionnaire Studies

In the preceding chapters we have dealt largely with research on teacher behavior toward students who are objects of contrasting teacher expectations or attitudes. As we have shown, expectations and attitudes, once formed, can cause the teacher to behave in ways which will produce self-fulfilling prophecy effects. Although we have presented a large body of data on the ways that teachers interact with students toward whom they hold particular expectations or attitudes, we have not said much as yet about how teachers form and change those expectations and attitudes. What student attributes cause a teacher to adopt a given expectation or attitude toward him? How stable are teacher expectations and attitudes once they have been formed? Teacher interview and questionnaire studies which have addressed these questions are reviewed in the present chapter.

ATTITUDINAL REACTIONS TO
TYPES OF STUDENTS

In Chapter 1 we noted that Feshbach (1969) had undergraduate female education majors read paragraphs describing sixteen fictional students and then rate these fictional students on a series of rating scales. The teachers most preferred students described as rigid, conforming, and orderly; then students described as attentive, passive, and acquiescent; then students described as flexible, nonconforming, and untidy; and lastly students described as independent, active, and assertive. Among other things these data have been used to support the notion that female teachers are biased toward girls and against boys, preferring traits associated with the female sex role and rejecting traits associated with the male sex role. This study has spawned a number of replications and elaborations which have led to refinements of its results, showing that they apply to only certain kinds of individuals.

First, a study by Good and Grouws (1972) showed that the results generalized to male student teachers. Using Feshbach's sixteen paragraph descriptions of fictional students, Good and Grouws asked twenty-two male and fifty-five female student teachers to rate the fictional students. The findings replicated those of Feshbach. Again, the student teachers preferred passive and compliant students to more independent and more demanding ones. However, as we will see later in the chapter, teachers do respond favorably to students who are independent workers and generally mature students if they are attentive and willing to comply to teacher requests. Teachers do not like independent students who are aggressively assertive. Furthermore, there was no sex difference. The male student teachers showed the same pattern of preferences as the female student teachers. There was a small and nonsignificant trend for the males to respond slightly more favorably to nonconforming male students, but overall their reactions to these fictional students were strikingly similar to those of the female student teachers. This is but one finding in a larger pattern that will be reviewed in the following chapter showing that male teachers tend to have the same preferences and the same classroom interaction patterns toward boys and girls as do female teachers. Thus the findings regarding teacher preference of students cannot be attributed to discrimination based on sex by female teachers; instead, they represent an interaction between the role of the teacher, the role of the pupil, and the male and female sex roles as they are defined in our society. Regardless of sex, teachers tend to prefer compliant and cooperative children and to reject independent and assertive children. This was also seen in the study by Kelly (1958), who found that students characterized as conforming, compulsive, rigid, and insecure were given higher grades than their measured achievement warranted.

So far, the data from this line of research suggest that American adults generally are likely to prefer compliant and cooperative children over independent and assertive ones. However, a follow-up study by Beigel and Feshbach (1970) illustrated that this tendency may be peculiar to student teachers (and, by implication, inservice teachers). This study replicated Feshbach's original work except that three different groups of respondents were included: a group of student teachers comparable to the subjects in the original study, a group of undergraduate psychology majors (comparable to the student teachers in being college students but differing in their choice of major), and a group of Teacher Corps interns who had had special training stressing tolerance for divergent attitudes and cultural mores. In this study the original findings replicated only for the student teachers.

The psychology majors and the Teacher Corps interns did *not* show the same marked tendency to prefer passive, conforming students. Thus, to date at least, this preference pattern appears to be unique to student teachers in traditional teacher training programs. Apparently there is something about the students who go into these programs and/or the content of the programs themselves which causes student teachers to adopt their particular pattern of preferences. The fact that the same pattern did not appear in psychology majors who were of similar age and social status suggests that the finding is not a general one, and the fact that it did not appear in Teacher Corps interns shows that it is not general to all teachers, either. It is probably true that the Teacher Corps lays greater stress upon tolerance for differing attitudes and practices than more traditional university based teacher training programs, but the latter programs, particularly in their educational psychology courses, also stress this point. Thus the difference in findings does not seem likely due to a difference in the philosophies espoused by the trainers, although it may well be that the Teacher Corps's training in this particular area is more effective than the typical university based program. However, there is good reason to believe that individuals who elect to go into the Teacher Corps differ in many ways from typical preservice teachers in university based programs, so the difference could be partly or totally due to a difference in the salient characteristics of these two kinds of teachers. One way to test this out would be to expose university based preservice teachers to the same sequence of training that Teacher Corps interns get and then test them with the Feshbach technique to see if the Teacher Corps's training succeeded in eliminating the typical pattern of preference for compliant and cooperative children over other types of children.

Helton (1972) conducted a study which combined Feshbach's methodology with measurement of the attitudes of attachment, rejection, indifference, and concern, described in the previous chapter. Fifty-three third- and fourth-grade inservice teachers responded to Feshbach's sixteen descriptive paragraphs (adapted so that half were presented as males and half as females), and then rated each "student" on six-point scales for each of the four attitudes. Helton's results confirmed the ones reported above for preservice teachers and showed that they also were true for inservice teachers. Passive, dependent, rigid, conforming, and orderly students of both sexes received high attachment ratings and low rejection ratings. Flexible, nonconforming, and untidy students were rated lower, especially if they were boys, and active, independent, and assertive students were also rated lower, especially if they were girls.

In general, student personality variables were the most important characteristics determining the attachment, rejection, and indifference ratings, but student *academic* aptitudes and achievement were more important in determining the concern ratings. These data fit with the behavorial data presented in Chapter 5. In the same vein, high achievers were most frequently mentioned in the attachment group, and the teachers were generally more concerned with the academic problems of girls but more concerned with the personal and social problems of boys. The teachers stated high concern for and willingness to do remedial work with certain students that they were unenthusiastic about (low ability students and flexible, nonconforming and untidy students) but not for certain other students (the active, independent, assertive students). These findings agree with the data of Chapter 5 suggesting that concern students are perceived as low achievers who make legitimate demands and need help, while rejection students are perceived as students who make illegitimate demands. Thus in its broad general findings, at least, Helton's study confirms both previous findings regarding teacher preferences for Feshbach's student types and profile descriptions of the students whom teachers select for nomination into the four attitude groups (certain other findings from Helton's study are not so consistent with Feshbach's results or with the behavioral data described in Chapter 5, but most of these involve second- and third-order inter-actions among teacher attitude, student sex, student ability, and student behavior, which were less important than the more general findings reported above).

Levitin and Chananie (1972) used somewhat different methods but reached similar conclusions to those in the above studies, which used Feshbach's method. In this study, forty female elementary school teachers were asked to react to descriptions of fictional students. Half of the students were male and half were female. Within each sex of fictional students, half were portrayed as aggressive and half as dependent. In general, dependent students were preferred to aggressive ones. Sex of student was also a factor, however. Aggressiveness was less rejected in boys than in girls, and it was judged to be typical of boys. Meanwhile, dependency was judged to be typical of girls. Thus, although in general the teachers preferred dependent to aggressive children, within sex there was a tendency to be relatively more favorable or less rejecting towards students who were portrayed as typically sex-typed rather than students who were portrayed as behaving atypically or inappropriately for their sex.

In summary, the data from several questionnaire studies confirm the suggestions in the previously reviewed behavioral studies that teachers tend to prefer compliant and cooperative children and to reject assertive and active children. Because of the nature of the sex roles defined by our society, this also means that teachers tend to prefer girls over boys, although the study by Good and Grouws and the studies to be reviewed in Chapter 7 show that this is a function of the teacher role rather than the teachers' sex as such. Male teachers show the same pattern of preferences as female teachers. Also, the questionnaire studies confirm the suggestion we made in Chapter 5 that one important difference between concern and rejection students may be the assertion or acivity variable. Low achievers who are dependent and compliant tend to be objects of teacher concern, but teachers tend to reject children who are overly active and assertive, especially if they are low achievers. The data from student teachers and inservice teachers generally correspond quite closely, as would be expected, but studies from other samples show that many of the attitudes and preference patterns seen in student teachers and teachers are unique to these in-dividuals and not common to American adults generally. It remains to be shown why this is so. It may be a function of the direct instruction given to preservice teachers or the indirect socialization into the teacher role that occurs in the process of becoming a teacher, or it may reflect a general difference between individuals who choose teaching as a career and individuals who choose careers in other professions. Most probably it is some combination of these two general sets of influences. In any case, it is a question worthy of research interest.

STABILITY OF TEACHER ATTITUDES

The question of the stability of the teacher attitudes of attachment, concern, indifference, and rejection was raised in Chapter 5, although only in the context of determining whether placement of students into the four attitude groups would remain stable for two separate school years and in two separate teachers. Good (1972) has investigated the stability of these attitudes in the same teachers with regard to the same groups of students. Early in the school year and then again seven months later in the spring, twelve junior high school teachers were asked to rank the students in the last class that they taught each day on expected achievement, concern, and indifference, and they were also asked to indicate whether or not they wanted the student to remain in their classroom (attachment plus rejection). Stability coefficients were highest for what they expected achievement to be (significant for all twelve teachers) and for whether or not they would prefer to keep the student in their classroom (significant for ten of the twelve). Stability was more variable for concern (six of twelve significant) and for indifference (eight of twelve significant). The stability coefficients for the total group of boys and girls respectively were .71 and .56 for achievement, .30 and .27 for concern, .67 and .45 for keeping the student in class, and .48 and .44 for indifference.

Analysis of movement patterns showed that girls tended to move up and boys down on the measure of desire to keep the student in class, and, to a lesser extent, in the achievement rankings. At the end of the year the teachers also ranked the students on how active the student was in contributing to the verbal interaction in the classroom, on how much effort the student expended in doing his schoolwork, and how attractive the student was.

High achievement rankings were correlated with how well-known the student was, with how much the teachers wanted the student to remain in their class, with how high the student ranked on verbal contributions to class and effort, and, to a lesser extent, with how physically attractive the student was. All of these fit in with previously reported findings. Students listed as best known to the teachers tended to be high achievers and/or to be listed as concern students, to be toward the positive end on the stay-in-class measure, to be verbal contributors to the class, and to be ranked as making good effort in their work. These best known students also showed very low but positive correlations with the physical attractiveness ratings.

The concern students showed the least powerful and interpretable set of correlations with the other measures, with all correlation coefficients being between −.17 and .27 Coefficients with the other measures were mostly negative at the beginning of the year but positive at the end of the year, at first suggesting that the concern students became more positive in the eyes of the teachers as the year progressed. However, stability for concern students was low, and a finer analysis showed that the students who were primary objects of teacher concern at the beginning of the year were seldom the same students who were primary objects of teacher concern at the end of the year. Thus, teacher concern showed low stability. It is unknown why this was so, although it may be that as teachers become concerned about students they do things that eliminate some of the problems the students are having, so that the students improve and therefore become less worrisome to the teachers. Other interpretations are possible, however.

Students rated as those whom the teacher would like to retain in class (attachment as opposed to rejection) were high achieving, were well-known to the teachers, were verbally active in contributing to discussions, and were hard working. These children also showed low positive correlations with physical attractiveness ratings. Thus these data show a general positive halo effect, as would be expected for students whom the teachers particularly liked.

Good's data on the characteristics of students in the four attitude groups supplement and reinforce the data reported previously, as do his data showing that teacher concern is relatively unstable compared to the other three attitudes. They do not add much to the profiles of the students in these four groups, however. Additional data describing the stability of teacher attitudes has been provided in a study of elementary and secondary student teachers (Good and Limbacher, 1973). Significant stability correlations on the four attitudes were found in both groups of student teachers, except that secondary student teachers' ratings of concern were not stable across time. Thus ratings from both secondary teachers and student teachers show that concern classifications are much less stable than the concern classifications of elementary teachers. It is not clear if the results are due to systematic differences in teachers at these two levels, systematic learning differences, the less time that secondary teachers spend with students, or a combination of factors. However, it is clear that concern classifications are not stable in secondary settings. The concern group remains particularly ill-defined, with low achievement being the only consistent correlate. It seems established at this point that concern students are low achievers whom the teacher has not rejected, but little is known about what positive qualities they may have which cause teachers to develop positive concern about them.

The preceding studies have all been related to Feshbach's four student types and/or to Silberman's four teacher-attitude types. There are several additional questionnaire studies which asked teachers to react to the behavior that they perceived in their students. These are reviewed in the following section.

TEACHER REACTIONS TO STUDENT BEHAVIOR

The previous studies all dealt with teacher reactions to descriptions of students given to them by the experimenter (except the Good, 1972 and Good and Limbacher, 1973 studies which allowed teachers to describe their naturalistically formed expectations of students but using forms supplied by the investigators to do so). Studies reviewed in the present section were naturalistic ones in which the teachers involved were reacting to their everyday students on the basis of the impressions they had formed during classroom interaction with them. Although teachers form an infinite variety of specific impressions about individual students, certain student characteristics are noticed rather generally because they are important to the role of teacher and student and are likely to become involved in the interaction between the teacher and the student.

Research in Britain (Morrison and McIntyre, 1969) has shown that teacher reactions tend to fall into three major clusters: pupil attainment, both in general and in different subject areas; general classroom behavior and attitudes toward teachers (courtesy, cooperation, trustworthiness, persistence, attentiveness); and cheerfulness, leadership, popularity, social confidence, and cooperation with peers. Thus the student's general achievement, his cooperation and general interaction with the teacher, and his cooperation and general interaction with peers are three major variables of interest to teachers. Generally, teachers make a more uniform generalized assessment of a girl than of a boy (teacher attitudes in these three domains are more likely to be highly intercorrelated when girls are involved). This is another individual instance of the more general rule that boys are more variable than girls on almost any variable measured (Maccoby, 1966). Teacher perceptions here are probably accurate. Sex-role pressures are likely to product high intercorrelations among school achievement, cooperation with the teacher, and peer popularity in girls, but not necessarily among boys.

Also, younger teachers tend to be more concerned about classroom behavior, while older teachers are more concerned about achievement. These two clusters are generally more important to teachers than the student's peer popularity. Morrison and McIntyre (1969) asked a sample of British elementary school teachers to rank order the student attributes that were of most concern to them. The nine attributes. of highest concern were, respectively, general ability, carelessness, laziness, talkativeness, cooperativeness, persistence, courtesy, ability to use language, and originality. These all relate either to the general achievement cluster or to the cooperation with teachers cluster. Traits such as social confidence, sociability, and popularity, which are related to the peer adjustment cluster, were rated lower on the list. Thus variables of most concern to the teachers in the process of enacting the teaching role were rated highest. Several studies have questioned teachers regarding the relationships they perceive among various student behaviors. One was reported in the previous chapter, concerning the attributes of students whom teachers assigned to the attachment, indifference, concern, or rejection groups. Several others are discussed below.

Barnard, Zimbardo, and Sarason (1968) asked second- and third-grade teachers to rate twenty-four student attributes according to how they were related to student anxiety and student intelligence. Fourteen of the traits were significantly related to teacher perception of intelligence, while none were significantly related to measured anxiety. This shows, among other things, that teachers do not know how to assess student anxiety accurately. They can assess intelligence, however, and even those who cannot do so very accurately usually have access to IQ scores in the student's cumulative file. These teachers said that high-IQ children learned quickly, paid attention, retained material, overachieved, and were ambitious. Thus they associated greater effort, and not merely greater ability, with high IQ. Although there is some correlation, this probably represents considerable halo effect, since it seems unlikely that student intelligence and student effort would be very highly correlated even at the early grades. Evidence of halo effects is underscored by the other significant differences in the ratings of traits associated with IQ. The teachers stated that the brightest children daydreamed less, were less dependent, more aggressive, more sensitive, more mature, more sociable, more popular, and more active. All of these traits are known to be generally unrelated to intelligence, yet the teachers rated the brightest children more positively on each of them. Thus a child of high intelligence, assuming that he is reasonably cooperative toward the teacher and does not present a serious behavior problem, is likely to be perceived as generally better adjusted and more preferable than his classmates.

Sears (1963), as part of a larger investigation, studied the student characteristics that were associated with teacher liking for students. She found that school achievement was a significant correlate for girls of both average and superior aptitude and for boys of average aptitude but not for boys of superior aptitude. Results from other studies suggest that this finding is probably due to the presence among the group of high aptitude boys of a subset who were assertive and nonconforming, thus threatening the teacher's authority. Getzels and Jackson (1962) also found, in their study of high aptitude students, that the more conforming and compliant students were more preferred by their teachers than the less conforming, more creative students.

The degree to which students independently engage in doing their work approached significance in all groups except the girls of superior aptitude, where the relationship was almost significantly negative. Here again, sex role enters the picture. Teachers apparently like independence in boys (provided that it is not combined with behavioral nonconformity), but do not like it in girls where it is less consonant with the sex-role stereotype. The most preferred girls were the most passive and compliant ones. Other data showed that the generally brighter and generally more cooperative children were preferred over the less bright and less cooperative children. Several other aspects of the data also suggested that the teachers preferred children who were bright but anxious or dependent. For example, self-concept was positively associated with teacher liking for average boys but negatively associated for high aptitude boys. Similarly, a need for structure was positively correlated for the average aptitude boys. In general, Sears's findings can be summarized by stating that teachers preferred children who were achieving well, who posed no control or discipline problems, and who gave evidence of "needing" them. In short, the teachers preferred the children who were more reinforcing to them.

Barclay, Stilwell, Santoro, and Clark (1972) studied the relationship between teacher ratings, peer ratings, and observed classroom behavior of 700 high achieving elementary school students. These data show that both teacher and student perceptions are generally accurate when they deal with observable behaviors. Girls judged to be shy and reticent did not raise their hands seeking to respond to questions very often, while girls who answered many questions were seen as striving for leadership and as being somewhat disruptive. Girls who were not paying attention, whispering, squirming around, and fidgeting were seen by their peers as possessing artistic, intellectual, and leadership skills, but they received lower ratings by the teachers. Here again, teacher ratings are seen to be highly affected by whether the students reward or interfere with teachers' ability to function successfully in the teacher role.

Boys who were frequently called on to answer questions viewed themselves as above average on enterprising and leadership skills. Boys viewed by both teachers and peers as disruptive often talked out loud, turned their backs on the teachers, and showed generally disruptive behavior. Both boys and girls who were classified as extroverted raised their hands more often, talked out loud more often, and stood up at their desks more frequently then their classmates. Boys and girls judged to be introverted tended to pay more attention to the teacher, to volunteer less frequently, and to squirm, fidget, and make noise less often. Thus introversion-extroversion is one of the easier student attributes to judge, and it is also one of the more important ones in determining the quantity and quality of a student's interactions with his teacher (see Chapter 8). All in all, the perceptions of peers were quite accurate and perceptions of teachers were mostly accurate, although when students presented behavior problems this sometimes prevented teachers from fully appreciating (and perhaps even from seeing) their positive qualities.

Lippitt and Gold (1959) studied the relationship of student power in the peer group to teacher-student interaction. Students rated their classmates on the degree to which they were able to get peers to do what they wanted them to do. These ratings were highly correlated with ratings of social popularity. The children were generally pretty accurate in their perceptions of how they were rated by others.

Interaction analysis revealed that the teachers paid more attention to the social behavior than to the academic performance of low status pupils, but they reacted differently to these low status pupils according to sex. Low status boys tended to receive primarily criticism, while low status girls tended to receive support. These findings are reminiscent of the differences between the concern and rejection groups reported in Chapter 5. Further observation showed that the low status girls were generally passive and withdrawn in their peer relationships but warm in their relationships with the teachers. In contrast, the low status boys were generally more aggressive and troublesome in the classroom. Thus the teachers were responding with affection to little girls who seemed to be asking for it and not getting it from their peers, while responding with rejection to boys who presented behavior problems. All of these data are quite consistent with those presented previously.

Several studies have provided evidence that when students depart from teacher expectations, either by violating preestablished expectations or by changing their preestablished behavior patterns, the effect on the teacher's perception is likely to be negative. This is true even when the change in the student behavior is positive!

This was first noted by Rosenthal and Jacobson (1968). Independent judges rated the students in the *Pygmalion* study on a scale of the degree to which the student looked "Mexican." Correlation of these ratings with students' expectancy advantage in the experimental and control groups showed that the children who looked most "Mexican" were among those who made the greatest gains if they were assigned to the experimental groups. However, despite these gains in achievement, these children were not rated higher on teacher ratings of curiosity, and, in fact, had a tendency to be rated somewhat lower, despite their achievement gains. As Rosenthal and Jacobson put it: "It seemed almost as though, for these minority-group children, intellectual competence may have been easier for teachers to bring about than to believe."

Other data in Rosenthal and Jacobson's study showed similar results. Children's gains in IQ were correlated with teachers' perceptions of their classroom behavior, separately for upper- and lower-track children and for experimental and control children. Among the upper-track children in the experimental group, greater gains in IQ were accompanied by more favorable teacher ratings. In contrast, greater IQ gains in the lower-track control-group children, where no special gains were expected by the teachers, were accompanied by *unfavorable* teacher ratings. This unexpected achievement gain by children who were expected to show poor gains produced a negative rather than a positive response in the teachers. The reasons for this are unclear, but it is certainly not an isolated finding. Recall the Brophy and Good (1970a) findings that high achieving students got more praise and less criticism than low achieving students, even when success rates were taken into account. Here again, common sense would predict that the teachers would be happy about unexpected successes, but the data suggest otherwise.

Jeter and Davis (1973) replicated many of the results from our initial study. In particular they found that lows received more criticism than highs following wrong answers and that lows had more answers not followed by teacher feedback than did highs. Thus, it seems that some teachers cannot react immediately and appropriately to lows' academic responses in public situations. We would suspect that these teachers would be able to react adequately to lows' private responses (seatwork conferences, homework, test papers), but research is needed on this point. If private use of praise and criticism matches public behavior, then lows are highly likely to become passive and resistant in school settings.

The *Pygmalion* findings were replicated in a dissertation by Shore (1969). In this study Shore measured teachers' expectations for student achievement and asked them to make a number of student behavior ratings similar to those used by Rosenthal and Jacobson. A month later the teachers were given their students' actual IQ and achievement data and were asked to rate the students again. Shore found that when the teachers had held negative expectations for students who were actually performing well, the teachers did acknowledge their level of achievement, but they rated the children lower in personality and adjustment. Here again, children who performed "too well" were down graded in the teachers' ratings.

Related findings were reported by Leacock (1969) in a large scale study of low and middle income black and white students in the second and fifth grade. In general, teacher ratings of like and dislike for the students paralleled social stereotypes. As previously reported, the black children were rated lower than the white and the lower SES children were rated lower than the middle SES children. However, a finer analysis showed that the children with *more* ability in the low income and black groups were most likely to be objects of teacher rejection. For example, at the fifth-grade level the favored children in the middle class school had an average IQ of eleven points higher than the rejected pupils. Meanwhile, at a low income black school, the favored fifth graders had an IQ ten points *lower* than the rejected children. Furthermore, even though the rejected children had an IQ almost ten points higher than their positively or neutrally viewed classmates, their reading achievement was slightly lower. Although other interpretations are possible, this may well have been a result of self-fulfilling prophecy effects. Teacher resentment of the high ability students among the low income blacks may have led to inappropriate treatment which resulted in these students' failure to achieve at a level that their IQ scores would predict.

An alternative hypothesis would be that these bright students were more capable of perceiving and reacting to inappropriate teacher behavior, and that they responded to teacher rejection with hostility of their own. Other interpretations similarly built upon assumptions about what may have taken place as the school year went on could be constructed. However, the study by Rubovits and Maehr (1973) suggested that the teacher reaction was based squarely on race-connected expectations rather than on student behavior. Recall that in this study teachers worked with groups of four students whom they had never met before and only spent a short time with the students, it was unlikely that there was enough time to allow much of an opportunity for the teachers to develop particular perceptions about the individual students. Thus the teacher ratings in the study were likely conditioned largely by their preexisting expectations concerning blacks and whites. In this study the white students labeled as "gifted" were praised much more frequently than the black students labeled as "gifted." The gifted black children also received more criticism than any other children. Also, while white gifted children received more teacher attention than white controls, black gifted children did not.

Taken together, the data from these studies suggest strongly that children who violate teacher expectations for performance are likely to suffer teacher rejection, even when the violation is in the form of good performance when poor performance was expected, and even when the student performance is accurately perceived by the teacher! Research clearly is needed on this phenomenon, so that its causes can be understood and so that it can be eliminated eventually through proper teacher training. Some hypotheses for it were advanced in Chapter 4, but so far they have not been systematically studied, nor have any other explanations for the phenomenon been researched. An explanation based upon cognitive consistency and ego defense mechanism notions would be relatively easy to construct if the phenomenon proves to be universal, but data are still too sparse to give an indication of whether or not they are in fact universal.

ACCURACY OF TEACHER IMPRESSIONS

Studies of the accuracy of teachers' impressions concerning student achievement potential or personality characteristics have yielded varying results depending upon the child variables being rated and the experiences to which the teachers were exposed. Hawkes (1971) gave sociometric questionnaires to fifth and sixth graders in four classrooms and collected IQ scores, achievement test data, and teacher perceptions of the social and academic adjustment of the children and of their willingness to work. He found that the teachers' perceptions of student adjustment were moderately related to achievement and IQ, and that teacher ratings of desire to work and IQ were moderately related to each other. Also, the children rated as well-adjusted by their teachers were also rated as most popular by their peers on the sociometric measures. These data suggest that the teachers were successful in separately rating student intelligence, motivation to work, and general personal adjustment, and that their ratings of each of these were relatively accurate. There was little evidence of the general halo effect that appears in many studies. There is some data to suggest that certain teachers' attitudes toward students may depress their ability to perceive students appropriately. These teachers tend to overjudge those pupils they most prefer and underjudge least preferred students. Teachers strongly biased in either direction tend to be the least accurate judges (Gronlund, 1950). These data suggest that strong preferences may distort reality.

Putnins (1970) collected data suggesting that teachers who are more accurate in judging sociometric popularity are generally better teachers. A pool of twenty-four sixth-grade teachers were asked to rank their students in sociometric popularity, and these ranks were then compared with the ranks obtained from the students themselves to get a measure of teacher accuracy. Each teacher's classroom was observed for two thirty-minute periods. These observation data revealed that the more accurate teachers were more indirect in their approach to student motivation and control, that they more often expressed acceptance of their students' ideas and feelings, that they criticized their students' academic responses less frequently, and that they tended to use longer and broader questions and to apply frequent positive reinforcement immediately before and after students responded to questions. Thus, in general, the more accurate judges of student sociometric popularity seemed to be generally more student-oriented and warmer than the less accurate teachers. Thus teachers differ in their accuracy of perception of student popularity, and this accuracy is associated with differential patterns of classroom interaction with students.

Several studies have collected data on teacher accuracy in predicting student achievement. One was conducted on a group of ten primary school teachers in Scotland (Wilson, 1969). Teachers' rankings from the first few weeks of school correlated .45 through .88 with arithmetic scores and .33 through .85 with reading scores on tests administered at the end of the school year. A second set of teacher ratings taken four months later showed higher correlations, at least for those teachers who were initially lower. This second set of ratings correlated .79 through .96 for arithmetic and .63 through .89 for reading. Thus these ten teachers showed variable accuracy in their ability to predict end-of-the-year achievement after a few weeks with the children, but all showed moderately high to high correlations after a semester.

Somewhat lower correlations were reported by Jackson and Lahaderne (1967), who asked teachers to estimate children's IQ's and achievement. Teacher estimates correlated .39 with girls' IQ's and .44 with boys'. Their estimates correlated .31 through .37 for girl's achievement in reading, language, and arithmetic, and they correlated .45 through .51 for achievement in these three areas by boys.

Our own studies have produced generally higher correlations. In the Brophy and Good (1970a) study, the rank order correlation coefficient between teacher rankings of expected achievement and total scores on the Stanford Achievement Tests administered at the end of the year was .77. This is comparable with Wilson's (1969) finding suggesting high teacher accuracy after several months of experience with the children.

Even higher correlations were obtained in the follow-up study (Evertson, Brophy, and Good, 1972). Table 6.1 shows correlations between the three sets of teacher rankings taken during the first semester of the first grade and the children's rankings according to their performance on the Metropolitan Achievement Tests administered early in the fall the following year when they were in the second grade. Several aspects of these data are interesting and notable.

First, the correlations are generally quite high. Even the least accurate teacher (teacher number four) showed a correlation of .49 between her first set of rankings and her children's rankings on tests given a year later. The correlations for the other teachers were considerably higher. Second, again with the exception of teacher number four, who started lower than the others, the correlation coefficients remained

TABLE 6.1.   Correlations between Teachers' Rankings from the First Semester of the First Grade and Achievement Test Data from the Beginning of the Second Grade (from Evertson, Brophy, and Good, 1972)

TEACHER	CORRELATION BETWEEN SEPTEMBER RANKING AND 2D GRADE RANK[a]	CORRELATION BETWEEN NOVEMBER RANKING AND 2D GRADE RANK[a]	CORRELATION BETWEEN MARCH RANKING AND 2D GRADE RANK[a]
1	.92	.87	.86
2	.73	.89	.80
3	.72	.78	.77
4	.49	.60	.67
5	.91	.90	.86
6	.76	.77	—
7	.64	.62	.65
8	.62	.57	.73
9	.87	.90	.91

[a] Spearman's Rho rank correlation coefficients between first grade teachers' rankings and rankings of student performance on the Metropolitan Achievement Tests administered at the beginning of the second grade.

stable or became only very slightly higher across the three sets. That is, in general the teachers were not much more accurate in judging the children's ultimate achievement levels in March than they were back in September. The basic reason for this is that the initial set of correlation coefficients were quite high in the first place, much higher than we had expected on the basis of the data reported above. We had expected that the teachers' forecasts would be generally accurate, but we did not expect them to be quite so accurate as they were so early in the year.

We do not know why the teachers in this study were more successful at predicting student achievement than teachers in the other studies reviewed. If anything, they should have been less successful for at least two reasons. First, the children were only in first grade, and the teachers had less information to use on them because they had not yet established a "track record." In contrast, Wilson's teachers were drawn from several elementary grades, and the teachers in the Jackson and Lahaderne study were estimating the IQ and achievement of sixth graders.

A second reason for suspecting that the teachers would be less successful in forecasting achievement was the fact that we had selected three schools involved in the study because they contained particular kinds of student populations. One effect of this selection was to restrict the range of individual differences within a given school (and, by implication, within each teacher's classroom) thus making the teacher's job of ranking the students on expected achievement more difficult.

Nevertheless, the teachers were remarkably successful at predicting the achievement of their children. This was true even though the children were first graders and even though the rankings were taken after only a few weeks of school. We can offer no explanation for the uniquely high correlations that these teachers produced except to suggest that they were remarkably accurate judges of student achievement potential. This accuracy was sufficiently intriguing, however, that it led to a subsequent study designed to discover the student attributes that teachers attend to and use in forming impressions about students with whom they have not had prior experience or knowledge (Willis, 1972). This study will be described in some detail later in the chapter.

STABILITY OF TEACHER IMPRESSIONS

Whether or not teachers' impressions of students are accurate, they tend to be relatively stable over time. One big reason for this is the first impression or primacy effect (Asch, 1946). That is, once a teacher forms a clear-cut impression of a student, this impression is likely to stay with the teacher. For example, Murray, Herling, and Staebler (1972) had elementary school teachers observe videotapes of a boy performing a task. Some teachers saw a tape in which the boy gradually improved, starting slowly but gradually increasing his percentage of correct responses. The remaining teachers saw the opposite pattern, in which the boy started out doing well but began making more and more errors as the task progressed. After viewing the tapes the teachers were asked to recall the number of items that the boy had succeeded on, to predict his score if given a similar task, to estimate his IQ, and to estimate his academic achievement. Although each boy had fifteen successes and fifteen errors on the total of thirty trials, he was evaluated differently by the two groups of teachers depending upon which order of success and failure they had observed. Although there were no significant differences regarding predicted performance, predicted IQ, or predicted academic achievement, the teachers showed a primacy effect in their estimates of performance on the task. That is, the teachers who observed the boy initially doing well "remembered" more successes than did the teachers who first observed him doing poorly. The authors note that, if these findings can be extrapolated to the classroom, a student who performs well early may be viewed more favorably by teachers than one who shows improvement as he continues to work on the task, and a student who regresses in his schoolwork may continue to be evaluated more highly than a student who has progressed and demonstrated improvement over time.

Primacy effects were also dramatically demonstrated in two studies by Feldman and Allen. The first (Feldman and Allen, 1972) involved sixth graders who were tutoring second graders, attempting to teach them the trapezoid concept. Unknown to the sixth-grade tutors, the success of the second graders were experimentally manipulated. Some tutors experienced success on each of two sessions, some experienced failure on each of two sessions, some experienced success on the first session and failure on the second, and some experienced failure on the first session and success on the second. After tutoring, the tutors were asked to fill out rating scales on how smart they thought their tutee was, how much they liked him, and how much they enjoyed teaching him. As expected, tutors who experienced success on both trials rated their tutees high, and tutors who experienced failure on both trials rated their tutees low. However, the data for the other two conditions showed a primacy effect that goes against common-sense expectations. Second graders who first showed success and then failure were rated by their tutors as smarter, better liked, and more enjoyable to teach than second graders who first showed failure and then success.

In a follow-up study (Feldman and Allen, 1973), adult subjects watched filmed tutoring lessons showing one of the four conditions mentioned above. Some subjects observed both parts of the lesson continuously, while others did not see the second part until two days after they had seen the first part. The primacy effect was again observed. Regardless of whether the subjects saw the two sessions at the same time or whether they saw them two days apart, their ratings of the student's ability were determined by his performance on the first part of the lesson, regardless of his performance on the second part.

Thus first impressions tend to persist even in the face of disconfirming evidence, at least when they are well-formed. This primacy effect of first impressions is probably one of the reasons that teacher impressions of students tend to remain relatively stable over time. Stability in teacher assessment of achievement potential was suggested indirectly by the data in Table 6.1 showing correlations of first-grade teachers' rankings on expected achievement with achievement test data from the beginning of the second grade. More direct data on stability in these rankings is given in Table 6.2, which shows the intercorrelations of the September rankings with those taken in November and in March, as well as the numbers of children who moved between the top and bottom thirds of the distributions. These data show that stability in teacher rankings was quite high. The impression held after a few weeks of school was sustained throughout the school year.

Table 6.2 also shows that only nine students moved between top and bottom thirds. Two boys and four girls moved up, while three boys and no girls fell from the top to the bottom third. Thus the incidence of movement between the top and bottom thirds was very small (below 4 percent), and upward mobility was easier for girls than boys.

The latter finding is not merely an artifact of where the students were placed initially. This would occur, for example, if the girls had been ranked generally lower than the boys on the initial rankings, so that upward mobility would be more likely for girls than boys on a chance basis alone. However, initially the teachers assigned equal percentages of boys and girls to the high and low groups with only a very slight bias toward the girls. This is seen in Table 6.3. These data correspond nicely with the previously mentioned findings by Good (1972) that teachers were more attracted to girls (and, to a lesser extent, perceived them as more capable) as the year progressed.

Although equal percentages of children were rated in the high and low third within each sex, more boys rated at the extremes. That is, the teachers initially judged more of the boys to be either high or low achievers, while they saw more

TABLE 6.2.   Stability and Change in Teachers' Rankings of Students According to Expected Achievement (from Evertson, Brophy, and Good, 1972)

TEACHER	CORRELATION BETWEEN TIME 1 AND TIME 2[a]	CORRELATION BETWEEN TIME 1 AND TIME 3[a]	MOVE FROM TOP THIRD TO BOTTOM THIRD		MOVE FROM BOTTOM THIRD TO TOP THIRD	
			Sex	Rank Change	Sex	Rank Change
1	.95	.87	—	—	M	19–8
2	.90	.81	—	—	M	23–8
3	.83	.74	M	5–19	F	19–8
4	.86	.84	M	6–18	—	—
			M	7–22		
5	.95	.93	—	—	F	29–6
6	.97	—	—	—	—	—
7	.95	.93	—	—	—	—
8	.96	.86	—	—	F	27–9
9	.95	.84	—	—	F	21–4

[a] Spearman—Rho rank correlation coefficients.

TABLE 6.3.   Teachers' Rankings for Boys and for Girls in September and in March
(from Evertson, Brophy, and Good, 1972)

| | SEPTEMBER | | | | MARCH | | | |
| | Boys | | Girls | | Boys | | Girls | |
	N	%	N	%	N	%	N	%
High	35	35.5	29	29.9	28	28.3	36	37.1
Middle	27	27.3	41	42.3	31	31.3	37	38.1
Low	37	37.4	27	27.8	40	40.4	24	24.8

of the girls as being average. With time, the distribution of the rankings changed, so that more girls were perceived as high achievers and fewer as low achievers, while the boys showed a general drop in the rankings. This can be seen by comparing the September rankings and the March rankings in Table 6.3. The girls clearly were perceived more positively than the boys at the end of the semester than at the beginning. These data are but another example of the more general finding that girls outperform boys in the early grades of American elementary schools. This point will be discussed in the following chapter.

Despite these noticeable sex differences and the movement of a few students from one extreme to the other, the teachers' expectations showed remarkable stability from September through March. This led us to conclude that the September rankings represented genuine expectations rather than mere guesses, and that they were generally accurate (as noted in Table 6.1, later achievement testing bore out these conclusions). Self-report data from the teachers also suggested that these early rankings represented true expectations. For example, most grade repeaters were ranked low in the September rankings even though they were doing relatively well at the time. When questioned about this, teachers explained that the initial good work by these students was deceptive because they had had the work the previous year, and that by the end of the year they would be doing poorly compared to the rest of the class. This was in fact the case.

As mentioned previously, we were quite impressed with the teachers' abilities to predict the achievement potential of first graders without a previously established "track record" on the basis of a few weeks of observation of them. These forecasts were both stable and accurate, leading us to wonder "how did the teachers do it?"

CORRELATES OF EARLY TEACHER IMPRESSIONS

Relatively little information is available about how teachers judge children's performance potential when they enter school. Goodwin and Sanders (1969), as reported in Chapter 1, asked teachers to rank the relative importance of several sources of information in forming impressions of students. The teachers stated that SES was the most important variable for predicting success at the first grade level, followed in order by I.Q., standardized test scores, age, sex, anecdotal notes, and grade point average. Since only some of these sources of information would be available to a teacher meeting a student entering school for the first time, it may be inferred from their data that teachers would judge potential according to SES, age, and sex, in that order. These indicants would seem to be fairly useful in a classroom containing a heterogeneous socioeconomic mixture, although they would be less useful in a classroom made homogeneous by *de facto* segregation and/or a tracking system.

Long and Henderson (1972) asked 120 white elementary teachers of both sexes to rate the usefulness of pupils' race, class, test data, and classroom behavior for predicting their school performance. The subjects used a five-point scale to assess the probability that children just entering school would be reading at grade level by the end of the second grade. The fictional "children" were all males designated by their first names and their race. In addition, paragraphs describing these fictional students contained readiness test scores (three levels), information on classroom activity levels (active or passive), and information on attentiveness (attentive or inattentive). The "children" were also described as being middle class or lower class. Each subject rated twelve of these fictional "children."

The data revealed that readiness test scores were by far the most important predictors of expected achievement. The teachers predicted high achievement when they saw high readiness scores regardless of all other factors. The ratings were significantly affected by the children's attentiveness and activity level scores also, however. The more active and attentive "children" were rated higher than the more passive and inattentive "children" (in this study, activity level was presented as a positive variable and did not imply rule breaking or other threatening assertiveness that makes negative impressions upon teachers). There were some interactions, however. Passive high scorers got especially high predictions compared to active high scorers, and attentive high scorers got higher predictions than inattentive high scorers. The attention effect was stronger among the medium and high scorers, while the activity effect was stronger among the medium and low scorers. Thus active, low scoring "children" were especially likely to receive higher expected achievement scores than passive, low scoring "children."

Neither race nor social class affected the ratings of expected achievement in this study. This may be because the study was conducted in an academic setting, and the respondents avoided using these indicators so as to avoid making socially undesirable responses. However, the data reviewed on I.Q. and socioeconomic status in Chapter 1 suggest that race and SES are important only in the absence of more specific and more reliable information. The teachers in this study were provided with such information in the form of readiness test scores, so it may be that race and SES information was largely ignored because readiness test data were available.

Willis (1972) conducted a large-scale interview study in an attempt to determine what attributes of children teachers attend to and use in forming impressions about their achievement potential and their personality traits. The interviews were conducted with teachers working in predominately white middle class schools at the first-grade level. All teachers were female. The schools were located in a large urban school system or in a suburban school system immediately adjacent to it. The study was conducted at the first-grade level in these schools because they did not have kindergarten, so that the teachers were unfamiliar with the entering first graders (although they may have taught older siblings previously).

Teachers were contacted at three points in time during the first semester. The initial interview was conducted during the first week of school, when the teachers had had only a few days of contact with the students and before test data were available. The second interview was conducted several weeks later, shortly after the results of readiness tests were made available to the teachers. The final set of interviews was taken toward the end of the semester. Thus the data represent the teachers' initial impressions of the children, their impressions of the children modified by knowledge of the children's scores on readiness tests, and their impressions of the children after a semester of work with them, respectively. A total of seventy-four teachers were included in the study, divided into two subgroups. One group received an interview, in which the interviewer, at each of the three time points mentioned above, went down the class roster with the teacher and asked her to state whatever she had to say about each individual student. These interviews were tape recorded and later transcribed. Nine of the transcripts from the first set of interviews were presented in Chapter 1. In addition to responding to the interview questions, each time they were interviewed the teachers also ranked their students on expected achievement. They also ranked their students on the four attitudes items described in Chapter 5 on the final interview. The free response interview format was chosen for this subset of teachers in order to avoid cuing responses or "putting ideas into their heads." By simply asking each teacher to say what she had noticed about each student, Willis got the teachers' impressions in their own words. They were not given adjective description lists or ranking scales to make them think about student attributes that they might not otherwise have thought about on their own. Thus, the interview data were purely naturalistic and are extremely valuable for this reason. They have the drawback, however, of requiring the development of coding systems to code the responses that were given freely, so that the teachers' spontaneous comments are collected at the cost of greater time and expense and greater difficulties in analyzing the data.

To complement the data on the twenty-eight teachers interviewed, forty-six additional teachers were asked to respond to a questionnaire involving ranking their students on a variety of bipolar adjective description scales. These have the opposite advantages and disadvantages of the interview data. They are easy to administer and score, but they do not represent data taken spontaneously from the teacher and phrased in her own words. However, the dangers of introducing undesirable method variance by "putting ideas into the heads of the teachers" through the use of adjective ranking scales were minimized by using scales that previously had been shown to reflect student attributes that teachers typically talk and think about. Furthermore, the two sets of data address many of the same problems and can be used in tandem to investigate the effects that the contrasting methods of getting information from the teacher may have had on the resultant data.

Ninety-five percent of the students were white, although only two-thirds of the teachers were white. This was because the district had initiated a teacher crossover plan in response to governmental pressures for desegregation. In addition to the data from the interviews or questionnaires, student variables studied included sex, race, teacher ranking on the expected achievement and attitude scales, readiness test scores, and grade repetition. Grade repeaters were removed from most analyses because they were not new to the teachers and thus were not comparable with the rest of the children when teacher reactions to new students were being investigated. To facilitate further the comparability of the questionnaire data from different teachers' classrooms, a five-point forced choice format was used for the questionnaires: Teachers were asked to place two students in the highest and lowest categories, five students in the second highest and second lowest, and all of the rest of the students in the middle category.

In short, this produced a forced normal distribution in the teacher rankings on each of the adjective-description scales included in the questionnaire study. A total of thirty bipolar scales were used in the questionnaires, but only twenty were used at a time to help minimize the work required of the teacher. Many items appeared on the first and second administration, the first and third administration, or the second and third administration. Thus most items were repeated twice. The achievement rankings were similar to those used in previous studies, although the teachers were allowed to circle the names of children that they felt they could not distinguish between (thus tied ranks were allowed).

The data from these two sets of teachers were analyzed to identify what teacher attributes were noticed and used in forming impressions about the children, how these impressions were affected by knowledge of the children's scores on readiness tests, and how accurate and stable these impressions were across the first semester of school. Data on these issues will be presented separately for the interview and the questionnaire teachers, since different methods were used and different teachers were included in the two groups.

Stability of Achievement Expectations

Stability coefficients for the teachers' rankings of expected achievement at three different time periods in the semester are presented in Table 6.4 These coefficients show that stability was quite high across the three samples for both groups of teachers and for both boys and girls, although especially high between time two and time three. The latter finding reflects the effects of receiving readiness-test data upon the teachers' achievement expectation estimates. Teachers' initial impressions of the children were modified in some cases by the children's performance on the readiness tests (and perhaps by the students' classroom behavior between the first and second

TABLE 6.4.   Stability of Teachers' Rankings of Expected Student Achievement Across Three Time Samples[a] (from Willis, 1972)

| | QUESTIONNAIRE | | | INTERVIEW | | |
	Time 1–2	Time 2–3	Time 1–3	Time 1–2	Time 2–3	Time 1–3
Boys	.69	.82	.64	.68	.86	.60
Girls	.67	.81	.61	.68	.85	.58

[a] All N's exceed 250; all r's statistically significant at $p < .01$.

ranking; the independent effects of classroom behavior and readiness tests cannot be singled out in this design). After this, their achievement estimates remained highly stable through the end of the semester. Given that the children were first graders with whom the teachers were previously unfamiliar, these stability coefficients seem quite high. Was it because the teachers could quickly and accurately judge the achievement potential of most of their students, or because early impressions exerted a primacy effect that tended to stay with the teacher throughout the semester (with some minor modifications when the readiness tests became available)? This question is dealt with in the following section.

Accuracy of Achievement Expectations

Correlations between the teachers' estimates of expected achievement and students' scores on the Metropolitan Readiness Tests are shown in Table 6.5. Comparing these data with the data in Table 6.4, two findings are worth noting. First, given the paucity of data upon which to base their observations, the teachers' estimates of achievement potential were considerably accurate (at least insofar as the readiness test scores reflect this potential). Second, although the initial rankings made after only a few days of school are both statistically and practically significantly correlated with readiness test scores, the data of Table 6.5 underscore the fact that the teachers' estimates were influenced by the readiness test scores once they became available.

Taken together, the data in these two tables show that the impressions teachers

TABLE 6.5.   Correlation of Metropolitan Readiness Test Scores and Teacher Rankings of Expected Student Achievement Across Three Time Samples[a] (from Willis, 1972).

| | QUESTIONNAIRE | | | INTERVIEW | | |
	Time 1	Time 2	Time 3	Time 1	Time 2	Time 3
Boys	.63	.80	.75	.60	.79	.72
Girls	.56	.75	.71	.61	.79	.78

[a] All N's exceed 200; all r's statistically significant at $p < .01$.

gained from teaching students for just a few days were sufficient to allow them to formulate not only stable but accurate assessments of student ability. The correlations between teacher estimates and measured ability are not extremely accurate, of course; they are significantly improved by the introduction of readiness test data, and there is still considerable room for error and for self-fulfilling prophecy effects. Nevertheless, it appears that most teachers are capable of making a generally accurate assessment of a child's abilities and potential simply on the basis of observing him in the classroom for a few days. This finding naturally raises the question "how do they do it?" To begin to find out, Willis assessed the relationships between the teachers' achievement expectations and their other perceptions about the students. These data help identify those student attributes and behaviors that teachers attend to and use in forming judgments about the achievement potential of students.

Correlates of Expected Achievement

Correlations between the bipolar adjective descriptions used with the questionnaire teachers and the achievement rankings that these teachers made are given in Table 6.6. All of these adjective descriptions are significantly correlated with teacher rank-

TABLE 6.6.   Correlations of Adjectives from Adjective Description Form with Teacher Achievement Rankings Across Three Time Samples (from Willis, 1972)

	TIME 1		TIME 2		TIME 3	
	Boys N = 522	Girls N = 480	Boys N = 552	Girls N = 506	Boys N = 512	Girls N = 476
Very attentive to class proceedings/Does not pay attention	.70**	.70**	.72**	.71**		
Gets along well with others/Fights argues, shows aggressive behavior	.21**	.37**			.18**	.28**
Very self-confident/ Lacks self-confidence	.70**	.65**			.68**	.62**
Active participant, often makes comments or asks question/ Very quiet	.50**	.39**	.49**	.39**		
Very obedient/ Disobedient, defiant	.34**	.45**			.29**	.34**
Has very good self-control/ Restless, hyperactive can't sit still	.34**	.40**	.34**	.45**		

TABLE 6.6—continued

Good looking/ Unattractive	.30**	.34**				
Large/ Small	.20**	.15**				
Mature/Immature	.71**	.71**	.66**	.67**		
Works very well without constant teacher supervision, follows instructions easily/Does not work well without constant teacher supervision	.75**	.76**			.76**	.69**
Industrious, always tries to do his best/ Lazy, often doesn't do his best			.56**	.61**		
Leader/Follower			.49**	.46**		
Easily understood, speaks very clearly/ Very hard to understand (whispers, uses baby talk)			.56**	.48**		
Has many friends/ Has few friends			.54**	.46**		
Very neat/ Very messy			.57**	.61**	.51**	.53**
Best Reader in class/ Poorest Reader in class			.85**	.85**	.86**	.85**
Very healthful/Frail, not healthy					.37**	.38**
Very cautious, careful/ Very impulsive					.43**	.44**
Helpful, assists teacher or other children voluntarily/ Not notably helpful, does not assist teacher or children voluntarily					.54**	.52**
Creative, imaginative/Not notably creative or imaginative					.62**	.64**

* $p < .05$
** $p < .01$

ings, although some of these correlations are quite low, being statistically significant only because of the large numbers of children involved. The data from time one are particularly instructive, since these were taken after only a few days of experience with the children and were uncontaminated by teacher knowledge of the children's scores on the readiness tests. These data show that student attention to the teacher, student self-confidence, maturity as judged by the teacher, and student ability to work well without constant supervision were the most important correlates of teacher judgment of student ability. Of lesser importance were the degree to which the student asks questions or actively participates in discussions, the degree to which he is obedient or compliant, his appearance (good looking versus un-attractive), and the degree to which he gets along with his fellow students. Student size was the least important of the variables studied, although even here the larger students were ranked significantly higher than the smaller students. It is worth noting that at this point in time, before teachers' expectations have jelled and before they have seen test results, the correlations with criterion scores show a very wide range, with teachers concentrating on student attributes fairly directly relevant to classroom achievement and concentrating less on attributes less related to achievement. While this remains true as a general statement in the later rankings, the later rankings show more evidence of halo effects. At times two and three, the highly rated students were more likely to be seen as "all good" and the lowly rated students to be seen as "all bad" than in the first set of rankings. Thus, these data suggest that halo effects in the teachers' ratings develop increasingly over time. In the initial rankings the expected achievement scores were based primarily upon student attributes directly related to school achievement, but in the later rankings a number of personality variables that are at best tangentially related to achievement nevertheless showed strong correlations with achievement rankings. In short, it appears that the teacher does not retain her initial global assessment of the child throughout the semester. Instead, her initial assessment is based primarily upon achievement relevant attributes, but as this assessment becomes more secure it also becomes more global and begins to include personal attributes less directly related to achievement. Apparently, children who succeed in school become increasingly perceived as positive on most measures, while the children who fail in school become more negatively perceived as times goes on.

The data discussed so far, in which teachers were responding to a predesigned questionnaire asking them to rank their students on particular adjective descriptors, were complemented by the interview data in which the teachers freely described the students in their own words. The data from the twenty-eight teachers interviewed were tape-recorded and transcribed, and the transcriptions then were coded according to commonly observed categories. These included comments about the physical characteristics of the child (size, hair color or style, clothing, general attractiveness), comments about the family (broken home, older parents or grand-parents, parental cooperation, teachers' familiarity with the family), comments about the child's physical condition (vision, speech, and so on), comments about his social-emotional characteristics (maturity, independence, extroversion, politeness, and so on), comments about the child's interaction with peers (prosocial versus anti-social), comments about the child's attitude toward school (likes school, tries hard versus gives up, has or has not self-confidence), comments about the child's class-room behavior (behaves well versus behaves mischievously, seeks attention, is hyperactive, and so on), comments about school readiness (either general statements about the child's readiness or statements about specific skills), comments about the child's verbal skills, comments about his work-related skills (follows directions, pays attention, works independently, works neatly, finishes on time), comments about the child's ability (general comments about ability, fears that the child may fail, suggestions that he is underachieving and can do better, suspicions of perceptual problems or learning disabilities, and so on), and miscellaneous comments about the child's personal characteristics or about idiosyncratic events concerning the child that the teacher has observed and remembered.

This coding yielded a total of 249 variables (although many of these were combination scores, so that the actual number of different variables is lower). Of these, forty showed statistically significant correlations between teacher comments in the first interview and the expected achievement rankings made during that interview. In general, the free response comments of the teachers bear out the data reported above from the questionnaire teachers, although they also add certain variables not included in the questionnaire.

Variables from the interviews which correlated above .30 with achievement expectation rankings included the following: comments about perceived maturity, total negative comments about social-emotional development (minus), total negative comments about classroom behavior (minus), positive comments about readiness for school, negative comments about readiness for school (minus), positive comments about work-related behavior when doing assignments, negative comments about work-related behavior when doing assignments (minus), positive comments about ability, negative comments about ability (minus), total positive statements about the child, and total negative statements about the child (minus). With the exception of social adjustment, these variables used by teachers to predict student achievement closely correspond to the four major variables used in the first set of questionnaire data (attentiveness, self-confidence, maturity, and ability to work independently). Thus, the questionnaire data and the free choice interview data yield very similar patterns of correlates with rankings of expected achievement.

Student variables correlated with expected achievement lower than .30 but still statistically significantly included the following: race (whites expected to do better than blacks), broken home (minus), total negative statements about the family (minus), independence (in self-care rather than in work), total positive comments about social-emotional characteristics, total negative comments about attitude and motivation (minus), good behavior in the classroom, inability to perceive likenesses and differences (minus), inability to color or draw well (minus), poor motor coordination or writing (minus), the ability to be an alert, close observer, total positive statements about school readiness, inability to follow directions well (minus), failure to pay attention (minus), belief that child will need a lot of readiness work (minus), fear that child may fail or have to be withdrawn from school (minus), total positive comments about ability, and total number of idiosyncratic interactions with the child that the teacher reports (minus). Most of these correlates conform to common-sense expectations based upon the relationship between the student variables and student achievement or upon stereotyped expectations regarding achievement (race, broken home). The final variable (number of idiosyncratic interactions with the child that the teacher remembers) has a negative relationship because the majority of the interactions classified in this category were negative, suggesting that the student was likely to become either a concern or a rejection student.

Taken together, Willis's data suggest that teachers are generally accurate in assessing student learning potential simply because they use appropriate and reliable criteria in making their judgments. Although influenced to a minor degree by factors such as race, intact versus broken home, physical attractiveness, and physical size, the teachers' rankings are much more closely associated with student variables known to be related to student achievement (attentiveness, self-confidence, maturity, and ability to do assigned tasks). Furthermore, the evidence suggests that the teachers were judging the students' actual long range potential rather than merely their short range scores on readiness or achievement tests. Although teacher observations of various aspects of school readiness were correlated with achievement rankings, the correlations were not nearly so strong as those for the factors mentioned above. Thus, the teachers' judgments appeared to characterize the children's general levels of ability (or IQ's if you will), and they seemed to be able to distinguish successfully between general abilities and the more specific readiness skills that primarily reflect home background and preschool experience differences rather than ability differences.

The teachers' abilities to make these discriminations were seen not only in the correlational data, but also in the comments that they made about the children. Very frequently they would state that a given child had not yet settled down in school, had not yet learned school routines, or was temporarily behind the rest of the class because he had not been to kindergarten, but they would state with confidence that the child would be doing well by the end of the year. Thus teachers were depending more on the student's general self-control, school motivation, and (especially) learning abilities as demonstrated in the classroom than on the presence or absence of certain specific knowledge or skills. To the extent that the concept of general intelligence has validity, it appears that teachers can judge it fairly accurately on the basis of observation of children in their classrooms.

CORRELATES OF TEACHER ATTITUDES

In addition to the achievement rankings, the twenty-eight teachers in the interview group were asked to nominate three children to each of the four attitude groups of attachment, concern, indifference, and rejection. Differences between these children and the rest of the children on teacher comments made during the third interview at the end of the first semester were then assessed to determine the student characteristics of children assigned to these groups (Willis and Brophy, 1974).

The sex distribution in the nomination of students to the four attitude groups was similar to that reported in Chapter 5. Altogether there were 341 boys and 296 girls in the classes surveyed. Of these, 32 boys and 32 girls were nominated to the attachment groups, 42 boys and 22 girls to the concern groups, 30 boys and 23 girls to the indifference groups, and 37 boys and 25 girls to the rejection groups. Although the differences are not large except for the concern group, the data generally re-affirm the higher saliency of boys and the tendency of teachers to be more concerned about and have a generally more negative attitude towards them. Teacher comments about the children assigned to the four attitude groups are presented below, separately by sex.

Regarding boys assigned to the attachment groups, the teachers made more positive comments about their clothing, more often said that they had an immature appearance, more often stated that they had a visual impairment or required glasses, less often stated that they were quiet, more often assigned them as leaders or classroom helpers, more often described them as helpful with other children, more often described them as busybodies, more often stated that they knew left from right and could stay within lines on a tablet, more often stated that they did not draw well, more often made negative comments about their reading ability, more often stated that they volunteered information during classroom discussions, more often mentioned a perceptual problem or learning disability, more often mentioned positive classroom behavior, more often mentioned positive social behavior, and more often mentioned the student as a high ability student (this was confirmed by these students' significantly higher Metropolitan Readiness Tests scores). In general, these qualities fit the stereotype of the attraction student as a high ability student who is well-adjusted to the school situation, conforms to the teacher's rules, and "rewards" the teacher by being somewhat dependent upon her and by doing well in his school-work. The only negative ability comment concerned reading progress, and this would appear to be relative rather than absolute in view of the more general picture of high ability. Thus, the picture here is more one of concern about getting the child to maximize his potential rather than concern about getting him to meet minimal requirements. Other data suggest that the teachers favored the attachment students, at least by the end of the semester. Note that even though these students were perceived as being busybodies, they were more often assigned as leaders or helpers than their classmates. The comments about clothing suggest that these students were generally of higher socioeconomic status than their classmates.

In commenting about girls assigned to the attachment group, teachers described them as larger than average, as more attractive than average, as having interested, cooperative parents, as having a visual impairment or requiring glasses, as having been to kindergarten, as not knowing how to write their name, as being creative and imaginative, as being alert, close observers, as liking stories, as being able to work independently on assignments, as being of generally high ability, as coming from generally good families, and as being high in expected achievement (this was borne out by the Metropolitan Readiness Tests scores.) In addition, the teachers had significantly more positive comments and significantly fewer negative comments about these girls than about their classmates. Here again, the girls in the attachment group appeared to be high-ability students who conform to and reward their teachers. Again, there is evidence that they come from higher social class families and that they are perceived in a generally positive way, even including physical attractiveness.

In general, the attachment group data for both boys and girls conformed closely to the data reported previously.

Boys in the concern group were especially likely to be described as being of average size, being reared by grandparents or older parents, having a speech impediment or using baby talk, being generally immature, being active and vivacious, seeking teacher attention, being able to use and keep up with school supplies, being dependent in schoolwork and needing help from the teacher, needing reassurance and approval, being of generally low ability, needing readiness work, having a positive attitude toward school, having generally poor health, having generally poor social-emotional development, having generally poor oral and verbal skills, having generally poor skills in the area of independent work, and having generally low abilities (this was confirmed by generally lower Metropolitan Readiness Tests scores). In addition, the teachers made generally fewer positive comments and generally more negative comments about these children (although the negative comments were confined almost completely to their abilities rather than to their personalities or cooperation with the teacher). These data strikingly confirm the previously suggested picture of concern students as low ability students who are dependent upon the teacher and who are perceived as making legitimate demands because they generally conform to classroom rules but are in need of help due to low ability.

Teachers described girls in the concern group as being more likely to be nonwhite than white; they mentioned the parents' occupation more frequently (generally in a negative sense); their parents were described in generally positive terms; they tended to be from large families; the teachers reported that the size of the family was one of the problems confronting the child; the child was more likely to have a speech impediment or to use baby talk, to be more dependent, quieter, lacking in self-confidence, to be dependent in work, to need help from the teacher, to have a generally positive attitude toward school, and to have poorly developed verbal skills (these girls also had significantly lower Metropolitan Readiness Tests scores). Even more than the boys, the concern group girls showed a pattern of low achievement in combination with dependency upon the teacher for both emotional and academic support. In general, the data on concern students in this interview study bear out conclusions reviewed earlier suggesting that such students are low achievers who depend upon the teacher to tell them more or less continually what to do. This dependency is expressed in inhibited, socially approved ways; concern children do not present behavioral problems and are not assertive or intrusive like children in some of the other attitude groups.

Boys in the indifference group were described as more likely to be blond haired, to have a "blank" eye expression, to appear immature, to be neat and clean, to have a working mother (which the teacher perceived as a problem for the boy), to be reared by grandparents or substitute parents, to have a disinterested or uncooperative parent, to have a visual impairment or need glasses, to have a speech impediment and/or use baby talk, to be a sociometric loner, to be anxious to please, to be in poor health, to have negative attitudes toward school, to have failed to live up to the teachers' initial expectations, and to have poor verbal skills. Also, in their total comments about such children, the teachers more often mentioned their physical description, more often and more negatively commented upon their health, more often made negative comments about their work-related behavior, and made more total negative comments about them. Nevertheless, the Metropolitan Readiness Test scores of these boys did not differ significantly from those of their classmates.

These data suggest a pattern of contrasts between the concern and indifference boys. Although both groups were perceived as lacking certain skills (especially the concern students), the children differed in their response to the teachers (at least teachers perceived that they did and reported this in their interview responses). Concern children were clearly dependent upon the teacher and showed this in their classroom behavior. The indifference students apparently did not respond to the teachers in ways that were rewarding to them. Note that the teachers perceived the needs of these children quite clearly, and even rated them as anxious to please, and yet they responded with indifference rather than with concern. Clues for an explanation of this appear in the teachers' perception that these students had blank facial expressions (suggesting that they did not respond to teachers' overtures), that they had poor attitudes toward school (the indifference group boys were the only group to be rated significantly different from their classmates on this variable), and that they had failed to meet initial expectations. Apparently on the basis of their appearance and observations of their early work, the teachers developed moderate to high expectations for these students (and the readiness tests scores suggested that these students were equal to their classmates, in contrast to the concern students). However, these boys apparently responded inappropriately (from the teachers' point of view, at least), to the teachers' overtures (blank expression, negative attitudes), conditioning the teachers to stay away from them.

Recall the earlier experiment by Yarrow, Waxler, and Scott (1971) which showed that teachers returned more frequently to children who gave them a positive response than to children who did not. It seems likely that this phenomenon was going on here, and that it exerted a strong primacy effect in conditioning the teachers to avoid and become indifferent about these boys, even though they clearly perceived their needs for help in certain areas. The teachers seemed to feel that these boys wanted to be left alone and/or disliked the teachers, so they began to avoid them.

The girls in the indifference group were described as more likely to be non-white than white, as not liking school, as giving up easily when working on assignments, as lacking self-confidence generally, as not being prepared for school, as not knowing their colors or numbers, as being creative and imaginative, as being of generally low ability, as being children that the teachers did not frequently interact with, and as presenting problems in their classroom behavior. The teachers' general feeling that these children were deficient in readiness skills was borne out by their significantly lower scores on the Metropolitan Readiness Tests. Here again, we see a pattern in which the teachers clearly perceived that the children were in need of help, and yet they responded with indifference rather than concern.

Again, the difference seems to be in the response of the children to the teacher. Whereas the concern group combined low ability with dependency and positive response to the teacher, the indifference group combined low abilities with misbehavior in the classroom and negative attitudes toward school. Comparing the indifference children with children in the other groups, the distinguishing factor seems to be a negative response to the teacher and/or to school in general. Apparently, when teachers encounter such attitudes and do not succeed in changing them, they tend to respond with indifference ("if they don't like it they can lump it"). If these data are typical of the general state, they imply that teacher indifference toward indifference group students is not a benign indifference occurring simply because the child is nonsalient and the teacher is too busy interacting with everyone else. Instead, the indifference appears to be a defense mechanism to protect the teacher from continued frustration and rejection by indifference group students. Apparently, unresponsive and/or sullen behavior by the students in interaction with the teachers early in the year "turns off" the teachers, conditioning them to minimize their interactions with these students in the future and to develop an attitude of indifference rather than concern for their problems even though their problems are accurately perceived.

Boys in the rejection group were described as more likely to be nonwhite than white, as coming from intact families in which both parents were living, as being immature and not well-adjusted, as being independent, as being loud or disruptive in the classroom, as being relatively inactive and not vivacious, as being unlikely to be assigned as a leader or helper, as having difficulty in getting along with others, as being talkative, as not knowing likenesses and differences, as not knowing how to write their names, as not knowing left from right or how to stay within lines on tablets, as being unable to use or keep up with school supplies, as having weak reading abilities, as needing extra help because of generally low ability, as needing readiness work, as being likely to fail or have to be withdrawn from school, as having deteriorated in their work since the beginning of the year, as being either notably healthy or having poor health, as lacking in readiness skills, as having poor verbal skills, as being physically unattractive, as presenting classroom behavior problems, as generally lacking in school readiness, as presenting problems in their behavior during work assignments, and as being of generally low ability. In addition, the teachers remembered both more positive and more negative contacts with these children, they had more total negative comments about them, fewer positive total comments about them, and more total comments about them (positive plus negative). *These children did not differ significantly from their classmates on the Metropolitan Readiness Tests scores despite the teachers' comments about low ability.*

These comments are strikingly similar to the patterns observed and reported earlier, in that they show a general halo effect of rejection, but tempered by occasional exceptions in which the teacher makes positive statements in certain areas (as if she is trying to balance her presentation by finding something positive to say about the child). The halo effect is seen in the teachers' repeated mention of lack of specific skills or general low ability in these students; in contrast to teacher perceptions, these boys did as well as their classmates on the readiness tests. Thus teachers' perceptions here were distorted by their attitudes of rejection toward these boys. Also, the previously suggested patterns of contrast between the rejection students and the concern students can be seen in the data on these rejected boys. Instead of being quiet and dependent on the teacher like the concern students, these boys are more assertive, perhaps even loud and disruptive, and they present frequent classroom discipline problems. Their interpersonal problems are not confined to their interactions with the teachers, as with the indifference students, since they are also described as having difficulty getting along with their classmates (read "argues and fights frequently"). Thus, the problems that these boys present are frequent and serious enough for the teachers to respond with an attitude of rejection ("I wish I could get him out of my room"), rather than an attitude of concern.

It is noteworthy that both the concern and rejection boys are described as in need of readiness work and extra help generally, but only the rejection boys are described as likely to fail or to have to be withdrawn from school. This implies that the teachers have positive expectations of success in their efforts with concern students, but they do not have such expectations for whatever efforts they may be making to give needed help to the rejection students. Also, bear in mind that it is the concern students and not the rejection students who actually have low abilities as measured by the readiness tests; the rejection students do not differ significantly from their classmates despite the teachers' beliefs that they are of generally low ability. Apparently boys who present severe discipline problems create a strong halo effect in which the teacher attributes low abilities and lack of readiness to them also despite the evidence from the readiness tests. This was the only group where the teachers' perceptions of ability did not match the readiness test data. The frustration and aggravation caused by these boys was sufficient to impair the teachers' judgments regarding their ability, even though the teachers were quite accurate in their judgments regarding other children.

The girls in the rejection group had patterns featuring frequent negative comments about the families (broken home or poor parental cooperation), and they were described as being busybodies, as not liking school, as giving up easily, as lacking self-confidence, as being playful and mischievous, as not being prepared for school, as not being adjusted to school routines, as not knowing colors and numbers, as not knowing likenesses and differences, as being alert, close observers, as not volunteering information to the class, as failing to pay good attention, as being likely to fail or having to be withdrawn from school, as being able to do more than they were doing, as having poor school attitudes, as having poor school readiness, as having poor work behavior, and as having poor general abilities. Again, the teachers made significantly more negative comments, significantly fewer positive comments, and significantly more total comments about these girls. Also, again despite the teachers' comments about abilities, these girls did not differ significantly from their classmates on the readiness tests. Although it shows up in somewhat different variables, the general pattern for the girls in the rejection group is quite similar to and has the same interpretive implications as the pattern for boys. In contrast to their classmates, these girls appeared to present more behavioral and disciplinary problems, to be underachievers, and in general not to "go along with the program." As was the case with the rejection group boys, the teachers tended to rate the rejection group girls as having low abilities (although sometimes they described them as underachievers, rather than as low ability children), even though they did not differ significantly from their classmates in their readiness test scores. The contrast with the girls in the concern group parallels the contrast between the concern and rejection boys. Concern girls have low abilities, but rejection girls do not. The teachers are apparently rewarded by the concern students' behavior and develop concern and the habit of spending a lot of time with them, while they are put off by the behavior of the rejection students and develop an attitude of rejection toward them.

In each case, teacher attitudinal reactions to the four types of students are readily explainable on the basis of the behavior of the students (*as perceived by the teachers*). The two major variables involved seem to be the students' general level of success in school and the students' tendency to reward the teachers in their personal contacts with them. The attachment students achieve both. The concern students have difficulty in school but are personally rewarding to the teachers, so the teachers become concerned about them and spend much time with them. The indifference students do not provide this kind of rewarding interpersonal contact, so that teachers develop indifference and do not spend much time with these children, even though they perceive them as needing extra help. The rejection students not only do not provide positive experiences in interpersonal contacts with the teachers; they also cause frequent classroom disturbances, and they generally are discipline problems. The teachers respond to this by rejecting the students to the point of wanting to get rid of them, and by projecting a number of traits, especially low abilities, onto them which they do not in fact possess (at least as a group). Teacher perceptions are generally accurate for the first three groups, but the children in the rejection group apparently are sufficiently threatening to the teachers to impair the accuracy of their perception and to cause them to project inappropriate and incorrect attributes to these students. This extends even to the teachers' judgments of the abilities, which are usually quite accurate.

All in all, the data from the previous study bear out implications drawn from earlier work by Silberman, Jenkins, and ourselves, although they provide much more direct data on some questions, particularly the question concerning the differences between concern and rejection students. They also provide some positive descriptors of the indifference students, whereas previous research had identified only low frequency of contact as a regular characteristic of this group. The characteristics mentioned above for the indifference group help explain just why the frequency of contact with these students is as low as it is (along with the Yarrow, Waxler, and Scott findings reviewed earlier). Across attitude groups, one of the major findings of this research is that the particular relationship between a teacher and an individual student is extremely important in affecting the teachers' attitudes toward that student, independent of such general student characteristics as achievement, race, sex, and so on. It appears that children who reward teachers are liked and sought after by them, while children who do not reward teachers are avoided and/or rejected by them. Also, although some relationships do exist, the attitude data are primarily independent of the achievement data; teachers' attitudes toward the students seem to be more dependent upon the personal qualities of the students and the reactions of the students to the teacher than upon the students' achievement. Expectations are quite closely tied to individual achievement for the most part, but attitudes are not. A high achiever is not necessarily going to be liked by a teacher, nor is a low achiever necessarily going to be rejected. Depending upon the student's responses to the teacher, a high achiever can just as easily be treated with indifference by the teacher, and a low achiever can easily become the object of teacher concern rather than rejection.

GENERAL TEACHER EXPECTATIONS

So far we have been discussing teachers' attitudes and expectations toward individual students. However, as was mentioned in Chapter 6, teachers' expectations toward their entire class are also important, perhaps more important in some cases than their expectations for individual students. Research by Good and Dembo (1973) has shown that teachers do differ in their general expectations for success or failure in teaching the curriculum to their students, and that these expectations affect the ways that they teach their students. Student behavior, then, is an important variable in the formation of teacher expectations. However at some point, rather early in the year, teacher expectations take on an independent reality for some students so that teachers overreact to the complex student behavior stimulus (rejection students are the prime example.) Theoretically, the formation of adverse teacher reactions can be explained in terms of S–R theory, but teacher overreaction (distortion of reality) seems to suggest that in some instances teacher expectations do function as a "true" independent variable (more on this in Chapter 10).

Subjects for this study were 163 teachers with at least one year of teaching experience who were working on an advanced degree in a summer education course. The teachers filled out a questionnaire which included a few items related to their expectations regarding success and failure in teaching curricular material to their students. One question asked the teachers to state the percentage of their students that they expected would fail or just get by in an average year. The alternatives provided for the teachers to check in answering this question were 10 percent, 15 percent, 25 percent, 35 percent, and 50 percent.

Sixty percent of the teachers chose the first alternative (10 percent), indicating generally positive expectations for teaching success. Another 25 percent chose the second alternative, 12 percent chose the third alternative, and the remaining 3 percent chose the last alternative (stating that they expected half of their students to fail or just get by). Thus although expectations were generally positive, 40 percent of the teachers were willing to admit that they expected at least 15 percent of their students to fail or just get by.

The responses to this first question might have been affected somewhat by social desirability, since responses to a related question suggested a somewhat less favorable picture. This second question asked the teachers to state the percentage of students in their classes that would "really master the material you present." Thus, in this question the teachers were asked to say how many students they really expected to succeed with, while in the first question they were asked how many they thought would fail. The response alternatives provided to this second question were: 15 percent, 25 percent, 45 percent, 70 percent, 95 percent.

In contrast to the responses to the first question, which were bunched in the first two alternatives, the teachers' responses to this second question were more spread out. The numbers of teachers who responded to each of the five alternatives listed above were, respectively, 20 percent, 16 percent, 21 percent, 37 percent, and 6 percent.

Thus 36 percent of the teachers expected that only a fourth of their students would "really master the material," and more than half of the teachers expected that only 45 percent of the students would do so. The teachers generally expected a normal distribution in student mastery of material that they presumably were to *learn*. Only 6 percent of the teachers expected to see 95 percent of their students "really master the material."

Earlier we suggested that less competent or insecure teachers might lean on the high achievers in order to provide reinforcement. Another question in the Good and Dembo data is related to this idea. The question began by stating that teachers often attempt to secure model answers from students in order to get a discussion started, to illustrate correct answers, or to motivate the class. The teachers were then asked what percentage of the class could be depended upon to provide such model responses if called upon to do so. In responding to this question, 39 percent of the teachers said that only the top 10 percent of the students could do so, and another 31 percent said that only the top 20 percent of the students could do so. Thus 70 percent of this sample of teachers thought that only one-fifth of their students could be depended upon to come up with an appropriate answer in the circumstance mentioned.

Other questions were concerned with teacher strategies for dealing with low achievers.

The teachers were asked to choose which of the following four alternative methods of dealing with lows would be appropriate:

1. Call upon lows less often than other students, but call upon them when they are likely to know the answer.
2. Call upon lows equally without concern for whether they know the answer.

3. Call upon lows more often than other students, but call upon them when they are likely to know the answer.
4. Call upon them equally, but call upon them when they are likely to know the answer.

The numbers of teachers selecting these four alternatives were, respectively, 34 percent, 4 percent, 3 percent, and 59 percent. Thus, 96 percent of the teachers favored calling on lows only when they were pretty sure that lows knew the answer, and only 4 percent suggested calling on lows without taking this factor into account. This is probably an appropriate strategy for dealing with lows who lack confidence and are hesitant to participate, but it is probably less appropriate for lows who are uninhibited or who are underachieving because of poor motivation.

The 34 percent of teachers who would call upon lows less often in addition to calling on them only when they probably knew the answer are the ones most likely to show generalized expectation effects and to teach lows inappropriately. The largest group of teachers opted for calling on lows equally, but only when they were likely to know the answer. Only 3 percent of the teachers suggested calling on lows *more* often than other students, even though this response alternative also mentioned calling on them only when they were likely to know the answer. Thus, it seems that teachers in general hesitate to put lows "on the spot" very often, *even when they think they know the answer.*

These interview data tie in with the behavioral data from several studies showing that teachers usually do not compensate for differences between high and low achieving students in rates of seeking response opportunities and initiating contact with teachers. In fact, data on the measure of "direct questions" usually follow the pattern suggested in the Good and Dembo questionnaire data: Usually there is no group difference, and when there is a difference it tends to favor the highs over the lows, despite the fact that highs always call out more and answer more open questions.

These questionnaire data also suggest that teachers seem to be well aware of the need for lows to achieve success experiences, but to be much less aware of the need for lows to be prodded into regular participation in classroom interchanges by being called on more often.

The Good and Dembo questionnaire data are of unknown generalizability, because the teachers involved may not have been representative of teachers in general and because the specific questions included in the questionnaire might have forced responses which would not have appeared in a differently worded questionnaire. However, to the extent that they are generalizable, they suggest that most teachers routinely expect sizable numbers of their students to fail or just to get by in learning the curriculum, and that less than half of the teachers expect their students really to master the material.

The teachers also tend to feel that only the top 20 percent or so of their students can be depended upon to give a good answer, to begin a discussion, or to provide a model for classmates. Finally, they tend to agree that low achievers need to be brought along slowly and carefully, and that they should be called on only when they probably know the answer. Thirty-four percent of the teachers believe, in addition, that low achievers should be called on less frequently than other students.

It is tempting to speculate about the reasons for these beliefs. Depending on which aspect you wish to stress, the data can be interpreted as showing teachers to be realistic in their expectations and at least partially appropriate in their strategies for dealing with low achievers, or they can be interpreted as showing teachers to be cynical or unnecessarily pessimistic in their expectations and to be uncomfortable in dealing with low achievers or to reject and to avoid them. In any case, it is clear that teachers differ considerably in the kinds of general expectations for success and failure that they hold for their own teaching.

As stated previously, we believe that this general expectation probably affects the degree of actual success that teachers achieve in meeting their objectives. Some data already exist to support this contention, particularly the studies by Palardy and by Doyle, Hancock, and Kifer reviewed earlier. The Palardy study showed that teachers who expected boys to learn to read as well as girls did better with boys than teachers who did not expect boys to do so well as girls, and the Doyle, Hancock, and Kifer study showed that teachers who generally overestimated their children's IQ's and had generally high expectations were more successful in teaching the curriculum to their students than were teachers who had lower expectations.

This general expectation factor is being investigated in a large-scale study of teacher effectiveness in the early elementary grades (Brophy, 1973).

SUMMARY

In contrast to the previous chapter which dealt with observed behavioral reactions of teachers to student behavior in the classroom, the present chapter discussed the findings of teacher questionnaire and interview studies. Although less direct than the behavioral studies, these studies are helpful in identifying the dynamics underlying dyadic teacher-student interaction and in isolating the student characteristics that teachers attend to and use in forming impressions about students.

Several studies used Feshbach's story descriptions and agreed in finding that teachers and student teachers tend to prefer rigid, conforming, and orderly students to those who are more assertive and independent. Other studies using different methods have borne out these results, and also the finding that teacher preferences for students are partially mediated by societal sex roles. That is, characteristics that are associated with boys are more preferred or at least tolerated in boys than in girls, and vice versa.

Data from several studies suggest that students who have established a well-formed and somewhat rigid set of expectations and attitudes in their teachers tend to produce negative teacher reactions if they begin to behave in ways that do not fit these well-established expectations or attitudes, even when their behavior change is in a positive direction. These data, which go against common sense expectations, suggest that teacher attitudes and expectations toward students function as defense mechanisms (among other things), so that a negative teacher response is produced when their veracity is called into question. This includes changes for the better in students from whom the teacher expects only negative behavior and/or failure.

Studies of teacher accuracy in judging student ability and other characteristics have produced mixed results, although the ones dealing with student ability have shown generally impressive correlations between teacher rankings and student ability as measured by objective tests. However, analyses of teachers who differed in their degree of accuracy have shown that the more accurate teachers tend to be better all around teachers as judged by process observation measures. Teachers' impressions of students tend .to be quite stable, although part of this stability is probably due to a strong primacy effect that has been observed: teachers form strong first impressions of students on the basis of their early contacts with them, and these impressions tend to stay with the teachers in most instances. This is partly because these first impressions are usually accurate, judging by the correlations between early impressions and tested abilities later in the year, but they are not always accurate and, in particular, are likely to be inaccurate when the student is the type of student whom the teacher responds to with rejection. Apparently, teachers form a generalized negative halo effect about rejection group students, so that they see them as "all bad," regardless of their objective characteristics.

A study by Willis (1972) designed to discover the student attributes that first-grade teachers attend to and use in forming impressions about students' achievement potential revealed that teachers can make quite accurate achievement potential judgments after only a few days of experience with the children, although their accuracy is not so high as it is after they have received readiness test information. The data also revealed that the teachers can accurately distinguish between ability and readiness, identifying those students who have high readiness but lower ability because they have been well-coached at home and also those students who have high ability but low readiness because they have received little or no preparation for school in the home.

Some of these teachers were also questioned about children whom they assigned to the four attitude groups of attachment, concern, indifference, and rejection. These data showed that the attachment students, as previously hypothesized, are especially likely to be the kind of high achieving and conforming students who frequently reward teachers. Also, as previously hypothesized, the concern and rejection students, while similar in some ways, differ in certain key variables that make a difference to the teachers. Concern students tend to be of low ability but to be dependent students who come to the teachers for help and who "reward" them by being heavily dependent upon them. In contrast, the rejection students tend to be of somewhat higher ability but to have negative attitudes toward school and teachers as well as a tendency to create discipline problems in the classroom through disruptive behavior. Because these students not only cause discipline problems but also fail to provide the teacher with rewarding experiences in their interactions with them, they tend to be rejected, even though many of them are high ability students. The indifference students appear to be students who do not respond at all or at least do not respond favorably to early teacher overtures in dyadic interactions, so that they condition the teachers to avoid them in the future. Teachers accurately perceive the personal characteristics and individual needs of such students, but, in contrast to their reactions to concern students, they respond with indifference, apparently because these students "turn them off" by responding to them with indifference or hostility.

In addition to the many studies of teacher expectations about individual students, Good and Dembo (1973) studied teacher expectations for the general performance of students in their classrooms. They discovered that teachers differed in their expectations, some expecting to succeed with most or all of the class and some expecting to succeed with only a small part of the class. When questioned about how they would handle certain situations, teachers' responses were related to their expectation statements. Teachers were especially likely to say that they would call upon low expectation students only when they were pretty sure that the students knew the answer, and that they would hesitate to push such students for fear of embarrassing them before their classmates. These data suggest that teachers are likely to treat low expectation students inappropriately, especially in public response opportunity situations. This probably explains the consistent finding that low expectation students have fewer public response opportunities than high expectation students, at least after the first few grades. The data also suggest that teachers having a low expectation for the class in general, such as teachers working in low SES schools where morale is poor and where no one is expected to achieve very highly, are likely to be heavily influenced by their expectations to the point that their teaching style is more appropriately characterized as custodial rather than instructive.

chapter 7

The Influence of the Sex of the Teacher and Student on Classroom Behavior

So far we have discussed how teachers form primarily cognitive expectations and primarily affective attitudes toward their students on the basis of the student characteristics that they perceive. Except for the sections on group characteristics (sex, SES, race) in Chapter 1, we have focused so far upon *individual* student differences in achievement and personal attributes. In the present chapter we will discuss at length the effects of the *group* variable of the sex of the students upon teacher perceptions and teacher treatment of students. We will also investigate the teacher's sex as a relevant variable in classroom interaction, giving particular attention to the often-voiced hypothesis that the sex of the teacher and the student should interact such that male teachers will be more successful with male students and female teachers with female students.

Like almost everyone else in our society, teachers enter their classrooms with certain preconceived notions about the differences between boys and girls. Of all the variables that can be used to divide people into groups, sex is probably the most fundamental and pervasive. Boy and girl babies are treated differently (and in some ways begin to act differently) practically from the time they emerge from the womb. We are taught to believe that boys will be aggressive, physically active, and interested in the manipulation of physical objects, while girls will be quieter, more conforming, and more interested in verbal and symbolic activities. The stereotypes are accurate to some degree, since they are borne out by research data on children's behavior and interests (Maccoby, 1966).

There has been periodic speculation about the explanation for these sex differences and the implications they may have for school organization and teacher training. As far back as 1909, Ayres (1909) expressed concern about the lower reading achievement and greater incidence of reading problems in boys in the elementary grades. Impassioned concern about this and related problems has been expressed in volumes such as *Reading Rights for Boys* (Austin, Clark, and Fitchett, 1971) and *The Feminized Male* (Sexton, 1969). Is all this concern justified?

SEX DIFFERENCES IN ACHIEVEMENT IN ELEMENTARY SCHOOL

The problem does seem to be real enough. Several studies carried out in this country have shown that, even though there is no sex difference in general intelligence or ability, girls tend to outperform boys in the early elementary grades, especially in reading and other verbal skills (Gates, 1961; Maccoby, 1966; Stroud and Lindquist, 1942). Also, boys are much more frequently referred for remedial reading help and much more frequently diagnosed as having reading or learning disabilities (Blom, 1971).

Writers attempting to explain these sex differences have cited three main factors, either singly or in combination: there is a sex difference in maturation that favors girls over boys; a conflict exists between the sex-role expectations that our culture applies to boys and the student-role expectations that schools apply to all students; and the statistics show that the great majority of early elementary school teachers are female.

Although girls do mature earlier than boys in some areas, there is little reason to postulate a maturational difference in capacity for learning to read in the early grades. As we shall show below, boys can learn to read just as well as girls, if they are properly motivated and taught by teachers who expect them to do well.

Maturation might have an indirect effect, however, to the extent that it affects such factors as physical hyperactivity, short attention span, or other stylistic variables that might affect school learning. It does appear that boys have more difficulty than girls in maintaining the physical inactivity and the sustained attention to verbal instruction that school requires. However, it remains unclear as to how much if any of this difference is due to maturation. Sex differences on such stylistic variables may result from the differential socialization and experiences to which boys and girls are exposed in our society. Cross-cultural research has shown that most sex differences, including many that are ordinarily thought of as biological, are acquired through deliberate instruction or unconscious conditioning during the process of becoming socialized to one's culture.

In contrast to the relatively weak case for maturation, there is considerable evidence to support the idea that sex differences in school performance can be explained by the relative compatibility of sex-role expectations and student-role expections. The behavior expected of students in the early elementary grades is much more compatible with the "nice little girl" stereotype than it is with the attributes and behavior expected of boys in our society. Furthermore, this fact is as clear to children as it is to adult psychologists and educators. Research by several different investigators (Brophy and Laosa, 1971; Kagan, 1964; Kellogg, 1969; Stein and Smithells, 1969) has shown that children of both sexes associate school and school-related activities, especially those connected with reading, with the feminine sex role. That is, both boys and girls see school as a female-oriented institution. Also, in the early elementary grades, boys are much more likely than girls to reject their teachers and to have negative attitudes toward school (Gregersen and Travers, 1968).

These attitudes apparently affect the way boys and girls approach school-related tasks. Stein, Pohly, and Mueller (1969) investigated the reactions of sixth-grade boys and girls to tasks that had been labeled as either masculine or feminine. They found that children of each sex thought that it was more important to do better on tasks defined as appropriate for their sex, and that they expected to do better on these tasks. In addition, the labels carried over into performance for boys, who actually did do better on the tasks labeled as masculine.

In a follow-up study, Stein (1971) investigated sixth and ninth graders' reactions to three school subjects identified as masculine (mechanical, athletic, and math) and three identified as feminine (reading, artistic, and social skills). Again, the students stated that they felt it was more important to do better in the subjects associated with their sex and that they expected to do better in these subjects. They also stated that they would be satisfied with a lower performance in the subjects associated with the opposite sex.

Research by Graf and Riddell (1972) showed that sexual appropriateness of the task affects performance as well as attitude. In this study, male and female college students were presented with essentially the same math problem, except that sometimes it was presented in terms of buying fabric to make a dress and at other times in terms of computing charges from a stockbroker's sale. There were no sex differences in success rates in solving the problem, although there was a nonsignificant trend for more males to solve the male version of the problem and more females to solve the female version. There were significant differences, however, in the time taken to solve the problem. Males averaged 67.5 seconds to solve the yardage problem and 70.4 seconds to solve the stock problem, while the corresponding figures for females were 69.5 seconds and 96.3 seconds. Thus females could solve the problem as quickly as males when it was presented in a context familiar to females, but not when it was presented in a context unfamiliar to females. These data confirm earlier findings by Milton (1958) showing that, within both sexes, the more masculine individuals are better at solving mathematical problems but that the influence of sex typing on females disappears when the content of the problem is made relevant to the female role.

All of the studies reviewed in this section show that there may be sex differences either in general achievement or in achievement in particular content areas, but they also strongly suggest that these sex differences result from culturally determined sex roles rather than from biological differences between the sexes.

Cross-Cultural Data

Several cross-cultural studies also suggest that the degree to which the student role is identified with either the male or the female sex role is an important determinant of school success. Two studies carried out in French-Canadian schools (Lambert, 1968; Wisenthal, 1968) found no sex difference in reading attainment. These schools have sexually segregated classes, with boys being taught by male teachers in what is described as a "male" environment with "male" attitudes. Kagan (1969) also reported no differences between boys and girls in the early grades in a school on the island of Hokkaido in northern Japan. He reported that a majority of the early elementary school teachers there are male but did not report on the local relationship between sex-role expectations and the role of the student in school.

Peck (1971) presented data on socioeconomic status and sex differences in aptitude and achievement in seven countries. Data were taken in Brazil, England, Italy, Mexico, Yugoslavia, and in two parts of the United States. Although the usual SES differences were observed, there were no systematic sex differences on objective tests of aptitude and achievement in either ten-year-olds or fourteen-year-olds, nor were there any consistent trends. These data provide more evidence that observed sex differences within a given country are the result of sex-role learning and no biological sex differences. Interestingly, in most countries the earlier reported tendency for teachers to "downgrade" boys by marking them lower than their measured achievement would predict was observed in most countries, despite the lack of sex differences in aptitude or measured achievement. This tendency was especially marked in the United States at both locations.

The cross-cultural research that demonstrated most clearly that sex differences in early school achievement are culturally determined was the study by Preston (1962) and by Johnson (1972). Preston compared the reading achievement of fourth- and sixth-grade German and American students and found that the sex difference data usually seen in our country were reversed in Germany. The German boys outperformed the German girls in reading achievement and had fewer problems of reading disability or reading retardation than the German girls. In attempting to explain these data, Preston mentioned two main possibilities: the majority of teachers were male, and reading and school success are more closely identified with the male role in Germany than in this country.

Johnson (1972) compared several aspects of reading achievement in second, fourth, and fifth grade students in the United States, England, Canada, and Nigeria (all English-speaking nations). He found that girls did better in the United States and Canada, but that boys did better in England and Nigeria. The latter countries have more male elementary teachers than the United States and Canada, but, like Germany, they also stress school achievement as an expectation for young males.

Summing up the data reviewed so far, we note that better reading performance by boys has been associated with the presence of male teachers and with culturally determined sex-role expectations that make reading and school achievement compatible with the male role rather than defining them as primarily female.

DO FEMALE TEACHERS DISCRIMINATE AGAINST BOYS?

As mentioned previously, writers concerned about the relatively poor achievement of boys in our early elementary grades have cited not only possible maturational differences and the conflict between the student role and the male role as our society defines it; they have also pointed to the fact that the vast majority of our early elementary school teachers are women. Many believe that this factor is primarily responsible for the tendency for school to be defined as a female-oriented institution. An implication of this line of reasoning is that, if we had more male teachers working in the early elementary grades, the achievement of boys would improve and the tendency of children of both sexes to see school as a primarily female institution would disappear.

The call for more male elementary teachers is sometimes supported by other reasons than concern about school being identified as a female-oriented institution. Many writers have suggested that women are less able to handle boys effectively because they are less familiar with their attitudes and values and less able to empathize with them. Still others have gone further and suggested that women discriminate against boys, being predisposed to treat them ineffectively and unfairly either out of ignorance or outright hostility. To support this view, these writers cite many studies of teachers' attitudes and behavior toward boys and girls. These studies can be interpreted as showing that teachers are biased against boys, are unable to teach them effectively, or are "sexist" in trying to force feminine values upon them. But this is only one interpretation. As we shall show later, the same data can be interpreted in other ways that do not involve the idea that female teachers discriminate against boys or are incapable of handling them appropriately. First, however, let us look at the data usually cited as evidence of the need for more male teachers in the elementary grades.

Several studies have shown that female teachers or student teachers are more favorably disposed toward girls and female qualities than toward boys and male qualities (Arnold, 1968; Datta, Schaefer, and Davis, 1968; Jackson, Silberman, and Wolfson, 1969). Kaplan (1952) found that the aggressive child was annoying to almost three-fourths of the elementary teachers (primarily female) surveyed. Feshbach (1969), in a study of student teachers' preferences for different kinds of children as students in their classes, found that teachers preferred rigid, conforming, orderly, dependent, passive, and acquiescent children over flexible, nonconforming, untidy, independent, active, and assertive children. Not only did they prefer to have such children in their classrooms; they also believed that such children would be more popular among their peers and would be more generous in their interactions with peers. These attitudes were expressed despite a slight tendency for the student teachers to see the boys as more intelligent than the girls.

The latter finding from Feshbach's study is something of an exception. Ordinarily, whenever a sex difference is discovered in teachers' ratings or expectations for boys and girls, the girls come out ahead. Lehman and Witty (1928) found that teachers generally overrated girls and underrated boys. This same finding was seen in the previously discussed studies by Palardy (1969), who asked first-grade teachers to express their expectations regarding reading achievement in the first grade, and by Doyle, Hancock, and Kifer (1972), who asked teachers to estimate the IQ's of the boys and girls in their classrooms. Thus when a sex difference is operating it appears that teachers are more likely to overrate the intelligence and potential of girls and underrate the intelligence and potential of boys.

Similar findings have been discovered in studies of grading practices. Boys receive lower grades even though there are no consistent sex differences in measured achievement (McCandless, Roberts, and Starnes, 1972; Peck, 1971). Carter (1952), studying six algebra classes taught by female teachers, found that boys were assigned lower grades than their measured achievement would indicate. Carter also found this tendency in classes taught by male teachers, but here the downgrading of boys was much less. Garner (1935) reported similar findings.

Findings concerning grades are somewhat curious in view of the fact that several of the studies reviewed in the previous chapter as well as a study by Kremer (1965) suggest that teachers prefer students who are appropriately sex typed to students who are not. Kremer asked junior high school teachers to select adjectives that they felt would be descriptive of good male and female students. Their adjective descriptions showed striking sex typing. The adjectives most frequently used to describe "good" male students were: active, adventurous, aggressive, assertive, curious, energetic, enterprising, frank, independent, and inventive. In contrast, the adjectives most frequently used to describe the typical "good" female student were: appreciative, calm, conscientious, considerate, cooperative, mannerly, poised, sensitive, dependable, efficient, mature, obliging, and thorough. These data suggest that teachers should generally prefer and be likely to give the highest grades to students who most nearly fit these ideal types. This apparently is the case for girls, but not for boys. Although teachers may value curiosity, frankness, independence, and inventiveness, they tend to reject boys that they perceive as too assertive or aggressive. Thus, to the extent that a teacher's grading is influenced by sex typing in her students, she is more likely to be positively disposed towards a "normally" sex-typed girl than towards a "normally" sex-typed boy.

Hadley (1954), studying twenty classrooms taught by female teachers, found that the teachers rated the students they liked best higher than the students they liked least. Also, the girl students in this study were generally both more liked and given higher grades than the boys.

One possible explanation for such findings is that teachers are affected by student conduct when assigning grades in academic subjects. Research by St. John (1932) and by Hess, Shipman, Brophy, and Bear (1969) showed that conduct grades were much more highly correlated with academic subject grades for boys than for girls, and that boys received lower grades on their report cards than their measured achievement at the end of the year would indicate. It should be noted that these data do not necessarily indicate teacher discrimination against boys. If teacher grades are based primarily upon test scores from teacher-made tests given during the school year, and if boys do less well on these tests than girls (because of lesser effort, lesser motivation, or whatever), then the teachers' grades would be justified, despite the boys' performance on achievement tests given at the end of the year.

The studies reviewed so far are often cited as evidence that female teachers discriminate against boys, either because of their sex per se or because of their behavior. A different set of investigations is often cited as evidence that (female) teachers in the early elementary grades cannot teach boys so successfully as they teach girls.

ARE FEMALE TEACHERS INEFFECTIVE WITH BOYS?

Innovative Methods of Teaching To Help Boys

Several studies have been conducted which involved innovations in teaching young boys but which did not include the use of male teachers.

Dykstra (1967) experimented with several methods of teaching reading in grades one and two. He reported that, regardless of method, girls were more ready to read on entrance into the classroom and were more successful in reading achievement (although the girls' achievement advantage disappeared when scores were adjusted for their initial advantage in readiness). Thus none of the methods tried succeeded in bringing boys' reading up to par with that of girls.

Strickler and Phillips (1970) experimented at the kindergarten level, using two all-boy classes, two all-girl classes, and two mixed boy-girl classes, one with male-oriented activities. The latter included wrestling and large-muscle physical exercises, male tasks such as building and repairing, male-oriented crafts, and work benches and tools. Adult male figures were also involved with the cooperation of male teachers, administrators, and community resource persons. The data revealed a more positive and enthusiastic attitude towards school on the part of the boys in the all-boy classes, as evidenced by increased attendance and class participation and better class morale. Fewer emotional problems were observed in both the all-boy and the all-girl classes. This was believed to result from the stronger emphasis placed on the particular needs of each sex in these segregated classes. The results were not as strong in the boy-oriented mixed classes, although these classes seemed more relaxed, the boys seemed to enjoy them and participate more, and the girls seemed to enjoy the program as much as the boys. Thus, this experiment produced evidence of improvements on several affective measures, although no achievement improvement was reported. The authors also report improvements in the attitudes towards sex-typed behavior on the part of the teachers, who learned to accept the idea that boys generally will be more active and less neat than girls.

Similar results were obtained in a similar experiment by Ring (1970). This involved an all-boy first-grade class with the classroom and curriculum planned particularly to meet the needs of boys. Ring reports notable improvements in affective measures of both the students' attitudes towards school and the teachers' attitudes toward sex-typed behaviors. Again, however, no evidence that the innovations had produced improved achievement is reported. Thus this study and the previous one showed that sex-segregated classes can lead to improved school attitudes in both boys and girls and to improvement in teacher acceptance of male sex-typed behavior, although neither study produced evidence that boys show improved achievement in these classes. The following series of studies does show such achievement effects, however.

Stanchfield (1969) attempted several innovations in first-grade reading instruction aimed at improving the reading achievement of boys. In one study the children were segregated into different classes by sex (but otherwise taught with traditional methods and materials). Despite this innovation, the reading achievement of the boys was no different than it had been earlier. The experiment was repeated the following year, this time with an additional innovation: the boys' classes used readers containing stories especially written to appeal to boys' interests. This time the achievement scores suggested some slight improvement, but it was not strong enough to reach statistical significance.

Encouraged by these findings, Stanchfield and her associates worked to adapt the reading materials (they were judged to be interesting to the boys but too difficult for beginning reading), and to develop a variety of support materials to be used in addition to the readers themselves. These involved flannel board activities and puppets, listening skills exercises, practice exercises planned for use by individual children, slides, and a variety of media. Eventually this special early reading system, originally written specifically for boys, was used in Los Angeles schools for introductory reading with boys and girls. This time very encouraging results were achieved: both boys and girls in the experimental group got higher reading scores than control groups using the state texts. This meant, among other things, that the boys in the experimental group scored higher than both the boys and the girls in the control group (Stanchfield, 1973). Subsequent work involved extending the program down to the kindergarten level, and again the experimental children of both sexes achieved significantly higher scores than the control group children. Use of the program in Los Angeles city schools over the last several years has produced high reading achievement scores in the children and eliminated sex differences in the reading scores of the boys and girls involved (Stanchfield, 1973).

Stanchfield's research and development, which has continued over a ten-year period, has probably been the most intensive and successful of the intervention approaches designed to reduce the high rates of difficulty that young boys typically have in American schools. It might have been helpful if, in addition to providing stories of interest to boys, the investigators had also added stories, models, or other stimuli calculated to help the boys associate reading as a male activity.

This suggestion stems from a study by McCracken (1973), which showed that sex segregation alone can reduce the tendency for boys to see reading as a female activity. This study compared boys taught in all-male classes in the first three grades with control boys taught in coeducational classes (all boys were taught by female teachers), using a task designed to discover whether books, word and letter cards, and other symbols associated with reading were considered to be male or female by the boys. All significant group differences in this study showed that boys in the coeducational classes were more likely than boys in the all-male classes to associate reading-related items with the female sex role. However, significant differences appeared mostly on the items actually used in the grades (reader, phonics workbook, library card), and did not generalize to other reading symbols, particularly those associated with adults (newspapers, magazines, novels). Thus, while sex segregation alone did have some effects on the sex typing of reading, a program featuring a more systematic attempt to portray reading as an activity appropriate to males might have had stronger effects.

Materials of greater interest to boys might improve their attention during reading groups. Turnure and Samuels (1972), in a study of the reading group attentiveness of first graders, found that the girls were more attentive than the boys even though there was no sex difference in reading readiness. Furthermore, attentiveness scores from the group observations were correlated with reading achievement scores taken at the end of the year. Girls achieved more than boys, and the more attentive children achieved more than the less attentive children within both sexes. Low attentiveness was a particular problem for the boys, however.

A study by Glick (1972) showed the particular importance of early reading for boys in our culture. To assess the meaning and effects of success or failure in reading in the early grades, Glick studied general self-concept, academic self-concept, attitudes toward teachers, attitudes toward school, attitudes toward peers, perceived parental behavior, and attributed peer interaction in the classroom. Comparisons were made within sex between children who had made gains in reading versus those who had not. The general findings were that when girls made good gains in reading, this led to improvements in other areas, but failure to make good gains did not lead to problems in other areas. In contrast, good gains in reading did not lead to good gains in other areas for boys, but failures in reading did lead to trouble in other areas. More specifically, the boys who had not made good reading gains became more unfavorable in their attitudes toward teachers and peers. Meanwhile, girls who had made gains in reading showed positive changes in attitudes toward teachers, peers, and school in general. Changes in self-reports of parental behavior were mixed for good male readers but primarily negative for poor male readers, while these parental perceptions were primarily positive for both good and poor female readers. Thus, in general, reading success had limited good effects for boys while failure had widespread negative effects. Meanwhile, reading success had widespread good effects for girls while failure had only limited negative effects. These data point up the particular importance of developing better methods to minimize failure in early reading among boys in our culture.

Others have also tried homogeneous grouping by sex, with mixed and mostly negative results. Lyles (1966) reported that boys in all-male classes had slightly better achievement in language arts and math than boys in control classes, but the differences were not significant. The teachers were favorable to the homogeneous grouping arrangement, however, because they felt that it made for fewer discipline problems, greater individualization of material to student interest, better attendance, less classroom withdrawal, and a generally better classroom atmosphere. Of twenty-one teachers surveyed, sixteen preferred the sex segregated classes, two were impartial, and three preferred mixed classes.

Tagatz (1966), however, produced results in flat contradiction to those of Lyles. In this study segregation of first and second graders by sex made no difference whatever in measured abilities or personality measures, and the teachers generally were opposed to the idea of sex segregated classrooms. It should be noted that self-fulfilling prophecy phenomena might have been at work in these two studies; perhaps the differences occurred because the teachers in Lyles's study were favorable to the idea while those in the Tagatz study were not.

Another study (Kernkamp and Price, 1972; Price and Rosemeier, 1972) produced mixed results. In this study, first graders were taught in all-boy or all-girl classes for a year, and then were taught coeducationally the following year. The same teachers taught both years. Standardized achievement data showed no differences on the Gates Reading Test or on four of the five language arts subtests of the Stanford Achievement Test. However, the all-boy classes did better than the controls on the spelling subtest of the Stanford Achievement Test and also on the total reading score from this test. Thus, there was at least some evidence of advantage to the boys in the sex segregated classes. However, girls outperformed the boys in both the experimental and control groups on the Stanford arithmetic test, so that the advantage to the experimental-group boys was confined to only certain aspects of language arts.

Classroom observations suggested that the homogeneous grouping was of benefit to the boys but not to the girls. The boys in the experimental classes showed more positive task behavior than the boys in the control classes. Also, the authors felt that the experimental boys were less hesitant and shy about speaking up in the classroom, less easily discouraged, less likely to drop a task quickly, and less likely to leave their seats to socialize or to investigate in the classroom. They also presented fewer behavior problems than the control boys, who frequently caused disruptions by teasing the girls. Despite the latter observation, the authors felt that the girls dominated the coeducational classes, inhibiting the boys both academically and socially. The data for girls suggest that the sex segregated classes were less beneficial for them than the coeducational classes. The all-girl classes showed generally less distraction and better concentration, but these gains were achieved at the expense of reduced verbal assertiveness and gregariousness and less positive task-oriented behavior. In concluding, the authors suggested that the boys did better in an open structure where there was less concern for time, while the girls seemed to be more positively task oriented, more apprehensive about conformity, and more in need of structure. The girls wanted the teachers to tell them what to do next, while the boys wanted to make suggestions themselves.

Taken together, the data on sex segregation do not seem to justify this rather radical intervention strategy, since the effects are weak in intensity and mixed in direction. One innovation seemingly worthy of more attention is the attempt to reach boys by providing them with reading materials that they can identify with and find interesting. Note that Stanchfield began to get positive results when this innovation was added, even though no positive results were obtained previously by using sex segregated classes alone. The interest factor appears to be especially important for boys. Asher and Markell (1973) studied the degree of interest that fifth graders had in various topics and then gave them passages to read on these topics. They then tested them on the material, analyzing to see what relationship existed between interest in the material and scores on the reading comprehension test. Comprehension scores were higher for high-interest material than for low-interest material in both sexes, but in girls the difference was small and nonsignificant. Thus it is especially important to see that boys are provided with reading materials which will capture their interests.

Most of the data reviewed so far suggest that girls outperform boys in early reading in our society, regardless of attempts by the (female) teachers or the school to change this. However, data from Stanchfield's project show that the poor performance of boys is not necessary or unchangeable. The previously described work by Palardy (1969) is another example. He showed that boys achieved as well as girls when their teachers expected them to do so, but they did not match the girls' achievement when their teachers expected them to do less well. Thus teacher expectations partially determine the reading achievement of first-grade boys.

Also, although Dykstra (1967) did report an initial readiness advantage for the girls when they began first grade, this readiness advantage has not appeared in several other investigations. Studies by Felsenthal (1970), Konski (1951), and McNeil (1964) all reported no initial difference between boys and girls in reading readiness at the beginning of reading instruction. Nevertheless, in all three of these studies the girls outperformed the boys after a year of reading instruction by (female) first-grade teachers.

Several experiments suggest that self-paced, individualized learning strategies might be more successful with boys than the more traditionally used methods. Two of these were conducted at the level of higher education rather than at the level of beginning reading, but they are instructive nonetheless. Thrash and Hapkiewicz

(1973) evaluated a mastery learning strategy for teaching educational psychology to undergraduate and inservice teachers. They found that the students were generally favorable to the mastery learning approach (especially the undergraduates), and that males rated it significantly more highly than females. Thus, this individualistic strategy was especially popular with males. A second experiment, by Blitz and Smith (1973), involved dentistry students taking a course in oral pathology. Half took the course with a programmed text approach and half took it through computer assisted instruction. Course performance was then related to the personal attributes of the students. It was found that the more deferent, orderly, nurturant, and endurant students performed better with the programmed text, while the more aggressive students performed better in computer assisted instruction. These findings suggest that boys would be particularly amenable to computer assisted instruction.

This was precisely what was found by Fletcher and Atkinson (1972), who studied the reading achievement of first-grade boys and girls taught either with traditional methods or with computer assisted instruction. Their data suggest that computer assisted instruction was more effective with both girls and boys, but especially with boys. Thus there appears to be something about the individualistic learning styles and/or the special equipment involved in computer assisted instruction that appeals especially to male learners. This effect has been observed both in first graders and in college students.

The experiment by McNeil (1964) was particularly instructive on this point. After determining that there was no initial difference in reading readiness between kindergarten boys and girls, McNeil used a specially developed method of programmed individual instruction to teach the children beginning reading. The boys and girls made similar gains in this program, with the boys actually doing slightly better. Thus the children entered first grade with the boys being equal or even a little ahead of the girls in their progress in learning to read. Yet, after a year of instruction in a traditional first grade taught by female teachers, the girls were significantly ahead of the boys.

Children's Perception of Teachers' Behavior Toward Boys and Girls

These data give rise to speculation about why most (female) teachers in the early elementary grades do not produce so much achievement in boys as they do in girls. McNeil himself tried to develop an answer to this question by gathering data on the teachers' and students' perceptions. He found that teachers rated the boys lower than the girls on readiness and motivation, suggesting that they probably had lower expectations for the boys' achievement in the first grade. The child perception data showed that the children thought that the boys more frequently received warnings and criticism from the teachers than the girls, and that the boys got fewer opportunities to read during reading instruction. In a related study by Davis and

Slobodian (1967), interviews with first-grade children yielded similar results. Boys were perceived as receiving more negative comments from teachers, as getting fewer opportunities to read, and as being poorer readers than girls. Thus in two separate studies, first-grade children agreed that boys received more criticism from teachers and received fewer opportunities to read during reading instruction.

Davis and Slobodian checked out the accuracy of these child perceptions in their study by collecting observational data on reading groups in the classroom involved. The observational data did not bear out the children's beliefs. The teachers gave boys and girls equal opportunity to read and respond during reading instruction. Furthermore, there were no sex differences in the teachers' rates of accepting, rejecting, or ignoring student contributions, nor in their response to disruption of the reading group, even though the boys interrupted many more times than the girls.

Similar behavioral data were reported by Good and Brophy (1971a). Again, there were no significant differences in the ways teachers treated boys and girls in first-grade reading groups. Sex differences in reading groups were also investigated in our first- and second-grade follow-up studies. In the first-grade follow-up (Evertson, Brophy, and Good, 1972), there were no statistically significant sex differences in interaction patterns during reading groups, even though some of the typically found sex differences appeared in the data for general class activities. The second-grade follow-up (Evertson, Brophy, and Good, 1973), revealed only one statistically significant reading group sex difference: The teachers were more likely to stay with girls following initial failures but more likely to give the answer or move on to someone else following an initial failure by a boy. Other reading group measures, dealing with such factors as the frequency of interaction and the amount of praise and criticism directed at the students, showed no significant sex difference. Thus it appears that the differential reading achievement of boys and girls in the early grades cannot be explained by differential treatment during reading instruction, despite the beliefs of the children. The sex of the student appears to be unrelated to teacher behavior during reading instruction, at least for teacher behaviors which have been studied to date.

If teachers do not discriminate against boys in first-grade reading instruction, why do the children think that they do? The answer probably lies in the limited ability of first-grade children to discriminate particular teacher behavior during reading groups from more general teacher behavior and from their own perceptions of teachers. Given some of the teacher attitude data reviewed above, and given the sex differences in interaction patterns with teachers during general class activities (to be reviewed in the following sections), it is likely that young children of both sexes come to see girls as more preferred by teachers and more successful in school than boys. Thus even though there may be no actual differences in the ways teachers treat boys and girls during reading instruction, young children are likely to *believe* that such differences exist if they believe that in general, teachers favor girls and discriminate against boys.

FEMALE TEACHERS' BEHAVIORAL INTERACTIONS WITH BOYS AND GIRLS

Studies by many investigators, including some by ourselves and our colleagues, have revealed certain systematic differences in the amount and kinds of contacts that boys and girls have with female teachers.

Teacher Discrimination against Masculine Behavior

A study by Fagot and Patterson (1969) was one of the few to show clear-cut female bias in teacher behavior. This research involved observation of female nursery school teachers dealing with three-year-old boys and girls. Observers watched the kinds of behavior that the children engaged in and the amount and kind of reinforcement that teachers gave to particular child behaviors. The children's behavior was classified as masculine, neutral, or feminine, depending upon the degree to which a particular behavior was associated with one sex role or the other. Thus the data could yield information not only on the amount of teacher reinforcement going to boys and to girls but also on the kind of behavior that was reinforced.

The authors reported that the total amount of positive reinforcement given to the children did not differ by sex, but that there were differences in the patterns of reinforcement. The teachers were much more likely to reinforce behaviors associated with the feminine sex role than behaviors associated with the masculine sex role. When the teachers reinforced behaviors identified with one or the other sex role, 83 percent were reinforcements of feminine behavior. There was no over-all sex difference in amount of reinforcement, however, because the boys received many more reinforcements than the girls for neutral behavior (behavior not associated with either sex role).

The teachers reinforced the girls 353 times for feminine behavior and only 10 times for masculine behavior. This tendency to "feminize" the girls is not surprising, given the pervasiveness of sex typing in our culture, although the figures do seem rather extreme. The real surprise, however, comes in the data for boys. The teachers reinforced the boys only 33 times for masculine behavior, but they reinforced them 199 times for feminine behavior. Thus the teachers were tending to "feminize" the boys as well as the girls.

This "feminizing" tendency on the part of the teachers was not effective, however, despite its consistency. There was no evidence that the boys became more feminine in their behavior preferences as the school year progressed. Apparently these teacher reinforcements were overridden by peer reinforcements. The authors noted that the children tended to reinforce one another largely within sex, so that most peer reinforcements of girls came from other girls and most peer reinforcements of boys came from other boys. These peer reinforcements were mostly for sex appropriate behavior, so that, in the case of the boys, they were reinforcing one another for masculine behavior and thereby working against the influence of the teachers. This peer reinforcement, along with all of the other pressures toward sex typing in our society, apparently was enough to negate the effects of the teachers' behavior and prevent them from "feminizing" the boys.

Teacher discrimination against boys at the preschool level was also observed in the study by Yarrow, Waxler, and Scott (1971). Recall that in this study the adult caretakers were supposed to be nurturant toward all children during the nurturance condition and nonnurturant toward all children during the nonnurturance condition. However, they deviated from these instructions in response to the differential behavior of the students, and the sex of the student was one important factor. Boys drew out much more nonnurturant behavior from the teachers under both conditions. They were generally more salient than the girls, and they had generally stronger modifying effects upon adult behavior. In addition, the adults initiated more negative contacts with the boys, criticized them more frequently, and generally were "harder" on them.

Another study suggesting favoritism of girls by female teachers in preschools was conducted by Biber, Miller, and Dyer (1972). This study involved fourteen classes of four-year-old children in one of four different types of preschool programs. Observation of teacher-student interaction revealed that the girls received more instructional contacts from the teachers in all four programs, and that they received more positive reinforcement for instruction in all but one of the programs. There was no sex difference on a measure of reinforcement per instructional contact, however, indicating that the basic findings reflected a higher frequency of instructional contacts with girls rather than a tendency of the teachers to be more positively reinforcing with girls when they did come in contact with them.

A fourth study done at the preschool level, which took into account child behavior as well as teacher behavior, produced results similar to those typically found in elementary classrooms (Serbin, O'Leary, Kent, and Tonick, 1973). Here, fifteen white female preschool teachers were observed interacting with lower middle class and working class preschoolers (98 percent white). Observations focused on situations in which a dyadic teacher-child interaction was initiated by child disruption (ignoring teacher, destroying equipment, aggression toward others) or dependency (crying, proximity to teacher, soliciting teacher attention). Teacher responses coded included praise, loud reprimands, soft reprimands, yelling, extended instruction, brief instruction, long conversation (noninstructional), short conversation, touching the child, hugging the child, restraint, helping or doing things for the child, and removing the child from the group.

Classes were observed from three to six hours over a three-week period. Several interesting sex differences were noted:

1. Boys showed more aggression and ignoring of teachers and less proximity to teachers; there were no differences in crying or solicitation of teacher attention.

2. Teachers reacted more often to aggression (significantly) and to destruction and ignoring (non-significant trends) by boys than girls. They also were given many more loud reprimands *per behavior* than girls. Thus, teachers were more attentive and punitive towards male misbehavior, although such behavior probably was typically more intense and disruptive.

3. There were no significant sex differences for praise, hugging, or brief conversations, although each mean score was higher for boys. Also, teachers significantly more often reacted to boys' solicitations for attention and had significantly higher rates of extended conversations, brief instructions, and extended instructions with *boys*. All fifteen teachers had significantly higher rates of attention to positive behavior for boys, as well as to negative behavior.

These data suggest that student sex differences are due to student differences in salience, with boys being more salient and therefore more likely to receive teacher attention and response to *either* positive or negative behaviors. As a result, their data often suggest mistreatment of boys by female teachers, when a broader data base would have shown that the teachers were merely reacting to more frequent and intense initiations by boys, thus "favoring" boys in positive as well as negative reactions.

Teacher Criticism of Boys

Three studies comparing the interactions that boys and girls have with their female elementary schoolteachers have produced a remarkably consistent set of results (Felsenthal, 1970; Jackson and Lahaderne, 1967; Meyer and Thompson, 1956). Each of these investigations revealed that the boys had more interactions with the teachers than the girls. This difference was seen in all types of contacts but was especially pronounced in the negative contacts involving teacher warning or criticism directed at boys.

Boys are far more likely than girls to be warned or criticized for misbehavior. Nevertheless, they are also called on more frequently and more frequently have procedural and work-related contacts with the teachers.

Despite the large sex difference in teacher criticism, there appears to be no complementary difference in teacher praise. Most studies find no sex difference or even a slight tendency for teachers to praise boys more frequently than girls. This latter trend was noted in both the Meyer and Thompson (1956) study and the Felsenthal (1970) study, as well as in a study of Headstart classrooms by Meyer and Lindstrom (1969) and in fifth- and eighth-grade classrooms studied by Delefes and Jackson (1972). Thus the criticism data cannot be taken as evidence of clear-cut teacher bias against the boys.

Other studies (deGroat and Thompson, 1949; Lippitt and Gold, 1959) also show that more teacher criticism is directed at boys than at girls. Furthermore, there is even some literature to suggest that the sex difference in teacher criticism is not only quantitative but qualitative. Teachers are more likely to use a harsh or angry tone when criticizing boys but more likely to direct criticism toward girls in a more conversational tone (Spaulding, 1963; Waetjen, 1962).

These sex difference findings in research by other investigators have been confirmed and extended in studies by ourselves and our colleagues. For example, our initial study (Brophy and Good, 1970a) showed that boys had more interactions of all kinds with the teachers than girls, and received significantly more teacher criticism (although much of this was directed particularly at the low expectation boys). The boys also received more praise than the girls in this study, although the difference was not significant.

A finer analysis of the teacher criticism data from this study showed that the majority of it went to the boys in the low expectation group. Of the contacts that these boys had with their teachers, 32.5 percent involved criticism, while the corresponding figures for high expectation boys were 13.3 percent, for low expectation girls 16.2 percent, and for high expectation girls 8.3 percent, respectively. Thus teachers criticized the low expectation boys in almost a third of their interactions with them, while their criticism rates for the other three groups were much lower. Even if the high criticism rates for these boys were due solely to a higher rate of misbehavior on their part, the teachers were using ineffective strategies for dealing with them. Instead of working to eliminate misbehavior through rewarding appropriate behavior and other more effective behavior-modification techniques, the teachers had apparently drifted into a pattern of criticizing but tolerating misbehavior from these boys. This very probably reinforces negative expectations and increases alienation, while at the same time leaving the rate of misbehavior unchanged.

Much of the teachers' disciplinary efforts with these boys boiled down to an exercise in labeling the misbehavior rather than changing it. This usually results in reinforcement of the misbehavior rather than its reduction (Kounin, 1970). One teacher, for example, actually predicted her problem before it happened. When certain of her children were inattentive while she was giving seatwork directions, she responded by predicting that they would miss crucial parts of the directions and would then have to come up to her later because they would not know how to do the work. She went on to explain that this not only was unnecessary but was a double-edged nuisance, because she was going to be teaching a reading group and the children coming up to see her would interfere with her ability to teach the reading group! Having said all of this, the teacher then went on to finish her seatwork directions, ignoring the *continued* inattention of these same individuals who triggered her original statement.

She was right. As soon as she began teaching the reading group, the inattentive children began coming up to her for individual help with their seatwork. She responded by providing this help upon request, thereby effectively negating her ability to handle the reading groups efficiently and at the same time reinforcing the behavior of the children coming up to her for help.

This apparently is relatively typical. Both Garner and Bing (1973a) and Martin (1972) found that classrooms typically have a small group of children, usually primarily or exclusively boys, who receive the great majority of the criticism that the teacher directs toward individual students in the class. Martin even suggested that the frequent finding that boys have more interactions with teachers than girls might be due to the large differences in number of disciplinary contacts that teachers have with this relatively small group of boys, and he also noted that the typical finding of greater teacher criticism toward boys is more correctly understood as greater teacher criticism toward a subgroup of disruptive and misbehaving boys rather than toward boys as such. In any case, data from several sources suggest that certain boys in each class are especially likely to get very frequent teacher criticism, and that these boys are especially likely to be low achievers.

Our follow-up studies produced typical sex difference results. The first-grade boys (Evertson, Brophy, and Good, 1972) received significantly more praise than the girls, but they also received significantly more behavioral warnings and criticisms as well as significantly more criticism of their seatwork. There was no difference on the measure of warning over warning plus criticism, however, suggesting that even though the teachers criticized the boys more frequently, they were not harsher or more intense in their criticism.

As was expected from previous research, the measures of frequency of interactions with the teacher favored the boys over the girls on most measures, but only one of these differences reached statistical significance. Thus in this study sex differences were more notable on the qualitative than the quantitative measures of teacher-student interaction.

A finer analysis of teacher criticism data showed that the majority of teacher criticism of boys was directed at the high and low expectation groups. Boys in the middle group received relatively little criticism. This again points up the finding seen in several studies that students in the middle groups tend to have less intense affective relationships with teachers. The more active, high achieving children, especially boys, tend to get a lot of both praise and criticism from the teacher. The more active low achievers, especially boys, tend to get a lot of criticism. Low achieving girls are less likely than low achieving boys to be criticized, but their classroom experience is also relatively unproductive.

Sex Differences Indicated in Other Variables

A similar pattern of sex differences was noted in the data from our second-grade study (Evertson, Brophy, and Good, 1973). Here again, the boys' means exceeded the girls' means on most measures of quantity of interaction, significantly so for the measures of teacher-initiated work interactions, teacher-initiated procedural interactions, and recitation opportunities. Boys also received significantly more praise than girls for both their work and their behavior and significantly more criticism for their misbehavior. With the exception of the criticism data, these findings could even be interpreted as favoritism toward boys.

In this connection, it is of interest that the girls exceeded the boys in their tendencies to seek out the teachers and create interactions with them (both work and procedural interactions) rather than wait for the teachers to come to them. Such data can be interpreted in at least two different ways, depending upon what is seen as antecedent and what is seen as consequent. It may be that the girls are seeking out the teachers more often all along, and that the teachers try to compensate by seeking out the boys to initiate more contacts and by praising them more frequently in an attempt to motivate them. On the other hand, the whole process may have begun with the teachers tending to seek out and praise boys more frequently, perhaps causing the girls to feel neglected and therefore to begin to seek out the teachers more often in order to get more contact and possibly more praise.

In any case, in addition to the differences in quantity of contact and in teacher praise and criticism, there were some differences on measures of the teachers' persistence in working for a response. During reading groups, the teachers were more likely to respond to a girl's reading failure by giving a clue or providing a second response opportunity, but they were more likely simply to give the word or to call on somebody else in a similar situation with a boy. Also, in general class activities the teachers were more likely simply to repeat the question after an initial failure by a girl, but they were more likely to give help in the form of a clue or to rephrase the question following an initial failure by a boy. Thus the teachers appeared to have somewhat higher expectations and greater persistence in seeking responses when working with girls. These qualitative differences were somewhat unusual, although the sex differences on quantitative measures and on teacher praise and criticism were typical.

Cosper (1970) studied videotapes of sixteen forty-minute classes held by each of four female fifth- and sixth-grade teachers working with 105 gifted students. Significant sex differences were obtained on ten of thirteen measures. The teachers initiated significantly more talk with the boys, discriminated significantly between the boys and the girls in favor of the boys, and were more restrictive towards the girls. Also, the boys initiated more interactions with the teachers than the girls did. Thus, in this study, the female teachers involved actually favored the boys over the girls on every measure which showed a significant sex difference. Perhaps these unusual findings were obtained because the classes were for gifted students. Most classrooms contain a group of low achieving, acting out boys who are the targets of most teacher criticism. Perhaps these gifted classes contained none or only a very few such boys. In any case, the female teachers in this study favored the boys, not the girls.

A study by Abbott (1968) also yielded mildly positive findings. This study involved an all-boy kindergarten class with a male teacher and male aides and an all-boy first-grade class who had attended both kindergarten and first grade with a male teacher and male aides. These two classes were compared with matched control boys who had attended coeducational classes. The experimental boys scored higher than the control boys on a measure of masculinity (significantly for the first-grade boys), and showed a slight tendency to view school objects as more masculine than did boys taught in coed classes. Thus the boys in the all-boy classes had a slightly stronger general masculine identification and a tendency to identify school as a masculine place in comparison to the control boys. There were also some differences between the two groups on several measures of attitude and personality traits, but these differences did not always favor the all-boy classes and were generally mixed in direction. No achievement data were taken. Thus, in this study the masculinized environment produced a more masculine sex role identification in the experimental boys, but it did not make any clear-cut improvements in attitudes or personality, and no achievement data are reported.

A later report on the same program (Greeley Public Schools, 1969) notes that the experimental boys showed higher masculinity scores and better attendance than the control boys, but no significant differences in achievement.

Smith (1970) studied twenty male and twenty-one female fifth-grade teachers in an investigation of the relationship between teacher sex and sex role preference, general self-concept, and science and mathematics achievement in fifth-grade boys. Teachers were matched on such variables as age, marital status, psychological feminity, years of teaching experience, years of teaching fifth-grade, and educational credentials. Also, their classes were matched on variables such as intelligence, chronological age, sex balance of the students, class size, parental educational level, and an index of school-pupil population stability. Thus, in this study both the teachers and classes were quite carefully matched to hold constant possible sources of variation which might complicate or confuse the attempt to relate student measures to teacher sex.

Findings were mixed. The boys with male teachers had lower scores on psychological effeminacy and higher scores on school-related self-concept measures, and they also outperformed control boys in mathematical problem solving. However, no differences were found on two measures of peer related self-concept factors, in mathematical computation scores, or in science achievement scores. Smith's data are among the most impressive available to support the notion that exposure to male teachers would improve the school environment for boys. However, even in his case the positive results were mostly confined to affect and not to achievement measures, and with the very large number of subjects involved (567 boys), the group differences he obtained might be of minimal practical significance even though they were strong enough to reach statistical significance (a negligible group difference can be statistically significant when large numbers of subjects are included in the study).

Crawford, Elliott, and Johanson (1972) studied the influence of male teachers acting as classroom aides responsible for tutoring children in reading and related skills. The experiment took place in all six elementary grades. Each classroom was assigned aides who came to meet with small groups of three or four boys to provide remedial instruction and also to attempt to motivate them and generally "turn them on" to reading. These aides were all males. At the end of the year the boys in the experimental classes were compared to boys in control classes (matched by age, grade, and achievement scores) who had received reading instruction in the regular school reading program. These analyses showed that the experimental group made significantly higher reading achievement scores in all six grades, and the investigators also report the development of positive attitudes in students and parents that they attribute to the program. These data are consistent with the suggestion that male teachers be introduced to the elementary classroom. However, it is possible that the gains made by the experimental boys in this study had nothing to do with the fact that the aides who tutored them were male. Their gains might have resulted purely and simply from the extra tutoring they received, and might have been achieved just as well if the aides had been female. Since a female aide control group was not included, there is no way to disentangle the effects of the program of tutoring from the effects of the sex of the tutor.

The findings reviewed so far in this section provide some support for the idea that infusion of male teachers into the elementary schools might improve the achievement and affect of boys, although the findings regarding achievement are notably weak. Furthermore, all of these studies share a common weakness in that they investigated only boys. Since it is possible that gains made by boys might have been obtained at the expense of the girls, it would seem that both boys and girls should be included and evaluated in any innovative study related to the sex of the teacher.

All in all, the data supporting the "need" for male teachers in the elementary schools seem weak to us. Some of the affective gains are questionable (given what is included on measures of masculinity, many would argue that it is better for both the individual boy involved and for society in general to decrease rather than increase masculinity scores, unless they are very low). Also, the evidence for an achievement advantage to boys taught by males is not very impressive, and it is more than offset by the parade of negative results to be reviewed below.

McFarland (1969) studied the influence of male participation in first-grade classrooms on academic achievement, personality, and sex-role identification. Although both experimental and control classrooms had female supervising teachers, the experimental classrooms were assigned male student teachers. Assignments were made so that a male was present in the classroom throughout the day. Similar assignments were made for female student teachers in the control classes. Reading test scores showed no significant differences between the two groups.

Jones (1971), working in a secondary school, found striking quantitative differences favoring boys. Every measure of frequency of all kinds of interactions favored boys, with the difference significant for direct questions, open questions, callouts, student-initiated procedural contacts, teacher-initiated work contacts, and total positive teacher-student contacts. Furthermore, boys received more behavioral warnings and criticism than girls, as usual. There were no significant sex differences on qualitative measures of teacher behavior. It is notable that Jones' study used student teachers, showing that even beginners, despite recent course work, show the same patterns as more experienced teachers.

SUMMARY AND INTERPRETATION OF STUDIES INVOLVING FEMALE TEACHERS ONLY

So far we have reviewed the literature that is typically cited to substantiate claims that female teachers are ill-equipped to teach boys or that they are likely to discriminate against them. As far as they go, these data hang together to form a consistent picture. Boys usually do not achieve so well as girls in the early grades, especially in reading, even though they do in other countries and in classes where their teachers expect them to, and even though they usually enter first grade equally as ready to read as the girls. Interview and questionnaire data show that female teachers prefer students who show qualities associated with girls and are annoyed by behavior usually associated with boys.

In one study (Fagot and Patterson, 1969) the teachers were shown to be systematically "feminizing" the boys, as well as the girls, even though their behavior was not effective in changing the boys involved. Studies of teacher-child interaction in the classroom have repeatedly shown that teachers are more critical toward boys than girls, especially toward low achieving boys. The classroom behavior data are not all negative, however; studies also show that teachers usually have more contacts with boys and sometimes not only criticize but also praise them more frequently than they praise the girls.

Taken together, the data reviewed so far are almost completely consistent with the suggestion that more male teachers should be teaching in the early elementary grades. However, the data are only suggestive, not conclusive. All of these studies purporting to demonstrate female discrimination against boys involved mostly or only female teachers. Without a male comparison group, these studies provide no *direct* evidence about what the effects of male teachers might be. It is reasonable, of course, to hypothesize that the presence of male teachers in early elementary school classrooms would improve the motivation and performance of boys and eliminate the present sex differences that exist in early elementary-school achievement. However, one could also hypothesize that the presence of male teachers would make no difference whatsoever, or even that males would discriminate against their female students. In fact, Preston's (1962) data from schools in Germany would support the latter hypothesis.

Obviously, research on the behavior and effectiveness of male teachers is needed. The few studies of this type which have been carried out are reviewed in the following section.

STUDIES COMPARING MALE AND FEMALE TEACHERS

Effects on Achievement

Several studies have attempted to determine what effects the presence of a male teacher in the classroom would have upon student achievement. Shinedling and Pedersen (1970) investigated the reading achievement of fourth-grade boys with male teachers versus fourth-grade boys with female teachers. A general trend suggested improved achievement among the boys taught by male teachers, although the sample was small and the differences were not significant or barely significant at best.

Clapp (1967) conducted an extensive study involving nineteen male and thirty female fifth-grade teachers and found no evidence that the presence of the male teachers improved reading achievement in the boys.

Bennett (1967) studied the effects of male versus female teachers upon the achievement of fifth graders. He found that students with female teachers showed greater overall achievement than students with male teachers and that girls outperformed boys. There was no interaction, however; boys did not do better with male teachers than with female teachers, either absolutely or relatively.

Peterson (1972) studied the effects of the sex of the teacher in a task involving tutoring first- and fifth-grade children in paired associate learning. Although the girls scored higher than the boys at each grade level, the sex of the teacher made no difference on the achievement of either boys or girls.

Asher and Gottman (1972) conducted two studies of the effects of male teachers on the reading achievement of fifth graders. The first study compared the reading achievement of students taught by ten male teachers with that of students in the same school taught by female teachers. The second study was conducted the following year in the same school, this time with thirteen male teachers. In both studies the sex of the teachers had no effect on the reading achievement of either male or female students. Being taught by a male teacher did not improve the performance of the boys.

Lahaderne and Cohen (1972) studied the effects of fourteen male and thirty-nine female fifth-grade teachers on a variety of measures. Most measures showed no effect of the sex of the teacher, but those which did generally favored the female teachers. In particular, both boys and girls taught by female teachers had higher scores on a science achievement test and more positive attitudes toward school than boys and girls taught by male teachers. Thus, once again, this study produced no evidence that male teachers would improve the performance of male students.

Sweely (1970) studied the effects of sex of teacher on the self-concepts of twelve-year-olds. He found that the girls had significantly higher self-concept scores than the boys, but that there was no interaction across classroom or across sex of teacher for student self-concept scores. Male teachers had no differential effect on the self-concept scores of children of either sex.

Effects on Sex-Role—Stereotyped Learning and Behavior

Brophy and Laosa (1971) conducted an extended case study comparing kindergarten children attending a school taught by a husband and wife team with kindergarten children attending a more typical kindergarten taught by a female teacher only. The children at the former school not only were exposed to a male teacher; they also were exposed to a variety of activities included because they were relevant to the interests or abilities of boys. The play yard contained much equipment for large muscle activity in addition to the usual swings and slides. This included ropes and rope ladders, an obstacle course, a fort, a work bench equipped with tools and materials, and many homemade equipment items fashioned from rocks, wood, tires, and rope. The children had helped construct much of this equipment under the direction of the male teacher. Ordinary ongoing activities usually included a construction project in which the children participated, using real tools with which to build a functional equipment item.

In addition, the usual kindergarten curriculum was supplemented with opportunities to participate in male-oriented activities such as working on simplified science experiments; taking apart old clocks, radios, and appliances; building simple machines such as levers, ramps, and pulleys; and competing in races and sports. Both boys and girls participated in these activities, although they were included to get more male-oriented activities into the curriculum.

Comparisons between children attending this school and children attending the female-taught traditional school were made in two separate years. Measures taken on the children included sex typing of their interests and preferences, mental ability patterns, sociometric play patterns and friendship choices, attitudes toward school and school objects, task persistence, level of aspiration, and achievement motivation. In short, the research was heavily focused on the abilities and attributes which are associated with the male and female sex roles in our society and which are believed to be acquired through imitation of adult models and reinforcement by adult socializing agents.

Despite the conscious attempt by the male teacher to inject male-oriented activities into the curriculum and to make the school generally more interesting and relevant to the boys, there was very little evidence that his presence affected either the boys or the girls in his school. There were no effects on the children's sex-role differentiation, interests, or motivational measures. There was a very slight effect on the measures of mental ability patterns, with the children taught exclusively by a female teacher making relatively greater gains in verbal areas, and the children in the school taught by the husband and wife team making relatively greater gains in spatial ability. This finding was consistent with predictions based on the fact that girls generally do better than boys on verbal measures, but boys generally do better than girls on spatial measures (Maccoby, 1966). Even this mental ability pattern finding, however, while statistically significant, is of dubious importance. The actual score differences were quite small and can easily be explained on the basis of the differences in the curriculum between the two schools. That is, they were probably not due to the presence of a male teacher as such. It is likely that a female teacher who included the same kinds of activities in her curriculum would produce the same kind of gains in spatial abilities.

Perhaps the most important finding of this study is a negative one, concerning the male teacher's failure to affect the children's attitude toward reading. Knowing that children tend to see reading as a female-oriented activity, the male teacher attempted to change this by deliberately reading aloud to the children for a fifteen-to-twenty-minute period every day. Whenever story reading or any other reading was included in the day's activities, the male teacher made sure that he rather than his wife did the reading. He did so with the conscious and deliberate intention of attempting to associate reading with the male image and the male role. Despite these efforts, however, the boys and girls in his school still associated books and reading with the female sex role (Williamson, 1970).

Thus the sheer presence of a male teacher in the classroom, even when reinforced by a deliberate attempt to socialize the children, was ineffective in changing the sex-role stereotyping of reading in our society. This finding is reminiscent of the data of Fagot and Patterson (1969), showing that consistent reinforcement by female teachers did not succeed in "feminizing" nursery school boys.

Greenberg and Peck (1973) conducted a study similar to that of Brophy and Laosa, except that they were primarily interested in changing female rather than male sex-role stereotyping. The results were markedly similar. In this study a special curriculum was developed and teachers were consulted in an attempt to minimize sex differentiation and rigid sex typing regarding sex roles in preschools for children aged three through five. Despite intense and ingenious attempts to get the children to change their standard sex-role stereotypes (including, for example, the use of uniforms associated with particular jobs and the taking of pictures of children while wearing these uniforms or while engaging in sex-typed behavior), the treatment failed. First, the children never spontaneously engaged in opposite-sex-typed behavior, although they did do so under prodding from the teachers. Second, although the curriculum lead to cognitive gains, a retesting on a measure of traditional sex typing in occupational roles showed no change despite the length and intensity of the treatment.

The data reaffirm once again that sex-role differentiation is a pervasive and powerful complex of motivations acquired through socialization in our culture, and that it is not easily changed through exposure to a model or even through deliberate reinforcement.

An interesting twist to research in this area was added by Walberg, Welch, and Rothman (1969), who not only studied male teachers but measured their heterosexual interests. These authors studied student achievement in high school physics classes taught by male teachers who had taken a test measuring heterosexual interests and activation. They found that the achievement of girls in these classes was unrelated to the scores of teachers on this test, but that boys taught by teachers with high scores achieved more than boys who were taught by teachers with low scores. This suggests, at first glance anyway, that male teachers, or at least those with high "heterosexual" interests, will foster boys' achievement in physics.

Even this conclusion is questionable, however, because of some ambiguity about just exactly what the test was measuring. Most of the items involved interest in and involvement with the opposite sex, so that the test primarily measured heterosexual activity rather than the personality and behavior traits associated with the male role in our society (competitiveness, aggressiveness, mechanical and spatial orientation). Also, the scores on the test correlated negatively with age ($r = -.62$), so that the high scoring teachers were generally younger than the low scoring teachers.

Studies of Teaching Ability and Studies of Discrimination against Boys

The suggestion that female teachers are less able to teach boys successfully or are predisposed to discriminate against them assumes implicitly that male teachers will not show these same tendencies. Although much of the data on female teachers alone supports this hypothesis in an indirect way, only studies comparing the behavior of male and female teachers toward male and female students can provide direct evidence on the question. So far only a few such studies have been completed, but their results are rather consistent.

Earlier we noted that boys tended to be assigned lower grades by teachers than their measured ability and/or achievement would predict. We also noted that this may or may not reflect teacher discrimination against the boys, because it is possible that the boys do less well on teacher-made tests given during the school year, even though they may do as well as girls on norm-referenced tests given at the end of the year. In any case, two studies have compared the grades assigned by male and female teachers to male and female students. Arnold (1968) reviewed research at the secondary level suggesting that male teachers assigned lower grades to children of both sexes than female teachers. He followed up this work by studying the grading of male and female elementary school teachers. In contrast to previous findings, he found a slight tendency for male teachers to give higher, rather than lower, marks than female teachers. However, there was no interaction between teacher and student sex. Neither male nor female teachers tended to favor either boys or girls in their marking.

Edmiston (1943), studying grading by male and female junior high teachers, replicated the finding that boys get lower marks than girls. However, like Arnold, he found that teacher sex was unrelated to the grades received by the students. Male teachers were just as likely to grade boys lower as were female teachers. These two studies strongly suggest that the lower grading of boys that is frequently observed cannot be attributed to discrimination against boys by female teachers; male teachers show the same tendency.

A few studies have investigated process variables of teacher-student interaction to see if male and female teachers treated male and female students differentially. Griffin (1972) studied interaction in sixth- and eleventh-grade classes. As expected, he found that male teachers were generally more direct and authoritarian, while female teachers were generally more indirect and warm. However, it had also been predicted that teachers would be more direct and demanding with male students and more indirect and courteous with female students, but such differences were not observed. Few significant differences related to student sex were observed, and these did not fall into an interpretable pattern. Thus although sex differences in teacher behavior were observed, no interactions between sex of teacher and sex of student were reported. There was no evidence, in other words, that male teachers treated male students more favorably than female teachers did.

Three studies have been located which were planned explicitly to see if male and female teachers treated male and female students differentially. Stasz, Weinberg, and McDonald (1973) studied the effects of the sex of student teachers on achievement and teacher evaluation by high school students. Each student teacher taught a two-week course which met for an hour each day. Students took a verbal aptitude test before the course and completed a teacher rating scale and a second achievement test after the course. In all, data were accumulated on a total of twelve courses, each taught by a male and a female teacher.

The achievement data showed that the sex of the teacher was relatively unimportant. Main effects were obtained twice; in each case the students taught by a male teacher performed better than students taught by a female teacher. Significant interactions between the sex of the teacher and student were also obtained only twice and with mixed results. In one case students performed better when taught by a teacher of the same sex, while in the other case they performed better when taught by a teacher of the opposite sex. For the other eight courses, no main effects or interactions involving teacher sex were observed on the achievement scores. Thus the data provided evidence of a slight edge favoring male teachers over female teachers in effectiveness, but only in a larger context in which the sex of the teacher appeared to be rather unimportant. Also, the data provided no support for the interaction hypothesis; only one significant interaction showing better achievement by students taught by same-sex teachers was obtained, and this was contradicted by the other significant interaction. Here again, there was no evidence to support the idea that male teachers teach boys more successfully than female teachers.

Male teachers did have an edge in the evaluation data from students. A significant main effect was found on only four of the twelve courses, but all four of these favored male over female teachers. Thus there was a tendency for male teachers to be more popular with their students than female teachers. However, here again there were no interactions. That is, there was no tendency for boys to be especially partial to male teachers or for girls to favor female teachers especially.

Teacher popularity with students was general rather than related to sex of teacher or sex of student. All in all, this study produced slight evidence favoring male teachers, just as the earlier reported study by Lahaderne and Cohen reported evidence slightly favoring female teachers. However, neither study produced inter-action evidence to suggest that male teachers are more effective with male students or that female teachers are more effective with female students.

Etaugh and Harlow (1973) studied the relationship between teacher sex and behavior and school attitudes and behavior. This study involved eighty-seven fifth and sixth graders who were taught concurrently by two male and two female teachers throughout the school year. Ability tests and attitude scales were administered in the fall and spring, and teacher-pupil interaction was observed during the school year. The observation data showed no student sex differences on attendance, ap-propriate reading and writing, hand raising, or inappropriate behaviors. Nevertheless, boys were scolded more often than girls (by both male and female teachers), called on more often than girls (only by male teachers), and praised slightly more than girls (only by female teachers). Thus the male teachers in this study showed the same tendency to be more critical toward boys and to interact with boys more frequently that has been observed in female teachers. Furthermore, they actually praised the boys less than the female teachers did. Thus these observational data pro-vide no evidence to suggest that female teachers discriminate against boys as such or that male teachers act differently from female teachers in this respect.

This study did obtain an interaction in the student ratings of teachers; boys rated male teachers more favorably and girls rated female teachers more favorably. How-ever, comparisons between father-present and father-absent boys yielded no dif-ferences in classroom behaviors or in attitudes toward school or teachers.

The abilities test data produced results similar to those reported by Brophy and Laosa (1971). Boys outperformed girls on the spatial relations subtest of the primary mental abilities test, as expected, on both pretests and posttests. However, analysis of change over the year showed that girls and father-absent boys improved on this subtest while father-present boys did not. Even though the math and science courses in this study were taught by male teachers, the data provide some evidence for a male role model effect. If the differences were due to the curriculum and instruction alone, the father-present boys should have improved at the same rate as the girls and the father-absent boys. The greater improvement in spatial abilities in the latter two groups suggests that greater opportunity to observe and interact with a male model and/or to become involved in male-oriented activities are related to student gains in spatial abilities. Although this effect is relatively minor in its impact, the fact that it appeared in two quite different studies by different investi-gators suggests that it is genuine. The reasons for it remain unclear, however, especially the question of whether the effect is produced by the curriculum or by the presence of a male teacher as such. It is possible, for example, that Etaugh and Harlow would have obtained the same results if their math and science courses had been taught by female teachers.

Indirect evidence of a similar sort in the area of mathematical ability has been reported by Husen (1967). Among hundreds of other correlations in this international study of mathematics learning in twelve countries, Husen found that math achievement by students in a given country was correlated with the percentage of male math teachers in the country. More specifically, Husen noted that Japanese students scored highest and American students lowest in math among the twelve countries studied, and that Japan had the highest percentage of male teachers while the United States had the lowest percentage. Like the preceding data, these results suggest that male teachers may be more successful than female teachers in teaching male-oriented content, although they do not provide direct evidence that teacher sex as such has any important effects. A variety of differences between the cultures and educational systems of the twelve countries involved allow for several different kinds of interpretations of the findings, however, including several that do not involve any consideration of sex of teacher at all.

The final study comparing male and female teachers to be reviewed is a dissertation by Sikes (1971). This study was explicitly addressed to the question of whether observed student sex differences are attributable to discrimination against boys by the female teachers studied in previous research, or, instead, if they result from the conflict between the male role and the role of the student as they are respectively defined in our society. Put more simply, the study asked "do boys have trouble with female teachers because they are female, or simply because they are teachers?"

The research was a naturalistic observation study using the Brophy-Good system of interaction analysis. Data were collected in sixteen seventh- and eighth-grade classrooms in four junior high schools in a metropolitan school district. The students were mostly from Anglo, middle to upper-middle class families. The sixteen teachers included four male and four female math teachers and four male and four female social studies teachers. They had been selected from a list of Anglo teachers with one to five years of experience teaching average classes in their respective subjects.

Teacher-student interaction in each classroom was coded one hour a day for ten days, beginning the seventh week of classes. For purposes of investigating questions regarding teacher sex and student sex, analyses of variance in the dependent measures of teacher-student interaction were performed, using teacher sex, student sex, and subject matter (math versus social studies) as independent variables. There were numerous differences between the two subject matter areas and numerous interactions between sex of teacher and subject matter. However, let us concentrate on the findings regarding student sex differences and on the interactions between teacher sex and student sex.

Regarding student sex differences, the findings frequently reported elsewhere were demonstrated clearly in this research: males had many more contacts with the teachers than females. This was true not only for criticism and contacts related to misbehavior but also for academic contacts, both teacher initiated and student initiated. Measures of student contact with teachers regularly favored the boys, and in most cases the sex difference was statistically significant.

In contrast to these consistent quantitative differences, there were few significant sex differences on qualitative measures of interaction. The only one related to the teachers was that the boys received a higher percentage of abstract (process) questions relative to frequency of product or factual questions. Thus the boys not only had more response opportunities in general, they also had a greater proportion of those involving complex or abstract questions.

Two other measures showed a sex difference in willingness to guess when unsure of the answer. The boys had a significantly higher percentage of wrong answers over wrong answers plus failure to respond, while the girls had a higher percentage of failures to respond over total number of response opportunities. Thus, when unsure of themselves, boys were likely to make some kind of response, even though it might be wrong, while girls were more likely to remain silent. This difference in classroom behavior is consistent with many of the other kinds of differences that have been noted between boys and girls in our society.

The girls had a higher proportion of positive contacts with their teachers than the boys did. This difference was due to the greater percentage of negative contacts, particularly criticism for misbehavior, involving boys.

In summary, the student sex differences in Sikes's research parallel the data typically found elsewhere. Boys had many more contacts with teachers and were more active in the classroom than girls. They received notably more criticism, but they also received more of other kinds of contacts, including positive ones.

So far we have discussed only student sex differences. What about the sex of the teacher? The findings here were very clear-cut and convincing: of sixty-two measures of teacher-student interaction, only one showed a significant interaction between teacher sex and student sex. The presence of male teachers did not alter the patterns of interaction that boys and girls had with the teachers. Boys had more interactions and received more criticism from male teachers as well as female teachers. The one significant interaction actually favored the female teachers: they were more likely to seek out male students for work-related contacts (presumably to check their work and provide help if needed) than they were to initiate such contacts with female students.

Thus the often predicted interaction between sex of teacher and sex of student did not materialize; there was no evidence that male teachers were more sympathetic to boys or better than female teachers at diagnosing or meeting their needs. Female teachers were doing a better job with the boys on the one variable that showed a significant interaction. Furthermore, inspection of the group means on the other sixty-two measures did not suggest even a trend for male teachers to be better with male students. If anything, the opposite was the case.

Our View of the Data

In our view, the data reviewed in this section clinch the argument that the frequently observed differences between boys and girls in achievement and performance in the classroom cannot be attributed to female teachers' discrimination against boys or inability to handle them. The data also suggest that the presence of a male teacher in the classroom, without any other changes, will make no difference in the behavior or achievement of boys.

Data from several studies show that male teachers treat boys and girls differentially in quite the same ways that female teachers do. Thus, it seems that writers describing the "plight" of boys in the schools have overemphasized the fact that most of the teachers are female and put too little stress on sex roles and the roles of teachers and students. It appears that the viewpoints and behavior of both male and female teachers are largely controlled by the expectations of the school as an institution.

To the extent that boys have difficulty adjusting to school in the early grades, the problem probably results from conflict between the role of the pupil as defined by the school and the male sex role as defined by our society. The fact that most early elementary school teachers are female apparently has little or nothing to do with it. Unless other things change too, adding more male teachers to the schools is unlikely to make much difference (excepting a massive influx which was part of a radical change in the status quo). To make a real difference we would have to do a better job of training teachers (both male and female) to compensate for and overcome the conflict between the student role and the male sex role as it presently exists in our society, and/or change our societal sex-role expectations for boys to make them more compatible with school interests and achievement.

STUDENT SEX DIFFERENCES: SUMMARY

Data from many different studies and many different educational levels agree in showing certain common sex differences in classroom interaction patterns. The primary difference is quantitative: boys tend to have more interactions of all kinds with their teachers than girls. This difference is especially pronounced, however, for interactions involving behavioral criticism and control of misbehavior. Boys are much more often warned or criticized for misbehavior than girls. The data of several studies show clearly that this finding is not attributable to discrimination against boys by female teachers; male teachers also criticize and warn boys more frequently about misbehavior. Thus, the sex difference is due to the more frequent breaking of classroom rules by boys.

The fact that boys also have more frequent work and procedural interactions with the teachers is probably related to the more general findings that boys tend to be more active and assertive than girls (Maccoby, 1966). The bulk of the boys' advantage here is in student-initiated contacts. That is, boys are more active and probably more forceful in asserting themselves and gaining their teacher's attention.

This points up another general finding that runs throughout most of our research and which we believe helps to explain the findings of other investigators: teachers appear to be primarily *reactive* rather than proactive in their interpersonal interactions with students. That is, individual differences in students make differential impressions on the teachers and condition them to respond differentially. Most differential teacher behavior toward students appears to be of this reactive variety. Apparently, as Jackson (1968) has vividly described, the pace of classroom interaction is so rapid, and the teacher is so continually bombarded with complex and sometimes conflicting demands, that he may be able to do nothing more than simply react just to keep up. Despite occasional attempts to portray the teacher as an absolute monarch autocratically dominating his students, observational research by ourselves and others more often pictures him as someone who is frantically trying to keep up with events over which he has only partial control. Thus most of the teacher's behavior is reactive; relatively little of it is proactive in the sense that it reflects his deliberate planning and control.

Taken together, the data suggest that student sex differences are to be explained by differences in the attitudes and behavior of the students themselves, and these in turn are to be explained largely by differences in the sex-role expectations and socialization practices that are prevalent in different cultures. Thus there is no reason to believe that male teachers would handle boys any more effectively than female teachers.

This conclusion pertains to the boy from the normal, intact family, of course, and not necessarily to a boy being raised in a family without a father or father figure with whom to identify. Male teachers might well be particularly helpful for boys from such families, and their presence in schools serving populations with high percentages of fatherless homes would likely be especially helpful.

Boys with fathers at home, however, are unlikely to change their school achievement and behavior merely because they are taught by a male teacher. Meaningful change with these boys would require changes in societal sex-role expectations or changes in teacher training. The former seem unlikely in the short-run future, although we do seem to be in a long-run period of change in which sex-role differences are gradually narrowing. Perhaps in the future, as already is true in the present in some cultures, school success will be expected of young boys as well as young girls.

Attacking the problem through teacher training is a more promising short-run possibility. Certainly the research of Palardy (1969), as well as certain aspects of other investigations reviewed previously, showed that boys can learn as well as girls if properly taught. Observation of teachers who are successful in teaching boys might reveal their methods, and these methods might then be taught to prospective teachers. Many would question, however, whether this effort would be worth the trouble. Considerable data show that the initial superiority of girls gradually disappears until the boys catch up and eventually pass them in most areas of achievement (Maccoby, 1966). This is partly because more boys repeat grades or drop out of school, but mostly because boys tend to catch up. Thus although the problem might be serious in certain individual cases, the initial school difficulties of boys in our culture do not imply a permanent disadvantage and are not a cause for serious concern. Equalizing the achievement of boys and girls in the early grades may not be a goal worth the effort necessary to achieve it.

On the other hand, some things can be done which are probably worthwhile, particularly ridding the schools of unnecessary rituals, restrictions in speech and movement, needless regimentation, overconcern with form rather than substance of responses in written work, and other "Mickey Mouse" aspects that unnecessarily irritate children in general and boys in particular. Some of this is already being accomplished in the movements toward making learning less passive and more active and moving toward more informal and inquiry-oriented teaching, with a consequent reduction in unnecessary dreary drill. Children will probably not learn any more (or any less) under these new methods, but they will probably enjoy learning more while doing so, especially the boys.

Further Notes Regarding Boys

So far in our discussion of the differences in classroom interaction patterns involving male and female students, we have stressed mostly the main effects of sex differences and have not said much about the interactions between sex and achievement (or teachers' expectations for achievement potential). Thus we have stated, for example, that boys are more salient than girls in the classroom, more active in seeking and getting contacts with teachers and in getting response opportunities, but also are criticized more frequently for misbehavior. We have also noted that in general teachers tend to overestimate the achievement potential and intelligence of girls and underestimate that of boys and have lower expectations for boys than for girls of equal ability. In addition, teachers tend to have more negative attitudes toward boys, particularly regarding their school motivation and their potential for classroom disturbances and management problems.

These findings are remarkably consistent across many different studies by many different investigators, and they stand as general sex differences. However, there is an additional complication which we have alluded to at times but have not specifically discussed: teachers' expectations and attitudes usually interact with the level of achievement of boys much more than with the level of achievement of girls. Thus, for example, while boys in general are more salient in the classroom, the high achieving boys tend not only to be more salient, but to be seen as active, well-adjusted, successful, and generally positive in the eyes of the teacher. The low achieving boys are also more salient, but they tend to be seen as lazy, immature, maladjusted, and troublesome.

Part of this greater polarization of teacher attitudes toward boys as opposed to girls is probably based on real differences. A large volume of data bearing on sex differences on biological, psychological, and educational measures shows that in general boys are more variable than girls (Maccoby, 1966). Thus even on a variable where the boys' average is the same as the girls' average, there are likely to be more boys at both the high and the low extremes, with the girls being bunched more toward the middle or average figure. This widely observed sex difference has cropped up regularly in research by ourselves and others on sex differences in the classroom.

In particular, the low achieving boys stick out as a special group in almost every study that has investigated them specifically. In our first study (Brophy and Good, 1970a), for example, this group of boys raised their hands to seek a response opportunity less than half as often as their classmates but were criticized more than twice as often. Investigation of interaction between sex and achievement level in our subsequent studies has always shown the same general results. Teachers criticize boys as a group more than they criticize girls as a group, but a very large portion of the criticism directed toward boys goes to the few boys who are in the low achieving end of the boys' group. Similarly, in the several studies that have shown teachers to praise boys more than girls, most of the praise went to the boys in the high achieving end of the boys' group. In many ways, insofar as teacher-student interaction data are concerned, it makes sense to speak of low achieving boys and high achieving boys as separate groups rather than to speak of boys as a single group (Good, Sikes, and Brophy, 1973).

Part of the reason that boys are more salient in the classroom is that they are more active, and therefore more likely to take actions that thrust themselves upon the teachers' attention. It is difficult not to notice a high achieving boy who continually raises his hand and/or calls out high quality answers, or a low achieving boy who is disobedient and defiant. This activity factor alone may explain the differential saliencies of boys and girls in the eyes of teachers.

However, theoretical extrapolation from the findings that boys are generally more variable than girls leads to an additional hypothesis that might help explain boys' greater salience. To the extent that boys are more variable than girls, they are less predictable. To the extent that they are less predictable, they have a greater potential for surprising teachers with unexpected behavior. This surprise element is frequently mentioned in conversations with teachers ("you never know what he's going to be up to next"), and it may be an additional reason for the greater saliency that boys have in the teachers' eyes.

The implications for teachers from the data regarding sex differences in the classroom would seem to be different for high achieving and low achieving boys. With high achieving boys, the teacher's main problem will be to keep them from dominating the classroom discussion and the teacher's attention. This should not be done through suppression, of course, but through making creative use of the talents of these boys by giving them challenging assignments or enabling them to assert academic leadership in the classroom in more positive ways, such as tutoring their classmates who need help or undertaking difficult projects.

With low achieving boys, the problem is usually to help the teacher stop thinking of the "low achiever" label and of the behavior problems that these boys present, and start thinking more about how to teach them the curriculum. Work by Kounin (1970), our own treatment study described in Chapter 9, and data from various other sources all suggest that behavioral problems tend to disappear if the teacher can concentrate on working with the student to improve his academic achievement. What frequently happens instead, of course, is that the teacher begins to react to the low achieving and misbehaving boys as "problem" students and to become hypersensitive and hypercritical toward their poor achievement and their misbehavior. This in turn leads to increased criticism rates and increased punitiveness by the teachers and to increased resentment and discouragement in the students. The pattern we have previously described, in which the teacher and student get into a rut featuring continual criticism of the same behavior which is continually repeated but not changed, becomes the norm for these low achieving boys in too many classrooms.

While it is necessary to eliminate the misbehavior of these boys if it is too disturbing or disruptive, the teacher's main goal in breaking out of an established rut with such boys should be to pay less attention to their behavior and more attention to their achievement and see that this change in his orientation is communicated to the boys themselves. If the teacher can succeed in doing this, he will find that most of the boys' misbehavior disappears.

Further Comments About Girls

In this chapter, and in the book generally, we have given far more attention to boys than to girls. This has been due in part to the previously mentioned facts that boys tend to be more salient in the eyes of the teachers, and that the more spectacular sex difference data usually involve boys. Another reason is that much of our research has been done at the elementary school level, and we have addressed ourselves to the suggestion that female teachers at this level discriminate against boys. A third reason, again connected with our emphasis on the elementary level, is that the male sex role for boys at this age, as defined in our society, and the student role, as defined by the school, tend to be in conflict, whereas the female sex role and the student role are quite compatible at this age.

These factors in combination tend to focus the attention of investigators and educational commentators upon boys in the elementary grades, to the relative neglect of girls. This is unfortunate, because more research on appropriate teaching of girls is needed. The present trend toward women's liberation will probably correct the problem, but at present, despite girls' early advantage over boys in the early grades of school, they progressively fall further behind as they get older. Studies on sex differences in adults show that males are more likely than females to reach their full intellectual and creative potential and more likely to become prominent in the arts, sciences, and professions (Maccoby, 1966). Thus the apparent advantage that girls enjoy in the early grades does not hold up over time.

One main reason for this is the gradual change in the relationship between sex role and student role. As boys get older and move into high school and college, the conflict that once existed between the student role and the male sex role disappears as achievement in school becomes perceived as a stepping-stone toward later achievement as the family breadwinner, and as an occupation becomes a basic part of the sex-role expectation. In contrast, the harmony between the student role and the female sex role that exists when young girls are in the first few grades of elementary school gradually becomes reduced, so that by high school and college they suffer conflict between the demands built into the student role (compete for grades and prepare yourself for a full-time occupation) and the female sex role (avoid competition for grades and other activities that might make you unattractive or threatening to boys, and prepare yourself to be a wife and mother).

Classroom interaction data from several studies show the behavioral correlates of these phenomena. Girls are usually less active than boys, so that boys dominate most of the interactions with teachers and most of the contributions to discussions. In seeking approval, girls are much more likely than boys to try to cope via withdrawal and other avoidance-oriented strategies rather than through more direct, approach-oriented strategies (Lahaderne and Jackson, 1970).

Teachers at all levels can probably be helpful to girls by stimulating them to be a little more active in the classroom and by making systematic efforts to observe and get to know each of their girls as individuals. We speak of making a systematic effort because this is what will be required. If the teacher merely passively reacts to the differential pressure that different children give her, she will be spending most of her time with boys. Many girls will not come to the teacher; the teacher will have to go to the girls. We believe that this effort is worthwhile, however, since we cannot afford to allow overly restrictive sex-role expectations to pressure girls into hiding their abilities or talents under a bushel.

The process of socialization to the newer, less restrictive sex roles and to the women's liberation phenomenon that we are presently experiencing needs to be begun early. In the readers and other books used in the early grades, boys are typically pictured in dominant or leadership roles, with girls pictured in passive or follower roles. This situation will no doubt change gradually, since our society seems to be becoming increasingly aware of the tremendous waste of potential talent involved in our present restrictions on women. In the meantime, however, teachers can help by encouraging girls to speak their minds, by calling on them to participate if they do not volunteer, by assigning them to leadership roles for group projects, and by taking similar actions that will help break them out of a passive set.

Also, teachers can help broaden the horizons and perspectives of young girls by noting that girls can become doctors, scientists, lawyers, and so on. (If you ask preschool and early elementary-school girls what they would like to be when they grow up, they mention mother, teacher, stewardess, movie star, nurse, and secretary in almost 100 percent of their responses. They practically never mention professions that are presently dominated by males but are increasingly opening up to females.) Teachers can help break this set by deliberately suggesting these alternatives to their girls and by exposing them to learning experiences such as stories involving females in leadership positions, compositions about or discussions of the work of female scientists, and so on.

One final word of caution on this topic: Teachers should be careful, especially with preadolescent and adolescent girls, in pushing them to participate actively and become competitive in the classroom. The potential gains here could be more than balanced off by problems of social embarrassment or rejection (real or imagined), especially with a girl who has formerly been "teacher's pet" and who is trying to change her image with her peer group. Teachers should stimulate even these girls to be more active in the classroom, such as by encouraging them to ask questions or to share interesting personal experiences with the class when relevant, but they should be careful not to call on these girls too often to the point that the girls become perceived as "teacher's pet" or as "Miss Know-It-All." They should be doubly careful not to place such girls in a position of being in conflict with classmates (such as by asking them to correct their classmates' papers or to help another student who is having difficulty answering a question).

DIFFERENCES BETWEEN MALE
AND FEMALE TEACHERS

As noted previously, there is no evidence to support the claims (other than in nursery school studies) that female teachers discriminate against males or that male teachers teach boys differently than female teachers. However, some data do exist to show that there are more general differences between male and female teachers. Data are largely fragmentary and suggestive, but they do hang together enough to suggest some implications regarding teacher training and placement of teachers in certain classrooms.

One set of data comes from the Sikes (1971) study described above. Although interpretation is somewhat hampered by many interactions between sex of teacher and subject taught, there were some general differences between male and female teachers worth noting. First, the female teachers' classes seemed to be more active, with greater student involvement and greater student willingness to initiate inter- action with the teachers. Students initiated more comments and questions in the female teachers' classes, had more response opportunities, and initiated more private contacts with the teachers. Also, they were more likely to take a guess when unsure of their response, while they were more likely to remain silent in a male teacher's classroom. Thus, the students apparently felt safer in guessing in the female teachers' classes.

Student perception data supporting these classroom observation results were reported by Veldman and Peck (1964). Students rating their student teachers showed no overall preference for student teachers by sex, nor did they consider teachers of either sex to be more poised, systematic, or knowledgeable about subject matter than teachers of the opposite sex. However, they did rate female student teachers as more cheerful, more friendly, more interested in them, and more democratic in their teaching procedures. Nevertheless, they did not prefer female to male teachers.

Inspection of other data makes it difficult to interpret the finding that students felt more at ease in female classrooms. Female teachers were more likely to praise correct answers from the students, and they more often failed to give any feedback following a wrong answer. This suggests that during question-and-answer sequences, the female teachers praised the student if he responded correctly but merely went on to someone else if he gave a wrong answer. This suggests the "right answer syndrome," in which teachers are primarily oriented toward getting the right or expected answer than toward teaching the relevant concept.

Male teachers more often failed to give feedback to students, but this happened mostly after correct or part-correct answers. Female teachers, in contrast, more often failed to give feedback after the student had responded incorrectly or had failed to answer. Following wrong answers or failures to respond, male teachers were more likely to provide process feedback, to give explanations, or clear up the student's misunderstanding. In general, in failure situations male teachers were more likely to provide abstract feedback or to provide a second response opportunity by asking another question, while female teachers were more likely to give the answer or call on someone else. Thus female teachers responded more appropriately to success situations, where they were more likely to provide feedback and/or praise, while male teachers responded more appropriately in failure situations, where they were more likely to stay with the students and work to improve their responses.

These findings tie in interestingly with a simulation experiment by Brandt (1971). In this experiment volunteers drawn from an introductory psychology course were asked to teach a discrimination-learning task to a child that they could neither see, hear, nor talk with. Communication with the child (who did not actually exist) was accomplished through electronic equipment. Half of the children were described to the teachers as overachievers, and half as underachievers. Feedback to the teachers was experimentally controlled so that half of them thought that their student was successful in learning the task, while half thought that their student was unsuccessful.

Following the experiment, the volunteers filled out questionnaires concerning their perceptions and attitudes regarding the experience. In general, the teachers stated that they enjoyed working with the successful students more than with the unsuccessful ones, and they rated the successful ones as being better motivated. Both male and female teachers reacted similarly to these questions. However, a sex difference was observed in the question regarding preferences for working with underachievers versus overachievers. Female subjects stated that they would prefer to work with overachievers, while male subjects stated a preference for working with underachievers. The sex difference in these preferences ties in nicely with the behavioral differences between male and female teachers noted in the Sikes study.

Sikes's data also corroborate the observations of Adams and Biddle (1970) and Griffin (1972). Adams and Biddle (1970) reported that male teachers spent more time talking in the classroom (presumably lecturing) than female teachers, and that they spent a greater proportion of their time disseminating information as opposed to dealing with procedural matters. They also found that the classrooms of male teachers were more centrally organized and teacher dominated than the classrooms of female teachers.

Griffin (1972), further analyzing the Adams and Biddle data, found that male teachers tended to be more direct and authoritarian while female teachers tended to be more indirect and warm. Nevertheless, teacher popularity investigations tend to favor male teachers over female teachers. This has been reported not only in the study by Stasz, Weinberg, and McDonald (1973) reported earlier, but also by Leipold (1959) and by Yee (1968). Other studies have found no difference (Veldman and Peck, 1964) or have found that students prefer teachers of the same sex (Etaugh and Harlow, 1973). Thus although the findings are weak and somewhat mixed, there appears to be a tendency for students of both sexes to prefer male teachers even though the female teachers are generally warmer.

A study by McKeachie and Lin (1971) suggested that teacher warmth is differentially important for different kinds of students, at least at the college level. They found that a warm, personally oriented style was generally effective for women teachers, but for male teachers this style was effective only for female students and for male students who had high affiliation needs. Warmth in male teachers was unrelated to their success in teaching other male students.

These data suggest that there may be a few regular differences between male and female teachers in the ways they approach teaching and act in the classroom. These differences tend to be in their general approach to teaching and in teaching style, however, and are largely unrelated to the sex of the student. Also, although not enough data are yet available on such differences in teaching to allow us to state this conclusion with much confidence, it appears at least that classroom-relevant sex differences in teachers are fewer and less significant than sex differences in students. Individual differences in teachers, including sex differences, tend to be submerged within the teacher role when teachers are working in the classroom.

SUMMARY

This chapter was addressed primarily to the "problem" decried by many educational observers suggesting that elementary school is inappropriate to the needs of boys. A large body of research was reviewed showing that there are indeed sex differences, with teachers holding more negative attitudes toward boys, especially regarding their potential as behavior problems. Other research suggested that teachers underestimate boys' intelligence and achievement potential, and grade them lower than they grade girls who achieve at an equal level on measured achievement.

Classroom observation data were also reviewed, showing that boys generally are more salient and active in the classroom, but that they also get much more teacher criticism than girls. However, they also often get more praise. In general, the behavioral findings are rather mixed and do not provide much support for the idea that female teachers treat boys inappropriately. Most, if not all, of the sex differences in classroom data can be attributable to student sex differences in classroom behavior.

Because until recently almost all elementary school teachers in our country have been females, and because most of the data referred to above therefore came from classes taught by female teachers, many observers took this to mean that female teachers, as females, discriminated against boys. Furthermore, studies in which female teachers made deliberate attempts to make the curriculum and/or the school environment more relevant to boys' needs usually did not affect the typical sex-difference findings, suggesting that female teachers might not be able to teach boys successfully. However, several studies investigating the effects of male teachers have shown that the presence of a male teacher as such makes little difference; classrooms taught by male teachers showed the same pattern of student sex differences as classrooms taught by female teachers had shown in the previous literature. Thus, the teacher's sex as such appears to be largely irrelevant as an explanation for the well-documented student sex differences that have been reported in many different studies by many different investigators.

Other data, including some cross-cultural studies, suggested that the main explanation for student sex differences in school achievement lies in the degree of correspondence (or lack of it) between the role of the student as defined by the school and the sex roles for boys and girls as defined by society. Societies which do not define sex roles the same way that our society does do not show the same pattern of sex differences in school related data. In Germany, for example, where reading and school related activities are considered part of the male sex role, boys tend to outperform girls in the early elementary grades, in sharp contrast to typical findings in American schools.

Thus we conclude that male teachers as such will make little or no difference in affecting the typical sex-difference patterns of students found in studies of American elementary schools, until and unless our society changes its sex-role expectations for young boys and girls. Fortunately (in our view, at least), some change seems to be taking place at present, with the more rigid sex-role differentiation that typically existed in the past beginning to break down so that sex-role differentiation is likely to become less extreme and less important in the future. The women's liberation movement will probably speed up this process.

Although studies looking at the interaction between sex of teacher and sex of student showed little or no evidence that male teachers favored male students or that female teachers favored female students in any general sense, there is some evidence to suggest that male and female teachers differ from each other in certain other ways, unrelated to the sex of their students. Although the few studies done so far must be taken as merely suggestive rather than conclusive, it may be that male teachers are more achievement oriented than female teachers, and therefore more concern about putting across the material and about working with students to get responses and see that they understand. To this extent, the teaching of male teachers is more appropriate than that of female teachers. However, there are also suggestions that male teachers may be too dominant and/or forbidding in their classroom manner, because students apparently feel freer to contribute to discussions and make comments in the classrooms of female teachers than in the classrooms of male teachers.

Also, there are suggestions that female teachers tend to praise more and in general respond more appropriately to student success, while male teachers tend to work more persistently for response and generally teach more appropriately in situations involving student failure.

To the extent that these teacher sex differences hold up, they have implications for teacher training. Female teachers may need special work on dealing with students in failure situations, while male teachers may need special work on encouraging students to participate and on praising more frequently in the classroom.

In general, differences between male and female teachers seem to be less frequent and less intense than differences between male and female students. We believe that this is because the teacher role tends to submerge individual differences, including sex differences, so that teachers are much more similar to one another when working in the classroom than they are when outside the classroom.

chapter 8

Individual Differences
and Their Implications
for Teachers and Students

So far we have presented a wealth of data on how student individual differences can influence teacher perceptions and behavior. Although we have occasionally noted that not all teachers respond to a given student or a given student behavior in the same way, we have mostly stressed student attributes that are likely to have predictable, similar effects upon teachers if they do have any effect at all. This is valid up to a point. As a group, teachers hold roughly the same values and opinions that other adults in our society hold, and thus they tend to react positively to behavior that is generally valued and negatively to behavior that is generally condemned. Consequently we are safe in predicting that all or almost all teachers will find it easier to like and respond favorably to a bright, outgoing, and mature child than to a classmate who is nervous and insecure or hostile and aggressive. Similarly, we are safe in predicting that most if not all teachers will be more comfortable and at ease in continuing an interaction with a confident child who is providing interesting and appropriate answers, and appearing to be enjoying himself, than they will be with a child who appears fearful, uncomfortable, or unable to understand.

Another factor that enables us to make general predictions about teachers as a group is the pervasiveness and influence of the teacher role. As noted in the previous chapter, the commonalities in teacher and student roles as defined in our society, and the restrictions that these roles place upon the behavior of the various individuals in classrooms, make it possible for us to predict certain aspects of teacher and student behavior in the classroom with great accuracy.

Thus, up to a point, it makes sense to consider teachers simply as teachers, without worrying too much about their individual differences. However, individual differences exist, despite the clearly defined teacher role. Anyone who regularly visits classrooms knows that no two classrooms are alike, even in schools serving homogeneous populations. The reason is individual differences in teachers: each teacher has his own unique personality and approach to the classroom, and the teacher is the major factor in determining each classroom's atmosphere and the kinds of classroom activities that go on within it.

Although differences between teachers are obvious to the most casual observer and are a common topic of conversation among both teachers and students, relatively little is known about such differences and their implications for students' attitudes and achievement. It is known that the teacher's personality and classroom approach sets the tone for the class. Although most teachers are primarily *reactive* in their differential responses to individual students, these individual differences exist within a more general classroom atmosphere and classroom style which are set largely by the teacher.

This was shown clearly in a series of studies of teachers' leadership styles conducted in the forties by Harold Anderson and his associates. One study (Anderson, Brewer, and Reed, 1946) showed that teachers maintained their leadership styles (dominative versus integrative) from one year to the next, even though each new class of students was different from the last. In contrast, the students were more flexible. They perceived each new teacher's style and quickly adapted themselves to it, so that they could move from a teacher who used a predominantly dominative style to a teacher who used a predominantly integrative style (or vice versa) with relative ease.

Thus the teacher sets the tone for the classroom as a whole, while individual differences among the students determine the quality and quantity of interactions that each individual student will experience *within the range possible in that classroom*. For example, one teacher dispenses frequent and effusive praise, while another praises only rarely. The general rates of praise in the two classrooms are determined by the teachers, not the students. However, within each classroom, certain students will regularly get more praise than others.

MATCHING TEACHERS AND STUDENTS

Consideration of individual differences in *both teachers and students* raises the fascinating possibility of optimally matching teachers and students. That is, interactions between particular teacher and student characteristics might make it possible, if prediction and measurement were sufficiently accurate, to match students and teachers so as to insure maximum benefit and satisfaction for *both*.

For example, suppose that two students were being assigned to two teachers' classrooms. If we knew enough about individual differences in both teachers and students, we might be able to predict with confidence that student A would do better in the classroom of teacher A and that student B would do better in the classroom of teacher B. This would make the school year more profitable and enjoyable for both the teachers and the students involved. This idea of matching students and teachers on key characteristics is obviously a logical and attractive one, at least at the theoretical level (Hunt, 1971; Lesser, 1971; Sperry, 1972; Thelen, 1967). However, as we shall see, the limited and spotty knowledge presently available *from the classroom* is not sufficient to allow much practical application at present.

The idea of grouping pupils for instruction on the basis of ability or aptitude has been commonplace for a long time, but the idea of optimally matching teachers and students on the basis of individual difference variables is a relatively recent one. Thelen (1960) performed one of the first studies of this type. He allowed teachers to select students on the basis of their "teachability" as the teachers saw it. Thus teachers were able to select students who were most suited to their teaching aims and philosophies. As a result, the teachers were more satisfied, they liked their students better, and they gave higher grades. Also, the students were more orderly and manageable and were more satisfied with the activities conducted in their classes. Thus this selection procedure led to affective gains: the experimental classes were more cohesive, with teachers and students liking each other better. These affective gains were not necessarily accompanied by achievement gains, however. Achievement gains depended upon the purposes of the teachers. When the teacher strongly stressed achievement, the "teachable" classes did achieve at high levels. However, many classes did not achieve so highly, primarily because the teachers did not stress achievement so strongly as social emotional or other goals. In any case, the results of Thelen's experiment were encouraging, and they generated interest in the possibility of optimizing education through matching teachers and students.

Rubin (1971) provided related findings showing that self-selection increases the success of teacher training programs. In this experiment inservice teachers were given one of three types of treatment: an inservice program that reinforced their already preferred teaching styles, an inservice program that directly counteracted their preferred style, or an inservice program that was selected because the teachers involved thought it would be most useful. Analysis of teaching effectiveness showed that teachers allowed to use their preferred style were equally successful, but that training was largely unsuccessful in changing established patterns. Teachers trained in styles that counteracted their already preferred patterns tended to use their preferred patterns rather than the patterns that they were being trained to use. Judgmental rating data showed that teachers trained in the style which they already preferred rated the training program as most worthwhile, while those trained in the contradictory style rated it as least worthwhile. As was found by several other investigators, the high anxiety students preferred the more structured kinds of teaching situations.

Other studies involving student choice of instructional method have been less successful. James (1962), using a military population taking an aviation course, allowed the subjects to choose between receiving the material in written form or in lecture form. The students who were taught in their preferred forms did not achieve more than the students assigned randomly, however. Similarly, Tobias (1972) reported negative results in two studies. The first involved giving elementary students a choice between learning spelling with an aural or a visual instructional method, and the second involved giving college students a choice of responding to programmed instruction by making responses and getting corrective feedback versus merely reading the program with all of the response blanks filled in. Each study showed no significant difference in achievement between students taught with the method they had selected and students assigned randomly.

The matching studies that we have discussed so far have involved matching on the basis of *free choice* and *similarity*. Teachers were allowed to select students or students were allowed to select instructional methods on the basis of congruence with their own perceived needs and goals. The work of Thelen and Rubin in particular involved matching on the basis of similarity. The benefits (to teachers, at least) of allowing teachers to select their students seem obvious. Matching on the basis of similarity also has both face validity and considerable experimental support, particularly in the work of Byrne and his associates, showing that similarity produces mutual attraction, as a rule (Lindzey and Byrne, 1968; Marlowe and Gergen, 1969). That is, the more similar two people are to each other, the more likely they are to like each other. At the very least, matching on a similarity basis should lead to affective gains.

An alternative approach to optimal matching involves placing students with undesirable characteristics in the classrooms of teachers who are likely to change these characteristics, For example, schools often will deliberately place a misbehaver in the class of the teacher who is the best disciplinarian in the grade or place a fatherless boy in a class taught by a male. Other examples, to be discussed below, include the deliberate placement of students with certain teachers in an attempt to raise their conceptual level (Hunt, 1971) or to make them less impulsive and more reflective in their approach to problem solving (Yando and Kagan, 1968).

In the sections to follow, we will review research on individual difference variables in teachers and/or students that affect student product outcomes or teacher-student interaction processes. In each case we will first consider the available data on the general effects that individual differences among teachers are likely to produce, and then we will take up the question of interaction between teacher types and student types that might have implications for optimal matching.

MATCHING BASED ON INDIVIDUAL DIFFERENCE VARIABLES

Leadership Style

Teachers vary widely in their leadership styles. One of the most famous studies of leadership style, although it was not conducted in the school setting, would seem to have direct implications for the classroom. In this research (Lewin, Lippitt, and White, 1939) adult leaders supervised teams of boys working on group construction projects. The adults used three leadership styles. In the *authoritarian* style the leader assumed full responsibility and took full personal control. He issued detailed orders about what to do and how to do it, leaving no room for the boys to deviate from instructions or make contributions of their own. In the *democratic* style the leader assumed ultimate responsibility but shared decision making with the group. He led by posing questions, seeking group consensus, and stimulating the boys to create and implement their own ideas about completing the project. He kept the group problem centered and was the ultimate authority, but he sought to get them to solve problems on their own as much as possible. In the *laissez-faire* style the adult abandoned his leadership role by avoiding taking responsibility for the project and by adopting a passive, uninvolved stance. He not only did not tell the boys what to do; he refused to provide structure, to make suggestions, or to give help in answering their questions. Thus he left them on their own without providing leadership.

The findings showed that the democratic and authoritarian styles resulted in better products than the laissez-faire style. Boys working under the laissez-faire condition usually failed to accomplish their task because they were a leaderless group. They often fought among themselves without achieving consensus or arriving at solutions or went off individually in many directions at once without organizing for efficient work. While most had a good time and did a lot of "horsing around," they got little or nothing accomplished.

Boys working under an authoritarian leader showed a very different pattern. They followed the detailed instructions the leader gave them and consequently succeeded regularly in completing the assigned tasks. Thus, from the viewpoint of efficiency in seeing that the group achieved its task, the authoritarian style was quite effective. However, other evidence indicated that this productiveness was achieved at a cost. Observers suggested that these groups had an atmosphere marked by anxiety and tension, even though the work was being accomplished. The validity of these observations was reinforced by data on what occurred when the leader left the room. On these occasions groups under authoritarian leaders showed a tendency to "blow up," so that fights, arguments, name calling, and scapegoating were frequent.

Groups working under democratic leaders showed the positive features of the other two styles without the negative features. First, they were generally quite productive. Their success in achieving group goals almost (but not quite) equaled that of the authoritarian groups. The slight reduction in efficiency is understandable in view of the time taken by democratic leaders to get suggestions from the group and seek consensus before proceeding. This slight loss in efficiency was compensated, however, by the excellent group atmosphere that democratic leadership produced. Observations indicated a pattern of harmony and mutual cooperation. More impressively, when the leader left the room, these groups tended to continue working and/or to discuss and agree on plans, even though the adult leader was absent. Thus groups working under democratic leadership learned to function independently and showed no tendency to "blow up" when the leader left the room.

The implications of this research seem straightforward. Laissez-faire leadership tends to create chaos and confusion. Authoritarian leadership achieves efficient productivity but at the cost of frustration and a generally negative group atmosphere, leading to outbreaks of aggression when the leader is absent. In contrast to both of the above, democratic leadership appears to be successful in enabling groups to reach production goals but without the cost of frustration and aggression. In fact, it seems to have the added advantage of teaching the group to function more maturely, cooperatively, and independently in the leader's absence as well as in his presence.

Do these experimental data on leadership styles in a summer camp apply to the teacher's leadership style in the classroom? A review of a large number of studies comparing authoritarian versus democratic leadership styles (Anderson, 1959) showed that the classroom data generally bore out predictions that would be made from the experiment. Regarding productivity (student achievement), there appeared to be no clear-cut general difference between two styles. Some studies showed that authoritarian teachers produced more achievement than democratic teachers; other studies showed the opposite. The most simple conclusion seems to be that these styles interact with certain student characteristics so that there is no general advantage to either style with regard to student achievement (productivity).

The picture was much clearer, however, in affective data on student attitudes and classroom atmosphere. Here, as in the experiment, the classroom studies favored the democratic over the authoritarian style. Although there were exceptions, teachers with democratic styles generally were preferred to those with authoritarian styles, and they generally created more positive classroom atmospheres characterized by greater student enjoyment and cooperation and less competitiveness and frustration.

The exceptions to the preceding general statement about democratic versus authoritarian leadership styles also tend to hang together rather well. A good example is the work of Grimes and Allinsmith (1961), who studied third graders in two schools using contrasting approaches to reading instruction. One school stressed a phonics approach and the other a whole-word, look-say method. In addition to these differences, the authors noted that the schools featuring phonics instruction had "a more authoritarian atmosphere and a more traditional program." Schools included in the study were balanced on SES, so that this variable could not bias the results.

Student success in the two types of programs was related to the personality variables of compulsiveness and anxiety. Compulsiveness was measured by a parent rating scale on child variables such as perfectionism, irrational conformity to rules, orderliness, punctuality, and need for certainty. Anxiety was measured with a children's anxiety scale. Analysis showed a clear interaction between student compulsiveness and anxiety and school structure. The highly compulsive students showed generally higher achievement than the less compulsive students, regardless of school structure, but the difference was especially pronounced in the highly structured schools. Thus highly compulsive students did better in highly structured school environments.

Similarly, highly anxious students showed lower achievement levels than their less anxious classmates, but the difference was especially large in the unstructured schools. That is, highly anxious students did relatively better in the highly structured schools than in the less structured schools. Thus, while a democratic leadership style and a child-centered approach may be more successful in general, it appears that highly compulsive and/or highly anxious children do better (at least in terms of achievement) in more authoritarian, teacher-dominated classrooms.

Related findings were reported by Feitler, Wiener, and Blumberg (1970), who asked public school teachers and college students about the kinds of classroom settings that they preferred. The results showed a relationship between interpersonal needs and classroom preferences. As predicted, subjects with high control needs preferred more structured situations, with the teacher in a position of control. Subjects with low control needs selected settings in which the teacher's position of control was less obvious. Thus some teachers, as well as some students, feel more comfortable in more teacher-dominated classroom settings.

Similar results in college students were reported by Wispé (1951) and Smith (1955). In each of these studies, college students who preferred structure and showed generally authoritarian tendencies on personality tests responded more favorably to structured classroom formats (highly organized versus loosely organized classroom activities in one case, and lecture versus group discussion techniques in the other). Similar results were obtained by McKeachie (1958). All of these experiments suggest that the students who prefer and do well in highly structured classrooms tend to be personally insecure and fear failure. This fear leads them to prefer the highly structured classroom where student responsibilities are very clearly delineated. This enables the students to know exactly what to expect and exactly what will be expected of them, thus minimizing ambiguity and anxiety. Fear of failure, and especially free-floating anxiety, are sharply reduced when a person is given explicit expectations and instructions which allow him to meet demands and avoid failure successfully.

Tuckman, Cochran, and Travers (1973) made comparisons between open classrooms in grades one through five with traditional classrooms serving similar students. They found that in addition to being more flexible in the use of space and in the organization of classroom activities, the teachers in the open classrooms were rated as more creative, warmer, and more accepting. The students in the two types of classrooms did not differ on achievement or problem-solving skills, but the open-classroom children had more positive self-concepts and more positive attitudes toward school than the control children. Carbonari (1973) also showed that both teacher and student personality variables are related to preferences for open versus traditional classrooms.

Tuckman (1969) studied the interaction between teaching style and abstract-independent versus concrete-dependent personality patterns in high school students. Student self-report data and student grades showed that in general the students studied preferred nondirective teachers, were more satisfied with courses taught by nondirective teachers, and earned higher grades in these courses. This main effect favoring the nondirective teachers was much more potent than the interactions observed, although there were interactions. The latter showed that the concrete-dependent students tended not to differentiate in their preferences for teachers or in their performance in the different teachers' courses, but that the abstract-independent students tended to prefer and to do better in the courses of classes taught by nondirective teachers.

Covington and Jacoby (1972) studied the differential course preferences and behavior of college students who were either high in independence and low in conformity or high in conformity and low in independence. A personality inventory was administered to a large introductory psychology course, and twenty students in each of these two extreme groups were selected for study on the basis of their scores on the achievement by independence scale and the achievement by conformity scale. The course was run on a contract system which provided a large number and variety of options. Students could choose both the amount of work that they were willing to do (each option was worth so many points, and grades were related to the total number of points earned), as well as the kind of work that they wanted to do in order to earn a given number of points. Several interesting findings emerged, although there were no differences on total points earned (and therefore no differences in course grades) between the two groups.

The highly conforming students liked the contract system better than the highly independent and nonconforming students, apparently because they were relieved to be free of the pressure and uncertainty involved in competing for grades. Meanwhile, the independent nonconformers were somewhat frustrated because they tended to set unrealistically high goals for themselves and then failed to meet them. Analysis of the types of work selected showed that the conforming students more often picked projects requiring convergent thinking, while the independent students tended to pick ones that called for divergent, innovative thinking. Also, conforming students maintained a greater dependency and reliance on external authority (more time spent reading the textbook even though it was not required, rated the text as more useful, reported a stronger feeling of obligation to meet the standards and expectations of the instructor). Thus this contract system apparently was especially successful with highly conforming students. It probably would also be successful with most other students; the authors point out that the high independence-low conformity group were unusual students who were somewhat unrealistic in their goal setting abilities and generally anti-authority. Thus there is reason to believe that this contract arrangement would work well with most students, with the exception of those, like the independent nonconformers in this study, who do not set realistic goals for themselves.

Dowaliby and Schumer (1973) found that student anxiety was related to achievement in an introductory psychology course. Subjects for this study were students in one of two sections of the same course. One section was taught with a clearly teacher-centered method, while the other was taught with a clearly student-centered method. Analyses of the relationships between student anxiety scores and course exam scores showed that the teacher-centered mode led to better learning in high anxious students while the student-centered mode produced better learning for low anxious students.

All of the preceding studies suggest that the degree to which the student needs or desires *structure* is an important variable that interacts with the teachers' structured versus unstructured teaching style in determining student affective reaction and in some cases student performance in courses.

A series of studies by Fiedler (1973) has shown that the effectiveness of a given leadership style will vary with situational variables as well as with personality variables of the group members. Most of his research has compared the relative effectiveness of task-oriented versus relationship-oriented leaders. Task-oriented leaders are primarily concerned with the details of job completion, and relate to group members largely in terms of their roles in completing the task at hand. In contrast, relationship-oriented leaders subordinate task completion concerns to concerns about establishing and maintaining good relationships with each of the group members. Studies by Fiedler and his colleagues have shown that the relative effectiveness of these two leadership styles varies with the quality of the relationship that the leader has with the group members, the degree of structure involved in the task, and the relative power that the leader holds in relation to other members of the group. When these variables interact in such a way as to produce either a very favorable or a very unfavorable situation, task-oriented leaders do better. However, in more moderate situations, relationship-oriented leaders do better than task-oriented leaders. Thus, leadership style appears to be an important teacher variable, but it does not have any simple and straightforward relationship with product measures, except for the general tendency for democratic leaders to be preferred to authoritarian leaders. Other effects of leadership style, particularly effects on group or individual achievement, involve complex interactions between leadership style, situational variables, group relations variables, and the individual patterns of needs and motives in the students.

Convergent–Divergent Thinking

Related to the preceding studies on the preference for structure are several studies dealing with the preference or tendency to be convergent versus divergent in one's thinking. Persons favoring convergent thinking are oriented toward organized, deductive problem solving leading to convergence upon a single "correct" solution to a problem. In contrast, divergent thinkers are interested in and good at generating alternative strategies or solutions to problems. These two abilities are not mutually exclusive or even negatively correlated, but some individuals strongly prefer and/or excell at one as opposed to the other. This sometimes makes a difference in the classroom performance of students, depending upon the match between the teacher and student on this attribute. For example, Yamamoto (1964) studied arithmetic achievement in fifth graders in relationship to the convergent–divergent dimension. These data indicated an interaction; in particular, low divergent students achieved better in the classes of low divergent teachers than in the classes of high divergent teachers.

Joyce and Hudson (1968) studied the interaction between the personalities and intellectual styles of medical students taking statistics courses with those of their teachers. Four teachers were each studied over three successive classes. Investigation of final exam scores from these courses showed that students with high divergent scores did better when taught by the most divergent teacher and that, in general, convergent students did better when taught by convergent teachers.

Zussman and Pascal (1973) studied the effects of divergence and convergence in twenty teachers teaching forty-eight high school classes. They found that correlations between the convergent and divergent test scores were low, indicating that these are generally separate abilities. Several interesting interactions relevant to matching teachers and students were revealed. First, regardless of their own bias, teachers stated that divergent students participated more in class and made more original statements. In contrast, the convergent students were not named as better than the divergent students on any traits. Nevertheless, teachers stated that students whose convergent–divergent bias was the same as their own needed more attention from them, had a greater need for achievement, and achieved at a higher level than students with the opposite bias. Thus even though the convergent teachers recognized the greater creativity of the divergent students, they tended to prefer convergent students whose biases were more similar to their own.

The students reported that the divergent teachers presented material more rapidly, maintained a more tense atmosphere in the classroom by showing stronger likes and dislikes for their students, and were less organized and less concerned. In contrast, they described the convergent teachers as being more goal directed, as encouraging competitiveness, and as leaving the class with a greater feeling of accomplishment and satisfaction. These data would seem to largely favor the convergent teachers; however, like the teachers, the students showed a tendency to prefer teachers whose bias matched their own. The students rated the teacher whose bias was the same as their own as having greater diversity of interest and as teaching more democratically than they rated teachers with the opposite bias. Both the teacher and the student self-report data in this study reveal a fact about preferences that has been noted earlier: even when differences between two groups of teachers or students are perceived objectively, these differences are sometimes disregarded or even contradicted by halo effect in preference ratings. For example, the students in the previous study stated that the divergent teachers showed stronger likes and dislikes for students, creating a tense atmosphere in the classroom. Yet, the students with a divergent bias rated these teachers as teaching more democratically than the teachers with a convergent bias. Similarly, both types of teachers recognized that the divergent students made more frequent and more original comments in class, but the convergent teachers rated the convergent students as higher achievers. Thus even when differences are accurately perceived, similarity or other aspects involved in creating mutual attraction between teachers and students will sometimes produce a generalized halo effect capable of causing the person to ignore or forget about negative traits when rating his liking or disliking of a teacher or student.

Ycas and Pascal (1973) showed that convergent versus divergent bias in college students was associated with the kinds of courses and learning structures that they preferred. Convergent students expressed preference for methods such as lecture courses with a precise, methodical, well-organized professor; studies with another student that follow a set course plan with the stipulation that the student be dependable; and computerized instruction. In contrast, the more divergent students preferred such structures as student-dominated seminars with relaxed, easy-going, and stimulating professors; student-run and planned studies with another student with the stipulation that the other student be similarly freewheeling; and independent study courses set up to match the interests of the student.

Halpin and Goldenberg (1973) studied the attitudes toward students held by convergent and divergent undergraduate future teachers. Their data suggest that the convergent–divergent variable is likely to be an important one in affecting the quality of the relationship that such teachers have with their future students. The more divergent future teachers saw students as self-disciplining, provided that close, personal teacher–student relationships and mutual friendship and respect were established. They also viewed learning and classroom behavior in psychological rather than moralistic terms, and they felt that teacher–student interaction should be a two-way channel. They stressed flexibility in status and rules, a democratic classroom climate, and the importance of the individual. In contrast, the more convergent student teachers were more authoritarian, more pessimistic, more mistrustful of students, more likely to stereotype students on the basis of appearance, behavior, or SES, more likely to prefer impersonal rather than highly personal relationships, and more likely to view behavior in moralistic terms rather than to try to understand it. These data help explain the earlier reported findings that divergent teachers are generally more popular than convergent teachers as well as the interaction between convergence-divergence bias in teachers and in students.

Some related behavioral observations were reported by Gabbert (1973). These concern the differences between student teachers classified as either high or low on a scale of achievement orientation. Although this is not quite the same as the convergence–divergence dimension, teachers high on this scale are likely to be convergent teachers. Student teachers were observed while teaching in the elementary school classrooms to which they were assigned, using a version of the Brophy-Good Dyadic Interaction Observation System. It was found that teachers high in achievement orientation asked more direct questions and more product questions, while teachers low in achievement orientation elicited more correct answers. Teachers high in achievement orientation also gave more work-related contacts and more rejection. Thus in their classroom behavior these teachers appeared to be businesslike and problem centered. In general, they were the kinds of teachers that convergent-oriented students would prefer.

So far all of the data except that regarding preference for computerized instruction in convergent students seem to hang together. Recall from the previous chapter the experiment by Blitz and Smith (1973) who found that deferent, orderly, nurturant, and endurant students performed better with a programmed text, while more aggressive students performed better in computer-assisted instruction. Also, several studies found that boys seemed to be more positively oriented toward computer-assisted instruction than girls. These data would seem to predict that divergent rather than convergent students should prefer computerized instruction, but Ycas and Pascal found otherwise.

In general, however, data from several sources suggest that both convergent teachers and convergent students prefer a well-organized, businesslike, achievement-oriented classroom with a clear-cut structure established primarily by the teacher. In contrast, divergent teachers and students are less achievement and structure oriented, preferring instead a teaching approach involving minimal structure, highly personal interactions, and encouragement of everyone to follow his own interests.

Warmth and Enthusiasm

Two other teacher attributes that appear to have general effects are warmth and enthusiam. Reviews of the teacher effectiveness literature (Rosenshine, 1970; Rosenshine and Furst, 1971) have shown that these two variables consistently correlate positively with student achievement. Warmer teachers and more enthusiastic teachers tend to produce greater achievement gains. Also, they tend to produce better affective responses from their students, so that their classrooms show more positive atmospheres (Baird, 1973; Kleinfeld, 1972; McKeachie, Lin, and Mann, 1971; Sears, 1963; Sears and Hilgard, 1964).

Certain studies have shown that warmth is especially important with certain students, especially disadvantaged students or students who are targets of prejudice or discrimination. Kleinfeld (1972), for example, while finding that warmth was generally important for all students, found that it was particularly important, in fact essential, to teacher success with Indian and Eskimo students attending urban schools in which they were a minority. These students felt (and were) discriminated against and unwanted, so that teacher warmth was especially important in reaching them. Similarly, St. John (1971) found that black students responded more strongly and favorably to teacher warmth, in contrast to white students who were less affected by teacher warmth and more affected by the teachers' teaching skills.

Della Piana and Gage (1955) also found that teacher warmth is particularly important to certain students. Measures of pupil values revealed that some students were more concerned about feelings and personal relationships, while others were more concerned about achievement. Classes composed primarily of students concerned with feelings and personal relationships were likely to be especially accepting of teachers that they liked and rejecting toward teachers that they disliked on personal grounds. Teacher warmth was an especially important variable in determining their reaction here. In contrast, classes composed primarily of achievement-oriented students were less concerned with teacher warmth and gave it much less weight in responding to questions about how much they liked their teachers.

Amidon and Flanders (1961) related dependency in eighth graders to teaching style. One hundred forty students selected because they had high scores on a test of dependency proneness were assigned to one of four experimental conditions: direct teacher with clear goals, direct teacher with unclear goals, indirect teacher with clear goals, or indirect teacher with unclear goals. The clarity of the teachers' goals made no difference on the dependent variable of achievement in geometry, but these dependent students did achieve more when taught by the indirect teacher than when taught by the direct teacher. Indirectness as measured in the Flanders system includes many elements of warmth (praise, use of student ideas), and in view of the preceding data it seems likely that this aspect of indirectness rather than the relative lack of structure was the reason for the better achievement by the high dependency-prone students. The authors note that an earlier study of the same type by Flanders in which students across the full range of dependency were included found no difference among the four experimental conditions. Combining the two studies, it may be inferred that high dependency-prone students are especially sensitive to teacher behaviors such as praise, criticism, use of student ideas, and warmth generally.

Although some of the studies reviewed above suggest that warmth is especially important for teaching disadvantaged students, a few studies have come up with contradictory results. For example, in an experiment by Feshbach (1967), nine- and ten-year-old boys viewed films showing teachers who were either positive and rewarding or negative and critical toward students. After watching the films the children were observed for the degree to which they imitated the filmed teacher model during a standardized observation and then were questioned about their attitude toward the filmed teachers. Middle class and lower class boys showed clearly different responses to the two types of teachers.

The middle class boys imitated the warm but not the negative teacher, while the lower class boys did not imitate either teacher to a very large degree. However, in the preference interviews they expressed a preference for the negative teacher over the warm teacher. In attempting to interpret this surprising finding, Feshbach suggested that the behavior of the critical teachers may have been more similar to that of the mothers of the lower class boys or at least to their general expectations about female adults.

A similar experiment by Portuges and Feshbach (1972) yielded a somewhat different pattern of results. In this study, forty-eight white advantaged and forty-eight black disadvantaged third- and fourth-grade boys and girls individually observed two films, one showing a positively reinforcing teacher and the other showing a negatively reinforcing teacher. Then the children were allowed to play the role of teachers and were scored for the degree to which they imitated the distinctive behavior of the two teachers that they had seen on film. This time there were more clear-cut main effects rather than interactions. The advantaged white children imitated the filmed models more than the disadvantaged black children; the girls imitated more than the boys; and the positively reinforcing model was imitated more frequently than the negatively reinforcing model. These data support Feshbach's earlier findings showing a greater tendency for middle class than lower class children to imitate the model, but they do not provide replication for the earlier finding that the lower class children preferred the more negative model.

It is possible, of course, that Feshbach's earlier findings were simply a fluke. However, there are supporting data. Ostfeld and Katz (1969) studied the effects of mild versus harsh threats upon middle class and lower class preschool children. Confirming several previous studies, they found that mild threats were more effective than harsh threats with middle class children, but that harsh threats were more effective than mild threats for the lower class children. Additional support for Feshbach's findings was provided by Middleman (1972).

In this study ninety fourth-grade lower class urban children and ninety fourth-grade middle class suburban children were assigned to three experimental groups in each respective school. Each group was shown a videotape on which a teacher gave instructions to students about performing three simple tasks. The verbal content of the instructions was identical on all three videotapes, but the nonverbal communication differed. Through expression, gestures, voice tone, and other behavioral cues, the teacher presented the instructions in either a positive, a neutral, or a negative fashion. The children's productivity on the three tasks was examined, and they were questioned regarding their attitudes toward the teacher they watched.

The productivity data showed that the middle class suburban children were not affected by differences in the nonverbal communication styles of the teachers. However, the lower class urban children were *more* productive on one of the tasks under *negative* conditions. That is, they did better on a drawing task when the teacher presented the instructions in an authoritarian and hostile way rather than when he gave instructions in a neutral or positive manner.

The attitude data showed that the suburban middle class children most preferred the positive teacher, then the negative teacher, and lastly the neutral teacher. In contrast, the lower class urban children showed no particular preferences for any of the three styles.

Although the specific patterns of findings in these two studies differ, taken together they provide evidence that although a democratic leadership style and teacher warmth may be generally effective as teacher attributes, lower class children (some of them at least) may show better achievement and may actually prefer authoritarian teaching.

These social class differences in student attitudes towards teachers may be mirrored by similar social class differences in teacher attitudes toward children. Goldenberg (1971) administered the Minnesota Teacher Attitude Inventory to middle class master teachers and lower class teacher aides working in Head Start centers. Although the findings should be taken with caution because of the high probability that the responses were affected by social desirability sets, the data suggest that the middle class teachers were significantly more permissive and less puritanical in their outlook, more apt to take pleasure in the emotional aspects of teacher-pupil relationships, and less authoritarian in their attitudes toward children as compared to the lower class teacher aides.

Introversion–extroversion

Introversion–extroversion appears to be one of the more important and obvious dimensions of human personality. People who are talkative, outgoing, and sociable are strikingly and obviously different from people who are quiet, reserved, and inhibited. In the classroom extroverted students are likely to be the most active and salient, while introverted students are likely to be the least active students and the ones least likely to be noticed (they are probably also the ones most likely to be mentioned by teachers in the indifference group). Barclay, Stilwell, Santoro, and Clark (1972) found that student introversion–extroversion, as measured on a personality test, was evident in the classroom behavior of the students. Extroverts raised their hands more often, talked out loud more often, and were more prone to stand up at their desks. Introverts paid attention more often, volunteered less frequently, and squirmed, fidgeted, or made noise less often.

Entwistle (1972) studied the relationship between student introversion and achievement. His results suggest an age effect in which academic success in the primary school is linked to stable extroversion, while success at higher levels is more associated with introversion. However, this is an over-simplification of his results, since this simple pattern was complicated by a variety of interactions which indicated that the specific relationships differed with the intellectual level of the students, the type of school, the subject matter, and the teaching style of the teacher. Thus the age effect was a weak general tendency rather than a clear, strong relationship.

Given the fundamental importance of the introversion–extroversion dimension, it would appear especially likely to affect teacher-student interaction in ways that might make it useful as a variable for matching teachers and students. This possibility was investigated in the dissertation study by Jones (1971), who tested the hypothesis that teachers and students similar to each other on the introversion–extroversion dimension would share more optimal interactions than teachers and students who differed on this dimension.

Jones (1971) studied sixteen female student teachers and eight of each of their students in urban junior and senior high schools.

Both the student teachers and the eight students in their respective classrooms were specially selected from larger samples according to their scores on two subscales of the Adjective Self Description instrument (Veldman, 1970)—*introversion* and *efficiency (achievement orientation)*.

The sixteen student teachers were divided into four equal groups: high achievement-oriented introverts, high achievement-oriented extroverts, low achievement-oriented introverts, and low achievement-oriented extroverts.

The student teachers were asked to rate each of their students on a shortened form of the ASD during the sixth week of teaching. This short form included all sixteen items from the two scales previously described, along with an additional nine filler items which dealt mainly with physical attractiveness, nervousness and tension, and moodiness.

The eight students selected for special observation in each classroom were chosen according to sex and to their teacher's perception of their introversion and achievement orientation (ASD efficiency scale). The eight students selected were the boy and girl in each class that most nearly fit the definitions of the four categories of student teachers: high achievement-oriented introverts, high achievement-oriented extroverts, low achievement-oriented introverts, and low achievement-oriented extroverts. Thus the students were selected according to the same combination of two variables used to select the student teachers, except that both a male and a female student were selected in each classroom.

Based on the impressive volume of literature suggesting that similarity breeds attractiveness, it was hypothesized that teachers would interact more frequently and more positively with students whom they perceived as being similar to themselves in introversion–extroversion and in achievement orientation. It was also predicted that extroverted students and teachers would be more active in the classroom than introverted students and teachers, and that in general the introversion–extroversion variable would be more influential than the achievement orientation variable in influencing the quantity and quality of teacher-student interaction in the classroom.

To test these hypotheses, teacher-student interaction in the sixteen classrooms was observed with a revised version of the Brophy-Good Dyadic Interaction Observation System. Each student teacher was observed, during periods in which she was actually engaged in teaching students, until a total of 500 minutes of interaction had been coded. The coding took place between the eighth and eleventh weeks of the student teachers' experience in their classrooms.

Analysis of the rankings of pupils on the ASD measures of introversion and achievement orientation showed that these two measures were not related. The boys and girls included in each achievement group were evenly split between introverts and extroverts. Thus it appears that the four types of students included in the study are representative of the types of students likely to be found in all junior high and high school classrooms, rather than being unusual or rare types.

Differences between students rated high in achievement orientation and students rated low in achievement orientation were statistically significant on fifteen of the twenty-five teacher-student interaction measures studied. The high achievement–oriented students initiated more questions, made more comments, called out more responses, initiated more total contacts with the teachers, and in general had considerably more contacts with the teacher in *public* situations. In contrast, students rated low in achievement orientation initiated significantly more *private* procedural contacts with their teachers (but not more private work-oriented contacts).

There were also differences in the nature of the public contacts. Students rated as high in achievement orientation were asked more direct and more open questions, and were given more total contacts by the teacher. In contrast, students rated as low in achievement orientation were given more behavioral warnings and criticisms and more procedural contacts. Students rated low in achievement orientation received both more positive and more negative private contacts.

As predicted, the introversion–extroversion variable was more powerful than the achievement-orientation variable in its effects on teacher-student interaction: differences between the introverted and extroverted students reached statistical significance on twenty of the twenty-five measures. As predicted, the extroverted students had more contacts with the teachers. Seventeen of the measures were measures of quantity of teacher-student interaction, and all seventeen favored the extroverts. Of these, only the measure of teacher initiated product questions failed to show a significant group difference. Thus the extroverts had more of every kind of contact with their teacher, whether the contact was teacher or student initiated, and whether it dealt with work, procedural matters, or behavior. In general, extroverts were much more salient and much more active in the classroom than their introverted classmates.

Differences on qualitative measures were more mixed and less extreme. Extroverts had a significantly higher percentage of correct answers over total answers, even though they had many more response opportunities. This is not attributable to a difference in aptitude or achievement, since the groups did not differ in achievement orientation. Extroverts probably are more likely to take a guess when uncertain, and introverts probably are more willing to respond only when reasonably sure of being correct, so we would expect extroverts to make more mistakes and therefore have a lower percentage of correct answers than their introverted classmates. However, this was not the case.

Possibly the introverts were so insecure and shy in public response situations that they would respond only when absolutely certain of being correct, so that they may have remained silent or said "I don't know" rather than take even a small risk of being wrong. If this were true, it would reduce the introverts' percentage of correct answers.

Examination of the other two qualitative measures that showed significant group differences revealed that introverts were more likely to receive affirmation or praise following correct answers and less likely to receive no feedback at all following response opportunities. Thus although the introverts had fewer response opportunities, the data suggest that the teachers were attending to their answers more carefully and were providing feedback more regularly. Perhaps the introverts speak more softly or more slowly, hesitate more before answering, or indulge in other behavior that might indirectly force the teacher to pay closer attention and perhaps press him to make a feedback response more often.

The three measures of staying with students following an initial response opportunity showed no group difference on this teacher variable. Thus the teachers' tendency to interact more frequently with the extroverts did not also cause them to stay with these students longer while interacting with them. Nor did the teachers compensate for their reduced interaction rates with introverts by staying with them longer on the fewer occasions in which they did interact with them in public situations.

To summarize, the introversion–extroversion variable proved to be extremely powerful in determining the quantity and quality of interactions that students had with their teachers. Differences on quantitative measures were especially notable: the means favored the extroverts over the introverts on every quantitative measure. This does not imply that extroverts were being systematically favored, however, since these quantitative measures include warnings and criticisms. Thus extroverts had more negative as well as more positive contacts with teachers. They also had more correct answers per response opportunity. The introverts, however, were more likely to receive affirmation or praise following a correct answer and were less likely to be given no feedback at all following a response opportunity. As predicted, the introversion–extroversion variable was more powerful than the achievement-orientation variable in determining classroom interaction.

Teacher achievement orientation was significant on eleven of the twenty-five measures. The high achievement-oriented teachers asked more direct questions and fewer open questions, and initiated more "positive" private contacts with students. Students also initiated more private contacts with them. High achievement-oriented teachers also stayed with students more frequently following their initial answer, whether correct or incorrect.

These behavioral differences support the teachers' own perceptions of themselves as high and low achievement oriented. The contrast on all measures showing significant differences suggests that the high achievement-oriented teachers were indeed more concerned about achievement in their students and that they more frequently engaged in behavior likely to produce it.

The teacher introversion–extroversion variable was significant in separating the two groups of teachers on only five of the twenty-five interaction variables. As expected, extroverted teachers initiated significantly more total contacts with their students, especially more private contacts involving discussion of work. Their students reciprocated by also initiating a greater number of private work contacts.

Two measures favored the introverted teachers. First, students initiated more comments in general class discussions in the classes taught by introverted teachers. Also, the introverted teachers gave significantly more affirmation or praise following correct responses than did the extroverted teachers. It is possible that these two findings are causally linked, since if the introverted teachers were more likely to praise students, the students might be more likely to venture comments during class discussion. The first finding could also be explained differently, however. Perhaps introverted teachers were generally less dominant and slower to speak or respond in class discussions, so that students had more time or more opportunities to call out comments. Conversely, perhaps extroverted teachers tended to take greater command of the discussion or to move at a more rapid pace, thereby providing less opportunity for students to make comments on their own initiative. These are just post hoc guesses, of course; they cannot be answered unequivocally with the available data.

The behavioral data for both teacher achievement orientation and teacher introversion–extroversion support the teachers' own self-perceptions, since all the significant differences were predictable or at least consistent with the expected differences between the two groups. However, these variables produced fewer differences between the teachers than between the students. This again suggests that the teacher role homogenizes teachers' classroom behavior and masks individual differences.

We now turn to the primary question that Dr. Jones addressed in his dissertation: did teachers have more productive and positive interactions with students with whom they were more similar than with students with whom they were less similar?

Students' introversion–extroversion interacted significantly with teachers' introversion–extroversion on only four of the twenty-five measures. Introverted students initiated significantly more private contacts with introverted teachers, while extroverted students initiated more with extroverted teachers. Also, introverted teachers less frequently failed to give feedback to introverted students, while extroverted teachers less frequently failed to give feedback to extroverted students. Also, introverted teachers more often stayed with introverted students and asked an additional question following a correct answer, while extroverted teachers showed this pattern more frequently with extroverted students. There was a similar, but not significant, tendency on the measure of staying with students following failure.

Thus, on those few measures where significant interactions occurred, teachers did interact more positively with students who were similar to themselves on the introversion–extroversion dimension. This tendency was not very strong or widespread, however.

If the effect of similarity on teacher and student introversion–extroversion was weak, the effect of similarity in achievement orientation was nil. None of the interactions here reached the .05 level of significance; teacher and student similarity on achievement orientation did not affect the pattern of interaction in the classroom. The reason for this is the strong general effect of student achievement orientation, described previously. Teachers had more frequent and generally more positive contacts with high achievement-oriented students regardless of their own achievement orientation. Thus, in general, the consistent differences between high and low achievement-oriented students produced the same general responses from different kinds of teachers. However, there were some interactions between introversion–extroversion and achievement orientation which qualify this general statement.

First, student achievement orientation and teacher introversion–extroversion interacted significantly on two measures and showed nonsignificant trends on several other measures, all dealing with student initiation of contacts with teachers. The general nature of the interaction was that high achieving students initiated more contacts with introverted teachers, while low achieving students initiated more contacts with extroverted teachers. Differences were largest in the classrooms taught by introverted teachers. Introverted teachers had many more contacts with high achievers, especially high achieving extroverts. They also had notably fewer contacts with low achieving extroverts than with other types of students. Introverted teachers were especially likely to call on high achieving extroverted students during general class discussion activities. Thus it appears that they depended on these students to "get the discussion moving" and to provide them with reinforcement in the form of good or stimulating answers (see the Good and Dembo data in Chapter 6 regarding this point).

In contrast, extroverted teachers distributed their response opportunities rather evenly across the four types of students. Apparently these teachers felt more comfortable when leading discussions and did not fear the consequences of calling on students other than those in the high achievement-oriented, extroverted group.

Introverted teachers did initiate many private contacts with low achieving extroverted students, even though they seldom called on them during public discussion. Since the teachers saw these students as extroverted, it is unlikely that their unwillingness to call on them during public discussion resulted from fear of embarrassing them. As Jones (1971) suggested, this pattern instead may represent concern for classroom control in the introverted teacher. The introverted teacher appeared to "lean on" the high achieving extroverted students to keep the discussion moving, while she initiated more contacts with the low achieving extroverted students during periods of silent study and seatwork. Although much of this was no doubt an attempt to help the students with their work, it is likely that a control element was also involved. By frequently initiating private contacts with the low achieving extroverted students, introverted teachers could help insure that these students kept at their work and did not disturb their classmates.

Some of the other interaction data extend the previous suggestion that the high achievement-oriented teachers provide a more appropriate environment for learning than the low achievement-oriented teachers. Recall that in general the classrooms of the high achievement-oriented teachers featured more direct questions and more teacher initiated private contacts with students, more student initiated private contacts with teachers, and more frequent longer contacts with students following both correct and incorrect responses. Interpretation of these general findings is aided by significant interactions involving some of them.

First, although the high achievement-oriented teachers initiated more private contacts with their students generally, they did this less often with high achieving, introverted students. This seems appropriate, since such students apparently were capable of doing good work independently without much teacher help. In addition, however, the high achievement-oriented teachers called on the high achievement-oriented introverted students during public discussions just as often as they called on their classmates. This, too, seems appropriate, since such students need practice in making responses and contributions to these public discussions.

Also, high achievement-oriented teachers generally praised their students evenly, except that they did tend to praise the low achieving, introverted students more frequently. This again seems particularly appropriate: these teachers were giving special encouragement to the students who probably needed it most. Another significant interaction showed that the high achievement-oriented teachers were less likely to ask low achievement-oriented introverted students an additional question after they had made an initial correct response, although they were just as likely to stay with these students after they had failed to respond correctly as they were to stay with their classmates. Although their lower frequency of asking low achievement-oriented introverted students additional questions after an initial correct response might at first seem inappropriate, it must be viewed in the context of their previously noted tendency to praise these students particularly after they made a correct response.

Putting these findings together, it appears that the high achievement-oriented teachers' method of dealing with low achievement-oriented introverted students was "stay with them until you get a response, then praise them." This would appear to be quite appropriate, perhaps even ideal.

Along with the conceptual level test of Harvey and his associates (to be discussed on p. 262), the achievement-orientation scale of the ASD (Veldman, 1970) would seem to be a pencil-and-paper test which is capable of predicting teachers' classroom behavior, and which, therefore is potentially useful as a device for screening teacher candidates or matching them with specific students. This conclusion should be taken with caution, however, because the subjects of Jones's (1971) study were preservice student teachers rather than inservice teachers. The usefulness of the achievement-orientation scale (along with the other six scales of the ASD) for predicting the classroom behavior of inservice teachers is presently being investigated in an ongoing study of teacher effectiveness in the early elementary grades (Brophy, 1973).

Other Variables

Heil, Powell, and Feifer (1960) studied the interactions between three teacher types and four pupil types. Teachers were categorized as well-integrated (self-controlled), weakly integrated (fearful), or turbulent (generally defensive and tending to use intellectualization as their primary defense mechanism). Students were characterized as conformers, strivers, opposers, and waverers. The waverers were highly anxious children who showed variable patterns of behavior, while the other three groups were more consistent in their general styles.

Student achievement, teacher knowledge, and classroom rating measures were analyzed for main effects of teacher type and for interactions between teacher and student types. These revealed that the well-integrated or self-controlled teachers were the most effective with all types of students, while the weakly integrated or fearful teachers were the least effective. Interaction measures showed that the latter teachers were ineffective with all students except those identified as strivers, indicating that highly motivated students will persist in achievement-oriented behavior even with ineffective teachers. The teachers classified as turbulent were effective with both the strivers and the conformers (especially in mathematics and science), but they were less effective with the opposers and waverers because they were too intellectualized and withdrawn to provide the personalized treatment that these two types of students require. Analysis of the behavior of the well-integrated or self-controlled teachers who were most generally successful in producing student achievement gains revealed that their classrooms were marked by consistency, structure, routine activities, and general orderliness. This classroom environment appeared to be especially important in producing achievement in opposers and waverers.

Rexford, Willower, and Lynch (1972) showed a relationship between teachers' pupil control ideology and their classroom verbal behavior. On the basis of their responses to an attitude questionnaire, twelve secondary school teachers classified as having a custodial attitude towards classroom pupil control were compared with twelve teachers classified as having a humanistic attitude. As predicted, analyses of their classroom interaction patterns with the Flanders system revealed that the custodial teachers were more direct in their classroom teaching style than the humanistic teachers. However, the hypothesis that the custodially oriented teachers would show more teacher talk than the humanistically oriented teachers was not supported. There were no significant differences in teacher talk scores between the two groups.

Yando and Kagan (1968) demonstrated that impulsive children can become more reflective if placed in the classroom of an experienced teacher who is reflective. Impulsive individuals make quick decisions, often acting before taking all of the available evidence into account and thus frequently making needless errors. In contrast, reflective individuals take the time to examine carefully the available evidence before responding, so that they make relatively few errors. This variable, sometimes called "conceptual tempo," is relevant to the classroom because impulsive children have been found to make more errors in reading than reflective children. For this reason Yando and Kagan wanted to see if exposure to a reflective teacher would succeed in changing an established pattern of impulsivity. As noted above, placement of such children in the classrooms of reflective teachers did succeed in making them more reflective, at least when the teachers were experienced teachers (Yando and Kagan, 1968). Thus, exposing an impulsive child to the modeling and reinforcement that he will get in the classroom of a reflective teacher is one way that impulsive children can be made more reflective. However, this goal can also be accomplished more quickly and directly through explicit instructions (Meichenbaum, 1971).

Sarason *et al.* (1960) presented considerable evidence that highly anxious children need warm and personal treatment from their teachers and are likely to become especially anxious and unable to perform up to their capacity in testlike situations or in classroom environments which lack this warm, personal element. However, others, notably Grimes and Allinsmith (1961), have suggested that *warmth* is relatively unimportant to highly anxious students compared with *structure*: highly anxious students need highly structured situations in order to perform optimally. Grimes and Allinsmith argued that structure is the more important variable for highly anxious students and suggested that warmth showed up as an important variable in the study by Sarason *et al.*, only because these students attended extremely unstructured schools. It seems probable to us that both factors are important, since both would act to reduce anxiety. Teacher warmth provides a source of identification, comfort, and reassurance for the anxious child, while a clear structure provides the security that comes with knowing what to expect and knowing that one can cope with it. In any case, highly anxious children are likely to do best in the classrooms of teachers who combine these two attributes.

Belief Systems

A teacher individual difference variable that appears to be especially important for the classroom is the teacher's belief system or conceptual level (Harvey, Hunt, and Schroder, 1961). Using both projective tests and objective questionnaires, these investigators have developed measures to score individuals on what they call "belief systems," concentrating in particular on distinctions between abstract and concrete individuals. More concrete individuals tend to show more extreme and absolute, less flexible beliefs and attitudes than more abstract individuals. They also score highly on such variables as reliance on platitudes and normative state-ments, ethnocentrism, religiosity, and unquestioning conviction concerning the superiority of the American way of life.

By contrast, more abstract individuals give more individualistic and relativistic responses and tend to be more aware of the complexities involved in issues rather than seeing them as simple or one-sided. In general, most teachers (and people generally) that have been tested scored closer to the concrete than the abstract end of the continuum.

Several studies have been conducted relating teachers' scores on the abstract-concrete variable to their classroom style and/or their students' performance. In contrast to other pencil-and-paper measures of personality or cognitive style which have not fared well as predictors of teachers' classroom behavior, studies involving the concrete–abstract dimension have produced a set of notable and consistent results.

Harvey, White, Prather, Alter, and Hoffmeister (1966) classified teachers as either abstract or concrete on the basis of their responses to a paper-and-pencil test of belief systems. These data were then related to measures of classroom atmosphere in the preschool classrooms that the teachers taught. It was found that the abstract teachers were warmer, more perceptive of the children's wishes and needs, more flexible in meeting children's interests and needs, more encourag-ing of individual responsibility, more encouraging of the free expression of feelings, more encouraging of creativity; they also showed greater ingenuity and improvisa-tion in using teaching and play materials, invoked unexplained rules less frequently, were less rule oriented, determined classroom and playground procedures less often, were less in need of structure, were less punitive, and were less anxious about being observed. A factor analysis grouped these behaviors into three main factors: resourcefulness, dictatorialness, and punitiveness. This work was expanded in the following study.

Harvey, Prather, White, and Hoffmeister (1968) conducted a follow-up study of sixty-two kindergarten and first-grade teachers. Fifty of these had been classified as having concrete belief systems, while the other twelve were classified as having abstract belief systems. Ratings of teacher and student attributes were made by observers who visited each classroom for approximately two hours. The same observer rated both student and teacher attributes, although observers were instructed to observe the students and score them first before concentrating on the teachers.

The items on the teacher rating scale yielded three general factors. These included *resourcefulness* (use of physical resources, diversity of simultaneous activi-ties, encouragement of creativity, and ingenuity in improvising teaching and play materials); *dictatorialness* (need for structure, inflexibility, rule orientation, low encouragement of free expression of feelings, high teacher determination of class-room procedures, and use of unexplained rules); and *punitiveness* (low warmth, low perceptiveness of the students' needs and wishes, and punitiveness).

Hypothesized relationships between teachers' belief systems and these three aspects of classroom style were supported. Concrete teachers were less resourceful, more dictatorial, and more punitive than abstract teachers.

These data show that teachers' belief systems are related to their classroom styles. In particular, note that the relationships involve two of the classroom styles discussed previously. The dictatorialness factor corresponds to what has been called an authoritarian leadership style, while the punitiveness factor is simply the negative pole of teacher warmth. Thus, to relate this study to data described previously, it may be said that the teachers with more concrete belief systems tend to have more authoritarian leadership styles and to be less warm in their dealings with students than teachers with more abstract styles.

Student ratings were factor analyzed to produce seven factors representing aspects of student behavior: *cooperation* (immediate response to rules, overall adherence to rules, sustained activity, cooperation with the teacher, and adherence to the spirit of the rules); *student involvement* (enthusiasm, voluntary participation in activities, free expression of feelings, student voice in classroom activities, independence, information seeking, security, and task attentiveness); *activity level* (amount of activity and diversity of goal-relevant activity); *nurturance seeking* (guidance seeking and approval seeking); *achievement* (accuracy of facts, appropriateness of solutions, and integration of facts); *helpfulness* (considerateness toward classmates, cooperativeness with classmates, ability to take turns, and low levels of aggression); and *concreteness of response* (rote answers or solutions, orientation toward specific facts, and low novelty in answers or solutions).

As with teacher behavior, teachers' belief systems showed clear-cut and consistent relationships with student behavior. Students of the more abstract teachers were rated as more involved in classroom activities, more active, higher in achievement, less concrete in their responses, less nurturant seeking, more cooperative, and more helpful.

Finally, the correlations between ratings of teacher behavior and ratings of student behavior showed that teacher resourcefulness, dictatorialness, and punitiveness had consistent patterns of relationship with six of the seven student behavior factors. Teacher resourcefulness correlated positively with the positive student factors and negatively with the undesirable ones, while teacher dictatorialness and punitiveness showed the opposite pattern. All correlations were significant except those involving nurturance seeking and one involving student helpfulness, which correlated only $r = .02$ with teacher resourcefulness. The correlations for *student involvement* were especially strong ($r = .69$ with resourcefulness, $r = -.84$ with dictatorialness, and $r = -.73$ with punitiveness), as were those involving *concreteness in student responses* ($r = -.60$ with resourcefulness, $r = -.67$ with dictatorialness, and $r = .56$ with punitiveness).

The results of this study should not be accepted uncritically, since the same observers rated both the teachers and the students, and on the basis of only a single two-hour observation in each classroom. Nevertheless, the data show a remarkably consistent pattern of relationships between teachers' belief systems, teachers' resourcefulness, dictatorialness, and punitiveness in the classroom, and several measures of student achievement and classroom involvement. They also reinforce the data reviewed earlier concerning teacher leadership styles (authoritarian versus democratic) and teacher warmth (versus punitiveness).

This line of research was replicated and extended by Coates, Harvey, and White (1970), who found similar relationships between teachers' conceptual level and the classroom atmospheres of the classes that they taught in elementary schools.

Oswald and Broadbent (1972) showed that belief systems can affect a teacher's behavior in adapting to the requirements of a particular curriculum. In this research teachers varying in conceptual level were studied during learning activities intended to be minimally structured. It was found that the more concrete teachers tended to restructure such lessons so that they could play the role of teacher as they defined it, instead of using the less structured approach that the lesson called for. In contrast, the more abstract teachers altered their behavior relative to the nature of the lesson used. These teachers were more flexible, and especially were more comfortable and successful with minimally structured activities. More specifically, the concrete teachers taught more directly, engaged in more teacher talk, took more time to introduce activities, expressed less satisfaction with the activities, and attributed student gains to their own efforts rather than to students. Their comments about the activities suggested that the activities were too difficult and that the students needed readiness and preparation work before they could benefit from them. In contrast, the more abstract teachers commented favorably on the activities and on the creativity and generally good performance of the students. Compared with the abstract teachers, the concrete teachers spoke as if they saw themselves as striving to overcome difficult obstacles and difficult situations, and as having the idea that students must be made or forced to learn.

Related findings were reported by Murphy and Brown (1970), who related conceptual levels to the teaching behavior of 136 student teachers in home economics. Ratings of their tape-recorded lessons showed that the more abstract student teachers sanctioned search behavior by students more frequently, handled information by helping students theorize and express themselves more frequently, questioned for precise answers, and sanctioned attainment less frequently than the more concrete teachers did.

To the extent that such data are replicated, and to the extent that the paper-and-pencil measures of teachers' belief systems can be used to classify teachers reliably, it would seem that Harvey and his colleagues have the potential for coming up with a quick and easy-to-use measure for classifying teachers. Given only the data reviewed so far, the implication might be drawn that such a measure should be used for selection rather than classification. That is, perhaps future teachers who show up as concrete on these measures should be removed from teacher education programs because they are likely to be unresourceful, dictatorial, and punitive teachers. Such a conclusion would be premature, however, for three reasons.

First, measures of teachers' belief systems have not yet been refined to the point that they could be justifiably used as screening devices to eliminate potentially undesirable teachers. Second, it may prove to be relatively easy to eliminate undesirable teacher behavior through training. Third, many of the general findings reported so far do not hold up for certain subgroups of students. That is, some students actually prefer relatively punitive to warm teachers or relatively authoritarian teachers to democratic teachers. Furthermore, certain students appear to do better under these teachers than under teachers who are more generally successful.

Although these assertions would seem to violate both common sense and the general findings reviewed above, there are data to back them up. Thus if decisions about teachers are ever made on the basis of their scores on paper-and-pencil measures of belief systems, it just may be that the decisions will concern pairing teachers and students rather than deciding which potential teachers should be weeded out of teacher education programs.

Hunt (1971) has systematically investigated the idea that the optimal teacher for a student at a given point on the abstract–concrete dimension would be a teacher who is *slightly* more abstract than the student rather than an *extremely* abstract teacher. The rationale here is that the latter teacher might be too far removed from and too incomprehensible to the student, and therefore less effective in advancing his development toward greater abstractness than would a teacher who was closer to the student's present level and therefore perhaps more comprehensible to him.

Hunt is also systematically exploring and documenting the differences between types of students on the abstract–concrete dimension as they relate to the students' classroom behavior and to the kinds of teaching that would be most effective with students at a given level. The ultimate goal of this effort is to come up with information that would be useful in matching teachers and students so as to maximize student achievement and/or affective development in a given year.

In one study Tomlinson and Hunt (1970) examined the learning of constructs by matched classes of high school students taught with one of three methods varying in degree of structure. As predicted, there was an interaction between students' conceptual level and their concept attainment, with the more abstract students doing better in the less structured classrooms, and the more concrete students doing better in the highly structured classrooms.

Hunt and Hardt (1967) also observed an interaction between student conceptual level and degree of structure in the classroom, this time in disadvantaged high school students in the Upward Bound program. Some classes were highly structured, while others were very flexible. There were no overall differences between these two teaching approaches, but students low in conceptual level did better in the highly structured classes, while students high in conceptual level did better in the more flexible classes.

Phillips and Sinclair (1973) found that positive student perceptions of the classroom were more related to the match between student conceptual level and teacher conceptual level than they were to teacher conceptual level as such. Student perceptions were most positive when their teacher's conceptual level was similar to their own. The results were interpreted as supportive of Hunt's matching model idea.

Apparently students' conceptual levels can affect their performance on different types of tests and in different subject areas. Claunch (1964) found that abstract and concrete students did equally well on objective tests, but that abstract students did better on essay exams. If, as seems likely, concrete teachers give more multiple-choice exams than essay exams, concrete students may have good reason to prefer them to abstract teachers.

Another interesting effect of student conceptual level was noted by Pohl and Pervin (1968), who studied the grades of undergraduate males in various subjects. With aptitude controlled, they found that concrete students got higher grades than abstract students in engineering, while the abstract students got higher grades in the humanities and social sciences. No difference between the groups was observed in grades in the natural sciences. These data seem to fit nicely with those reported above, at least if the stereotypes about these subject-matter areas can be believed.

Of the variables reviewed in this chapter, conceptual level appears to be the most promising as a basis for profitably matching teachers and students.

DISCUSSION

Most of the studies reviewed in this chapter provide some support for the notion of matching teachers and students according to relevant personal attributes, although few relationships are strong and/or consistent enough to be practical at this time. Many of the expected classroom applications of theory and/or laboratory research have not worked out in practice, and many of the classroom matching experiments which have produced positive results are questionable because they may involve short-term gain at the expense of long-term loss.

One of the simplest and apparently most easily applicable theoretical principles is the similarity–attraction hypothesis. This predicts straightforwardly that people who are similar to one another on a given variable are more likely to be attracted to one another than people who are less similar, so that at the very least an improved classroom climate should be expected if teachers and students were matched so as to be similar on relevant variables. In practice, however, matching based on the similarity–attraction hypothesis has been generally unsuccessful. Jones (1971), for example, while establishing that introversion–extroversion was an important classroom variable, found little evidence that matching teachers and students on this variable would make much difference. Similarly, McDonald (1972) found that mutual attraction between teachers and students seemed to make little difference in their classroom interaction patterns. (See Chapter 5.)

Negative results regarding the matching possibility of several personality variables were reported by Poggio (1973). This study involved 11 teachers and over 600 sixth graders. The students took four math subtests from the Stanford Achievement Test Battery, and both the students and the teachers were measured for sociability, ego strength, dominance, outgoingness, sensitivity, and guilt-proneness on a personality questionnaire. Correlations between the students' personality variables and their math achievement scores were generally low. A few reached statistical significance, but none were high enough to be of any practical significance. Correlations between the six personality variables of the teachers and the four student achievement measures were even lower. Thus none of the six variables seemed to be very important or to be likely as a candidate for usage as a matching variable, at least so far as student math achievement is concerned (perhaps more positive results might have been obtained if classroom climate or other affective variables had been measured).

Thus optimal matching of teachers and students, while obviously a logical and exciting possibility, is impractical at present, at least as a generalized strategy, although the conceptual level variable appears promising. Optimal matching in special cases, of course, is demonstrably effective (placing impulsive students with reflective teachers, discipline problems with good disciplinarians, and so on).

SUMMARY

In the present chapter we reviewed individual differences in teachers and students that are known or suspected to influence classroom behavior and effectiveness.

Certain general traits which appear to be universally or almost universally associated with effectiveness include a democratic as opposed to an authoritarian leadership style (which does not produce better student achievement but does tend to produce better classroom atmosphere), teacher warmth and enthusiasm, and an abstract rather than a concrete belief system or conceptual style.

While these teacher traits are effective for most students, studies identifying subgroups of students for whom they are less effective than their opposites have been identified, so that exceptions to the general rules are known to exist. The latter point underlies an idea presently popular in educational research: attempting to match teachers and students on relevant variables in order to maximize cognitive and/or affective outcomes in one or both groups.

This could be done by matching students to teachers whose characteristics are opposite to their own (the "opposites attract" hypothesis), or by matching them with teachers who are similar on the relevant characteristics (the similarity hypothesis). Although "opposites attract" is a familiar homily and there are a few data to support the idea of matching students to teachers whose characteristics are opposite from their own, the vast majority of studies in the psychological literature favor the similarity hypothesis, suggesting that the more similar two people are, the more likely they are to like one another. An implication from this is that the more similar a teacher and student are, the more likely the teacher is to like the student and to have favorable interaction patterns with him in the classroom. However, classroom applications of this idea have been generally negative.

Apparently, the role demands and situation-specific behavior built into the teacher role limit the degree to which a teacher's individual characteristics show through in his classroom behavior. Thus two teachers will appear much more similar to each other when observed in their classrooms than they will when observed in a nonclassroom setting, and predicted interactions between teacher and student characteristics usually do not appear.

Although teacher roles tend to limit the degree to which teachers show their individual personalities in the classroom, the ways that different teachers define that role apparently exert strong effects on their classroom teaching style. High achievement-oriented and low achievement-oriented teachers differ from each other in their approaches to the teaching task. High achievement-oriented teachers show much more evidence of behavior reflecting concern about and attempts to promote student learning than low achievement-oriented teachers, who tend to be more concerned with classroom atmosphere and other affective variables. Teachers differing in conceptual level show similar differences in classroom behaviors. Of the variables studied, conceptual level seems most promising as a basis for optimally matching teachers and students. Even this work has not yet reached the level of practical application, however.

chapter 9

Promoting Proactive Teaching

INCREASING TEACHERS' AWARENESS
OF THEIR OWN BEHAVIOR

In the previous chapters we have described how group and individual differences in students can condition teachers to treat them differentially, often to the detriment of student achievement and/or motivation. However, we have consistently pointed out that such differential teacher behavior is typically unconscious, even when it is systematic and obvious to the classroom observer. As Jackson (1968) has pointed out, teaching involves such a rapidly paced sequence of action and reaction that the teacher is hard pressed simply to keep up, let alone monitor his behavior at the same time. However, the teacher must learn to monitor his behavior or at least to get feedback about it if he is to shape the pattern of interactions proactively in his classroom and not merely react to differential student behavior which in effect conditions him.

Teacher awareness is the key to achievement of this kind of proactive teaching, in our view. Once teachers are made aware of inappropriate teaching on their part, the vast majority are willing and eager to change. However, teachers typically do not get very much useful feedback (See Chapter 11). As a result, unproductive habits and teaching patterns sometimes persist indefinitely simply because the teacher himself is unaware of them and no one else makes him aware of them. In the present chapter we discuss this problem of teacher awareness and some of the reasons for it, describe treatment studies by ourselves and others which have succeeded in changing teacher behavior simply by making teachers more aware of their behavior, and present a general model for intervention when inappropriate teaching appears to result simply from lack of awareness on the teacher's part.

REASONS FOR LACK OF TEACHER AWARENESS

By now it should be clear that the attitudes and behavior of teachers and students are heavily influenced by the information that they have or think that they have on hand. We mentioned earlier that Feshbach (1969) found that teachers tend to project their own attitudes on to students in the absence of more specific and contradictory information. However, teachers here are acting just like anyone else. We all tend to make these kinds of projections in ambiguous situations. Chansky (1958) showed that students do the same thing. Students in a child psychology course were administered the Minnesota Teacher Attitude Inventory, a questionnaire designed to measure teacher attitudes on a variety of topics relevant to education. Its main focus is on the authoritarian versus democratic or child-centered approach to teaching. In addition to taking the MTAI themselves, the students were asked to predict the attitudes of their classroom instructor concerning child rearing (the instructor took pains to keep his attitudes to himself during the early weeks of the course when this experiment took place). Analysis of the results showed that students with high MTAI scores (indicating a more democratic, student-centered attitude) predicted that their teacher would encourage freedom in children, while subjects with low MTAI scores thought that their instructor would take a more clinical attitude toward children. They also tended to look upon the instructor more as a disciplinarian. Thus, in the absence of more well-defined cues about actual attitudes, individuals tend to project their own attitudes onto others.

Lack of well-defined cues is not the explanation for lack of teacher awareness, however. Over the course of the school year, teachers get much opportunity to interact with students and discover their characteristics and attitudes, and, as Willis (1972) showed, they are capable of accurately judging certain aspects of their students in a very short period of time. Thus low teacher awareness does not result from lack of opportunity to observe the student.

One factor, already mentioned, is the rapid pace of teacher-student interaction which makes it difficult for the teacher to monitor what is going on as it happens. Another factor is that the visual feedback provided by students is not very helpful and perhaps even misleading. Taylor (1968) found this in a study of three methods of measuring student attention during class. The three measures were student self-ratings, stimulated recall tasks in which videotapes of previous classes were played back to the student and stopped at certain points so that he could be asked what came next, and ratings of apparent attention shown by the student on films of these same classes. Here the ratings were made by neutral judges rather than by the teacher, and the ratings were highly reliable. Nevertheless, although the first two measures of student attention were highly intercorrelated and apparently valid, neither was very highly correlated with attention as judged by viewing the films. In other words, students who appear to be attentive to classroom discussion may not be, and those who might appear to be inattentive may actually be attending. This is probably a partial explanation for the finding of Jecker, Maccoby, Breitrose, and Rose (1964) that teachers could do no better than chance in judging student comprehension of material if they used only the visual clues provided by watching the students' faces. However, their judgment improved if visual clues were supplemented by asking the students questions about the material or involving them in discussion. Thus active interaction with the students which allows an opportunity to observe the student handling the material himself can produce accurate perception, but simple observation without such interaction is likely to be erroneous.

In this connection recall the data of Putnins (1970) showing that, among other differences, more aware teachers tended to use longer and harder questions than less aware teachers. In addition, the more aware teachers appeared to be better in all respects in that they were more student-oriented, warmer, and more rewarding in addition to their difference in questioning behavior.

Ehman (1970) also showed the problem of teaching awareness by comparing teachers, students, and classroom observers as sources of information. When questioned about various aspects of classroom interaction concerning the same class that the teachers and students had participated in and the observers had observed, the students and the observers agreed closely but neither agreed very closely with the teachers. Here again, teacher perception was not very accurate, probably because the teachers were too busy teaching to be very aware of what they were doing. As suggested in the studies reviewed in Chapter 6, however, teachers are quite accurate regarding certain aspects of the classroom, especially student ability. Baker (1972) found that teachers were more accurate than both parents and students themselves in judging student ability. In this study ten teachers, their sixth-, seventh-, or eighth-grade students, and the parents of these students were all asked to estimate student mathematical ability by indicating which mathematical objectives the student could and could not master. These predictions were then checked out with a mastery test, and it was found that teachers predicted with 48 percent accuracy, compared with 33 percent for students and 26 percent for parents. None of these figures are very high or impressive, but the teachers were clearly the best predictors, even better than the students themselves.

Defensiveness

Studies seem to indicate that teachers predict fairly accurately when asked about student ability and certain rather obvious student behaviors, but that they are relatively unaware of their patterns of interaction with students, especially individual differences with different students in their classrooms. So far we have discussed only what we believe to be the primary reason for this low awareness: the fast pace of classroom life which makes it difficult for teachers to monitor their own interactions. However, several studies have suggested an additional reason: defensiveness against perception of failure or other unpleasant classroom events. Johnson, Feigenbaum, and Weiby (1964) and Beckman (1970) conducted experiments in which teachers taught bogus students through a one-way window. The teachers never actually saw or interacted with the bogus students, but they did get feedback about student performance which led them to believe that they were either succeeding or failing in teaching the task. Posttask questionnaires revealed ego-defensive responses on the part of the teachers. They took personal credit for success when the student had succeeded in learning the task, but they blamed the student or factors other than themselves if the student failed. Again, this is not unique to teachers. Simon and Feather (1973) found the same tendency in students. Right before taking a test, undergraduates rated their ability, amount of preparation, the probable difficulty of the test, and their confidence or expectation for success. After receiving their grades they were asked to attribute causality for their performance by rating the relative importance of these factors and of luck. Their responses showed ego defensiveness; students tended to take personal credit for success by attributing it to their own abilities and efforts, while they tended to rationalize failure by attributing it to test difficulty or bad luck.

Furthermore, the findings concerning ego defensiveness in teachers are mixed. Ames (1973) criticized the studies by Beckman (1970) and by Johnson, Feigenbaum, and Weiby (1964) on the grounds that they were unrealistic laboratory experiments which did not allow the teacher-subjects to interact with and observe actual students. Consequently, he conducted a study designed to test whether or not teachers would take ego-defensive positions regarding their success or failure in teaching, but he used a more realistic teaching situation in which the teacher-subjects actually taught groups of students whom they could observe and interact with. His results were flatly contradictory to the ego-defensive position; the teachers took responsibility for student failure but credited the students when they achieved success. Similar findings were obtained by Beckman (1972) herself in a second study done under more realistic conditions than her first study.

However, studies using realistic designs have also obtained ego-defensive results. Quirk (1967) had student teachers teach three brief lessons to one group of ninth-grade boys and then teach three lessons to a different group. After teaching, the teachers were given feedback about student performance, sometimes being led to believe that they had succeeded well and other times led to believe that they had failed. Questionnaire data revealed that teachers in the success condition rated their teaching as better than teachers in the failure condition; rated their teaching as better than that of a reference group of teachers who supposedly had taught the same lessons the previous year; and reported that they "tried harder" to teach in the success than in the failure condition. There was also a near-significant tendency for teachers to rate their teaching performance in the success condition as better than their teaching performance in the failure condition. Thus these teachers were strongly influenced by the feedback concerning student performance in judging their own teaching success (appropriately so, given the shortness of the experiment and the absence of other relevant information). Just as the teachers tended to take credit for their success in the success condition, they tended to blame students for their failure in the failure condition. They rated students in the failure condition as less attentive, less cooperative, less interested, and less intelligent than the students in the success condition.

Similar findings were reported by Baldwin, Johnson, and Wiley (1970). When asked why students succeed in a particular subject area, teachers tended to attribute student success to teacher controlled variables such as their teaching methods. In contrast, they attributed student failure to student variables such as low intelligence, lack of readiness, poor motivation, and poor attention.

Mayhew (1972) conducted a study in which teacher defensiveness was partially reduced through treatment. The experiment began with a simulated teaching situation in which teachers were given an examination paper ostensibly written by one of their students and were asked to score the exam and to rate the student's ability (reading and math ability) and effort (work habits and cooperation). Half of the teachers were given exams showing 10 percent success, and the other half were given exams showing 100 percent success. Thus half were led to believe that they had failed to teach the student in question successfully, and the other half were led to believe that they had taught very successfully. The data on teacher ratings of students showed evidence of teacher defensiveness. Teachers attributed high ability and effort to students who had succeeded, and low ability and effort to students who had failed. Also, the successful teachers tended to praise both themselves and the students, while the unsuccessful teachers did not (they did not criticize themselves or the students, either, however).

After this experience, all subjects were exposed to nine hours of instruction in behavior modification. The course stressed, among other things, the importance of learning to view learning failures as informational feedback that the teacher can use to modify teaching strategies and not as threatening or critical. Following this instruction the experiment was repeated, except that all subjects were given examinations showing only a 10 percent score. The results showed that the treatment was a qualified success in reducing teacher defensiveness. Teachers still tended to attribute low ability and effort to students' failure, but this tendency was greatly reduced from the pretreatment rates. Also, the teachers became more self-critical. Following treatment, they were more willing to take personal responsibility for learning failure than they had been prior to the treatment. In general, the treatment was most successful in getting the teachers to take responsibility for student learning and begin to blame themselves for learning failure. Some defensiveness remained, however, in that they still tended to blame students also. Taken together, the studies reviewed above suggest that, at least in the absence of more clear-cut information, teachers are prone to take personal credit for student learning but to blame students for learning failures.

Lest we judge teachers too harshly, however, let us consider the findings of Ames and Ames (1973). Like the study by Ames (1973) mentioned above, the present study involved realistic teaching in which teachers taught short lessons to groups of eight children. Questionnaire data regarding attribution of causality for success and failure were obtained not only from the teachers but from observers who watched the teachers teaching the lessons. There were interesting differences between these two sets of data. The teachers did not take personal credit for success or blame the students for failures. Instead, they tended to explain both success and failure with reference to student characteristics rather than their own behavior. Thus failure was generally attributed by the teachers to poor student motivation and/or low ability, but student success was attributed to good student motivation and/or good ability rather than to good teaching. Thus the general finding for the teachers was a tendency to explain success and failure in terms of student variables rather than their own behavior. In contrast, observers tended to explain success and failure in terms of teacher variables. They tended to attribute success to good teaching and failure to poor teaching. Similar findings were reported by Beckman (1972) in her second study.

Both of these studies illustrate the power of the teacher role in structuring teacher perception and behavior during the act of teaching. It is noteworthy that although both studies found clear-cut differences in the perceptions of the teachers and the observers, the observers were themselves teachers (actually student teachers). Many had participated in the experiments themselves as teacher-subjects, so they had had experience in teaching and in dealing with student success and failure from the viewpoint of the teacher. Nevertheless, this experience did not generalize to their behavior when acting as classroom observers. The two perspectives on the classroom are considerably different. Teachers tend to be oriented primarily toward the material they are trying to get across and toward the apparent success and failure of their students in mastering this material, and they usually are not very aware of their own behavior. In contrast, the attention of classroom observers is focused much more upon the teacher than upon the students, so that they are more likely to explain classroom events in terms of teacher success or failure than student success or failure. These studies show the potential value of classroom observers as sources of objective feedback to teachers (assuming that the observers are trying to be helpful to the teacher and not taking a hypercritical attitude toward him). At the same time, however, they again illustrate how difficult it is for most teachers to monitor their own behavior during the act of teaching.

Students Condition Teacher Behavior

In the previous studies experimenters provided explicit feedback to teachers concerning their success or failure in teaching, and they showed that this feedback usually affected teachers' perceptions. Other studies have shown that teachers can be affected by student behavior that they perceive themselves, even if it is not specifically called to their attention by an experimenter or observer. Jenkins and Deno (1969) exposed teacher-subjects to classes who had been instructed to appear either attentive or disinterested. Unsurprisingly, the teachers who had taught in a class that appeared attentive and interested rated their teaching performance more highly than the teachers who taught in a class that appeared inattentive and disinterested. Related findings were reported by Herrell (1971). In this study the same guest lecturer, unaware of the experiment, lectured in two different psychology courses. One class was led to expect that he was a warm, friendly person, while the other was led to expect that he was a cold, indifferent person. Thus here the students were not even given specific instructions about how to react; they were merely given information about the personal characteristics of the lecturer. Nevertheless, this information was enough to affect student behavior, which in turn affected the behavior of the lecturer. Observation of his teaching behavior in the two classes showed that he was gradually conditioned by student response. In the class where he was expected to be warm and friendly, he gradually became warmer as the class progressed, while in the class where he was expected to be cold and indifferent, he gradually became colder as the class progressed. He was judged as warmer, more relaxed, and generally more competent during the latter segment of his lecture to the warm class than during this segment of his lecture to the cold class.

A more extended experiment of the same type was conducted by Klein (1971). This study involved twenty-four guest lecturers who were the subjects of the experiment. The subjects lectured to a class of students who were actually confederates of the experimenter following instructions to vary their behavior at different points in the lecture. During times when positive behaviors were to be shown, the students tried to appear attentive, to maintain eye contact with the lecturer, and generally to give evidence of interest in his presentation. During periods of negative behavior the students tried to appear restless, inattentive, bored, and generally disinterested. These conditions were invoked at various times during each lecture. Again, the evidence showed that student behavior conditioned teacher behavior. Three of four hypotheses were confirmed: (1) Teacher behavior changes as a function of changes in student behavior; (2) Teacher behavior is more indirect during periods of positive student behavior than during periods of negative student behavior; (3) Teacher behavior is more positive during periods of natural student behavior (when the students merely followed their own inclinations rather than deliberately simulated either positive or negative behavior) than during periods of negative student behavior. A fourth prediction, that teacher behavior would be more indirect during periods of positive student behavior than during periods of natural student behavior, was not confirmed. This most probably was because the students were generally positive during their periods of natural behavior. Klein reported that there was little difference between student behaviors in the natural and the positive conditions. This is readily understandable. Given the nature of the experiment, most students would probably be quite sympathetic to the lecturer-subject, even if they were uninterested in his presentation!

The previous three studies all involved experimental manipulations of some kind. However, Oppenlander (1969) produced naturalistic evidence that student differences force changes in teacher behavior in different classes. This study took place in the top and bottom classes of the sixth grade in a school that practiced tracking. The top class contained the top 20 percent of the students and the bottom class contained the lowest 20 percent. The same four teachers taught arithmetic, science, social studies, and language arts to these students. Each class was observed for five full class periods with a version of the Flanders system. Results did not bear out the main prediction that teachers would be more indirect in the high ability classes, but several differences were observed. Teachers in the high ability sections started out less direct but became more direct over time, but when they worked in the low ability section they started out more direct but became less direct over time. These effects were rather general across the four teachers. The data for the low ability classes were understandable in view of the frequently heard advice that teachers be tough at the beginning of the year and loosen up later, especially when dealing with low achievers or classes that have frequent behavior problems. However, the data for the high achieving classes remain a mystery. It is possible that the teachers were too indirect and had to tighten up somewhat in order to regain sufficient control, or perhaps the data were related to unknown and uncontrolled differences in the curriculum being taught at the time of the experiment. In any case, the study illustrates that different types of classes change teachers' styles somewhat, although the findings are not in agreement with what would be expected from the laboratory studies which would predict that teachers would be warmer and more indirect in the high achieving classrooms.

CHANGING TEACHER BEHAVIOR BY INCREASING TEACHER AWARENESS

The studies reviewed previously in this chapter and in the book in general underscore the point that much teacher behavior is unconscious. If one assumes (as we do) that this factor, and not callousness, indifference, or irresponsibility, is the major cause of inappropriate classroom teaching, it follows that much inappropriate teaching can be eliminated simply by making the teacher aware of what he is doing. Although relatively limited, the available literature strongly supports this idea.

Emmer, Good, and Pilgrim (1972) demonstrated the effects of set induction upon teacher behavior. Student teachers working in high school English classes were given instructions intended to induce either a set toward pupil achievement (concentrate on getting across the material and on seeing that the students master it) or on student attitudes (concentrate on making the material enjoyable to students and on motivating them to participate in class and enjoy it). Although there were no significant effects on product measures of student attitude or achievement administered early and later in the semester, the data did show significant process differences in teacher behavior. Teachers with the achievement set asked more convergent questions and stayed with students more often following failure and in general appeared to be primarily concerned with working to get the students to master the material. In contrast, student teachers with the attitude set asked fewer convergent questions, allowed more pupil-to-pupil interaction, and were generally more indirect. Thus the treatment did succeed in affecting the teacher behavior, although no significant product outcomes were observed.

Specific Information and Prescriptive Advice

Hoyt (1955) studied the effects of teacher knowledge about students on pupil achievement and attitude. One group of teachers was urged to avoid obtaining any information about their pupils other than what they could see in the classroom; another was asked to limit their information to copies of achievement and IQ tests plus what they could see in the classroom; and a third group was given considerable information about the students in addition to IQ and achievement data. Teachers in the third group also participated in discussions about the students with the experimenter. Hoyt found that giving teachers more information about students improved student attitudes toward teachers, but it made no difference on student achievement. Thus in this study greater information about students led to affective but not achievement gains. This may have been because simple provision of information about students without prescriptive advice about how to treat them might not be a strong enough treatment to affect student achievement. The increased knowledge about the personal characteristics of the student would be likely to increase teacher interest in the student, and therefore lead to affective results, but without diagnostic and prescriptive information about teaching the student, there is no particular reason to expect achievement gains.

Tilton (1947) tried to manipulate intraclass individual differences in teacher-pupil interaction. He asked each of six elementary school teachers to concentrate specifically on three or four students in each class and to try to increase the arithmetic performance of these students. The treatment was unsuccessful; the arithmetic achievement of these specifically identified students was not affected by the treatment. Here again, the treatment was global rather than specific and prescriptive. The teachers were asked to try to increase arithmetic performance, but they were not given specific instructions about exactly how to go about doing this.

This point is illustrated in a two-year longitudinal study by Gordon (1970) concerning information about musical aptitude in beginning music students. In this study the teachers were given information about some of their students from a musical aptitude profile which contained diagnostic descriptions of each student's strengths and weaknesses and prescriptive implications for how he should be taught. As a result, teachers were able to plan objectively their treatment of these experimental students to match their musical strengths and weaknesses. In contrast, they had to rely on their subjective judgments in planning instruction for control students. The result was significantly higher musical achievement for the experimental students about whom teachers had objective knowledge concerning musical aptitudes. Thus prescriptive advice about what to do, and not mere provision of information about students, appears to be essential for insuring effective change in teacher behavior.

This was also brought out in a study by Tuckman, McCall, and Hyman (1969). In this study teachers classified as high or low in their initial accuracy regarding their perception of their own behavior were given one of three treatments: direct feedback based upon observations by observers using the Flanders system; instruction in the use of the Flanders system but without direct feedback concerning their own behavior on these variables; or the opportunity to listen to tape recordings of classroom interactions but without any training in the Flanders system and without any feedback about their teaching. The data revealed that only the group given direct feedback about their teaching showed changes in their behavior, with the least accurate teachers showing the most change. Thus the combination of dissonance created by showing teachers that they were not teaching as they thought they were with specific, prescriptive information about how to change was effective in producing change, while less specific treatments were not.

Studies which have provided this kind of specific information have been generally successful. For example, Gage, Runkel, and Chatterjee (1960) succeeded in getting teachers to change their behavior by presenting them with feedback from their students. Feedback was acquired by asking students to rate their teachers on twelve aspects of teacher behavior (such as "acts disappointed when a pupil gets something wrong," and "explains arithmetic so pupils can understand it"). After collecting these pupil perceptions the investigators communicated them to the teachers, so that each teacher could see his pattern of teaching strengths and weaknesses as the students perceived it. Data from a readministration of student ratings of teachers following the treatment procedure showed that, in the eyes of the students at least, the teachers had made a significant improvement on ten of the twelve behaviors studied.

Ojemann and Wilkinson (1939) gave teachers detailed information about one member of a number of pairs of matched students in their classes. The students were high school students matched on age, achievement, and intelligence. In addition to this information, the investigators knew about the students' personality characteristics, personal problems, and home backgrounds. For the experimental student in each pair, the investigators shared this extra information with the teachers and made suggestions about how to use it to individualize and optimize better the teaching of these students during the school year.

Data on the students were collected at the beginning and end of the year, and these showed that the experimental students made significantly greater achievement gains, had more favorable attitudes toward school, and showed fewer indications of personality conflicts than their matched controls. Thus this combination of selection of specific students for treatment and giving specific instructions about the treatment to be implemented was highly successful.

In a study similar to our own treatment research to be described below, Withall (1956) demonstrated the effects of information and suggestions to teachers on the participation rates of students. After observing in several classrooms, he identified eight students in each class who had very low rates of classroom participation and communicated this fact to teachers, suggesting that they attempt to increase the interaction rates of these eight students. The results showed a dramatic increase in the participation rates of these students. Furthermore, a "radiation effect" (a change in teachers' behavior toward nontarget students which was related to changes in their treatment of target students) was observed: the teachers' general interaction rates with all of the students in the classes rose significantly. Thus the treatment not only got the teachers to interact more frequently with the eight students singled out for special mention; it also increased their general rates of interaction in the classroom.

CHANGING TEACHER BEHAVIOR RELATED TO TEACHER EXPECTATIONS

A Treatment Study

In Chapter 4 we described our unsuccessful attempt to show gradual polarization of high and low expectation students as the first semester progressed in nine first-grade classrooms (Evertson, Brophy, and Good, 1972). We will now describe the results of a treatment study conducted during the second semester in eight of those nine classrooms (one of the teachers in the upper-middle class white school transferred out of the district at the end of the first semester).

Methods

The treatment involved an interview in which each teacher was given feedback about her interaction with certain students (Good and Brophy, 1972b). Two groups of students that she had been treating somewhat inappropriately were described to her, and suggestions were made about how she could treat them more appropriately. The feedback and suggestions were based on the behavioral data collected in the first semester, so that they were founded on behavioral evidence. There was no attempt to artificially manipulate teacher expectations or to give teachers fictitious information.

In a sense, then, the treatment was very similar to what a supervisor does when he observes the teacher and then makes suggestions. A major difference, of course, was that our treatment advice had forty hours of classroom observation behind it, not just a short visit or two, which is usually all that a supervisor has to go on.

A single interview was selected as the treatment because one of our interests was to come up with a method that could be used easily by supervisors or others in a position to give teachers feedback after observing them in the classroom. Survey data from several sources show that effective supervision methods are sorely needed. Most teachers are rarely or never observed and given feedback by supervisors (McNeil, 1971). Furthermore, teachers tend to reject the supervisor feedback that they do get, often because they do not agree with the values or criteria that the supervisor uses in making judgments about their teaching (McNeil, 1971). As a result they usually do not change their teaching along the lines suggested, and they sometimes even deliberately move in the opposite direction (Tuckman and Oliver, 1968).

We had reason to believe that feedback based on data from our observations would be more acceptable to teachers than the feedback they usually get from supervisors. As we have pointed out elsewhere (Good and Brophy, 1970), supervisor comments too often boil down to "your way is wrong; do it my way" from the standpoint of the teacher. Criticism from even the most tactful supervisor will sometimes be seen this way by teachers, and many will become defensive or resentful.

Our treatment minimized this problem in two ways. First, it was based on objective observation of a large number of discrete interactions, rather than upon impressionist ratings or judgments. In fact, the classroom observers working in each teacher's classroom were not involved at all in the treatment, to insure that advice would be based strictly on the data and not be colored by personal impressions. Interviews were conducted by the authors, working from data sheets containing information about interaction in the classroom. We think that the objectivity of the data we were using reinforced the acceptability and credibility of the suggestions that we gave.

A second advantage resulted from our use of the individual student as the focus of analysis. By tabulating the teacher's interaction with each different student separately, we were able to show that teachers were teaching some students appropriately and others inappropriately. In making suggestions for improvement, we were in effect saying "you are doing a fine job with Arlene, now try to do the same kinds of things with Jere." This is much less threatening and more acceptable than "your way is wrong, do it my way."

The treatment was confined to a single interview because we wanted to see if teachers could change in response to feedback alone, without retraining or continuing feedback. Here again, the development of an intervention procedure that would have wide practical application was our primary concern. If it is true that much inappropriate treatment of individual students results from lack of teacher awareness rather than from unwillingness or lack of ability to do better, it follows that an intervention which simply provides teachers with *information* to make them aware of what they are doing should be enough to make them change.

The treatment was focused on two types of students in each classroom. The first (low participant group) included students who had very low rates of interaction with the teachers. These students did not volunteer to answer questions and seldom initiated interactions with the teachers. Correspondingly, the teachers did not seek out these students very frequently, either.

The low participant group was identified on the basis of quantitative measures of teacher-student interaction. A second group (the extension group) was identified on the basis of a qualitative measure: the teacher's willingness to stay with students and provide a second response opportunity when they failed on the first. The teachers usually did not persist in seeking responses from extension group students if they failed to succeed on their first opportunity. Instead of repeating the question or providing a clue, the teachers would give up on these students, giving them the answer or calling on someone else. We labeled these students the "extension" group because our advice to teachers was to *extend* their interactions with them in failure situations (we could also have called them the "give up" group).

Each classroom showed extreme variability on these measures, so that low participants and extension students could be identified in every teacher's class. There were also general differences from one teacher to the next, of course. For example, one teacher stayed with her students over 50 percent of the time following an initial failure, while another stayed less than 20 percent of the time. In the first teacher's class there were a few students (extension group) that the teacher stayed with only 20 percent to 30 percent of the time, while she stayed with a few other students over 90 percent of the time. The second teacher stayed with her extension group students less than 10 percent of the time, although she stayed with some of her other students 50 percent to 60 percent of the time.

The situation with the low participant group was similar. There were large differences between classrooms but even larger differences within classrooms, so that a group with strikingly low interaction frequencies could be identified in each class.

In each classroom at least two students, usually three or four, were identified for each treatment group. The number was dependent upon the data. If only two students in a given class stood out as having strikingly low rates of interaction with the teacher, these students alone comprised the low participant group. In another class where four students had strikingly low rates of interaction, the low participant group would contain four. This flexibility allowed us to be sure that each student included in a group was appropriately classified.

A total of twenty-one low participants and twenty-eight extension students were identified in the eight classrooms. The low participant group included fourteen girls and seven boys, while the extension group included eight girls and twenty boys. The predominance of girls in the low participant group was expected, since girls typically have fewer interactions with teachers than boys and are generally less likely to be salient in the classroom (see Chapter 7).

We do not know why the extension group contained many more boys than girls. The sex difference favoring girls in achievement at this grade level is one probable factor. Other things being equal, a girl is more likely than a boy to respond successfully the second time if a teacher repeats the question or gives a clue. Also, since the teachers were all females, it may be that they were more familiar and comfortable with the personal attributes and behavior of girls than boys. To the extent that the teachers were nervous or uncomfortable in dealing with boys, they would be less likely to persist in seeking responses from them than from girls.

These are only guesses, however. Although we have tried (through teacher interviews and rating scales), we have not yet succeeded in identifying any single attribute that extension group students share in common. It may be that student attributes interact with teacher preferences here, so that one teacher would easily give up on one type of student while another teacher would tend to give up on another type.

Both groups included students from all achievement levels. Based on a division of the teacher's rankings into high, middle, and low thirds, the low participant group contained seven highs, five middles, and nine lows, while the extension group contained nine highs, eight middles, and eleven lows. We had expected a more clear preponderance of lows, especially in the extension group, but, as explained in Chapter 4, most of these teachers did not treat low expectation students inappropriately.

Treatment Interviews

Treatment interviews were scheduled early in the second semester. Each teacher was seen individually in her own classroom after school. For each interview we prepared a list containing the names of *four* groups of students. On the left side of the paper were listed the names of the low participant students, and, under them, the names of the extension students. On the right side of the page, across from each of the respective treatment groups, were the names of two *contrast groups*.

The contrast groups contained the names of students that the teachers were treating appropriately in situations similar to those in which they were treating the treatment groups inappropriately. The contrast children were included on the lists for two reasons. The first was to stimulate each teacher's thinking and help her to see her own behavior more clearly. We reasoned that the opportunity to compare each treatment group with its contrast group would help the teacher gain insight into the reasons for her differential treatment of these two groups of students.

The other reason for including the contrast groups was our interest in providing acceptable and nonthreatening feedback to the teacher. The contrast groups allowed us to point to students with whom the teacher had been doing an especially good job. Further, in suggesting changes in behavior toward the treatment groups, we could say "you are already doing it with these contrast students; now try to do it with these other students too."

After assuring the teacher that we would later explain the basis for the grouping, we asked her to try to figure out the basis for the four groups. We wanted to see if the teacher would spontaneously notice anything in common among the students in a group, or any common difference between a treatment group and its contrast group. Such information would provide valuable clues about the student characteristics that affect the degree to which teachers will seek out students for contacts or persist in trying to elicit responses from them. The teachers were puzzled by this request, and most made vague responses. A couple of teachers did indicate that the low participant group contained "some of the shyest students in the class." Otherwise, the teachers were unable to indicate common characteristics within groups or common differences between contrast groups.

The teachers were then told how they had been behaving differentially toward each treatment group and its corresponding contrast group. We then questioned them about the degree to which they had been aware of their behavior and the degree to which they could explain it. About half of the teachers indicated awareness of their low rates of interaction with *some* of the low participants. Their responses included the following: "Deborah doesn't need help and doesn't want to be bothered by anyone. She is very independent." "Carla is very shy. She is extremely embarrassed when I call on her and she can't answer. I don't want to embarrass her." When a teacher was aware of her low rate of interaction with a given student, the student was typically a shy one that the teacher was afraid of embarrassing, although a few independent students were included here also. Usually the shy students were low achievers and the independent students high achievers, although this was not always so.

The low participant group also contained a number of unknowns in addition to shy and independent students. Teachers usually were not aware of their rates of interaction with these students, nor particularly aware of these students generally. They responded to questions about them with statements like "you know Sam there . . . I guess I don't interact much with him. I don't know him very well." These students sound like indifference students.

Attempts to get the teachers to compare the low participant group with its contrast group yielded no clear-cut contrast differences, although a few trends were evident. Contrast students were more likely to be described as independent than as shy, and they were not seen as likely to become embarrassed or upset if they could not answer a question. Thus they contrasted well with the shy students in the low participant group, but not with the independents or the unknowns.

After discussing the low participation students and their contrast group, we recommended to the teachers that they try to increase their frequencies of inter-actions with low participants by calling on them more frequently and initiating more private interactions with them. The teachers readily agreed to this with regard to the unknowns, but many had reservations when it came to the inde-pendent students (they don't need it—leave well enough alone) and especially the shy students (they will become embarrassed and upset).

One response here was that we shared the teacher's concerns but thought that these students' willingness to respond in public situations could be improved without endangering their security. We suggested that inhibitions do not disappear by maturation or just go away by themselves, and that they can be eliminated only with practice and exposure to public response opportunities, especially low-key opportunities that result in successful student response. Thus we encouraged the teachers not only to seek out the low participants more often for private con-tacts but even to call on them deliberately to increase their public response opportunities. We also reminded the teachers that they did not have to force a student to respond if he did start to become flustered; they could help him by giving the answer or providing a clue. After varying amounts of discussion, the teachers agreed to try to increase private and public contacts with low partici-pants, although a few teachers had reservations about a few students. The latter were mostly high achieving independent types, where the teachers felt (with some justification, we had to admit) that their contact patterns were already optimal.

We followed similar treatment procedures for the extension group, first dis-cussing the extension students and those in the contrast group and then suggesting that teachers be more persistent in working for responses with extension students rather than giving up after an initial failure.

The teachers could identify no common characteristics of the extension students and no common differences between them and their contrast group. Also, *none* of the teachers had any awareness of their tendency to give up easily with the extension group or to be especially persistent with the contrast group. Each teacher was surprised and mystified by the data on her behavior on this variable. A few said things like "that child makes me nervous," or "I don't know what it is about him—I just feel uncomfortable with him," about individual extension students, but they were unable to name any attribute that was common to all or most of them. The teachers' responses here were typical: so far every teacher that we have ever talked to regarding his tendencies to give up easily versus persist in seeking responses from students was unaware of individual differences until we called them to his attention, and was unable to offer any explanation for them afterwards. Yet, in most of the classrooms we have investigated, there have been huge individual differences on this variable. In several studies the percentage scores were so stable over time and based upon so many hours of classroom observation, that we are convinced that they represent systematic, real individual differences. Yet, their origin and maintenance remain unexplained. *Apparently, individual differences in the students condition the teacher into quite predictable behavior patterns, but without any awareness on his part.* We still do not know what these characteristics of the students are.

All the teachers readily agreed to become more persistent in seeking responses from the extension students, either by repeating the question or by providing help in the form of a clue or a new question. The teachers were in agreement that such persistence is usually a good strategy. Some seemed to feel this on an intuitive, common-sense basis, while others cited the importance of seeing that each student achieves frequent success experiences and drew the implication that the teacher should simplify a question until she reaches a level at which the student can respond. Thus, in contrast to the situation with low participation students, teachers readily accepted our advice about extension students, without attempting to justify their behavior or argue that it was appropriate for certain students.

The treatment interview was concluded after suggestions for change with the extension group were discussed. The list containing the names of the four groups of students was left with the teacher for her own reference.

Results

Data collection resumed shortly after the treatment interview and continued throughout most of the second semester. Observers coded classroom interaction but did not discuss the treatment with the teacher (in fact, observers did not know which students had been selected for treatment). There were no follow-up interviews, feedback conferences, or any other forms of intervention after the interview described above.

Each classroom was coded during February, March, and April, yielding a total of about forty hours of interaction for each class. Observers continued to code the teachers' dyadic interactions with every student in the class, not merely with the treatment students. This was because we not only wanted to note any changes in the teachers' behavior toward treatment students; we also wanted to check for radiation effects.

After all, our treatment involved disturbing a preestablished classroom ecology. Changes in the teachers' interaction patterns with target students could easily affect their interaction patterns with nontarget students as well. Such radiation effects could be either beneficial or harmful. We expected that any radiation effects resulting from the extension group treatment would be beneficial. If teachers succeeded in raising their rates of persistence with the extension students, it seemed likely that their general persistence rates would rise. In this way, the treatment would benefit not only the extension students but their classmates as well (assuming, of course, that staying with students to work for a response is a generally desirable strategy).

We were less confident about the effects of the treatment regarding low participants. If the teachers did change their behavior and call on low participants more frequently, would these students become more confident, or might they become threatened and even more avoidant than they were before? Further, if the teacher did begin to seek out low participants for more interactions, would this radiate so that she also would begin to have more individualized contacts with their classmates, as in the Withall (1956) study, or would this cause her to reduce her contact frequencies with other students? If the latter, the benefits to the low participants would be balanced by losses to some of their classmates.

Effects of the treatment were investigated by comparing data from the first semester (pretreatment) with data from the second semester (posttreatment).

To see whether the treatment affected the teachers' achievement expectations for target students, we compared the teachers' rankings collected in mid-November with the set collected in March after the treatment interview. These comparisons showed very little change in the rankings. There were a few minor up-and-down movements, but no clear trend for target students in either group to move either up or down. Thus, despite the considerable changes in teacher-child interaction patterns to be described below, the treatment did not affect the teachers' achievement expectations.

However, the treatment did not involve a direct effort to change teacher achievement expectations for target students. The intent was to change teaching attitudes (for example, it is okay to call on shy students) and behaviors. These efforts were clearly successful. Comparison of teacher-child interactions involving target students before and after treatment showed clear-cut treatment effects for both target groups. The most notable changes in teacher behavior with the extension group occurred on the measure of staying with students following an initial failure. Despite a marked tendency to give up easily with these students in the first semester, in the second semester the teachers stayed with these students just as often as they did with their classmates. Thus the treatment brought the extension students from a state of clear disadvantage to a state of parity with their classmates.

There were also some other changes in the teachers' treatment of extension students. The teachers called on them more frequently and initiated more contacts with them during the second semester, and they praised them more frequently than they had in the first semester. In addition to the increased praise, there was an improvement in the ratio of behavioral warnings to behavioral criticisms for extension students, suggesting an improvement in the teachers' attitudes toward them. In the first semester the teachers had been very likely to respond to misbehavior by extension students with criticism. In the second semester they more often confined their response to a mere warning.

However, despite these improvements, measures related to teacher attitude toward extension students showed that even after treatment these students were still at a relative disadvantage compared to their classmates. Extension students were more likely than their classmates to be criticized for failures to respond or for giving wrong answers, both before and after treatment. Also, the change in teacher behavior toward extension students was not accompanied by significant changes in the behavior of the extension students toward the teachers. The only significant change was on the measure of wrong answers over wrong answers plus no response. The extension students had been higher on this measure prior to treatment but evened off to a level equal to their classmates after treatment. This change may reflect a decrease in the extension students' willingness to take a guess when they did not know an answer. However, given the great increase in the teachers' frequencies of staying with these students, it is likely that the change occurred primarily because the teachers were now asking these students more questions that they could not answer.

On measures of percentage of correct answers and frequencies of reading errors, the extension students were similar to their classmates during both semesters. The same is true for their frequency of behavioral contacts with the teacher, even though the majority were boys and despite the higher-than-average teacher criticism directed toward this group. Apparently there is something about these students that made teachers hypercritical of them, but it was *not* a higher frequency of misbehavior on their part.

In summary, the teachers were able to significantly increase their rates of staying with extension students in failure situations. Following treatment, the teachers stayed with these students just as often as they did with their classmates. They also sought out these students for contacts more frequently, praised them more often, and were less prone to criticize them. Even after these changes, however, extension students still received more teacher criticism when they failed to respond correctly (but not more behavior criticism). There were no notable effects of the treatment upon the behavior of the extension students themselves.

The treatment was also successful in changing the teachers' treatment of the low participants. Seven of eight measures of quantity of teacher-student contacts changed in the direction of increased contacts, most of these significantly. As a result, on some measures the low participants achieved parity with their classmates, while on others they still remained below their classmates but not so far below as they had been during the first semester.

This activity on the part of the teachers produced some complementary behavior on the part of the low participants. Although the changes on student measures were not nearly so large and consistent as those on the teacher measures, low participants sought response opportunities and contacts with teachers more frequently after the treatment than before. Despite this improvement, however, the low participants remained generally below their classmates on these measures.

There were dramatic changes in the rates of teacher praise and criticism directed toward low participants. During the first semester low participants had been praised more frequently than average for their classroom behavior, but not for successfully responding to questions or completing seatwork (recall that inappropriate reinforcement is one indicant of low expectations). The posttreatment data showed dramatic rises in the measures of teacher praise for correct answers and good seatwork. There was also a corresponding drop on most measures of teacher criticism. These differences are probably related to the teachers' concern about pushing these students too hard and about making sure to encourage them when they showed signs of progress. It is of interest, however, that it took the treatment to bring out this concern: during the first semester the low participants earned special praise only for their behavior (conforming to classroom rules), not for their success in answering questions or completing seatwork. *Thus the treatment focused teacher attention more closely on the academic performance of these students.*

The data for the difficulty level of teacher questions showed mixed results. In general, the teachers asked low participants *more* difficult questions following the treatment. Thus, even though most of the teachers expressed fear of embarrassing the low participants during their interviews, this concern did not cause them to ask the low participants only easy questions during the second semester.

The measures of teacher feedback also showed significant and beneficial changes. During the first semester the teachers had more frequently failed to give feedback to the low participants after they made a response. Also, the teachers less frequently gave process feedback when they checked their seatwork. These differences disappeared following the treatment, again suggesting that the teachers began to pay more careful attention to the academic responses of the low participants and to make greater efforts to teach them during seatwork periods.

To summarize the teacher effects, the treatment produced more widespread changes in the behavior of teachers toward low participants than in their behavior toward extension students. The teachers not only called on low participants more often and initiated more individual contacts with them; they also asked them somewhat more difficult questions, praised them more frequently, criticized them less frequently, gave them more process feedback, and less often failed to give them feedback. Thus the treatment seemed to make the teachers generally more aware of and concerned about the achievement of the low participants.

There were also some effects on the students. Most notably, the low participants showed a drop in their percentage of correct answers. It is difficult to say whether this change was good, bad, or indifferent. Inspection of the percentage scores showed that the changes were general but rather small, especially in reading groups where most of the response opportunities occurred. During reading groups, low participants answered correctly 75 percent of the time during the first semester and 64 percent of the time during the second semester. Meanwhile, their classmates dropped from 75 percent to 70 percent. The change in the percentage of correct answers during general class discussions was much greater, however: low participants dropped from 71 percent correct to 55 percent, while their classmates only dropped from 70 percent to 67 percent. Thus one result of the teachers' asking low participants more frequent and somewhat more difficult questions was that their percentage of correct responses dropped.

Except for errorless learning advocates who believe that the rates of correct responses should approach 100 percent, most observers would see changes of this magnitude as positive and appropriate, indicating greater teacher efforts to get the most out of these students (assuming, of course, a generally supportive teacher and classroom atmosphere).

The posttreatment percentage for two classrooms dipped to 38 percent and 31 percent respectively, on the measure of correct answers during general class discussions. In these two instances the treatment apparently caused the teachers to push too hard. However, the means for the other six classes on this measure, and the means for all eight classes on the measure for correct answers in the reading group, were in the 50 percent to 80 percent range. Thus although one effect of the treatment was to lower the percentage of correct responses made by low participants, their posttreatment percentages were still comparable to those of their classmates.

Other changes in student measures were more clearly positive. Although the changes were not nearly so dramatic as those in the data for the teachers, the low participants became better behaved, more likely to seek response opportunities, and more likely to come to the teacher for help with their work during the second semester. The low participants were still less likely than their classmates to seek out the teacher during the second semester, but they were more likely to do so than they had been before the treatment.

In sum, the treatment had clearly changed the behavior of the teachers toward both target groups. We now turn to the question of how this change affected the more general classroom ecology. Did the effects radiate? If so, was it to the benefit or the detriment of the other students?

The data regarding radiation of effects for extension students generally supported our expectations that there would be some radiation, and that the radiation would be beneficial to all students. Seven of the eight teachers showed large gains in their percentages of staying with extension students in failure situations, while one teacher did not change her behavior. Of the seven teachers who began to stay with extension students longer in failure situations, three showed radiation effects such that they also tended to stay with other students more often than they had before. The other four teachers showed large gains for the extension students and little change for their classmates. The teacher who did not change her behavior toward extension students did not change her behavior toward classmates either.

Analysis of variables less central to the treatment of extension students showed that teachers tended to ask extension students more questions during reading groups following treatment. This increase was not at the expense of classmates except in one classroom, where the reading group response opportunities were more than doubled for extension students while being cut in half for their classmates.

In summary, the effects of the treatment for the extension students were rather general across teachers but mostly confined to the measures of teacher behavior in staying with students following failure. For the most part, the advantages accruing to the extension students as a result of the treatment were not gained at the expense of classmates (although there was one exception), and the extension group treatment sometimes radiated to the benefit of classmates.

The treatment regarding low participation students showed large gains in the frequencies of response opportunities and interactions that they were afforded by the teachers following the treatment. In a sense these quantitative gains were at the expense of their classmates, since the mean for the classmates tended to go down in most classes while the mean for the low participation students went up. However, the effect of the treatment was to more nearly equalize response opportunities in teacher-student contacts for low participation students and their classmates, rather than to make the teachers spend most of their time with the low participation students and begin to ignore their classmates. Further, as noted previously, even after the considerable improvement following treatment, most of the measures of frequency of contacts with teachers showed low participation students to be still behind their classmates even in the second semester.

The direct effects of the treatment on low participation students were general across teachers. The degree of change differed on different measures, but each teacher involved did show significant increases in providing response opportunities and individual contacts with low participation students following the treatment interview. Also, as noted earlier, the effects of the treatment on low participation students were more general than the effects of the treatment on extension students.

Gains in quantitative frequency of contacts with teachers for low participation students were sometimes at the expense of their classmates, but usually the change was such as to place the two groups in equivalent positions or to leave the low participation students still somewhat below their classmates, rather than to shift them to a position of advantage in comparison with their classmates.

CHANGING TEACHERS THROUGH FEEDBACK

The treatment interview was clearly successful in changing teacher behavior toward both of the target groups in the direction suggested. As a group, the teachers substantially increased the numbers of contacts they had with low participation students and substantially increased the percentage of instances in which they stayed with extension students in failure situations. Thus the consultation strategy of making teachers aware of their already established but inappropriate behavior patterns toward certain individual students was effective in getting them to change their behavior.

Along with the studies reviewed earlier, our findings illustrate that most teachers are willing to change their behavior if given specific feedback that they can perceive as relevant and credible. The data also reinforce our contention that most inappropriate teaching is due to lack of awareness in the teacher rather than to any deliberate callousness or inability to change.

We think that more such research on classroom intervention strategies is needed, but we would strongly argue that the time has come to call a halt to experiments which involve manipulating teachers' expectations or providing them with phony information. There appears to be little theoretical or practical advantage to be gained from continuation of such research.

In contrast, there is much to be gained from research which places the investigator in the position of being a partner and resource person to the teacher rather than a manipulator. Many classroom coding and rating instruments have become available in recent years which would allow an investigator interested in a treatment study to provide meaningful and useful feedback to teachers regarding their own behavior and to make rationally based suggestions for change. We would urge educational researchers to begin to do more of these kinds of studies.

A MODEL FOR INTERVENTION IN THE CLASSROOM

In describing the treatment results we have suggested an intervention model implicitly, and now we want to make that model explicit because we think it has general application potential. The steps in the model are as follows:

1. *Collect behavioral data on a representative sample of students or the entire class but maintain separate records for each individual student.* As we have argued elsewhere (Good and Brophy, 1971) data that describe how the teacher behaves toward the class as a whole (class averages) are not usually representative of teacher behavior toward individual students. And as we have seen in this book, teacher behavior toward subgroups of students is not representative of many teacher-child patterns that occur in the classroom. This strategy will not only provide a more representative picture of teacher and student behavior but will enhance the change agent's credibility by allowing him to talk about specific students, ideally including those that are of greatest interest or concern to the teacher. As has been pointed out elsewhere (Williams, Schmidt, Good, and Peck, 1970), consultants often damage their relationships with teachers by being manipulative or by dealing only with the problems they want to discuss to the exclusion of problems of more interest to the teacher. Although we stress behavioral (observational) data, it is conceivable that data such as student questionnaire responses or student test scores on specially designed performance batteries could be used for intervention purposes. Such data, though, should be drawn from a representative sample of students or from the entire class if they are to have maximal impact.

2. *Identify explicit problems or possible developmental points that appear in the data.* Obviously, a broad data collection plan will suggest a wealth of possible intervention possibilities and will provide base-line

data for comparing posttreatment behavioral responses. Although it is possible that a large number of teaching weaknesses will be identified, it is best to focus intervention efforts upon only a few. Too much negative feedback, despite the clinical skills of the consultant and the general openness of the teacher, is liable to overwhelm the teacher and have debilitating effects upon him. Having too many problems to work on at once produces an overload and a depressing effect; whereas concentration on a few problems makes it easier to identify and implement change-centered, concrete strategies for coping with these problems. Thus, after scanning the data, identify a few problems that have important theoretical value or that represent key problems that the teacher has to resolve before anything else can be dealt with (for example, management and control). A clear-cut focus on one or two problems also makes it easier for the consultant to construct the necessary graphs and tables that will help the teacher to see the effects of his behavior more clearly. Although the teacher's needs during treatment consultation sessions may make it necessary to abandon the prepared treatment for problems that are of concern to the teacher, the consultant should be prepared to discuss and clarify problems which he has identified as important. He may be able to convince the teacher quickly of their importance, even if the teacher has not considered them previously.

3. *If possible, find contrast groups to show good teaching behavior, making it possible to ask teachers to extend to new situations behavior that is already in their repertoire rather than to ask them to perform new behaviors.* Suggestions to change behavior often implicitly make the recipient of feedback feel that his behavior is inappropriate or inefficient. A much better strategy is to find examples of good teaching behavior (for example, they do wait for *some* students to respond) and to be prepared to contrast this behavior with inappropriate instances and to ask them merely to treat some students the same way that they are already treating other students. Obviously there will be situations in which the teacher does not express the target teacher behavior (for example, allowing students to evaluate their own work), but such cases will be the exception. Finding comparison data is just as easy when nonbehavioral data are used. For example, even if most students find a classroom uninspiring, typically there will be some who see it as a happy, productive place. Questionnaires that allow students to explain why they are satisfied and unsatisfied may identify systematic differences that can be corrected so that most or all students will begin to find the classroom enjoyable and rewarding.

4. *Express interest in the problem, but allow teachers to give explanations before suggesting changes.* In our treatment study we asked teachers to explain their behavior (for example, why they interacted more with some students) *before* suggesting changes. In general, the teachers

themselves will see that their behavior is not consistent with their intentions and will be motivated to try to change their behavior. However, if a consultant focuses on changing behavior before allowing the teacher to react to the data and to explain his behavior, he may convince the teacher that he is not interested in understanding the problem and only interested in manipulating the teacher. Often teacher comments will clarify questionable interactions and will elucidate treatment alternatives so that new problems are focused upon. Talking with and listening to teachers sets the stage for cooperative problem solving rather than the one-way evaluative comment that frequently produces aggressive behavior in teachers.

5. *Pinpoint differences in teacher behavior with contrasting students, and suggest change in teacher behavior with target students as a possible corrective step.* Having set the stage so that the teacher is interested in the problem and in remediating it, the consultant is now prepared to pinpoint *tentative* suggestions for changes in teacher behavior, curriculum materials, or other factors that may positively affect target students.

6. *If the teacher is agreeable, engage in mutual problem solving until explicit treatment procedures are agreed upon.* Teachers who are uninterested in the problem ("I agree that Ted and Alice have some problems, but these are minor compared to my problems with Ed, Bruce, and Karen") or who are generally unwilling to participate should not be forced or pressured to implement the suggested treatment.

Our assumption here is that, to be effective, treatment research must involve teachers who are willing to comply with treatment procedures that they themselves have helped to work out, and who believe that the procedures may help some of their students. It makes little sense to waste money and time coding in classrooms unless the treatment is consistently and willingly attempted by all teachers involved. Research in classrooms, from our viewpoint, should be engaged in by researchers and teachers who share a common interest in a problem and who want to find out what can be done to correct it.

7. *Specify exactly what the teacher will do to attempt to change student behaviors.* If several teachers agree upon the same change strategies, as was the case in our study, then data from several classes can be grouped together to study the generality of the treatment procedure. If teacher-consultant sessions lead to different strategies in different classrooms, the data will need to be analyzed separately.

Unless teachers and consultants agree on explicit strategies (names of target students should be written out, as well as teacher behaviors that are to be directed toward them; the frequency of contacts should be specified; and so on), teachers' interpretation of the treatment and the ways they attempt to change their behavior may vary widely from the consultant's interpretation, so that a definable strategy is not operative in the classrooms under study. Exclusion of disinterested teachers and close specification of target teacher behaviors will reduce error variance substantially and allow treatment effects to be observed more closely.

8. *Arrange to get posttreatment data to evaluate success in changing teacher and student behavior and to examine the data for radiation effects.* As we have suggested previously in this chapter, treatment data should be collected in such a way as to provide answers to three basic questions: (1) did teachers change their behavior in ways consistent with the treatment strategies? (2) did target students change their behavior as a result of changed teacher behavior? and (3) were there radiation effects (how were teacher interactions with nontarget students affected by the treatment)?

9. *Hold a debriefing session with the teacher to review the results of the study and to gain valuable clinical data from the teacher.* The teacher, for example, could provide insight into the difficulties that he encountered in changing his behavior and could suggest new ways in which to attempt similar remediation strategies in future research. Again, we emphasize that teachers and researchers working in tandem hold the key for effective classroom treatment research. Our experience has demonstrated that most classroom teachers are willing to engage in collaborative research even though they themselves are also subject to scrutiny.

There seems to be relatively little theoretical value or practical advantage to gain in continued manipulation of teachers' expectations or interventions involving giving some or all teachers phony information. Furthermore, there is nothing unscientific or theoretically objectionable about the researcher establishing a good personal relationship and discussing treatment procedures with the teacher, as long as the data collection is done by individuals who are not aware of the treatment or are otherwise "blind" so that they could not influence the outcome of the study.

SUMMARY

Due to the rapid pace of classroom interaction, ego-defensiveness, and other factors, most teachers are not very aware of individual differences in their patterns of contacts with individual students. This implies that simple provision of feedback should be enough to cause teachers to change inappropriate behavior of their own volition. Several studies were reviewed showing that this is generally true, provided that the information is perceived as relevant and credible by the teacher and that plans for change are specific and prescriptive. Detailed data describing a treatment study carried out by the authors were then presented, showing that teachers, as a result of feedback from structured observations, could change both quantitative and qualitative aspects of their behavior toward target students. Evidence of small changes in target students' behavior as a result of changes in teacher behavior was also reported. Radiation effects, the impact of the treatment of nontarget students, were also discussed, and it was observed that most radiation effects were positive. A model for treatment studies was elaborated and the need for involving the teacher as a partner in cooperative studies was stressed.

chapter 10

Classroom Research:
Some Suggestions
for the Future

Any series of research studies will raise more questions than it answers. The research reviewed in this book is no exception. Work by ourselves and others continues in this area, and as more data become available our understanding will become clearer. However, the book does provide some data that are consistent, clearly interpretable, and suggestive of ways to improve classroom interaction.

For example, the data reviewed here firmly support the view that differential teacher expectations and differential teacher behavior are real but are by no means universal. We know a number of ways in which teachers communicate inappropriate expectations in dissimilar ways and that some teachers do not communicate inappropriate expectations.

We know that patterns of interaction with teachers are greatly different for boys and girls and for high and low achievers. We also know that indifference, attachment, concern, and rejection students differ in their classroom behavior and that teachers treat them differently. Known also is that male and female teachers differ in some general stylistic ways, but that their behavior with boy and girl students is very similar.

For students in the same class, classroom life varies widely. Similarly, students in the same grade but with different teachers also have different classroom milieus. Some teachers ask 200 academic questions a day while others may ask but 20.

High participants in one classroom may only be moderate or even low participants in comparison to students in other classes.

Teachers are usually aware of their *general* instructional and behavioral objectives. However, it can be stated with some assurance that teachers in general are *not* aware of the *specific* ways in which they attempt to influence classroom behavior. They are especially unaware of the qualitative aspects of their interaction with students. However, teachers can be made aware of inappropriate behavior through structured observation and feedback procedures that can readily alter teaching style under appropriate conditions.

In Chapter 11 we will describe the implications that research data have for the classroom *teacher*. Meanwhile, the purpose of this chapter is to suggest general guidelines and specific *research* studies that seem necessary for improving our present understanding of individual differences in classroom performance and especially our knowledge about the types of teachers who are especially susceptible to expectation effects. Some of the needed research can be provided by analyzing data previously collected; however, most of the questions we will raise will require new data and new paradigms. Hopefully, this chapter will stimulate the interested reader to think about and possibly conduct research dealing with the formation, communication, or manipulation of teacher and student expectations and attitudes. Perhaps some readers will see the need for different, more rigorous, or more imaginative second-generation studies than those suggested by the authors. If so, our goal of stimulating others to go beyond our formulations will have been realized.

ANALYSES OF EXISTING DATA

Residual gain studies are planned to see if early teacher expectations are related to differential student achievement. One weakness here is that most of the classes in which we have collected early teacher rankings have been first-grade classrooms, where there are no good prescores to use as covariates for adjusting end-of-year achievement scores. Still, it is possible to generate residual-gain data using readiness scores as prescores, to see if students who were overranked (on the basis of readiness scores) or underranked by their teachers showed greater or lesser end-of-year achievement than children ranked "appropriately." Such a study would of course be a quasi-replication of the Doyle, Hancock, and Kifer (1972) study, and would provide limited but useful data about the influence of teacher expectations upon student achievement. In general, existing data will allow us to experiment with multiple regression models using sex, expectation, attitude, and other data to predict achievement gains.

In Chapter 9 we reported that target children in the treatment study did not move up in teacher rankings of achievement. However, teachers markedly changed their behavior toward target students, and minor changes in the target children's behavior were also evident. Limited data about the influence of the treatment on student achievement will be obtained by matching students in the treatment groups to controls of equal achievement rank to see if the treatment led to better than expected achievement in these students.

Also planned are general exploratory analyses of the interactions among sex, expectancy group, and attitude group in available data. These data need to be carefully examined for interpretable patterns which could provide the bases for future research.

COLLECTION OF NEW DATA

In our opinion there are several types of studies which would greatly expand knowledge about the influence of teacher expectations on student performance.

Presently the authors are engaged in two independent studies attempting to pinpoint behavioral correlates of teacher effectiveness. Data from two large metropolitan school districts have been made available to us. In one study teachers who have shown consistency for three years in the degree of learning gains they produce on standard achievement tests have been identified. These teachers, whose relative effectiveness is known, are being observed to see if they systematically differ in their classroom behavior. This data pool will eventually describe whether or not systematic differences in teaching behavior between effective and ineffective teachers can be isolated and will indicate if the profile of the effective teacher is the same in high- and low-SES schools (Brophy, 1973).

In the other study three criteria of effectiveness are being measured, with teacher age and experience, school SES, and student aptitude controlled (Good and Grouws, 1973, in progress). The three measurements of the criteria are student scores on the Iowa Achievement Test, a mathematics sentence completion task, and a classroom climate scale. The intent is to see if third- and fourth-grade teachers who are relatively high in producing standard achievement in math are also relatively high in producing positive affect in their students, high reading standard achievement scores, and higher scores on a different type of math test. Such data will provide some information about the general validity of teacher effectiveness. Perhaps to the extent that teachers are effective they are *generally* effective.

However, it is possible that effectiveness may be *specific* to particular dimensions, so that teachers who are effective in helping students to make extraordinary gains in reading achievement may be only moderately successful or even ineffective in helping students to gain mathematical concepts and insights. Other patterns are also possible. For example, student gains on standard achievement tests in mathematics emphasize basic computation skills, and such gains may come at the expense of their proficiency on a different type of math test (that is, teachers get gains by constant drill and repetition with little emphasis on understanding).

We do not yet know what patterns will emerge, but we do know that these basic data will tell us whether effective teachers share certain behavior patterns not evidenced in the behavior of less effective teachers. Also, data will be available to describe teaching effectiveness across different criteria.

Anticipating one possible use of this data pool, the authors are attempting to construct and to dimension a pen-and-paper measure of teacher expectations. Potential questions that will be embedded in a larger instrument for pilot testing are:

How many students do you expect to master the basic material you teach in the ——— grade?

When students fail to learn the material and are holding up the class, what do you do?

In public recitation sessions, when students give wrong answers do you deal with the failure (delaying other students) or proceed and deal with the student later (making him wait for feedback)?

Do male students in general have more trouble learning to read than female students?

Is it true that once a student falls a grade level behind, there is very little that a classroom teacher, without special help, can do to help the student achieve academically and to catch up?

The scale will be administered to teachers with known patterns of effectiveness (teachers who are generally obtaining relative high productivity from students, and teachers who have been observed to treat lows appropriately) to see if their general and specific expectations relate to their success in producing student achievement.

Obviously, such data would only be correlational, and high expectation scores might merely reflect the greater confidence that effective teachers have developed from their classroom successes. Use of such a measure with preservice teachers who have not built up experience, however, would help to get around this circularity problem. Laboratory teaching performance could be compared for preservice teachers who score at different points on the scale. Thus the efficiency of expectation scores for predicting behavior could be directly tested.

In any case, the collection of expectation scores would yield base line data for comparison in subsequent experimental studies. For example, if ineffective teachers are taught the same skills and behaviors that more effective teachers use, do their expectations automatically rise, or do basic attitudes and a failure orientation prevent their successful utilization of basic skills? Careful experimentation with ineffective teachers (some receiving behavioral skill training only; others receiving only treatments to raise their expectation for student performance; others receiving combination treatments) with variables such as teacher age, experience, sex, and selected personality dimensions controlled, will make it possible to draw out more fully the influence of teacher expectations on student performance.

OTHER AREAS THAT NEED RESEARCH

Broader Definition of Teacher Expectations

We now feel that measuring teacher expectations by having the teacher rank order the entire class in terms of expected achievement is too narrow a focus, and will not strongly predict teacher behavior in and of itself. Other, more focused questions, we feel, will provide some predictive power. Questions such as, "which students are unsuccessful learners with poor attitudes?" or "which students irritate you?" are more likely to be associated with differential teacher behavior. These questions are tapping attitudes and expectations that the teacher possesses. Simple rankings of students from highest to lowest may not include underlying teacher affective reactions to the students, and they do not provide information about what level of achievement teachers expect from students ranked low relative to their classmates.

We know that teacher expectation effects are not universal. Not all teachers are affected by their expectations. Furthermore, expectations about individual students are only a single aspect of the teacher's perceptual structure that influences his classroom behavior. Measures of many expectations (for example, role expectations, curricular restraints, classroom goals) in combination are likely to produce a better prediction of teacher behavior than any single predictor (for example, specific expectations for individual pupils). For example, we would predict that teachers who sought success in the classroom by creating an effective climate or by maintaining strict discipline would behave differently from those who concentrated on cognitive outcomes or who viewed IQ scores as real indicants of student performance. Similarly, teachers who do not feel limited by curricular restraints should differ from those who are overly conscientious about sticking to an established curriculum. Such different patterns of behavior would undoubtedly have different effects on different student outcome measures. Thus, predictions based on combinations of cognitive and affective variables are more likely to predict classroom events than those based on single variables. Clearly we would predict that when the distinct dimensions of a teacher's role perception are consistent and mutually reinforcing (IQ scores are real, the class should be taught as a class, I must keep pace with the curricular guide, and so on), behavioral predictions will be much stronger.

Our shift to a broader conceptualization has stemmed from a variety of sources. The major influences were our own data and talks with teachers. Clearly, for some teachers, their perceived inability to manipulate the curriculum or to individualize instruction were major detriments in and of themselves; low expectations for particular students simply exaggerated the problem. Also, empirical and theoretical work in Sweden by Lundgren (1972) and Dahlöff (1971) was influential in suggesting that the curriculum exerted real, measurable influences on teacher behavior. However, we suspect that teachers show wide individual differences in their susceptibility to curricular influences. Furthermore, the work of Philip Taylor and his associates (Taylor, Christie, and Platts, 1970) in England has shown that teachers' reactions to curricular influences and their pen-and-paper descriptions of effective teaching behavior predict differential teacher behavior. Thus we see our concern with teachers' expectations for specific students as somewhat parallel to Taylor's concern with teachers' perception of curricular influences. Both are seriously considering the teachers' perception of classroom events as a way of understanding why teachers behave as they do and why they have different effects upon students.

After reaching this conclusion, we were interested to find that others had reached similar conclusions. Lortie puts it this way.

We have yet to "map" the general outlines of teacher viewpoints and relate them to basic social variables. One does not object to the carefully targeted, theoretically designed study, but given our general ignorance of the world view of teachers, we are not likely to interpret findings from such studies with the appropriate level of sophistication . . . we need research on the world view of teachers with approaches (open-ended interviews, observation, analysis of personal documents, etc.) that make the researcher come to terms with the value hierarchies of teachers" (1973, p. 490).

Need for Multiple Dependent Product Measures

To learn more about the influence of expectation effects upon students, it will be necessary to include a variety of dependent product measures in future studies. In general, when researchers have included process measures, they have tended to use multiple measures. Hence a good deal is now known about the way teachers communicate expectations to students. However product measures have seldom been included, and when they are, typically only one measure is utilized. Thus the possibility that a given pattern of communication may affect cognitive and affective products differentially has not been widely explored. It would be beneficial for future studies to include a number of outcome measures (self-concept, school satisfaction, peer/teacher satisfaction, criterion referenced achievement tests, and change in student classroom behavior). Criterion referenced achievement tests seem especially relevant for testing expectation hypotheses. If teachers do not actively seek to influence students in the ways measured by investigators, there is little reason to believe that the classroom behavior of such teachers will be causally related to the researcher's dependent measures.

The Search for Determinants of Teachers' Reactions

Data have been presented to show that teachers can rank their students in order of achievement after only a few days of class and that these rankings are stable over time. Furthermore, the data reviewed in this book leave little doubt that teachers' expectations can become self-fulfilling prophecies by exerting influence on their behavior. However it is clear that some teachers do not treat low-achieving students in self-defeating ways even though the teachers perceive and report their relatively low performance levels. Thus teachers' low expectations do not act as causative variables independent of their teaching skill (especially their ability to deal with failure), experience, and personality. Previously we have described three types of teachers. Proactive teachers appear to be undeterred by their expectations for low achieving students, so that they spend more time interacting with lows than highs. Reactive teachers simply allow existing differences between high and low students to unfold, so that highs, due to their own initiative and ability, come to dominate public classroom life. A third class of teachers overreacts to student differences (in supplying qualitatively and quantitatively superior treatment to highs), thus exacerbating differences between students.

It would be of interest to observe the same group of teachers over consecutive years to see if they consistently react to high and low students the same way in different years. We suspect that proactive teachers and those who overreact would show stable behavior patterns, but that the reactors would show different classroom behavior if the composition of students changed markedly. There are data showing that, among a group of experienced teachers, roughly 50 percent were relatively consistent in their effects on student achievement scores over three consecutive years; however, the other teachers apparently were strongly influenced by the composition of each particular class (Brophy, 1973).

It would be of even greater interest to identify the *determinants* that predict teachers who form and communicate inflexible expectations to students. Above we reported our belief that broadening the teacher expectation variable to include a variety of teacher expectations about classroom life would yield more powerful data. Both cognitive and personality factors are involved. Rubovits and Maehr (1973) showed highly dogmatic teachers to be more susceptible to expectation effects than less dogmatic teachers, and Hunt (1971) showed teachers with low conceptual levels to be more negative and less flexible in general teaching style than teachers characterized by a high conceptual level. These teacher variables and others need to be studied if we are to understand teacher "typologies" that are likely to relate to expectation effects.

However, students, too, have different needs, personalities, aspirations, and coping behaviors. Some strive for teacher affection; others flee from warm, smothering teachers. Just as the curriculum may place real restraints upon teacher behavior, so may pupils. Furthermore, research has shown that the influence of teacher expectations (when communicated) is mediated by individual differences among students. One individual difference variable suggested by research is student accuracy in judging adult voice tone (Conn, Edwards, Rosenthal, Crowne, 1968). We would hypothesize that students who are teacher oriented would show more reaction and growth than students who are neutral or hostile toward the teacher and school. Student personality, cognitive complexity, and classroom salience may also be relevant factors.

A COMPREHENSIVE STUDY OF THE ABOVE FACTORS

Taking the above factors into consideration, we see the need for a large naturalistic study of at least 50 teachers (it would probably be necessary to test 200 or more teachers to obtain the relevant comparison groups) over two consecutive years. The general scope of the design is shown in Table 10.1.

The model explicated here suggests that certain restraints, including restraints that teachers place on themselves, lead teachers to develop a perceptual structure

TABLE 10.1.   Conceptualization of Some Variables that May Influence Classroom Interaction and Performance[a]

CONSTRAINTS	TEACHER RESTRAINTS	CLASSROOM PROCESS	OUTCOMES
Systems restraints	A. *Perceptual Structure*	A. Intensive observation of teacher behavior	A. Student growth on criterion referenced tests
Curriculum restraints	1. Role definition: teaching goals		
Pupil restraints		B. Intensive observation of student behavior	B. Student growth on cognitive/ problem solving tasks
1. Orientation toward school and teacher	2. Subject/ student orientation		
2. Anxiety		C. Stress on dyadic interaction and on identifying the teacher or the student as the initiator or cause of a given sequence of events	C. Satisfaction with school—classroom
3. Self concept	3. Attitudes		
	4. Beliefs		D. Student growth on school related self concept
4. Need achievement— aptitude	B. *Marker Variables*		
5. Demographic variables	1. Dogmatism		E. Moral development
	2. Cognitive complexity		
6. Social perceptiveness (alertness to voice cues, etc.)			F. Social development
	3. Conceptual style		
7. SES level	4. Anxiety		
	5. Need achievement		
	6. Demographic variables		

[a] This illustration is a simplified version of a model articulated at a research conference conducted at the Center for Research in Social Behavior at the University of Missouri in February, 1973. Participants other than the authors included professors: Bruce J. Biddle, University of Missouri; Philip H. Taylor and Bill Reid, University of Birmingham, England; Raymond S. Adams, Massey University, New Zealand; and Edward Scott, James Cook University, Australia. Professor Scott was especially influential.

that helps them decide how they should behave in the classroom, and that this complex belief structure will both determine what they will do and what the effects will be on students. The model presented above characterizes the various forces that *potentially* influence their classroom role. Some teachers emphasize cognitive goals; others attach importance to student affective growth. If this is true, pressure for students to internalize facts would be a relevant pressure for some teachers but not for others. We would assert that teachers who hold affective goals and who are not limited by curricular restraints will behave differently and exert different influences (as measured by student performance on end-of-year performance measures) than teachers who hold cognitive goals and who believe that they must adhere to the curriculum closely. The model also suggests, however, that classroom interaction is a dynamic process such that some sensitive teachers will form and reevaluate expectations concerning pupil abilities and interests from observing pupils in the classroom. *Moreover, those expectations form part of the cognitive structure the teacher brings to subsequent classroom meetings.* Such hypotheses can clearly be tested in the observation data. Thus such a plan would identify teachers who do or do not vary their behavior in line with student progress, allowing the determinants (personality, belief systems, and so on) that relate to different levels and patterns of classroom interaction and performance to be identified.

Clearly these results would help us to understand better the three types of teachers we described earlier (proactive, reactive, overreactive) by identifying personality, cognitive, or other behavioral correlates that are associated with each teaching style. Recognition of how these three types of teachers differ from one another would provide useful information for teacher training programs.

Others have also argued for comprehensive classroom studies that draw data from a variety of sources and have presented models for collecting and interpreting such data (see, for example, Jansen, Jensen, and Mylov, 1972). Classroom researchers are increasingly agreeing that major understanding will come only through carefully articulated programs of research.

SMALLER STUDIES

The model described above is complex and would involve a great deal of money and effort to sort out the various reciprocal effects and interrelationships that exist among teacher attitudes, teacher behavior, pupil attitudes, and pupil behavior. However, information about the impact of selected teacher attitudes and personality variables (with contextual variables controlled) upon classroom communication patterns and student outcomes would yield valuable theoretical and practical information. Well-controlled naturalistic studies involving just a few teachers could certainly identify variables that make teachers more or less susceptible to expectation effects and/or inappropriate teaching behavior. However, smaller studies, unless they are cumulative, systematic, and common in their instrumentation, may not sharply delineate cause-effect mechanisms. Other potentially useful areas of study well within the scope of a single investigator are explicated below.

Formation of Expectations

We now know a lot about how teacher expectations and attitudes are communicated once formed, but we need more information about the student characteristics that lead teachers to form initial impressions and about the events that lead teachers to change their expectations or attitudes. The results from Willis's dissertation (reviewed in Chapter 6) provide some information about child attributes that first-grade teachers attend to and use in forming impressions. It appears that teacher ratings are highly affected by whether or not students reward or interfere with teachers' ability to function successfully in the teaching role. Children who violate teacher expectations for performance are likely to suffer teacher rejection even when the violation is in the form of good behavior.

Needed are studies that combine process observation with open-ended teacher interviews. Intensive process examination of selected students would help to tie behavioral correlates to global teacher descriptions (for example, mature) and uncover possible cause-effect mechanisms that lie outside of teachers' awareness (for example, do children approach the teacher and in what way?).

Persistent interview techniques are especially needed. When teachers predict that students will do well or poorly, interviewers need to stay with the teacher and ask a series of questions trying to pinpoint the precise criteria that teachers utilized in forming their opinions. Again process evaluation would be helpful in allowing the teacher and researcher to identify the relevant attributes ("You say that Frank will do well because he is interested in school. How do you know he's interested? During the first week of school he raised his hand only an average number of times . . . he came to your desk only an average number of times," and so on).

Also needed are formation studies conducted with older students. Sixth-grade teachers and college instructors may use different behavioral cues for forming performance expectations.

Case Studies

We feel that extended study of teacher behavior toward special types of students and of the behavior of these students will provide useful information on the relative generality of teacher reactions. For example, we have expressed our own puzzlement concerning gainers and decliners. Given that teachers rarely change their expectations toward students, it is important to describe in detail those students who show considerable rise or fall over the course of a year. After coding the behavior of students in several different classrooms and identifying "movers," it would be fascinating to conduct detailed case studies of these students the following year (our measures yielded no information). One wonders if movers retain the status they had at the end of the first year at the beginning of the following year. For example, where would a student that rises from the bottom third to the middle third by the end of the year be ranked by his new teacher (at the bottom, or in the middle)?

Perhaps movers would show the same pattern the second year that they did in the first year. That is, in the case of gainers, the students might start out low both years and then gain in the teachers' estimation as the year went on. This suggests that something about these children makes a bad initial impression on the teacher, which is then changed as the teacher gets to know them better. We suspect that in any given study of teacher rankings over a period of time, the data will show some gainers and some decliners, but that the movers of one year will not necessarily be the movers of the following year. That is, early student behavior interacts in some complex way with (probably unique) teacher biases so that student potential is over- or underestimated for a few students. Still, it is possible that some, even many, of the movers may show the same pattern year after year. It would be very useful in this case to pinpoint the student characteristics which affect teacher expectations in this way. Similarly, whether or not movers are constant from year to year, it remains possible that the stimulus events that trigger false early impressions may be relatively uniform and identifiable through intensive case studies. We simply looked in too few classrooms to test such hypotheses. Here it would be necessary to survey a number of first-grade teachers in the spring and second-grade teachers in the fall to target several students for intensive observation.

A similar research model could be focused on rejection and concern students. As we have noted, the classroom behavior of these two groups of students is strikingly similar in many ways. Teachers, though, react quite differently to these two groups of students and apparently see them as being different than they really are. Teachers seem to see concern students as earnest but dumb or limited, and rejection students as unduly aggressive and undermotivated for classroom work. However, again it is important to note that the classroom *behavior* of these two groups of students is not that different (at least for behavior picked up in our coding system.

Case studies, especially early in the year, would be useful in seeing how student behavior influences teachers to develop attitudes of concern or rejection. Data explaining the formation of attitude labels would be especially useful if it is found that students who are rejection students one year are not rejection students the following year. Unfortunately, the data we have collected to date do not include rigorous stability data on attitude groups over consecutive years. Although we collected attitude data in first- and second-grade classrooms in the same schools, our methodological approach did not yield a large enough N to test hypotheses for two reasons: (1) several students in attitude groups were not present in the second grade in the following year; (2) in our attempt to get real rather than forced teacher attitudes, teachers were encouraged to list only a few students in each attitude group.

Data on the generality of any teacher attitude could also be obtained by asking team teachers or teachers and their student teachers to make independent ratings of students on parallel forms. However, such ratings at one point in time are relatively ambiguous because they provide no way of estimating whether general student behaviors or a few instances of intense but atypical episodes have heavily influenced teacher perceptions. Nevertheless, such information would be useful and easy to collect. To deal more directly with the generality of teacher reactions to students, it would be possible to get several teachers in junior high and high schools to provide their impressions of the same students. Especially interesting data could be collected if researchers collected differential reactions from students at the same time to see if differential ratings by team teachers are mirrored in differential student reaction to teachers.

Should rejection students be rejected again the second year, it would be important to look for signs of alienation and academic deterioration in these students. For example, we have stressed that their classroom profile in the first grade is very similar to that for concern students, and that academic indicators in particular are very similar. Those students who are rejected two years in a row may show lower end-of-year achievement scores than students (concern or first-year rejection students who were not rejected during the second year) who were very similar initially in the first grade. General behavior measures (not approaching the teacher in academic situations, not raising hands, making no response to academic questions, more misbehaving, and so on) might show that the coping skills of these students in comparison to other students are generally declining. Here we refer to comparisons between concern and rejection students who are promoted. We have noted that many rejection students in our study were forced to repeat the first grade. Obviously, rejection students who are retained would be likely to show lower achievement after two years than concern students who were promoted to the next grade.

Polarization

The preceding discussion of rejection students has suggested the need to conduct follow-up studies to identify the stimulus conditions that influence teachers to reject certain students and the need to conduct research on the stability of teacher rejection of students over consecutive years. Furthermore, the preceding discussion has suggested that systematic study of rejection students may allow for tests of polarization to determine if students who are systematically rejected progressively perform more poorly relative to other students. The general topic of polarization needs careful attention.

Our program of research has generated a wealth of data concerning the relationship between differential teacher expectations and attitudes and differential classroom behavior. It has also yielded interesting treatment data and a model for treatment studies. However, relatively little attention has been paid to polarization. Certainly if teacher attitudes (rejection) or failure expectations for certain students cause them to form rigid communication channels, then it should be possible to observe the influence of such communication on classroom behavior.

One suspects that if students are given up on in failure situations and criticized when they perform incorrectly, they will learn to remain passive and silent in response situations. However, to date no research data adequately test the polarization hypothesis in a given year or over successive years. Most of the data reported in this book, even the naturalistic studies, involved only a few weeks of observation and did not allow enough time to test polarization hypotheses. Even our own work often has involved only a few months or a semester of observation, and the data from the year-long first-grade study were contaminated by the treatment study during the second semester.

Naturalistic studies that carefully monitor the behavior of low achieving students with groups of teachers over an entire year and preferably over consecutive years are needed. If the form and effects of polarization and progressive deterioration can be observed and identified, it is possible to construct treatment programs designed to prevent or reduce these effects. At present there is only indirect evidence (Yee, 1968; Lundgren, 1972) that teachers' expectations become more rigid over time, and no evidence about the way in which polarization processes affect student outcomes. Much research, involving both naturalistic and treatment designs, needs to be conducted on this issue.

Teacher Expectations for the Entire Class

Stress has been placed on the fact that teachers' expectations other than expectations for individual students need to be investigated. It is known that global expectations have been related to differential student gain. Doyle et al. (1972) have shown that teachers who tend to overestimate the ability of students get better results than teachers who underestimate. Furthermore, Palardy (1969) has shown that teachers' low expectation for males' reading performance is associated with depressed reading achievement scores. In discussions with teachers, we have been struck by the frequent references made about the ability of the class per se. In talking about their role, teachers regularly report impressions about the interest of the class, the speed of going through the material, discipline problems, and so on in comparison to previous classes. Interestingly, favorable and unfavorable references to the present classes seem balanced across teachers as a group. Thus comments are not just defensive behavior—"I've got it rough this year: what can you expect?" Furthermore, teachers seem to react to classes in extreme good–bad ways. Few teachers point out the relative benefits or problems of this year's class compared to last (although this point needs empirical documentation). Exciting research questions include: What criteria do teachers use in reacting to a class as a whole? How soon do teachers form such expectations, and how stable are they? How do teachers communicate global class expectations? Elementary teachers' behavior with distinctly different classes (from the teacher's viewpoint) over consecutive years would be interesting data. At the secondary level (or in elementary schools that are departmentalized) it would be possible to assess teachers' expectations for the different classes and to study their behavior in high and low expectation classes. Also, comparing teachers' expectations for the class with objective data drawn from school records or collected by the investigator could yield useful information. The interaction of teacher expectations for individual students with teacher expectations for the entire class would be informative. Are teachers with generally favorable class expectations more or less likely to treat low expectation students in a dramatically ineffective fashion?

Steering Groups

The work of Lundgren and of Dahlöff in Sweden suggest that teachers pick certain students in order to cue their teaching tactics, especially to decide when to terminate parts of a unit and move to new topics. In short, they argue that the teacher picks a group in a class toward which to gear lesson level, tempo, and presentation style. In the context of the tightly controlled Swedish curriculum (and in mathematics classrooms), these researchers found that teachers geared their instructional effort at the students in the upper half of the lowest ability quartile in the classroom (10–25 percent ability level). In this country the qualities of such pace-setting students would probably vary widely depending upon a number of teacher and curricular variables. The extent to which teachers do use students in this way, the way in which the size and composition of the steering group varies with subject, grade level, and teacher variables, and the effects of differing steering groups upon various student outcome measures present explorable problems. Steering group research and global expectation studies would take on more importance if they included multiple teacher variables, complex behavioral process measures, and distinct outcome measures.

Open Classrooms

Given the present interest in exploring alternative school models, it would be useful to conduct basic expectation and attitude studies in open or individualized school models (for example, PLAN or IGE). It would be surprising indeed if indifference students (who initiate little contact with the teacher and reciprocally receive little teacher contact) do not exist in these schools. Teachers are still busy in these environments, and the cognitive complexity of three teachers tracking ninety students may even be more difficult than one teacher tracking thirty students. Data about the similarity of teacher performance expectations and attitudes for particular students and the behavioral treatment that different teachers (in the same teaching unit) provide individual students would yield a rich source for comparing the efficacy of such classrooms. Also work on the mechanisms through which teachers communicate expectations in such settings would be valuable (what type of learning choices are provided for high versus low expectation students, what type of feedback, and so on?). The style through which expectations are communicated may vary markedly in such environments, but it would be surprising if certain individual teachers or clusters of teachers did not communicate differential expectations.

Grouping Processes and Expectations

One wonders how grouping processes within the traditional classroom affect the communication of expectations. Teachers within traditional classrooms show large individual differences in the use of small group instruction. Some teachers rarely teach the class as a class (allowing several small subgroups to operate as the teacher moves from group to group); whereas, other teachers almost always teach the class as a class. Hudgins (1971) reminded us that, among other factors, inequality increases as size of the group increases and structured discussions lead to more equal participation than free discussions.

Relatedly, Jeter and Davis (1973) noticed that there was no small group instruction in their observation of ten fourth-grade teachers and raised an important question: When teachers characteristically group students for instruction, do expectations relate to differential teacher behavior as forcefully as they do when teachers teach the entire class?

Clearly, only more data will resolve this question. It would seem that a student's opportunity to be called upon as well as his general level of involvement would be greater in a teacher-led group of four than a teacher-led group of thirty. However, the teacher may systematically spend more time with certain groups of students and avoid other groups, so that low expectation students would be worse off in a small group instruction classroom than a whole-class instructional mode.

We suspect that, on balance, teachers' *use* of the method would be the key, not the method itself. Thus, communication of low expectations would be present in both modes of classrooms, although the determinants, the percentage of teachers who show the effects, and the way in which expectancies are communicated might vary across situations. Data on these points are needed and well within the scope of a single investigator.

Private Feedback: Homework

In Chapter 6 it was noted that teachers often have difficulty in reacting appropriately to the public responses of lows (for example, failing to provide feedback to lows or criticizing them when they respond inadequately). Unfortunately some teachers appear to systematically miss opportunities to reinforce lows even when they do provide correct answers. Some teachers seem unable to respond to success when they are expecting failure. One wonders if this phenomenon occurs in private situations as well. Perhaps these teachers, when they have time to react and think, can and do respond appropriately.

Studies of teacher feedback to students' homework would be relevant to see if differential amounts or quality of feedback is provided to high, medium, or low expectation students. Especially important would be data that pinpoint teacher feedback to lows when an unexpected success occurs. For example, how does the teacher respond to a homework paper when all of the assigned problems are attempted with 75 percent of the work correct (following two papers where only half of the problems were attempted and where only half of these were correct)? Teachers might *react* to the paper ("adequate"); be *proactive* ("Nice work!" "The paper shows a lot of work and progress." "Keep it up!"); *overreact* ("Why don't you do this all the time?"); or *fail to react* (make no comment at all). Private, written feedback as a mechanism for the communication of expectation effects seems an important and virtually unexplored area of classroom life.

Matching Teachers and Students

Parallel matching studies would make it possible to see if selected teacher types can more profitably deal with certain types of students. We do not refer here to the traditional forms of matching, where teachers who prefer to teach, for example, high achieving students, are allowed to do so without special planning or training. However, we do suspect that teachers who have strong preferences for teaching certain types of students may be especially helpful to these students under certain conditions. For example, the fact that teachers choose to deal with a specified group of learners may make it difficult for them to blame these students for failure and may motivate them to continue searching for new alternatives more persistently. There are data to suggest that teachers commonly blame students rather than themselves when students encounter difficulties (Good, Schmidt, Peck, and Williams, 1969; Quirk, 1967). In such dissonant situations more teacher involvement in the teaching task may be maintained when teachers are allowed to teach students whom they have selected to deal with because of special interest in their problem.

However, such matching studies typically are doomed to fail from the start because the teachers involved receive neither specified training nor specially designed materials. As a case in point, one project in New York City reduced class size to see if teachers in small classes could promote student learning more optimally than teachers in large classrooms. Teachers of large and small classrooms were found to exert equal influence upon students (that is, smaller classes did not produce greater learning). Interestingly, informal observation suggested that teachers in small classrooms taught just as they had traditionally taught in larger classes, and thus there were no special benefits for the students in small classes (Fox, 1967). Obviously if matching studies or treatment studies of any sort are to work, teachers need to be trained to take advantage of a unique environment or trained to deal with the special problems of specified learners.

Teachers have often been found to state strong preferences for certain types of learners. For example, Brandt (1971) reported that many experimental subjects stated a definite preference for working with under- or overachievers. Other research has shown that young teachers in training prefer to work with relatively passive, achievement-oriented children (Feshbach, 1969; Good and Grouws, 1972), but it has also been reported that certain teachers with unique backgrounds (Teacher Corps trainees) state preferences for more aggressive children (Beigel and Feshbach, 1970).

Research centered on teacher preferences and expectation for working with selected students, coupled with specific behavioral-skill training, might yield predictable patterns of success rates in ghetto schools or in other target environments. Such research, in addition to providing useful information about the influence of general teacher expectations and preferences on student achievement, might also at some point identify essential attitudes (interest in dealing with student failures) and skills (ability to wait silently for a low achiever to respond) that are successful in different environments.

We have noted that some teachers are more affected by their general expectations than by student performance, that other teachers are more affected by discrepancy between expectations and performance, and that still others are relatively unaffected by either factor. Designs focused upon matching teacher preferences for certain students and comparing how teachers treat preferred and nonpreferred students in equivalent circumstances (for example, when the student responds incorrectly) would yield more data about the interplay between preference and performance. Follow-up laboratory research using some of the procedures of the Brandt (1971) study but allowing subjects to teach preferred students would be especially useful to see if teacher interests and sensitivity to certain student problems allow them to deal with these problems more successfully than other teachers do.

That teacher preferences are real and exert influence upon teacher behavior has been demonstrated by Rubin (1971). The teaching effectiveness of structured and unstructured curricula appeared to be equal when teachers used their preferred styles. Highly anxious students preferred to teach in more structured situations. Furthermore, training was largely unsuccessful in changing already established preferred patterns.

These results do not show that teaching preferred students improves teaching behavior, but they do suggest that freedom to use a particular method is *potentially* important. These data also suggest that training teachers to perform certain activities may be very difficult, very expensive, and perhaps self-defeating. Matching self-expectations (for example, teaching goals) with school programs may become a more viable alternative than attempting to train teachers to be able to perform all behaviors and be all things to all students.

However, present data do not appear to support the idea of matching students and teachers on a wide-spread scale. The suggestions here are research possibilities, not immediate ideas for wide classroom practice. Matching makes the most sense from the standpoint of changing students who have undesirable characteristics in more positive directions (putting a fatherless boy with a male teacher, putting a hyperactive behavior problem with a good classroom controller, or putting an impulsive child with a reflective teacher); matching based on matching strengths with strengths appears to make less sense.

TREATMENT STUDIES: GENERAL COMMENTS AND SOME SPECIFIC PROPOSALS

Much research has suggested that teachers seldom use feedback information advantageously and indeed are often hostile toward those who attempt to influence and facilitate their classroom efforts. In Chapter 9 we discussed the model that we used for changing teacher behavior, and noted that the model was useful in changing teacher behavior. Apparently allowing teachers to see the discrepancies between their intended and their actual behavior and generally helping them to become more aware of what they and their students do by using structured observation to provide descriptive (as opposed to evaluative) information is a useful plan for unfreezing and changing teacher behavior. The model is to be especially useful when teachers are unaware of their behavior (for example, see the data on give-up students in Chapter 9), or when they can see that the objectively recorded data are self-defeating by their own standards.

However, when teachers are aware of their behavior and feel that their present behavior is appropriate, the model we suggest may not be universally useful. A partial test of the model's generality was present in the treatment for low participation students. The reader may recall that teachers were often aware of their behavior toward low participants and were confident in their treatment of some of these students. Unfortunately, there were not enough of these students to allow us to analyze the data separately for low participants whom teachers felt had no problems and who would not benefit from additional help, to see if teachers did in fact change their behavior toward these students.

However, by focusing upon the low participants' behavior, especially on their low initiatory rates rather than on the teacher's failure to seek them out, it was possible to interest teachers in an attempt to improve the initiatory rates of these students. Thus even when the teacher does not immediately feel that his behavior is inappropriate, it is still possible to focus on the behavior of target students (for example, failure to approach the teacher) and to see if the teacher would prefer or expect different types of student behavior. If teachers are concerned about such student behavior, it still may be possible to use the general treatment model and allow teachers to examine their behavior toward students who behave in the way the teacher desires to see if those interaction patterns provide clues for ways to work with the other students. However, the weakness of the treatment model in instances where teachers are aware of their behavior and satisfied with it illustrates the need for other change models. It is entirely possible that the teacher may be correct or justified in his beliefs. Teachers' claims of success, especially those that are based on reasonable or innovative practices, should be investigated, and those which appear to be valid should not be interfered with or criticized. Clearly more research is needed on change strategies.

Another weakness of our model is that awareness alone may not be enough. For example, in the case of rejection students, teachers can be given feedback data allowing them to see that the classroom behavior of these students does not differ greatly from that of concern students, and they can be shown data describing their behavior toward concern and rejection students. Such data presented objectively and sensitively might allow the teachers themselves to label their behavior as inefficient and to gain insight about other ways to act. But awareness alone may not be enough. Their reaction to certain student characteristics (nose picking, filth, smell, shouting) may be so strong that it negates their ability to work with them productively. Information creating the need and desire to change may need to be coupled with behavioral skill training (and perhaps desensitization procedures as well) before teachers can cope successfully with certain students.

As another case in point, teachers who find that they wait less longer for lows to respond may not be able to make immediate use of this information. Anxious teachers who are embarrassed by silence or who believe that students are excessively upset when they cannot respond may be unable to wait longer without special training and attitude development. Behavior modifiers report that some teachers cannot be simply told to reinforce children. Some teachers' lack of important behavior skills (appropriate voice, touch, warmth, and so on) prevents them from being appropriately reinforcing. Thus the treatment model we suggest appears to be generally but not universally applicable, and more research is needed before more elaborate and complex treatment models can be developed.

Treatment studies that both are procedurally simple and provide straightforward application will be especially useful. Obviously, if complex interpretations and expensive treatments are necessary, few teachers will have the time to undergo training and few school districts will have the necessary funds to hire clinical staffs to conduct desensitization activities. Thus as a starting point it seems reasonable to attempt to intervene in classroom problems with information strategies emphasizing information that can be controlled by teachers themselves if they are properly trained. This is especially important since more and more school districts have video equipment allowing teachers to form self-study groups to improve their instructional skills (extensive discussion of self-study groups is provided in Good and Brophy, 1973). Also, recent staffing models that call for team or instructional units can free one team member to collect the described data from time to time.

Although a variety of important treatment studies can be conceived and conducted, we will confine our discussion to a small representative sample that corresponds directly with problems that have been discussed earlier in the book.

Seating Location

As we mentioned in Chapter 1, some classrooms are marked by an action zone so that students who sit in the middle of the front row and in the middle row directly in front of the teacher's desk participate much more frequently in classroom discussion than do other students (Adams and Biddle, 1970). No doubt the physical environment affects student expectations and classroom interaction, but presently it is impossible to specify how the physical characteristics of the classroom influence behavior.

Students who do not have eye contact with the teacher may feel psychologically isolated, and the effectiveness of teachers' social reinforcements may vary with the distance between the teacher and the individual student who is the recipient of teacher praise. There is some evidence suggesting that student characteristics affect seating location when students are allowed to select their seat. Walberg (1969) presented self-report data suggesting that when students are allowed to pick their own seats, students who enjoy school tend to sit in the front of the room while students who dislike school tend to sit in the rear.

There is some reason to believe that teachers may group the classroom in such a way as to produce an action zone. Rist (1969) reported that teachers not only grouped students in achievement clusters but also pointed out that highs were seated closer to the teacher. In one of our studies (Brophy and Good, 1970a) a similar pattern was observed. However, even in elementary classrooms where the highs are not all seated close to the teacher, it has been commonly observed that highs do sit together in groups. It is possible that physical arrangements where students sit in achievement clusters may allow action zones to develop.

Although, if properly executed, it makes sense to group students for *instruction* during special instructional periods on the basis of their readiness for the task (for example, reading groups), it may be inefficient to group students in their *general class* seating location on the basis of achievement. Lows sitting next to highs, for example, may be motived by the general curiosity and high initiatory rates of highs. Also, with hand raisers spread throughout the classroom, teachers may spread their attention more evenly throughout the classroom and become more sensitized to low responders.

Very little systematic information is available to describe the seating arrangements (under teacher assigned and student selected conditions) of: high and low achieving students, high and low participators, concern and rejection students, attachment and indifference students. Interesting indeed would be naturalistic data describing where teachers place such students and where these students choose to sit. Particularly important would be naturalistic studies that also assess student reactions to individual teachers and subjects, to determine if general student preferences are influenced by their like or dislike of a particular teacher or subject. If such naturalistic research reveals that a student's or teachers' expectations influence seating location, a second generation of treatment studies could be designed to show how individual and class participatory rates, achievement, and attitudes are affected when seating locations are systematically varied. This kind of study could be done easily in junior and high school settings where students take several different subjects and probably have different seating in the different classrooms they attend.

Teacher Expectations and Grouping

The effect of homogeneous grouping practices on teacher expectations for student performance and subsequent teacher behavior are unknown. Studies of grouping patterns have not included process measures (Dahlöff, 1971). Research that characterizes teacher-student interaction patterns in heterogeneously and homogeneously grouped classes with content and student ability controlled could provide extremely valuable data about the influence of grouping on teachers' instructional behavior as well as on their attitudes and perceptions. As we and others have pointed out (see Good and Brophy, 1973) grouping students into classes on the basis of ability and reducing the ability range that a teacher has to work with has *not* systematically improved the achievement or attitude of students at any achievement level.

One wonders, for example, if average students in a heterogeneously grouped room share a different type of interaction with their classroom teachers than do students who are grouped into average tracks. Similarly, one wonders if the achievement expectations and general attitudes that teachers hold toward students in these dissimilar situations are similar. Do average students become indifference students when they are mixed with students who achieve both above and below them, or does an average track per se engender a general feeling of indifference from the teacher? Again, one wonders how teachers react to relatively similar students when grouping places them in dissimilar situations. Exciting data would be yielded by a design that compared the behavior of average students (or rejection students, and so on) and teachers' attitudes toward them in heterogeneously grouped classes, where the average students tended to sit together out of the teacher's central view, with those in heterogeneously grouped classes, where they were grouped in centered view, and with those in heterogeneous classes, where they were randomly seated. Then all these data could be compared to the general behavior of average students and teachers' attitudes toward them in homogeneously grouped classes.

Orientation

One wonders what would happen if elementary teachers spent the entire first week of school just getting to know students. As other students read independently and worked on review exercises, the teacher could spend his time talking informally with individual students about their interests, hobbies, or summer vacations, informing students about what they would be doing in class the next week, and soliciting their ideas about classroom policies and general projects they might want to work on during the year. Such a simple design would yield a variety of research questions, such as the following:

1. Do teachers who have such sustained but informal contacts with students show more open and benevolent attitudes toward students than teachers who start school in more traditional ways?
2. Do experimental teachers report more differentiated assessments of their students and less stereotypic global reactions than control teachers?
3. Do teachers in the experimental group show the ability to incorporate student ideas into the curriculum? Does this ability interact with cognitive, attitudinal, or personality measures of teachers?
4. Do students in the experimental teachers' classrooms, on the basis of felt board or questionnaire responses, see their classrooms as more relevant or interesting than students in control classrooms see their classes?
5. During the first instructional month, do students in the experimental group initiate more questions and generally behave more appropriately than control students?
6. Is there an interaction with grade level and orientation treatment such that younger children are not helped by the treatment but older elementary students are?
7. Does the orientation influence last past the first instructional month? Is there a need for an informal orientation feedback day once a month so that teachers and students can reopen communication lines?
8. Would the number of indifference and rejection students increase or decrease as a result of such treatment procedures?
9. What are the effects of the program on student outcomes (school satisfaction, and so on), and do these outcomes interact with teacher types?
10. If data were available, it would be interesting to see how teachers' expectations for the treatment class as a whole compared with their reactions to previous classrooms.

Previously it has been noted that teachers are sometimes unaware of their behavior toward students in general and that they often develop exaggerated or inaccurate impressions of selected students. What would happen if teachers actually became better acquainted with students under quasi-controlled conditions? Such a simple strategy could yield a great deal of information about the pervasiveness of teacher expectations when they have the opportunity to interact casually with classroom students.

Secondary Classrooms

Teachers in secondary schools have relatively little contact with students, and it would be difficult to conduct the orientation study described above at the secondary level. However, there are data to suggest that brief communications by teachers may have salubrious effects upon students (Alexander, Elsom, Means, and Means, 1971). The reader will recall that in this experiment forty college students were divided into twenty high and twenty low achievers. Matched pairs of high and low achievers were assigned to each setting. Students in the control group were not addressed before or after class, and their questions were answered politely but briefly during class. In contrast, the teacher made a point of learning and using the names of the subjects in the treatment group, and initiated conversations with each of them before or after class at least three times a week. Subjects given personalized attention by the teachers outperformed control students on the end-of-semester multiple choice examinations. The study showed that increased teacher attention was sufficient to influence student achievement. Unfortunately, process data were not included in the study, so it is not possible to specify if the classroom behavior of treatment students was also improved or if the instructor's behavior toward treatment students was influenced in unanticipated ways (that is, not part of the planned treatment) but observable ways.

Similar studies done with a variety of teachers, including process observation, and collection of pre- and postassessments of student expectations, course interest, and other product measures, would provide useful information about the efficacy of such general treatment programs. Such studies could also provide information about the kinds of teachers that can successfully communicate interest in students in believable ways. Individual differences in teacher's ability to pull off the strategy outlines above will probably be found. Moore and his associates have shown that the effectiveness of expectancy statements from adults is influenced by the degree to which the child believes or accepts the adult's statement. There is also some reason to suspect that teacher attention alone is unlikely to affect student effort, but that teacher approval and other evidence of positive feedback are likely to increase both expectations and performance (Moore, Gagné, and Hauck, 1973; Moore, Means and Gagné, 1973). Thus the affective communication and the credibility of the teacher (Alexander, Elsom, Means, and Means, 1971) are probably just as important as time per se. More studies will clarify the teacher attitudes and behaviors that mediate such effects and the types of students that are likely to be influenced.

It should be noted that general strategies as exemplified above are potentially useful, as teachers can use the strategy in the general course of running a class with no special intervention techniques. That is, the teacher does not have to develop highly specialized techniques for given students. However, although the results of general studies have been promising, their application in a public school setting where students are perhaps less motivated than college students remains to be demonstrated.

Student Behavior

In prior discussion we have focused upon changing teacher behavior in treatment studies. Obviously student behavior can be manipulated to make them more attractive to teachers. Little work in real classrooms has been focused on working with students directly. We know that relatively simple procedures can help children to cope with problems that might unnecessarily dampen the teacher's opinion of them. For example, Meichenbaum (1971) has helped impulsive children to modify their problem solving styles by teaching them to "talk to themselves" in using language to solve problems. Should subsequent research identify children who have been rejected for two consecutive years, it would be possible to intervene with these children a few days before school and teach them a few strategies for influencing teacher opinion favorably (raising their hands, sitting in the front row, talking with the teacher after class) and/or sensitizing them to the third-grade curriculum (reviewing the tasks that they would complete). A more complex design might include three experimental groups and one control group to assess the relative efficacy of different treatment procedures. One experimental group would be a treatment centered on rejection children alone, with teachers receiving no information. Another would involve meeting with teachers to explain the findings of the two previous years, to discuss potential strategies, and to make arrangements to code data to see if treatment procedures are helping the students. The third treatment could, of course, involve a combination strategy with both teachers and students receiving specific information. Criteria for assessing the adequacy of the treatment would involve comparing the behavior and achievement of rejection students with their performance in earlier years and collecting affective data from teachers and rejection students describing their reciprocal feelings toward one another. Research on gainers and decliners could proceed in a like fashion, preparing decliners for making a better impression on teachers and/or preparing teachers so that they do not respond inappropriately to such students.

The advantages of presenting teachers with information about their behavior have been pointed out. Students also may benefit from information about their behavior. To change students' expectations for their own behavior and subsequently their actual classroom performance, it may be more useful in some instances to deal directly with the student rather than attempt to influence students by affecting teacher behavior. As a case in point, investigation may reveal that some passive students in selected classrooms have low self-concepts and are fearful in public-response situations. One way to try to influence student performance is to sensitize teachers to the problem and to provide them with skills for dealing with it.

However, the same strategy used to provide teachers with information about inappropriate behavior can be used to sensitize students to their own problems. Securro and Walls (1972) have shown that students may profitably change their behavior when presented with information about their classroom behavior. These investigators had college students record the frequency of their contributions to classroom discussions and found this strategy was effective in increasing the responsiveness of shy, reticent students. An advantage of this method is that when students are recording their *own* response rates they are freed from the psychological pressure of peer and instructor scrutiny. Apparently the experience of coding their own behavior sensitized students to their problem and motivated them to do something about it. Incidentally, the tally itself may serve as positive reinforcement for verbal responding; thus, the student receives encouragement even if the teacher does not respond appropriately.

Obviously, other problems may be attacked by allowing students to code their own behaviors. Of course behavior modifiers have been advocating such strategies for some time now. Our additional interest in such research designs would be to couple the behavior recording process and changes in student behavior with changes in teacher and student expectations. If students change their behavior, it would be interesting to see if teachers change their expectations in measurable ways and begin to present students with new, appropriate challenges. Similarly, do changes in student behavior increase student expectations such that their general classroom coping and initiatory rates are affected in measurable ways? The theoretical interest in such data of course is to see if behavioral success and changes operate independently of teacher expectations. Teachers who form rigid expectations such that increased student capability is not noticed nor built on may necessitate intervention strategies that deal directly with student deficiencies. In such studies it would be especially important to see what difference, if any, increased student participation has on student interest and teacher attitude, as well as on student achievement (using residual gain comparing treatment with control students of similar pretreatment achievement level). More elaborate but realistic and potentially useful strategies have also been developed (Flowers and Marston, 1972).

Special Education Students

Presently there is a great deal of interest in moving special education students back into the regular classroom. Such involvement is predicated on a variety of beliefs such as: (1) segregation from normal public schools provides systematic feedback to special education students that they cannot learn or are inferior, (2) opportunities for self-development for certain special education are limited (fewer materials, excessive amount of time spent in travel rather than learning activity, unstimulating peers), (3) special education students will be more satisfied in an environment that accepts them as normal.

To begin with, it seems that few naturalistic data exist to support these assumptions. Clearly, we disapprove of needless student grouping, but the question remains. In public school settings with thirty classroom students, will special education students be accepted by peers and teachers as normal students capable of learning? Will their opportunity for learning and their self-image increase or decrease? All of these are researchable questions. Our beliefs without data lead us to predict that in some classrooms these students will meet a facilitative environment but in other classrooms they will be "branded" in invidious ways (sometimes with rejection, but sometimes with smothering sympathy). Data to explain the types of classrooms that are apt to provide good environments for these students are important.

Here, too, treatment studies could provide important information. Does material (written or conference discussion) presented to teachers before special education students enter the room help teachers to adapt to the situation appropriately? Do teachers and material interact so that advance information helps some teachers but not others? If so, what are the salient individual difference variables? Does what the teacher says to the class before special education students enter the class make a difference? Does too much emphasis, no matter how empathetic, create a difference that continues to exist, immutable to change?

It might be especially important to attempt direct countersocialization of teachers (for example, when these circumstances apply, explaining to teachers that children formerly thought of as normal but troublesome had become labeled as special education students and now this label was exerting expectation effects and would continue to do so unless they could prevent it). Similarly, direct intervention with students might have some lasting effects. Training special education students to act in key ways during their first few days in class might prevent or help to override low expectations that peers or teachers possess. The movement of special education students back into the standard school settings dramatizes both the importance of expectation research and the need for more knowledge about how expectations are communicated.

Peer Expectations

Peer expectations may also affect student performance, and it seems plausible that low achievers need some public success exposures if peers are to increase their esteem for them. Although very little is known about how students communicate their expectations to fellow students, the case study by Rist (1969) provided some interesting hypotheses. Much more naturalistic research is needed to pinpoint how peer expectations are communicated, to identify the nature and frequency of public success that must occur before peer expectations are substantively altered, and to suggest appropriate treatment strategies. Carefully designed research could provide data about the relative stability of peer and teacher expectations and the relative ease with which they could be modified. Such data would be especially useful in secondary classrooms, since there is much research to show that peer expectations are quite pervasive at this level (females masking their brightness to remain popular, and so on).

Teacher Training Research

Several types of research paradigms could be pursued in microteaching laboratories in university settings to identify the determinants that relate to the communication of low, inflexible expectations and the interaction of teacher expectations with personality variables and behavioral teaching skills. For example, some research has suggested that dogmatism (probably mediated by the subjects' susceptibility to the expectation set, their ability to reject contradictory evidence, and so on) is an important individual difference variable. Also, some classroom teachers have been found to react to low achieving students' failure by accepting inadequate performance (giving the student the answer or calling on someone else). Combining teacher variables with student behaviors would provide an opportunity to separate the various forces that potentially shape teacher-student communication patterns.

Table 10.2 shows a set of relationships from which a variety of treatment studies could be drawn. Any variable that has been associated with the communication of low expectations (smiling, inappropriate use of praise, inappropriate reaction to failure) could be studied in the program of research. Here it would be especially interesting to see if information per se would be sufficient to prevent the communication of low expectations, or if special training is necessary. For example, one wonders if teacher trainees who read detailed information describing the influence of teacher expectation effects (which called to their attention specific ways in which teachers had been found to communicate low expectations), would show classroom behavior that differed from trainees who had not read the material.

Behavioral data are needed to answer this question. Our hunch, at present, is that information per se would be effective for some variables (intermix high and low achievers in classroom-seating assignments), but that training (perhaps extensive) would be necessary if certain teachers are to improve their performance on selected measures (wait for a student to respond and feel comfortable with initial silence). Experiments could help identify those teaching variables associated with behavioral performance inadequacies, and other studies could provide information about the difficulty of improving performance.

We have talked about the distinction between a treatment involving merely providing information versus a treatment that would have to be more powerful because simple provision of information was not enough to get the teacher to

TABLE 10.2. Variables to be Studied in Microteaching Laboratories

TEACHER VARIABLES	TRAINING VARIABLE	STUDENT BEHAVIOR MANIPULATION	EXPECTATION TREATMENT	EXPERIMENTAL OUTCOME
1. General measure of expectations	1. None	1. None: here child variables could be studied	1. None	1. Criterion referenced measures of student learning in conditions when student learners were not used as confederates
2. Dogmatism	2. Information only	2. Have students emit a prearranged pattern of behavior	2. Identification of certain students as fast, medium or slow learners, and so on	
3. Anxiety	3. Indirect training (for example, Mayhew, 1972)	a. Percent of time they respond correctly		2. Change in teaching behavior over time
4. Cognitive complexity	4. Behavioral skill modeling	b. Pattern of response rates (increasing/ decreasing, success)		3. Change in student behavior
5. Prior experience in teaching/working with students	a. Demonstrated skill in increasing wait time for students to respond	c. Demonstrating predetermined patterns of behavior in certain situations (for example, in failure situations looking at the teacher versus looking at the floor)		4. Teachers' attribution of success/failure
	b. Demonstrated skill for working with students in a failure situation, and so on			5. Teachers' affective reaction to students
	5. Behavioral skill training (subject learns specific skills)			

change his behavior. *In the latter cases, information explaining why the treatment was not successful would be especially valuable.* Is it because the behavior is so very difficult that it cannot be changed without some kind of powerful treatment, or is it because the behavior is not so difficult to change in its own right but is in effect a defense mechanism or tied up with other defense mechanisms so that the teacher resists changing it? The answer to this question would have obvious implications for designing treatment programs.

In addition to providing information about the types of teachers who are likely to be influenced by low expectations, the paradigm outlined above could also be used to identify the characteristics of individuals who can bring about positive expectation effects as opposed to those individuals whose positive expectations do not have much if any effect.

One of the problems with short laboratory studies is that the subjects' compliance with the experimental set (when these are slow students) may be seen as intelligent behavior. Given that one is to teach students for an hour or less, it might be sensible to accept the set and ask brighter students more complex questions and generally show differential interaction patterns. *However,* the importance of such studies lies not in the initial pattern of differential behavior they effect but it resides in whether or not the initial set *prevents teachers from seeing relevant cues and adapting their teaching style accordingly.* Thus we would suggest that experimental laboratory studies be conducted so that subjects teach the same students for a period of time (for example, one hour each day for a week). Under these circumstances we would predict that some teachers would not be influenced by the initial set but that others would. In the second group we would predict that some teachers would, in time, correct their inappropriate behavior patterns as they received more student feedback. Accordingly, we would also predict that some teachers would not correct their interaction patterns and would continue to engage in the same pattern of self-defeating behavior. And if such studies were conducted for a sufficient period of time, students being taught by teachers with low and unchanging expectations would begin to show different behavior patterns as well. Identifying the characteristics of teachers who show these patterns would have important training implications. Also, such studies would have important theoretical value. For example, do expectations influence teacher behavior even when contradictory behavioral stimuli are present? These data could be used to indicate if expectancies in longer laboratory studies are controlled mainly by students so that a stimulus-response account seems most parsimonious, or if even in longer studies expectancies control how teachers perceive and react to student behavior.

The external validity of such studies could be extended by observing selected teachers (for example, those who are behaviorally restricted, those who cannot praise effectively, and those who are affected by low expectation states and who in turn reduce student performance) during their student teaching experience. Should the same patterns appear in the formative weeks of student teaching, then intervention should be applied at this level. Of some interest would be the relative ease of changing teacher behavior by delaying intervention strategies (pre-student teaching versus student teaching or post-student teaching). Competing theories provide different recommendations at this point. For example, if student teachers perceive themselves as generally effective and have a chance to practice selected inappropriate strategies, then such rewarding experiences may freeze their behavior. However, Fuller (1969) and Katz (1972) suggested that teachers proceed through a developmental cycle from relatively immature survival concerns to more mature teaching concerns. This suggests that information and skill training will be relatively ineffective until students are ready to learn the material. Studies as described above would help to clarify the generality of these two views and pinpoint teacher types that are most likely to be influenced positively by a particular strategy.

Focus on Individual Students

Our research model, coding system, the data we have collected, and the data that other investigators have collected on the interactions that occur between teachers and individual students show that it is practical and feasible to study the individual student systematically. Certainly the work of Flanders, Amidon, Bellack, Medley, and others who have produced systems for coding teacher behavior toward the entire class have contributed immensely to an understanding of what happens in classrooms and have stimulated a great deal of classroom research. We foresee the continued use of such systems when they provide relevant data on the hypotheses being tested, and obviously such situations are not infrequent (for example, is the teacher's behavior isomorphic with the goals of the experimental program, and so on?).

However, for testing hypotheses about the effects of specific teacher behaviors on different students or attempting to specify process teaching behaviors that may account for differential rates of student learning, it seems mandatory that investigators use coding systems that keep track of teacher contacts with individual students as well as systems that code teacher behavior toward the class as a whole. Even here, though, researchers should develop their own system or adapt an existing coding system so that relevant dependent measures that directly bear on hypotheses being tested are collected. Too often investigators use a coding system simply because it exists. Investigators, like teachers or anyone else, have difficulty in breaking a set and are unimaginative in coding and classifying data.

Our point is simple. It is possible to code the behavior of individual students in classrooms. The work has just begun, but at some point in time the collective results from numerous investigators studying individual students in the classroom may make it possible to elaborate more fully the type of interaction milieus that facilitate the growth of students varying in age, sex, socioeconomic status, aptitude, and personal traits. It seems that future investigations focused on individual students' behavior will greatly expand our knowledge of classroom behavior and learning. Techniques for studying individual students now exist; it remains for future investigators to modify and expand such systems and to use them in imaginative ways.

Cooperative Research and Treatment Studies

In addition to stimulating more research on individual students, we hope the book will stimulate more research that is useful to classroom teachers. We especially see the need for treatment studies that help teachers to become more aware of their behavior and to develop new instructional alternatives, while at the same time allowing investigators to explore topics of theoretical relevance. So much is unknown about classrooms it seems senseless not to test hypotheses in real classrooms when teachers are willing to participate as research partners.

We suspect that teachers' resentment of researchers is in part based upon teachers' experiences where researchers have manipulated them and misrepresented the purposes of data collection. That teachers react with little enthusiasm when they are requested to participate in research studies is hardly surprising if the teachers have no involvement in the study or have serious doubts about researchers' credibility. It would seem profitable for the research community to create new lines of communication with teachers by including them as partners in the research process.

Movement to cooperative patterns of research is seen as being feasible in that purely naturalistic hypotheses (how does the teacher normally behave?) are less relevant now that we have much information about basic day-to-day classroom behaviors (and, as we have seen, teacher behavior is largely reactive), but we know very little about what happens when that behavior is varied. Thus treatment studies conducted in ordinary classrooms are especially appropriate and needed at this point, especially those noting how individual students are affected by various treatments.

SUMMARY

In previous chapters we have shown that teachers are sometimes influenced by their impression of students. In the present chapter we have emphasized the need for expanding knowledge about the types of teachers who are likely to show expectation effects. It has been argued that teachers' expectations other than their expectations for individual students need to be studied, and that a combination of general affective and cognitive expectations is more likely to predict teacher behavior than a single set of expectations. It has been stressed that the communication of inappropriate expectations is influenced by the teacher's general expectation, but also by other personality and cognitive variables of teachers as well as by system restraints and pupil restraints. Furthermore, to understand the impact of low expectations upon student performance, it will be necessary to utilize a variety of outcome measures. Researchers have used few product measures in their studies, and affective variables have been especially neglected.

Paradigms have been suggested for exploring the determinants of classroom behavior, the effects of such behavior upon student performance, and the cause-effect relationships that exist between four classes of variables—teacher determinants, teacher behavior, student determinants, and student behavior and performance. Also, a number of studies have been suggested that could be conducted by single investigators. These studies dealt with: (1) exploring the determinants of teaching behavior; (2) making case studies of students who reflect highly salient characteristics (for example, students who move markedly on teacher rankings); (3) documenting the polarization hypothesis (do teachers discriminate more sharply in the treatment of high and low achievement students as the year progresses?); (4) extending expectation studies to include study of teacher expectations for the class as a whole and the communication of expectations in open or individual environments; and (5) conducting a variety of treatment studies which have suggested for changing teacher/student expectations and behavior.

The program of research described in the book has been successful in documenting the existence of differential teacher–student classroom interaction patterns. Subsequent research will have to show the types of teachers and students who are most susceptible to the effects and the impact that low expectations (either student or teacher) have on the performance of individual students and the class as a whole. Hopefully, some who read this manuscript will be encouraged to expand and clarify the data presented here.

chapter 11

Implications for Teaching

In the previous chapter we stressed the need for more knowledge about student and teacher characteristics that maximize the possibility for self-fulfilling prophecies. Indeed, the emphasis upon acquiring new information and new insights was so strong that the reader may be left with the feeling that practical implications will have to be gleaned from future research. We do not feel that this is necessarily so, however. The findings reviewed in Chapters 1–9 have *present* value for classroom practice. In particular, the documentation of specific ways in which teachers have been found to communicate low expectations to students seems to have particular value. Furthermore, the data presented in the book seem to clarify and focus major problems and dilemmas that teachers involved with classroom research face. *Problem recognition* has potential value in itself.

It is true that workable strategies of known generalizability have not been documented. Thus when we recommend practices for alleviating selected problems we will be skating on thin ice. The reader will recognize, then, that when we make prescriptive statements about desirable teaching behaviors, many of these recommendations flow from the authors' experience in classrooms, their observation of teaching, and their conversations with teachers: not all are backed by empirical data. However, most of the behaviors and attitudes that we suggest for teachers are data based or at least suggested by research.

In summary, then, in this chapter we attempt to spell out teaching implications. Data presented in Chapters 1–9 have been conservatively interpreted, but in this chapter we will at times go beyond the data in order to articulate our reactions more fully. Dependable knowledge exists about the communication of low expectations to students because much experimentation has focused on this problem. Much less is known about strategies for changing the attitudes and classroom behavior of teachers and students, because little research has been focused on these questions.

COMMUNICATION OF LOW EXPECTATIONS

Examination of studies of teacher treatment of low achieving students demonstrates that many teachers provide them with ineffective environments. Furthermore, teachers in various settings (kindergarten and secondary classrooms, low and high SES districts, homogeneously and heterogeneously grouped classes) have been found to communicate low expectations to certain students. Not all teachers show such effects. Fortunately, it appears that relatively few teachers overreact to the extent that they treat lows in grossly inappropriate ways. Also some teachers reach out forcefully and successfully to involve low achievers. However, teachers of the latter type are also relatively rare. Most teachers simply respond to (without enhancing) lows' present motivational and ability levels. These teachers communicate minimum expectations to lows, accept their mediocre performance, and indirectly (and without awareness) allow lows to remain passive and disinterested learners.

What then are some of the *observed* ways in which teachers have been found to communicate low expectations to students? Below we will list documented variables; however, it should be noted that some studies have not supported these findings: not all or even most teachers behave this way. But equally important to emphasize is the fact that all variables (except waiting less time for lows to answer) have been replicated in independent investigations showing that teachers as a group tended to show differential behavior toward high and low achieving students on the variable in question. Furthermore, even in studies where group effects were not found, it has been possible to find some teachers who do teach lows inappropriately. Thus the point that we have made throughout the book needs to be kept in mind: expectation effects are common but not universal.

Variables That Communicate Low Expectations

1. *Waiting Less Time for Lows To Answer:* Teachers have been observed to provide more time for high achieving students to respond than for low achieving students. The determinants of this behavior could include

excessive sympathy for the student, teacher anxiety, and lack of probing skills, among others. As with the other variables that appear below, the determinants of such behavior are largely unknown.

2. *Staying with Lows in Failure Situations:* In addition to waiting less time for lows to begin their response, teachers in replicated studies have been found to respond to lows' (more so than highs') incorrect answers by giving them the answer or calling on another student to answer the question. High achieving students in failure situations are much more likely to have the teacher repeat the question, provide a clue, or ask them a new question. Thus teachers have been found to accept mediocre performance from lows but to work with and demand better performance from highs.

3. *Rewarding Inappropriate Behavior of Lows:* In some studies teachers have been found to praise marginal or inaccurate student responses. Praising inappropriate substantive responses (as opposed to perseverance, and so on) when the childrens' peers know the answer may only dramatize the academic weakness of such students.

4. *Criticizing Lows More Frequently than Highs:* Somewhat at odds with the above findings is that in some studies teachers have been found to criticize lows *proportionately* more frequently than highs when they provide wrong answers. This is indeed a strong finding, for it suggests that lows' expression of risk taking behavior and general initiative is being discouraged. One would expect that lows might receive more negative feedback (but not necessarily criticism) simply because they emit more wrong answers. But the analyses alluded to here were controlled for the frequency of wrong answers and found that on a percentage basis lows were more likely to be criticized than highs. It is possible that the quality of lows' responses may have been lower, but criticism for a serious attempt to respond is an inappropriate strategy in any case. The seeming discrepancy between variables three and four may reside in differing teacher personalities. Teachers who praise inappropriate answers from lows may be mired in sympathy for these students, whereas hypercritical teachers may be irritated at them for delaying the class and/or providing evidence that the teaching has not been completely successful.

5. *Praising Lows Less Frequently than Highs:* Also in contrast to (3) above, some research has shown that when lows provide correct answers they are less likely to be praised than highs even though they provide fewer correct responses. The situation is clear for lows in certain classes. If they respond, they are more likely to be criticized and less likely to be praised; thus, the safest strategy is to remain silent, because here the teacher is likely to call on someone else.

6. *Not Giving Feedback to Public Responses of Lows:* Teachers in some

studies have been found to respond to lows' answers (especially correct answers) by calling on another student to respond. Failure to confirm their answers seems undesirable in that these students more than other students may be less sure about the adequacy of their response.

7. *Paying Less Attention to Lows:* Studies have shown that teachers attend more closely to highs (and, as we noted above, provide more feedback). Some data exist to suggest that teachers smile more often and maintain greater eye contact with highs than lows. Studies also show that teachers miss many opportunities to reinforce lows simply because they do not attend to their behavior. Such studies provide support for part of Rosenthal and Jacobson's original explanation of the *Pygmalion* results: positive expectations increase a student's salience and his opportunity for appropriate reinforcement.

8. *Calling on Lows Less Often:* Relatedly, teachers have been found to call on high achieving students more frequently than low achieving students. Although much of the difference can be explained by student differences, the data show that few teachers compensate for these student differences. The difference in public participation becomes more sharply differentiated with increases in grade level.

9. *Differing Interaction Patterns of Highs and Lows:* Interestingly, contact patterns between teachers and lows are different in elementary and secondary classrooms. In elementary classrooms highs dominate public response opportunities, but highs and lows receive roughly the same number of private teacher contacts. In secondary classrooms highs become even more dominant in public settings, but lows begin to receive more private contacts with the teacher. Perhaps at this level private conferences with teachers are a sign of inadequacy, especially if the teacher does not initiate many private contacts with highs.

10. *Seating Lows Farther from the Teacher:* Studies have suggested that when students are grouped randomly within classrooms, undesirable discrepancies in teacher behavior between high and low achievers are less likely. Perhaps this is because lows are sitting next to highly salient or "liked" students so that teachers are more likely to notice them and to maximize treatment of them as *individual* learners. Seating pattern studies have sometimes found that lows tend to be placed away from the teacher (creating a physical barrier). Random placement seems to reduce the physical isolation of lows and the development of sharp status differences among peers.

11. *Demanding Less from Lows:* Several studies have suggested that this is a relevant variable. It can be seen as an extension of the more focused "giving up" variable discussed above. This is a broader concept suggesting such activities as giving these students easier tests (and letting the students know it) or simply not asking the student to do academic work.

Also, sometimes if a low achieving student masters the elementary aspects of a unit he may be neglected until the elementary aspects of the next unit are dealt with. Teachers set different mastery levels for students. At times, however, being less demanding may be appropriate if initial low demands are coupled with systematic efforts to improve performance.

Obviously there are many additional ways that teachers communicate expectations to students. Single intense communications ("you can't learn anything!") may do more harm than the systematic occurrence of any of the variables listed above. And we know that such penetrating outbursts, although rare, do occur. We are reminded of the study that asked college students to recount their most negative life experiences and found that their most intense interpersonal problems (humiliation, and so on) were with teachers (Branan, 1972). Milder but frequent comments ("I can always depend on you." "Who can give the right answer?") are also telling. Future systematic research will undoubtedly uncover many other unstudied variables (for example, assigned versus freely chosen independent activities) that show teacher expectation effects for some students. However, the above studies suggest some of the documented ways in which teachers communicate low expectations to students.

Are These Behaviors Necessarily Harmful?

Given that some teachers behave as discussed above, it is important to question the effects of such behaviors upon students. Should teachers wait longer for low achievers to respond? Should they call on low achieving students more frequently? We turn to those questions now.

Some behaviors are categorically inappropriate. For example, failure to praise lows' correct answers and criticism of their wrong but serious response attempts are quite inappropriate teaching behaviors, because they discourage student participation. Class grouping patterns are undesirable when they segregate high and low students during all activities and establish unnecessary barriers that easily escalate into status cliques. Seating lows farther from the teacher seems decidedly self-defeating, since they typically possess shorter attention spans and are unlikely to seek out the teacher when they have problems.

Furthermore, demanding less than the student can perform seems to guarantee that the student will achieve less in a given time than he would if the teacher had structured more appropriate assignments (at times, though, teachers may have to demand less in the short run to heighten later performance). Furthermore, receiving feedback about the adequacy of one's response seems better than receiving no feedback. On theoretical grounds one can argue that nonevaluative feedback and attempts to help students develop their skills for self-evaluation are important (we agree). But in classrooms where other students regularly receive feedback, not getting feedback is discouraging. Also, attention (eye contact) and appropriate nonverbal feedback (smiling) would seem to be appropriate, encouraging teacher behavior.

However, we do not know the full effects of these teaching behaviors on students' classroom behavior, their affective feelings about themselves or school, or their achievement. As noted in the previous chapter, process (teaching behavior) and product measures (child achievement, and so on) have seldom been combined in the same design. Recognizing the lack of a data base, we would still suggest that paying less attention to lows, not responding or inadequately responding to their statements and work efforts, grouping them together so that they cannot learn from other students, and demanding less of them then they can produce, are not motivating behaviors of teachers. Rather, they are the behaviors that support a cumulative deficit process and explain why lows talk less the longer they remain in school.

Three of the variables (waiting longer for students, staying with them in failure situations, and calling on them more frequently) are more difficult to discuss because the contextual climate and the sequence of behaviors that precede or follow their occurrence are just as important as the emission of the variables themselves. Although we feel that teachers should wait longer for students to respond (lows in particular), we suspect that a curvilinear relationship exists such that, if the teacher waits too long, the child will feel sharply embarrassed and the strategy may do more harm than good. Rowe has shown that teachers who increased their waiting time were rewarded with longer and more appropriate student responses (perhaps students were learning that the teachers wanted to hear what they had to say). Thus there are data to suggest that extending waiting time (up to a point, at least) is desirable.

However, again we would suggest that *context* is the key. If the teacher frowns while waiting (anticipating failure) and fails to provide feedback if the student responds weakly, he is unlikely to improve student confidence. Teachers who are relaxed, who smile or nod their head expectantly while waiting for the student, and who provide appropriate feedback to the student's answer are more likely to obtain and continue to obtain student responses. Undoubtedly, waiting longer for students will increase the percent of students who attempt to respond in the short run; however, if the process is not a reasonably relaxed and satisfying experience, students will not keep responding. Concomitantly, students need to learn that teachers are interested in what they have to say (not just in the right answer) and that the recitation period is an exchange of ideas and information (not a critical evaluation). If these conditions do not exist, simply waiting longer for a student response is unlikely to do much good in the long run.

Should teachers stay with students in failure situations? We think so, but again the picture is complex. The process is the key. If the teacher stays with the student and the student continues to give wrong answers or remains silent, then little has been accomplished. Teachers who remain relaxed, wait a reasonable time for a response, and then repeat or rephrase the question or ask a new question and subsequently get a response they can reinforce are on the right track.

However, some students will be so passive and reticent that the teacher will have to work privately with them to make progress. To build their confidence in public, the teacher initially may ask them easy questions (teacher knows student possesses the answer). Similarly, teachers may need to ask these students value judgment or personal opinion questions that do not necessarily require specialized information for the student to respond (should we spend money to place a rocket on Mars?).

Infrequent public response demands may be appropriate for certain students if they are tied to a *comprehensive strategy* in that the teacher gradually increases the complexity of the response demand placed on these students. The point is that the presence or absence of any single teacher behavior, *independent* of other teaching behaviors and their collective effects upon student progress, is *unimportant*.

Should teachers increase the frequency of public-response opportunities for low achieving students? Logically, more involvement and responsiveness in class discussions should improve student achievement; however, the research on this issue is complex and suggests that sometimes participation is/is not related to achievement, and the relationship between verbal participation and improved student attitude is only slightly positive (Good and Brophy, 1973). Apparently, increased participation may even be harmful for some students (Schultz and Dangel, 1972). Certain anxious students (as the teacher's tendency to call on them increases) may begin to anticipate being called upon, become apprehensive, and lose track of the substantive discussion such that their achievement is depressed by calling on them more frequently.

We feel that lows should have more contact with the teacher (but not necessarily more public response opportunities) and that the student and his reaction to increased public response opportunities is the key to guiding teacher behavior. *There are no magic formulas that can be applied.* The important principle is that the student knows he is expected to answer when called upon and will attempt to provide an answer without excessive anxiety or discomfort. Again, the process is more important than the frequency of the behavior. Different teachers with the same or different students could reach this goal in a variety of ways. The ultimate question is: has the pattern of teaching been successful in improving the attention rate of the student (or his achievement, and so on)?

In summarizing, it is important to reiterate that *appropriateness* is better evaluated on the basis of a cluster of behaviors than a single behavior. A cluster of several behaviors in appropriate context may be useful in encouraging the efforts of low achieving students. The behaviors discussed in this section were those that previous research found to be associated with differential patterns of teaching highs and lows (other behaviors and strategies will be discussed later). We cannot yet say that these teaching behaviors are causes of student performance; however, available data suggest that their systematic presence or absence has the potential for encouraging or eroding the confidence of low achievement students.

WHY SOME TEACHERS FAVOR HIGHS

Previously we have made the point that not all teachers show strong expectation effects. Indeed, relatively few present grossly deficient environments for lows. Most of the potential development for lows which is lost is lost in more subtle ways. We emphasize this frequently to be sure that what the data do and do not represent are clearly understood. But we also wish to underline the fact that failure to react is probably the more important problem. In this section we will discuss some of the reasons why teachers allow many lows to remain on the sidelines. Undoubtedly the factors vary from teacher to teacher, but a discussion of several possible causes may help teachers to understand some of the subtle influences that may shape their behavior.

Highs Reward Teachers

A basic reason why highs attract more teacher attention and better teacher reaction resides in the fact that their classroom performance is qualitatively superior to that of lows and hence more rewarding to teachers. Teachers, like spectators at sporting events, are impressed by excellence, not mediocrity. Spectators vary in their preferences, with some being inclined to root for running teams, others for passing teams and still others for strong defensive teams. Although specific preferences differ, most fans respect and demand a winning team. From time to time a player may be applauded for *effort*, but the player sprawled on the field after a missed tackle is more often cursed than cheered.

Many teachers behave similarly in responding to student performance. Each will have his own pattern of specific preferences. Some may prefer passive, dependent students, while others like mildly aggressive ones. Some like boys, and others prefer girls. More generally, however, there is ample research to show that teachers like high achievers better than other students. Teachers usually try to minimize obvious favoritism, if for no other reason than to save these students from the problems that usually beset "teacher's pet." Nevertheless, we have seen that teachers consistently respond more favorably to hard working, responsive, dependable, high achieving students (see Chapters 5 and 6). Garner and Bing (1973 b) reported that teachers have most contacts with two types of students: intelligent, hard working, sociable, and independent ones; and disobedient but amusing and sociable ones. Other children are much less salient to the teacher.

However the independence referred to above is the behavior shown by sociable students who have general success in the classroom and who readily comply with teacher requests. Teachers do *not* generally like independent students who aggressively pursue their own individual interests (see Chapter 6). Students who are attentive, able to work independently, and compliant with teacher rules are especially likely to engender high positive expectations and favorable attitudes in teachers.

The performance of highs not only is qualitatively better than that of lows, but it also is probably more stimulating, so that some teachers may want to hear highs more frequently. For example, some teachers probably praise highs proportionately more frequently than lows because highs' answers are better, making it easier for teachers to respond positively. The previously reported finding that teachers were much more likely to ask highs additional questions after their initial response probably results in part because their comments are more relevant and because teachers are interested in what they say and want to hear more. Highs, especially at higher grade levels, are more likely to arouse genuine teacher interest ("I never thought of that before").

The literature reviewed earlier shows that highs receive more teacher contact in part because they initiate more contact. Teachers usually do not compensate for differences in student initiation rates, so that highs receive noticeably more teacher contact. Thus although some of the differences in quantity of contacts with teachers are due to student behavior, it is accurate to state that most teachers tolerate or passively accept these differences and in some cases allow them to widen. Such teacher behavior occurs not so much because teachers are unconcerned about lows but because they enjoy contacts with highs. These contacts are rewarding, and they subtly condition and reinforce teacher behavior.

Lows Present Difficult Problems

Contacts with lows may be unpleasant enough for some teachers that they begin to avoid these students. Teacher approaches to the student (or vice versa) may involve hostile, aggressive exchanges or disinterested passivity. Thus teachers may unconsciously form an adverse reaction to lows, because they are rejected by them and fail to receive desired responses from them. The result may be reduced public interactions with these students. This may be part of the reason why certain lows place themselves or are placed by the teacher in the rear of the room.

Thus the general unattractiveness of these students may lessen their involvement with teachers. (In this context we are referring to the behavioral attractiveness of students as opposed to their physical attractiveness.) Initially these reactions may be controlled more by the student than the teacher. Thus a few intense episodes (student misbehavior) may create a teacher expectation which then in turn acts as a self-fulfilling prophecy: "To reduce friction I had better not call on him." Data reviewed in Chapter 6 show that teachers do indeed form adverse reactions to students who do not satisfy their needs in interpersonal interactions, and that feelings of rejection are likely to occur early in the year and to remain present throughout the year.

Lack of Teacher Awareness

We have suggested that students' attractiveness or unattractiveness may subtly condition teacher behavior. (That students consciously or unconsciously can influence teacher behavior is well-documented: Emmer, Good, and Oakland, 1971; Jenkins and Deno, 1969; Jones, 1971; Klein, 1971.) We would suggest that a third dimension is equally important: lack of teacher awareness of their own patterns of classroom behavior. Teachers are unaware of many simple aspects of their classroom behavior, especially *qualitative* aspects of their interactions (Good and Brophy, 1973). For example, information about which students they stay with or give up on in failure situations comes as a surprise to teachers. Other researchers have demonstrated that simple measures such as the percent of time teachers talk or the percent of time they spend with various children are poorly recalled by most teachers (Emmer, 1967; Garner and Bing, 1973 b).

Teachers' lack of awareness about their behavior stems from two sources. The first and most pervasive reason is the hectic pace of classroom life. So much happens so quickly that it is difficult for a teacher to maintain a firm notion of the various interactions they have with the class and with individual students. Dreeben (1973) presents a good review of studies looking at the rapid nature of classroom interaction and the complex demands that busy environments place on teachers. He reminds us of Jackson's (1965) study wherein an elementary schoolteacher was found to have 650 interactions with individual students and about 1000 interactions with the class as a whole in one instructional day.

Complicating matters further is the fact that most teachers have not developed conceptual categories for labeling and understanding their classroom behavior as it unfolds. Artley (1972) has described this general problem and presented a sensible, usable strategy that teachers can apply mentally as they ask students questions during reading group instruction. However, in general, teacher-training programs have not helped students to develop conceptual labels that can be used while standing on one's feet teaching a class. For example, teachers who react inappropriately to a student's silence or incorrect response may not perceive their behavior as giving up. Their perception may be "keep the ball rolling," "don't embarrass the student," or simply an automatic response to their own vague feeling of uneasiness. The development of such conceptual labels (wait for a response, give up, stay with, do not demand too much, get a rewardable response, and so on) may help teachers to be more conscious of their behavior as it unfolds and better able to evaluate its effectiveness.

Teacher Competence in Dealing with Failure

The attractiveness of the student, and the lack of teachers' awareness about their own ongoing behavior are both important reasons accounting for why highs and lows receive differential treatment. Another important contributing factor is teacher competence, or the behavioral skills that a teacher possesses. The teachers may like lows and feel that it is important to work with them in failure situations but still not work with them because they do not know what to do.

This is probably because teachers, like anyone else, are better equipped to handle success than failure. Teacher-training programs typically do not provide teachers with techniques for handling student failures. As a result, too many teachers enter the classroom "right answer" oriented. Much has been written about how to present material, how to lecture, how to lead discussions, and how to question effectively, but comparatively little has been written about how to act when students fail to respond or respond incorrectly. Many curricula are written in a way which almost suggests that if teachers present the material "effectively," learning will be errorless. It is no wonder, then, that young teachers (and too often even experienced teachers) react with puzzlement and uncertainty when students give wrong answers.

For example, teachers learn in educational psychology courses about the general purpose and meaning of aptitude and achievement tests. They also learn about general evaluation procedures and develop skills for making their own tests. But they spend little time learning how to use test results for improving classroom instruction. Aptitude scores too often are used only to provide a base from which to develop superficial but rigid expectations for student performance. Trivial differences (such as between IQ's of 100 and 110) are emphasized, but the practical implications that score patterns represent are not. However, some refreshing changes from this tradition are beginning to appear (see Meeker, 1973).

Teachers, especially beginning ones, simply do not know how to respond to failure. They are trained in techniques for presenting material and evaluating learning, but by and large they do not learn sophisticated and comprehensive strategies for dealing with academic failures. Furthermore, they usually do not learn strategies for structuring the classroom so that they have time to work with students having learning difficulties without penalizing the progress of other students. Thus teachers often lack both the administrative know-how necessary to organize the classroom for individual instruction (for both fast and slow learners) and the specific skills for doing effective remedial work. Sperry (1972) noted that researchers historically tended to attribute student failure to their motivational or emotional problems rather than to teacher expectations, teacher behavior, or the curriculum. Thus part of the problem is that little research has centered upon alternative patterns of teacher behavior which might successfully overcome established patterns of failure.

Insufficient training in dealing with student failure is compounded by the fact that many teachers enter the classroom with intense unresolved personal problems of their own. Beginning teachers (unless their training program has helped them to work through early concerns) enter the classroom acutely concerned about whether they will be able to control students, about how they will impress fellow teachers, and about whether or not their students will like them (as opposed to more mature concerns such as how they can help students learn).

There is some research to suggest that excessive concern with self can interfere with a teacher's ability to perform effectively (Fuller, 1969). Teachers anxious about themselves may subconsciously repress student difficulties because they are so busy coping with their own problems. Student silence following a question, for example, is threatening. Not only do teachers not know how to respond to silence and to the possible wrong answer, but silence per se is a threat to the teacher's well-being. Student response, no matter how trivial, assures the teacher that "everything is okay." Thus the insecure teacher is likely to answer his own question or call on someone else rather than patiently wait for a response. Another indication that teachers are not equipped to deal with failure is a tendency to respond positively to student responses without regard to whether or not they are congruous with the teacher's original question (Bellack *et al.* 1966). Consider this teacher question. "In *your* opinion should we spend money on space flights?" An example of a congruous answer to this request for the student's own opinion would be, "I think. . . ." An incongruous response would be, "well, in the book the author said it would promote our technological growth" (the student neither disagrees nor agrees with the statement nor elaborates it in any way). Bellack *et al.* reported that *if* teachers evaluated a response, 80 percent of the time the evaluation was positive both when the student's response was congruous or incongruous with the teacher's original demand. Thus in that study, the degree of congruity was unrelated to a positive evaluation. Apparently, teachers reward student responses for reasons other than answering the logical demands imposed by the question.

Additional indirect support for the assertion that silence is threatening and student talk is rewarding is provided by the observation that it is very difficult for teachers to increase the length of time that they wait for students to respond (Rowe, 1972). Apparently there is some emotional resistance to doing this, because most teachers in a training program set up specifically to teach them to wait longer for responses made little or no progress. Further evidence that personal difficulties may impede teacher response to failure is provided by the previously reported finding that teachers fail to provide feedback to lows more often than to highs. Perhaps teachers who do not know how to react to marginal answers "solve" this problem by avoiding it. Instead of staying with the student and reacting to his answer, they just move on to someone or something else.

Obviously, some teachers do learn to cope with their anxieties and become secure enough to be able to shift their concern from themselves to their students. However, we suspect that many behaviors reinforced through habitual use become stable parts of the teacher's repertoire. Research on student teachers consistently suggests that student teachers' styles are heavily influenced by their cooperating teacher, and that inservice teachers teach basically the way they taught as student teachers (Peck and Tucker, 1973). Such findings are not surprising; if a strategy is *apparently* working, there is little reason for changing it. Thus if a teacher initially learns to handle "awkward" silence by quickly calling on another student, this is likely to become a permanent response pattern, especially since the teacher is unlikely to be aware that he behaves this way. And once on the job teachers are unlikely to get good, corrective feedback.

Low Expectations for Students

Of course the consistent theme of this book has been that low expectations for students are a prime source of differential teacher behavior. If teachers form a low estimate of a student, fail to reevaluate the validity of their label, and fail to develop active, conscious strategies for helping the student, undesirable effects are bound to follow. Teachers begin to anticipate failure, so they do not call upon these students, do not notice their successes, and/or begin to show some of the other behavioral indicators of expectation effects discussed in Chapter 4.

In combination, the other "causes" of differential teacher behavior previously discussed in this section are likely to lead to low expectations which may become self-fulfilling. For example, the busy teacher has little time to correct his misconceptions. Thus the impact of notable student behavior would seem especially important early in the year. Students who politely seek out the teacher for help may lead the teacher to expect warm, satisfying interactions. Students who approach the teacher hesitantly or with indifference or belligerence (I do not understand why we have to do this) may create unpleasant impressions. Teachers who are especially anxious about themselves or who do not know how to deal with problem students may cope by avoiding these students. Unfortunately, even accurate impressions (the student does not like me, he is hostile, he is a slow student) may lead teachers merely to blame students rather than to examine their own behavior as part of the problem. Thus teacher expectations (often formed on the basis of accurate observation of student behavior) may create cognitive anticipatory mechanisms, leading some teachers to exaggerate student difficulties and to treat them in such ways as to exacerbate the problem.

Expectations tend to be self-sustaining. They affect both *perception*, by causing the teacher to be alert for what he expects and to be less likely to notice what he does not expect, and *interpretation*, by causing the teacher to interpret (and perhaps distort) what he sees so that it is consistent with his expectations. In this way, some expectations can persist even though they do not fit the facts (as seen by a more neutral observer).

Summary

In this section we have argued that highs receive better treatment in part because of their own behavior and their general attractiveness to teachers. Teachers may have some minor aversions to selected lows, but a major related problem is that they do not possess specific and effective skills for dealing with failure. Their own resultant uneasiness and their students' discomfort in public situations subtly encourages teachers to avoid students who fail frequently and/or to react emotionally to their failure with sharp criticism. Furthermore, since classrooms are so busy and teachers possess few conceptual labels for monitoring their own behavior, teachers are largely unaware of their behavior. This lack of awareness allows the process to continue so that, ultimately, teachers overreact to student behavior (anticipating failure, and so on).

WHAT CAN TEACHERS DO?

The purpose of this section is to describe some of the things that a single, unaided teacher in a self-contained classroom can do to improve the environment of the classroom for both lows and highs. Emphasis will be placed upon dealing with lows, because their problems appear to be more widespread and intense. However, we believe that the recommendations that follow will in many cases benefit highs as well, and in no case will they penalize highs ipso facto.

Teachers we have previously labeled as proactive (reaching out to lows) do not appear to achieve their rapport with lows at the expense of highs. It is true that highs in these classrooms have less teacher contact, but their loss is compensated (from our perspective) by their active involvement in individual and peer group activities that help them expand their skills for self-directed and personally satisfying learning.

In the following parts of this section we shall first describe some attitudes that we feel teachers should develop (or communicate) and then suggest behavioral strategies for working with lows. But before presenting this information it is important to stress two approaches that we do *not* suggest, to make sure that we do not communicate false and unintended implications to the reader.

Equal Expectations and Treatment for All Students: No

First, we do *not* suggest that all students should receive equal (in the sense of *sameness*) classroom treatment. Some students will learn more quickly than others. Some will be relatively reticent but will learn mostly by listening and actively, but covertly, evaluating what they hear.

Paradoxically, the pressure for equal student performance is the source of invidious and self-defeating comparisons that eventually erode the confidence and motivation of many students. The fact that John scores below grade level on a given test need not necessarily upset him, but if Byron's score exceeds grade level and John is expected to achieve as well as Byron, John (or his parents) may be affected adversely. The expectation that all students should be at or above grade level guarantees that 50 percent of the students in the country will be considered failures. Furthermore, if the teacher believes (and communicates this belief to students) that test scores are evaluations of worth rather than feedback about learning progress, students will regard testing, reporting, or answering classroom questions as dangerous situations in which they may be "found out," rather than as chances to compare their ideas with others' and to perceive useful feedback. Thus the expectation that all students will achieve equally is unrealistic and self-defeating.

Carroll (1963) and Bloom (1973) have stressed that if students receive the same amount and quality of instruction, student aptitude and postinstruction achievement will be highly correlated. That is, if students receive the same amount and quality of instruction, the individual needs of the majority are not met and teachers will simply apply existing differences in students to shape learning outcomes subtly. Thus if teachers are to help lows to master the material (and if highs are not to be bored), teachers must necessarily behave differently toward students who master course material at different rates.

Similarly, teacher or school expectations that students learn best in quiet, passive milieus guarantee that some students will find the classroom stifling and unfulfilling. In fact, any strategy that is designed for all students categorically will insure failure for many. Teachers who assign all students the same frequency and type of classroom opportunities, as well as the same goals, structure the classroom so that many students will be over- or underchallenged. *Sameness* is not the answer. Sameness is inappropriate as an expectation and self-defeating as a strategy.

Our purpose in this section is not to specify how highs and lows should be treated but rather to point out the need for differential teacher behavior toward students with different needs. As we have seen, differential treatment is commonly observed. However, these differences in teacher-student interaction patterns often occur in the wrong direction. To reduce the complexity of the situation, we have used the terms "highs" and "lows." However, our use of these terms does not imply that the needs of these students do not overlap. *Clearly the needs of these students do overlap at times, and when they have similar learning needs they should receive similar teacher treatment. But the converse is also true. When students have different needs, they should receive different treatment.* We do not need to eliminate differences in teacher behavior; we need to identify *appropriate differences* in teacher behavior.

High Expectation for All Students: No

Positive expectations are not automatically self-fulfilling, and unrealistically high expectations may even be damaging. It has been shown consistently that teachers' low expectations are often linked with inferior teaching patterns, but we do *not* suggest that merely holding high expectations will magically help students reach new plateaus.

Readers with average mechanical and manipulative skills will readily recognize the dangers of unrealistically high expectations. Consider the Christmas toys or appliances that carry false advertisements such as "ten minutes of assembly time and your new —— will be ready to use." After struggling through incomplete directions and missing parts for an hour, the harrassed builder has but two choices: he can devalue his own ability and become willing to purchase only already assembled toys in the future (he gives up); or he can blame his failure on the manufacturer and vow never again to buy their products.

Students will respond similarly to unrealistically high teacher expectations. For example, in hopes of motivating student performance, a teacher might announce: "This story is so simple and interesting that all of you should finish it in half an hour." If some students need an hour to read the story, due to missing parts (they do not know the vocabulary) or misleading instructions (they do not find the story interesting), they also are left with two basic choices: they can pretend to finish the assignment and hope they are not "found out"; or they can continue to read while the teacher or their peers make remarks about their slowness or the delay they are causing. The student will feel bad either way, and if such events are repeated regularly, the slow student will tend either to accept his inferior status or to blame the teacher and school. He is also likely to become progressively alienated and to start looking forward to his chance to drop out of school.

The young child typically cannot identify the specific obstacles that prevent his "successful assembly," so that failure occurs for reasons beyond his control. He cannot generate strategies for coping with or solving the problem, and he must accept his inadequacy as inevitable or shift the blame to others. If he does the latter, it will likely be in an amorphous general way that helps him preserve some self-esteem but does nothing to help him learn to cope more positively. Thus we do not advocate that teachers, independent of changing their classroom behavior, adopt unrealistically high expectations for student progress.

Now that we have emphasized two attitudes that we do *not* advocate, we shall state some basic attitudes and expectations that we feel teachers possess when they function successfully in the classroom.

The Teacher Should Enjoy Teaching[1]

Teaching brings many rewards and satisfactions, but it is demanding, exhausting, and sometimes frustrating. It is hard to do well unless you enjoy doing it. Teachers who do enjoy their work will show this in their classroom behavior. They will come to class prepared, and will present lessons with interest and excitement. They will appear eager for contact with students, *keep track of students' individual needs and progress,* and take pride and satisfaction in helping them overcome learning difficulties. Difficulties and confusion in students will be perceived as challenges to be met with professional skills, not as irritations.

Teachers who really don't enjoy teaching also show it in their classroom behavior. They appear apathetic or negativistic, and act as if they are "putting in

---

[1] The material that follows through p. 349 has been adapted from pp. 86–95 in *Looking in Classrooms* by Thomas L. Good and Jere E. Brophy. Copyright © 1973 by Thomas L. Good and Jere E. Brophy. Reprinted by permission of Harper & Row, Publishers, Inc.

their time" on the job. They seem eager to escape the students when opportunities arise, and they may frequently assign busy work or needless recitations because they are unprepared or unwilling to teach. They seem unconcerned about students who are not learning the material, being content to rationalize rather than accept the challenge of finding another way to teach them.

The Teacher's Main Responsibility is to Teach

The teacher's job involves many roles besides that of instructing students. At times the teacher will serve as a parent surrogate, an entertainer, an authority figure, a psychotherapist, and a record keeper, among other things. All of these are necessary aspects of the teacher's role. However, they are subordinate to and in support of the major role of teaching. Important as they are, they must not be allowed to overshadow the teacher's basic instructional role.

It sometimes happens that teachers working with young children will become more concerned with mothering or entertaining the children than teaching them. In these classes much of the day is spent reading stories, playing games, working on arts and crafts projects, singing and listening to records, or holding show and tell and "enrichment" activities. Often the teachers basically do not like to spend time teaching the curriculum, and feel they must apologize to or bribe the children when lessons are conducted. This type of teacher is meeting his own needs, not those of the children. By the end of the year they will have acquired negative attitudes toward the curriculum, and will have failed to achieve near their potential. Teachers must have empathy and respect for their students. However, they must also expect students to learn and see that they do so.

At the higher grades, failure to teach is sometimes seen in teachers who have low expectations about their own classroom management abilities or about the learning abilities of a particular class. Where homogeneous grouping is practiced in a junior high or high school, for example, teachers assigned to a period with a low achieving class may sometimes abandon serious attempts to teach their subject. They may attempt to entertain the class, or else to act as a sort of proctor who is interested only in seeing that the noise doesn't get out of hand. Such behavior indicates a serious lack of confidence in the teacher, either in his own ability to motivate and control the class or in the students' ability to learn or to become interested in the subject matter. It represents a total surrender to failure expectations, in which emphasis has been switched from teaching the class to merely keeping the class happy.

The Crucial Aspects of Teaching are Task Presentation, Diagnosis, Remediation, and Enrichment

Failure to be clear about this point characterizes teachers who favor high achievers over low achievers or who pay more attention to answers than to the thinking processes that a student goes through in reaching an answer. Such teachers sometimes act as if students are expected to learn on their own with no help from them. If a student doesn't catch on immediately after one demonstration, or does not do his work correctly after hearing the instructions one time, they react with impatience and frustration.

Such behavior represents a fundamental misunderstanding of the teacher's basic role. The teacher is in the classroom to instruct. This involves more than just giving demonstrations or presenting learning experiences. Instruction also means giving additional help to those who are having difficulty, diagnosing the source of their problem, and providing remedial assistance to correct it. It means conducting evaluation with an eye toward identifying and correcting difficulties, and not merely as a prelude to passing out praise or criticism. It means keeping track of each student's individual progress, so he can be dealt with in terms of where he was yesterday and where he should be tomorrow. It means finding satisfaction in the progress of the slower students as well as the brighter ones.

Many aspects of teacher behavior indicate whether or not the teacher clearly understands what he is supposed to be doing with his students. The handling of seatwork and homework assignments is one good indicator. The purpose of such assignments is to provide students with practice on the skills they are learning and to provide the teacher with information about their progress. Teachers should monitor the students' performance, noting the particular error patterns that occur. This will identify each individual student's learning problems, and indicate which remedial actions the teacher should take. However, some teachers fail to use seatwork and homework in this way. They pass out the work and then collect and score it, but they don't follow up with remedial teaching. Students who succeed are praised, while those who need help receive only criticism and low marks. Seatwork thus does not lead to diagnosis and remediation.

Teachers can create negative attitudes toward seatwork assignments if such assignments are inappropriate or are not adjusted to individual differences in students' aptitudes and interests. Assignments should be made with specific instructional objectives in mind. This may mean separate assignments for different groups of students in a class. Assignments that are too difficult or too easy for a given student will not fulfill their instructional purpose.

Another important indicator is the way the teacher responds to right and wrong answers. When the teacher has the appropriate attitude, he accepts either type of response for the information it gives about the student. He neither becomes overly elated about correct answers nor overly depressed about incorrect answers. He uses questions as a way to stimulate thinking and to acquire information about student progress. Questions should come in sequences designed to see that both the students who answer them and the rest of the class who are listening develop a deeper understanding of the concepts being discussed. They should not be a series of disjointed "tests" or spot checks on the students' memories.

Inappropriate expectations can even be communicated through praise. Although praise and encouragement are important, they should not interfere with basic teaching goals. If the teacher responds with overly dramatic praise every time a student answers a simple question, the class will likely be distracted from the content of the lesson. A contest in which the more confident and outgoing students compete for teacher recognition and approval will probably result. The better strategy is to follow a simple correct answer with simple feedback to acknowledge that it is correct. The teacher should then advance the discussion by asking another question or adding information. Praise can be saved for times when it can be given more effectively and meaningfully, especially during contacts with individual students. Criticism, of course, should be omitted entirely. In general, the teacher's behavior during question and answer sessions should say, "We're going to discuss and deepen our understanding of the material," and not, "We're going to find out who knows the material and who doesn't."

When praise is given to students, it should be specific praise that reinforces their feelings of progress in learning new knowledge and skills. Empty phrases like "how nice" or "that's good" should be avoided in favor of more specific statements. Praise should stress appreciation of the student's efforts and the progress he is making, and usually should be focused on his more general progress rather than on single isolated successes. All of this helps to reinforce the teacher's role as a resource person who facilitates learning, as opposed to a judge who decides who has learned and who hasn't.

Teachers Should Expect All Students to Meet at least the Minimum Specified Objectives

Although all students cannot reasonably be expected to do equally well, reasonable minimal objectives can be established for each teacher's class. Naturally, most students will be capable of going considerably beyond minimal objectives, and the teacher should try to stimulate this development as far as their interests and abilities allow. However, in doing so, teachers must not lose sight of basic priorities. Remedial work with students who have not yet met minimal objectives should not be delayed or omitted in favor of enrichment activities with those who have.

Teachers with appropriate attitudes will spend extra time working with the students who are having difficulty. Their behavior when interacting with these students will be characterized by supportiveness, patience, and confidence. In contrast, teachers with inappropriate attitudes will often spend less time with the students who most need extra help. When they do work with these students they will tend to do so in a half-hearted way that communicates boredom, disappointment, or frustration. Such teachers are often overly dependent on achieving easy success and eliciting many right answers. They will need to change this attitude if they are to acquire the patience and confidence needed to do effective remedial teaching with slower learners.

Teachers Should Expect Students to Enjoy Learning

Teachers can and should expect students to enjoy learning activities, including practice exercises, and should back these expectations with appropriate behavior. This is one of the most common areas where teacher expectations become self-fulfilling. When teachers do have the appropriate attitude toward schoolwork, they present it in ways that make their students see it as enjoyable and interesting. Tasks and assignments are presented without apology as activities valuable in their own right. There is no attempt to build up artificial enthusiasm or interest; the interest is assumed to be already there. Comments about upcoming assignments stress the specific ways in which they extend or build upon present knowledge and skills. Comments about present work reinforce the students' sense of progress and mastery. The teacher doesn't try to give learning a "hard sell," or to picture it as "fun." He doesn't expect the students to enjoy it in the same way they enjoy a trip to the circus or ride on a roller coaster. Instead, he expects the quieter but consistent satisfactions and feelings of mastery that come with the accumulation of knowledge and skills.

The teacher with a negative attitude toward school learning behaves very differently. He sees learning activities as unpleasant but necessary drudgery. If he believes in a positive approach toward motivation, he will be apologetic and defensive about assignments and will frequently resort to bribery, attempting to generate enthusiasm artificially through overemphasis on contests, rewards, and other external incentives. If he is more authoritarian and punitive, he will present assignments as bitter pills that the students must swallow or else. In either case, the students will quickly acquire a distaste for school activities, thus providing reinforcement of the teacher's expectations. Other evidence of inappropriate teacher attitudes toward school activities include: a heavy stress on the separation between work and play, with work pictured as unpleasant activity one does in order to get to play; a tendency to introduce assignments as something the class has to do, rather than merely as something they are going to do; the use of extra assignments as punishments; and practices such as checking to make sure that everyone has signed out one or more books from the library. Teachers with negative attitudes also have a tendency to discuss academic subjects in a way that presents them as dull and devoid of content. For example, they tend to say, "We're going to have history," instead of "We're going to discuss the voyage of Columbus," or "Read pages 17–22," instead of "Read the author's critique of Twain's novel." All of these behaviors tell the student that the teacher doesn't see school activities as very interesting or pleasant.

The Teacher Should Expect to Deal with Individuals, not Groups or Stereotypes

As a rule, teachers should think, talk, and act in terms of individual students. This does not mean that they should not practice grouping, or that terms such as "low achievers" should not be used. It does mean that teachers must keep a proper perspective about priorities. Grouping must be practiced as a means toward the goal of meeting the individual needs of each student. Similarly, labels and stereotypes are often helpful in thinking about ways to teach individuals better. Ultimately, however, the teacher is teaching John Smith and Mary Jones, not Group A or "low achievers." The way teachers talk about students in their classes is an indication of how they think about them. If there is continual mention of groups to the exclusion of individuals, the teacher may well have begun to lose sight of individual differences within groups and to overemphasize the differences between groups. If this has happened, observers will note that the teacher has too many choral responses and not enough individual responses in group situations, that he has not changed his group membership in a long time, that groups are seated together and spend most of the day together, or that the teacher spends more time with the high group and less with the low group.

Similarly, it seems that teachers should carefully monitor and assess activities in which they teach the class as a class. There are times when it is very useful to teach the whole class. Positive instances might include (1) when the class has been carefully selected on the basis of aptitude and learning interests; (2) when new materials are being introduced; (3) when the independent work of individuals or small groups of students on similar topics can be integrated. However, as we have noted previously, student learning speed varies so greatly that the teacher who teaches the whole class always faces the dilemma of staying too long on the unit and wasting the time of students who master the material quickly or proceeding prematurely such that some students have not mastered the basic content.

Teachers with appropriate expectations see low IQ scores and poor previous achievement records not as evidence that the student can't learn but merely as signs that school was not a productive place for the student in the previous year(s). (The school and the student both failed.) Teachers who can accept this view are willing to examine their own behavior and curricular offerings as possible causes of student failure. Teachers also need to be alert to other biasing factors that may influence their behavior, for example: (1) dialect, race, and appearance *per se* are not predictors of student aptitude or attitude toward school; (2) sibling school behavior differs widely; (3) dramatic/intense interactions with individual students early in the year are especially likely to trigger unexamined and inappropriate expectations, etc.

Behavioral Strategies for Dealing with Lows

Helpfulness of Positive, but Appropriate, Expectations

Despite what has been said so far about confidence and positive expectations, there inevitably will be difficulties, and teachers must expect and be prepared for them. Positive expectations will go a long way toward solving and preventing problems, but they will not prevent or solve all problems. Expectations are not automatically self-fulfilling.

Positive expectations are necessary and important, however. To the extent that they initiate behavior that leads to self-fulfilling prophecy effects, they help prevent and solve problems that would otherwise appear. These benefits would not have been gained if the necessary positive expectations had not been there in the first place.

In addition, the effects of negative expectations must be considered. Where no negative expectations exist, undesirable self-fulfilling prophecy effects cannot occur. Where negative expectations do exist, however, some are likely to result in behavior that produces self-fulfilling prophecy effects, thus adding to the teacher's burden. In addition to problems that would have been there anyway, there are added problems caused by his own negative expectations.

An additional benefit of consistent positive expectations is that they cause the teacher to examine his own behavior and to ask what he might be doing differently to help the situation. This is an important function, since teachers, like everyone else, are strongly tempted to take credit for success but to blame failure on things other than themselves.

Such rationalizing is not particularly malicious and not confined to teachers. We all want to see ourselves as likable, competent, and successful, and we all tend to repress or explain away the things that do not fit this self-image. Such defensiveness is not necessary in teachers who adopt positive, but *appropriate*, *expectations* for their students. Because the expectations are appropriate, the teacher does not need to feel guilty or dissatisfied if slower students do not do so well as better students. Success is defined as progress in terms of the students' capabilities. Since the expectations are also positive, they continually remind the teacher to think in terms of forward progress and to analyze the problem and to question his teaching approach when progress is not evident. This helps him to stay on top of the situation and to adapt quickly to changes as they appear. The teacher will recognize and exploit breakthroughs as they occur and will respond to failure with a search for another way to do the job rather than for an excuse or "explanation."

In summary, even though appropriately positive attitudes and expectations are not automatically or totally effective by themselves, they are necessary and important teacher qualities. Teachers will not always succeed with them, but they will not get very far at all without them.

Teachers can avoid many problems by adopting appropriate general expectations about teaching, by learning to recognize their specific attitudes and expectations about individual students, and by learning to monitor their treatment of individual students. In particular it is essential that teachers remember that their primary responsibility is to teach, to help each student reach his potential as a learner. It is natural that teachers form differential attitudes and expectations about different students, because each student is an individual. To the extent that these are accurate and appropriate, they are helpful for planning ways to meet each student's needs. However, they must constantly be monitored and evaluated to insure that they change appropriately in response to changes in the student.

Need for Increased Teacher Awareness

We have taken time to review potential explanations for why lows receive relatively inferior teacher treatment and to sensitize readers to the extraordinarily complex problems and processes that teachers must deal with. With very few exceptions, teachers do not maliciously humiliate lows or consciously neglect them. Granted, there are notable examples of mindless behavior, such as when a teacher calls his superior groups "tigers" and "cardinals" while referring to his low group as "clowns" (Rist, 1969).

In general, teachers are dedicated, hard working people who care about the pupils they teach. We suggest that dismal patterns of teacher contacts with lows are identifiable and understandable but changeable. We have seen that teachers are drawn to highs because they are generally more reinforcing and likeable. Teachers tend to avoid and give up on lows because they expect mediocre performance and do not know how to deal with failure, and in some cases because their own confidence is so low that they cannot reach out and help these students.

Thus teachers need help in monitoring their own expectations and the consequences of those expectations. They do not need mindless criticism and abuse.

We have reviewed obstacles that prevent teachers from interacting more favorably with lows and have consistently pointed out that most inappropriate teacher behavior occurs because teachers are unaware of their behavior patterns and of other alternatives. We have also stressed that the data reviewed so far in this book are *not* a call for students to receive identical treatment or for teachers to adopt unrealistically high expectations.

Teachers need to become more aware of their classroom behavior in general and their interactions with lows in particular. As a starting point, teachers could review their behavior with an eye toward the results of studies previously reported in the book. Relevant questions to raise include the following:

Do teachers praise or encourage lows when they initiate comments?

Do teachers stay with lows in failure situations?

Do teachers stay with lows in success situations?

Do teachers avoid calling on lows in public situations?

How often do lows have positive success experiences in *public* situations?

Are lows needlessly criticized for wrong answers or failing to respond?

Are lows placed in a "low group" and treated as group members rather than as individuals?

Do teachers ignore the minor inappropriate behavior of lows, or do mild violations of classroom rules bring on strong reprimands?

How often do lows get to select study topics?

How frequently do lows have a chance to evaluate their own work and to make responsible (important) decisions?

Certainly, if teachers are to change their behavior they must become aware of it. Teachers may profitably increase their awareness by listening to audio tapes, viewing videotapes of their own teaching, inviting fellow teachers to observe in their classroom during free periods, engaging in informal discussions with students, and regularly soliciting anonymous feedback from students. Teaching, like anything else, can be studied, and teachers who are willing to study their own behavior and who seek feedback from others will gain valuable insights and new alternatives for increasing their repertoire of classroom skills.

Awareness of Student Problems and Difficulties of Changing Behavior

Students who are low achievers vary in their classroom behavior (some are passive; others openly aggressive and hostile) and the etiologies of their difficulties stem from a variety of multiple forces. The passive student and the belligerent student may behave in opposite ways even though the source of their problem (for example, relatively low aptitude, history of school failure, no athletic skill or other visible skill to compensate for their academic failure) is similar. And it is also possible to identify students who achieve at low levels and behave similarly but for dissimilar reasons. The diagnosis problem the teacher faces is complex, and there are no universal answers that can be applied in an unthinking fashion. To deal effectively with such students (or any student for that matter) it is important to know them as individuals.

Learning to Know the Low Achiever as an Individual

Too often teachers group and treat lows as though they were one student. It is especially important to learn about the *unique* needs and interests of students who have been turned off by school and who see school as an irrelevant or punishing place. Paradoxically, when teachers visit informally with students, it is rarely with lows. Perhaps because lows (especially in older grades) are often outwardly sullen or fearfully silent, teachers do not want to or are afraid to approach them. The paradox lies in the fact that most of these students want teacher contact but do not know how to obtain it, and that in general they are convinced that teachers like them less than other students and do not want to be bothered with them.

Therefore, a teacher must seek out the lows for extended and frequent informal discussions if he is to convince them that he is interested in them. Also, he will need to discover the unique individual interests of these students through such informal contacts if he wants to be able to channel these interests into school-related projects. The time investment that teachers make in learning about lows and becoming interested in them is a necessary and practical one that often brings rich dividends.

Even though to deal with a low achieving student and his problem the teacher has to deal with the individual students, we suggest three generalizations that may be helpful in reacting to a specific student's problem. Regardless of the student's specific problem (low motivation, physical deficit such as eyesight or hearing, low aptitude, intense anxiety, short attention spans) several common factors merit discussion. *First, students have had a chance to institutionalize coping strategies for minimizing the frustration they face in various situations.* Many students will simply not provide responses that can be evaluated (do not answer in class when called upon, do not hand in homework). Apparently students who react with passivity have been rewarded for such behavior and have learned that making no response is better than taking a chance. The teacher's task here is to *teach* students that their responses will not be sharply evaluated, and that responding is the way to get teacher attention and help. Rosenfeld and Zander (1961) presented data (student interviews) to suggest that students can distinguish between teacher disapproval of poor performance and teacher disapproval when the student had done the best he could. Disapproval in the latter situation produced negative student feelings.

Many lows initially played the academic game as best they could, but teacher or peer feedback proved so disheartening that they learned that an academic question avoided is an academic battle won. Teacher criticism of any serious response attempt is dubious in any situation, but especially for passive low achieving students.

Other students will react to threatening situations with different strategies. Some play the class clown and often supply clever but irrelevant responses. Such behavior protects their self-esteem and punishes the teacher for calling on them. Other students may respond to teachers with open hostility ("I don't know. Call on somebody who studies this stupid stuff."). Such behavior, although it may bring teacher criticism for rudeness and general attitude, does not bring negative teacher evaluation of the student's ability. And the teacher may provide indirect reward (if you read and improve your attitude you'd be one of the best students in the class!). Such behaviors prevent the student from being "found out" academically, and this may be more rewarding than attempting to respond or comply with teacher requests.

The point is that student behaviors that have been institutionalized through practice and reward are difficult to change. The first step in changing such response patterns is to recognize the coping strategy that the student uses and then systematically reward competing (for instance answering versus not answering) responses. Recognition of the problem helps the teacher to modify his expectations and perhaps change his behavior. However, eliciting the competing response is the trick.

Similarly, helping students to recognize the problem is a key to changing their behavior (although the directness that the teacher uses in confronting a student with his behavior should vary with teacher's skills, age of the student, severity of problems, and so on). However, just as the causes of low achievement vary widely, so do methods of discussing problems with students. Middleman (1972), for example, showed that students from different backgrounds may use different cues for judging teacher credibility. Thus the simple direct technique ("I'm concerned about your behavior in class; am I doing something that turns you off?" and then listening to the student) is probably the best strategy. Such a direct approach might provide teachers with: (1) concrete suggestions that they could immediately use in class to illustrate interest in the student ("you don't call on me early in the discussion," and so on); (2) a way of communicating interest in the student and showing a willingness to talk whenever he wishes to do so; and (3) a means to set up concrete goals for alleviating the problem.

Teachers need not confer with students about every problem. Indeed, shy, anxious students' problems might be intensified by knowledge that the teacher intended to call on them more, unless the teacher has well-developed clinical skills. However, meetings with students may be necessary in some cases (for example, student hostility, failure to turn in homework).

Teachers can also use general classroom discussion periods as a vehicle for learning about students' interests as well as providing shy students with an opportunity to express themselves and to gain confidence in public speaking in situations that do not require academic responses. Glasser (1969) discussed several types of group discussions that teachers can initiate to serve these dual purposes. Thus teachers can use class discussions as well as private discussions in order to learn more about students and to involve them in making decisions about classroom procedure.

Clarifying Goals

Another problem that many low achievers face is their belief that they cannot achieve, which leads them to *set unrealistically high or low goals in order to spare themselves from frustrating evaluations of ability.* Low goals guarantee success. High goals make failure excusable. Tyler's (1958) laboratory work suggested that low achievement students take longer to respond, are more likely to guess than reason, and are more likely to perseverate with primitive or inappropriate response strategies. Thus there is reason to believe that these students have given up on themselves. Just as they evoke strategies to avoid public failure, they also adopt strategies such as inappropriate goals to disguise failure to themselves. Like anything else, coping skills can and need to be taught.

Bradley and Gaa (1973) show that simple goal setting conferences may help students to set realistic goals such that achievement may be positively effected. This is not to suggest that teacher attention in a goal setting conference will alter student behavior. Time per se is not the key. But if in such conferences teachers communicate respect and interest in the student, focus on progress, help the student to develop realistic goals and establish mechanisms for appropriate self- and teacher feedback, such conferences may have beneficial effects.

The motivational importance of stating a personal expectancy for obtaining commitment and involvement in a task has been demonstrated (Zajonc and Brickman, 1969). The statement per se of commitment or expectancy may be the causal factor (Gurin and Gurin, 1970). A statement of intention may mobilize a student even if the stated expectancy is low. However there are some data to suggest that positive expectations (reasonable) are associated with greater involvement and persistence in difficult achievement tasks (Battle, 1965; Crandall, Katkovsky, and Preston, 1962). The reader desiring an extended discussion of the theoretical aspects of this research should consult Gurin and Gurin (1970).

Duel (1958) provided data indicating that opportunity for self-evaluation in a *nonthreatening* context can facilitate achievement. Furthermore, de Charms (1970) has described a program for increasing internal goal setting, better reality perception, personal responsibility for outcomes, and self-confidence. Treatment subjects showed gains on several measures as well as on the Iowa Achievement Tests. Interested readers may want to pursue this program as an instance of how teachers might attempt to help students set realistic goals. Thus teacher meetings with students can then be used to influence student achievement as well as for dealing with behavior problems. Face-to-face private conversations with students may be a useful strategy for involving students in the classroom if the teacher is willing to spend time with students in such ways, to listen to them (acting upon student suggestions when appropriate), and to use such meetings to develop specific expectations and programs of action.

Considering Student Interest

A third factor that seems to be widespread among students generally and low achievement students in particular is the *belief that school or teacher is disinterested in them and that what they think is not important to school personnel.* Morrison and McIntyre (1969) presented data reporting that 73 percent of low achievers think teachers think poorly of them whereas only 10 percent of highs feel this way. Doubtlessly figures would vary from teacher to teacher and from school to school; however, Morrison's data do summarize the problem. Teachers should be especially alert for opportunities to allow students to set class rules and to use their interests in mapping out learning experiences. Solomon and Oberlander (1973) argued that students are more favorably disposed toward teachers when they have a voice in classroom decisions. General tips on using student ideas and helping them to become more accurate judges of their own work are summarized by Solomon and Oberlander (1973).

The suggestion here is that teacher attempts to communicate with students may not make impressive, quick gains for some students because they have been alienated by the school process. For example, many students' failure experiences in school have been such that they never have been able to engage in *self-congratulatory* activity. Such behavior (I've done a good job, people need me) is necessary if our morale is to remain high. Many low achieving students have never experienced the satisfaction of completing a long and difficult assignment totally successfully. Furthermore, their failure may continually deny the minor satisfactions of classroom life. Such students rarely have the opportunity to read something for the fun of it (they are too busy finishing required material).

Expectations and Student Interests

Thus in some ways teachers might move faster by allowing student interests to dictate part of the curriculum. Initially, a better strategy is to keep expectations relevant to student needs and interests.

Sometimes even positive expectations are self-defeating. Teachers may consistently communicate that the subject matter is important, insist upon student learning, and make efforts to make the material interesting, but still find that students do not want to or cannot perform. The distinction between situations where the student cannot perform and where he does not want to perform is an important one, because different teacher strategies apply. Generally, when students do not perform because of a skill deficiency, teachers need to take remedial steps to assure that the students learn the necessary skills. At times the students may resist the teachers' remedial attempts (primarily because initially, unless the teacher is careful, the special attention only deepens the student's sense of failure). Nevertheless, the teacher should persist in trying to remedy skill deficiencies. This, we feel, is because *student interest in a subject usually comes about because the student achieves a modest degree of success in the subject* and not vice versa. Attempts to build student interest in a subject will fail unless the teacher also builds student skills so that he can achieve enough success in the subject to motivate him to persevere. Thus teachers need to communicate their genuine interest in the student and their personal enthusiasm for the subject and explain to the student why the material is necessary to master, but they always must back this with actions which will remediate the student's skill deficiencies in the subject.

In general, we suggest that when important skills are involved (reading, computation), the teacher *must* stay with the student (using his interests, adapting materials) and see that he masters the material. However, in situations when *basic* skills are *not* involved and when inadequate student performance is primarily *motivational* in nature, the teacher should take a careful look at his instructional goals. Most (appropriate) instructional goals involve the acquisition and use of *processes,* rather than rote learning of specific *content.* Usually there is no single way to learn the material most efficiently; however, some teachers present the curriculum in a "one road to learning" fashion, trying to force all students to learn the content in the same way.

Why, for example, do students in an art class have to draw the same daisy (unless the teacher unwisely wants to demonstrate the relative talents of students)? Why do all students have to do historical reports on Bach rather than Bacharach or some other composer that the student is interested in? Why do mathematical "thought" problems always have to involve questions that no normal student wants to think about (if a train in Quincy, Illinois, is going ninety miles an hour and a car in Owensboro, Kentucky, is traveling at seventy-five miles an hour . . .)?

Why should seventh-grade students who resist oral music classes because they cannot sing be forced to attend and sing? Rigid approaches to curriculum, such as in this example, probably will succeed only in causing students to internalize their resistance to music so that they will never enjoy it. Why not allow such students to spend time in appreciation courses, sampling a variety of musical expression and developing their own musical tastes?

It should be emphasized that using student ideas does not mean to water down the curriculum by repeatedly pursuing nonsubstantive topics. The suggestion is that student interests can be used to involve the student in a meaningful endeavor. We agree with Jackson (1973) that schools should provide students with satisfying day-to-day experiences, but that the chief goal of the school is to provide meaningful educational experiences.

Welch and Walberg (1972) demonstrated that student interest does not guarantee learning, but we feel it is an important first step. And if this first step is followed by appropriate teacher behavior (establishing clear learning goals, helping the student to evaluate his progress and to assume increasing responsibility for his own learning), meaningful student accomplishment will follow, thereby reinforcing the student's initiative. Behavioral accomplishment on meaningful tasks is the important goal, but when students have given up and make no serious attempts to master curricular material, use of student interest and getting them to try becomes especially important. But working on enjoyable tasks per se will accomplish but little.

Although the advice presented above is applicable to the teaching of all students, it is especially important that the growth of lows not be stifled by irrelevant curricular expectations. Lows have sufficient difficulty in mastering basic skills, so that whenever an opportunity occurs that allows them to learn or to do something in their own way the teacher should take advantage of it.

Obviously, finding and using student interests is not an end in itself. Even after identifying relevant student interests, teachers may find it difficult to relate these interests to the curriculum, in ways that increase the students' involvement as well as help achieve instructional goals. This takes much work. But teachers who know what individual lows like and dislike about school in particular and life in general have taken a major step in helping them to become more involved in school work.

Breaking Down Tasks into Specific, Small Steps

Lows who have been overwhelmed academically and who have well-developed failure expectations may not respond when the teacher allows them to pursue topics of personal interests, even if the teacher spends a great deal of time with them. Teachers need to initially gauge the responsiveness of lows when they begin to work with them, because some lows have been turned off by too much structure in the past and what they need is a chance to structure their own learning experiences, to pursue topics of interest, and to share with a teacher something that they are very interested in.

However, it is important to be aware of the fact that many lows perform slowly because even tasks that they are highly interested in may appear so complex to them that *they do not know where to begin.* Most lows benefit from direct teacher assistance in learning how to structure their work (how to organize a library search, how to limit a theme topic). If teachers are to break patterns of habitual failure, they must help these students set short-term goals that can be accomplished in a very short period of time, allowing students to develop "can do" attitudes, experience success, and gradually become addicted to learning. Besides helping these students to develop realistic, appropriate short-term goals, teachers should give them frequent and specific feedback about their progress toward these goals. Once this approach has begun to succeed, teachers can gradually increase the scope and complexity of goals and allow the student to assume more responsibility for structuring and evaluating learning progress. Many lows, but not all, will benefit from specific help in learning how to structure and attack learning problems in a step-by-step fashion. Marion Blank has written an especially useful book describing how teachers can break down childrens' resistance and respond to childrens' failure (Blank, 1973).

Spending More Classroom Time with Low Achievers

The material presented so far suggests implicitly that teachers should spend more time with lows than they presently do. Now we specifically and explicitly suggest that teachers in general need to spend more *classroom time* with lows than any other group of students. Stress has been placed upon the words *classroom time*, because although highs also need teacher consideration of their unique needs, much of this can be accomplished (especially in the older grades) through out-of-class teacher planning. Such planning needs to focus on developing sequences of instructional experiences that allow highs to develop increased capacity for independent study and self-evaluation. Because of their greater skills (and usually greater confidence and better motivation), highs can learn independently if teachers plan appropriate assignments and prepare necessary resource materials. Obviously, highs need and benefit from some direct supervision, feedback, and stimulation from teachers. But highs need less teacher aid than lows, and, if properly structured, increased opportunity for individual learning will foster, not restrict, their development. Lows need more direct instructional time than highs, and teachers should not feel guilty when they give lows the increased attention and time that they require. Teachers need to develop strategies for individualizing instruction so that the needs of highs and lows are met.

Setting Classroom Goals for Optimal Teaching of Both Highs and Lows

Teachers' decisions about organizing the classroom for learning can be pervasive. Classrooms are often dominated by group instructional activities. We acknowledged previously that there are many occasions when this is an appropriate strategy, but often it is not. Teachers who regularly instruct the class as a whole run several risks: that none of the unique interests of individual pupils are being satisfied; that the instructional pace is too fast or too slow for many students; and that instructional techniques are inappropriate for certain students.

We argue that teachers are more likely to interact with students in desirable ways if they break down the classroom structure and work mainly with individuals or small groups of students, allowing other students to work independently, in small groups, or to engage in peer tutoring activities. Clearly students need to know how to behave in such environments, and we have described techniques for implementing a small-group learning model within the limitations of a self-contained classroom elsewhere (Good and Brophy, 1973).

The expression of this plan is based upon the assumption that time spent in relevant task activity enhances achievement (Bloom, 1973; Carroll, 1963). Teaching the class as a class guarantees that in some instances students will be engaged in activities that they are not ready for or have already mastered. Such circumstances depress the learning progress of all students and lows particularly. Further, we suspect that school related affective feelings of students are largely tied to the amount of time they are engaged in challenging and respectable but manageable tasks.

However the model itself does not guarantee success. Teachers who do not rotate from learning station to learning station or who do not develop systematic strategies for updating learning centers and providing students incisive feedback about their individual work will fail to motivate many of their students. Again, we cannot guarantee this model or any model as *the* way to proceed. But we can say that a method that makes limited use of whole class instruction, coupled with frequent use of learning groups, independent study, and peer techniques can free the teacher to have time to deal with individual students.

Each teacher has to set realistic goals in his own setting. The teacher who has but three out of twenty students reading below grade level faces a different decision than does the teacher who has sixteen out of forty reading below grade level. In one case the teacher can give ample individual attention to lows without much risk of neglecting better students.

In the latter situation, the teacher will probably have to group students who share similar problems (no public speaking skills) or interests (advanced geological topics) and try not to lose contact with individuals in remedial or enrichment groups. Here teachers would need to survey regularly student progress and student interest to see if needs are being met. Obviously, feedback must be used to see if highs or lows are losing interest, and teachers may have to establish priorities when they do not have time to deal with all problems.

We do not ask teachers to create new problems (for example, indifference to highs) by dealing with problems that now have high salience. But we do feel that sensitive teachers can enhance the life in classrooms for lows without reducing it for highs. Indeed we see the two as highly interrelated. If teachers are to find time for lows they must involve highs in self-exploratory work and enlist them as instructional helpers from time to time.

Even if teachers can learn to monitor their own expectations, identify the interests of lows, use those interests in planning curricular activities, and structure the classroom so that they can spend more time with lows, two other major problems must be solved before lows can grow in the classroom.

Emphasizing Instructional Help, Not Sympathy

Sympathy alone is misplaced and self-defeating. Teachers who give easier tests to lows, who always ask them elementary questions, or who give up on them in public-response situations do not help and often worsen their plight.

Kleinfeld (1972) presented a penetrating ethnographic analysis of teacher behavior with Indian and Eskimo students experiencing cultural shock when moving from rural to urban schools, showing that sympathy alone was not enough to help these students. She found that the most effective teachers were those who took a personal interest in students, engaged in informal conversations with them, adapted instruction to their different backgrounds and achievement levels, and were highly supportive of student attempts to learn (avoided the use of criticism). From her observations the most effective teachers *first* established rapport with the students and *then* communicated an "active demand" to them. Teachers who failed to establish rapport with students (started with task focus) or who did not demand performance from lows were ineffective with these students.

In summary, she concluded:

the essence of the instructional style which elicits a high level of intellectual performance from village Indian and Eskimo students is to create an extremely warm personal relationship and to actively demand a level of academic work which the student does not suspect he can attain. Village students thus interpret the teacher's demandingness not as bossiness or hostility, but rather as another expression of his personal concern, and meeting the teacher's academic standards becomes their reciprocal obligation in an intensely personal relationship (Kleinfeld, 1972. p. 34).

Stephens (1967) reached similar conclusions, arguing that it is more important that the teacher be taken seriously and respected than be loved or admired.

Students need help to become academically more self-sufficient and need to be held accountable for their learning. They do not need sentimental behavior that protects them from failure so completely that they do not have a chance to develop their skills and abilities.

Creating an Appropriate Classroom Climate

Teachers have to *legitimize* the aid that they provide to lows, or else the lows (and other students, too) will interpret increased teacher attention as a sign that lows are hopelessly lost. This problem is quite complex, and although general suggestions can be made, teachers have to work out strategies that mesh with their personality and the characteristics of the students they teach. Kleinfeld, for example, argued that one way to reduce the debilitating effects of special attention to lows is to individualize much of classroom instruction so that teachers have periodic individual contacts with all students. In such environments more frequent and extended contacts with lows seem less out of place.

Some research has suggested that other students openly direct hostility toward lows, and that the process begins at an early age (Henry, 1957; Rist, 1970). Perhaps the best way that teachers can reduce student hostility and invidious comparisons is to *focus upon individual progress rather than relative progress.* Students should be taught to focus on their own progress over time (for example, looking at their handwriting in September and May, not comparing their work with another student's), so that the classroom norm becomes "do better than yesterday," rather than "outperform George." This is a difficult task to accomplish, because students (and teachers) are used to measuring their worth on a comparative basis with others. Nevertheless, if students are truly to grow in the classroom they must gain interest and skills in self-growth and self-evaluation. Obviously teachers who allow for individual assignments (students draw one of thirty objects, not the same one) will have an easier time inculcating interest in mastery rather than competition. As previously stated, it is important for teachers to become concerned about the process of learning, not just about learning products.

In summary, teachers need to create a credible environment where they can give lows the *initial* help they need and where all students can pursue important topics of special interest. If credibility is not established, teacher behavior toward lows, no matter how appropriate, will not help them and may convince them and other students that they are hopelessly incompetent. To establish a credible environment, teachers must communicate a respect for individual learning speeds and interests.

Enabling Low Achievers to Achieve Public Success and Recognition

As suggested in the preceding section, teachers must be aware of how other students feel about and treat lows. In the early grades the teacher may be able to influence the student's self-concept and achievement simply by dealing with the individual student more appropriately. As the student becomes older, the problem increases in difficulty. At older age levels the student's behavior is controlled by peer expectations and the communication of those expectations. Students who expect poor performance from a peer may behave in ways that make it more likely that the student will fail. When a low goes to the board to do a math problem, he may be accompanied by a chorus of hushed but distinguishable giggles. The shy, reticent student who does not respond immediately when called upon may automatically receive reactions of irritation from classmates or "Jane never has anything interesting to say" glances.

Teachers who create classroom climates that stress a basic respect for individual differences will minimize such distractions; however, inferior status may still be assigned to lows in subtle ways that keep their confidence low and their motivation eroded despite teacher attempts to work with them.

Teachers can help lows to achieve more self-respect and respect from classmates if they allow them to achieve notable *public* success from time to time. Doing this successfully involves much planning and work, for trivial or unsuccessful exposure of lows may deepen the problem. Public success is important and worth planning for, though. As we have previously noted, most of the successes of lows are private ones but most of their failures occur in public situations.

As a case in point, consider the shy, reticent student who seldom talks in class. Although there is typically no reason to try to make these students highly verbal, most will benefit from a few well-planned public successes. However, such a student must develop some skill or ability that he *demonstrates* if he is to become convinced and to convince others of his personal worth. Sympathy and public exposure do not work, but skill development and exposure may work, especially if the skill is one which other students value or wish they had.

Often teachers can use unique talents that students already possess (developing prints) or can capitalize upon the life styles of individual students (Kleinfeld, for example, reported that some teachers were able to increase the prestige of village students and reduce hostility toward them by making their skills such as "surviving in the wilderness" public knowledge). At other times, teachers will need to work with students for long periods of time to help them learn skills (for example, teaching a fifth-grade student how to run a projector, or allowing him to make a movie). Once the students have learned the skills, they can be allowed to demonstrate them publicly (showing a popular film and teaching the class how to run the machine). Repeated public successes involving such skills, especially those deemed important by the peer group, will do much to raise the self-respect of lows and the esteem with which they are regarded by their classmates.

Emphasizing Learning Sets in Early Grades

As we suggested earlier in the chapter, we are presenting our opinions, not data, in this chapter and much of our opinion is based upon hours of observation in elementary classrooms and interviews with teachers, as well as the data we have presented in this book. Such observations have led us to conclude that too much emphasis in schools is placed upon mastering the curriculum, *especially in early grades,* and too little emphasis has been placed upon helping students to develop appropriate learning sets. Of prime importance is that students learn to expect that they can achieve, to approach the teacher and to ask a question when they do not understand an explanation or an assignment, to understand that the classroom is a place where they can find answers to their own questions at times, and to understand that evaluation is simply feedback guiding future efforts, not personal ratings of one's value. Unfortunately we know that too many students learn quickly that they cannot achieve, that their behavior is controlled by external forces, that it is better to feign knowledge than to call for help when they need it, and that evaluation is not helpful feedback but a threat to their individual worth. Too much emphasis is placed on child achievement on standardized tests and too little emphasis upon the mastery of general coping skills. More attention and higher priorities need to be attached to the need for helping students to develop more favorable sets toward school and learning. Certainly there is a need for instruments and coding inventories that would allow "set behaviors" to be coded and there is great need for teachers, especially kindergarten and first-grade teachers, to place more emphasis upon helping students to develop school-related coping behaviors. These skills we believe are more important than short-term achievement in content areas.

SUMMARY

In this chapter we have argued that teachers are basically reactive in the class, largely allowing existing differences in students to unfold in the classroom. It has been suggested that the teacher's failure to intervene or to be more proactive in the classroom guarantees that the potential of certain students will remain untapped.

Note has been made of the fact that teachers should behave differently toward different students. However, it has been emphasized that observed differences in teacher behavior with high and low achieving students often do not make instructional sense.

Suggestions were made that unrealistically high or low expectations are self-defeating, and teachers were urged to develop appropriate expectations by carefully monitoring the day-to-day behavior of their students. Mention was also made of the fact that no set of teaching behaviors is universally effective, and that teachers cannot rely on formulas to dictate their behavior, but they must assess the appropriateness of their behavior with regard to how it affects student performance.

It was also argued that teachers need to pay close attention to the general coping behavior of students. Stress was placed on the teacher's role in helping students to develop confidence in themselves and to develop an openness to learning. Such openness and receptivity to seeking feedback and needed information would be in marked contrast to the defensiveness that many learners presently develop.

Thus in summary we have suggested if teachers are to help lows they must:

1. Become more aware of their own behaviors and biases and reject information that suggests children cannot learn ipso facto.
2. Possess and communicate positive expectations (enthusiasm for learning, and so on).
3. Take time to know students as individuals and allow student interests to influence curricular activities.
4. Organize classroom activities, so that they have time to interact with and establish appropriate goals for individuals or small groups of students.
5. Monitor the progress of all students regularly and adjust classroom schedules, so that major problems can be dealt with.
6. Develop specialized skills to help lows to accept teacher interest as credible, to overcome *institutionalized* resistance strategies, and to become more adept at setting personal goals and evaluating performance.
7. Provide an instructional climate wherein real demands are placed upon lows, so that other students can see their visible progress.

References

Abbott, L. Some effects of masculine influence on boys during the kindergarten and first grade. Unpublished Ed.D. dissertation, Colorado State College, 1968.

Adams, R., & Biddle, B. *Realities of teaching: Explorations with videotape.* New York: Holt, Rinehart and Winston, 1970.

Alexander, L., Elsom, B., Means, R., & Means, G. Achievement as a function of teacher initiated student-teacher personal interaction. Paper presented at the annual meeting of the Southwestern Psychological Association, 1971.

Ames, C., & Ames, R. Teachers' attributions of responsibility for student success and failure following informational feedback: A field verification. Paper presented at the annual meeting of the American Educational Research Association, 1973.

Ames, R. Teacher's attributions of responsibility. Unpublished doctoral dissertation, Indiana University, 1973.

Amidon, E., & Flanders, N. The effects of direct and indirect teacher influence on dependent-prone students learning geometry. *Journal of Educational Psychology,* 1961, *52,* 286–291.

Anderson, D., and Rosenthal, R. Some effects of interpersonal expectancy and social interaction on institutionalized retarded children. *Procedings of the 76th Annual Convention of the American Psychological Association,* 1968, *3,* 479–480.

Anderson, H., Brewer, J., & Reed, M. Studies of teachers' classroom personalities. III. Follow-up studies of the effects of dominative and integrative contacts on children's behavior. *Applied Psychology Monograph,* 1946, *II.*

Anderson, R. Learning in discussions: A resume of the authoritarian-democratic studies. *Harvard Educational Review*, 1959, *29*, 201–215.

Antes, J., Anderson, D., & De Vault, M. Elementary pupil's perceptions of the social–emotional environment of the classroom. *Psychology in the Schools*, 1965, *2*, 41–46.

Arnold, R. The achievements of boys and girls taught by men and women teachers. *Elementary School Journal*, 1968, *68*, 367–371.

Artley, A. Reading instruction and cognitive development. *Elementary School Journal*, 1972, *72*, 203–211.

Asch, S. Forming impressions of personality. *Journal of Abnormal and Social Psychology*, 1946, *41*, 258–290.

Asher, S., & Gottman, J. Sex of teacher and student reading achievement. Paper presented at the annual meeting of the American Educational Research Association, 1972.

Asher, S., & Markell, R. Influence of interest on sex differences in reading comprehension. Paper presented at the annual meeting of the American Educational Research Association, 1973.

Austin, D., Clark, V., & Fitchett, G. *Reading rights for boys*. New York: Appleton-Century-Crofts, 1971.

Ayres, L. *Laggards in our schools*. New York: Russell Sage Foundation, 1909.

Babad, E. Effects of learning potential and teacher expectancies in classes for the retarded: or,: The punishing expectancies. *Studies in learning potential*. Cambridge: Research Institute for Educational Problems, 1971, *2*, 1–21.

Baird, L. Teaching styles: An exploratory study of dimensions and effects. *Journal of Educational Psychology*, 1973, *64*, 15–21.

Baker, E. Parents, teachers, and students as data sources for the selection of instructional goals. *American Educational Research Journal*, 1972, *9*, 403–411.

Baldwin, T., Johnson, T., & Wiley, D. The teacher's perception and attribution of causation. Paper presented at the annual meeting of the American Educational Research Association, 1970.

Bales, R. *Interaction process analysis: a method for the study of small groups*. Reading, Massachusetts: Addison-Wesley, 1950.

Barclay, J., Stilwell, W., Santoro, D., & Clark, C. Correlates of behavioral observations and academic achievement with elementary patterns of social interaction. Paper presented at the annual meeting of the American Educational Research Association, 1972.

Barker, Lunn, J. *Streaming in the primary school*. Slough, Great Britain: NFER, 1970.

Barnard, J., Zimbardo, P., & Sarason, S. Teachers' ratings of student personality traits as they relate to IQ and social desirability. *Journal of Educational Psychology*, 1968, *59*, 128–132.

Battle, E. Motivational determinants of academic task persistence. *Journal of Personality and Social Psychology*, 1965, *2*, 209–218.

Battle, H. Application of inverted analysis in a study of the relation between values and achievement of high school pupils. Unpublished doctoral dissertation, University of Chicago, 1954.

Becker, H. Social-class variations in the teacher–pupil relationship. *Journal of Educational Sociology*, 1952, *25*, 451–465.

Beckman, L. Effects of students' performance on teachers' and observers' attributions of causality. *Journal of Educational Psychology*, 1970, *61*, 76–82.

Beckman, L. Teachers' and observers' perception of causality for a child's performance. Final Report, Grant No. OEG-9-70-0065-0-I-031, HEW, Office of Education, 1972.

Beez, W. Influence of biased psychological reports on teacher behavior and pupil performance. *Proceedings of the 76th Annual Convention of the American Psychological Association*, 1968, *3*, 605–606.

Beigel, A., & Feshbach, N. A comparative study of student teacher, teacher corps, and undergraduate preferences for elementary school pupils. Paper presented at the annual meeting of the California Educational Research Association, 1970.

Bellack, A., Kliebard, H., Hyman, R., & Smith, F. *The language of the classroom*. New York: Teachers College Press, 1966.

Bennett, D. A comparison of the achievement of fifth grade pupils having male teachers with those having female teachers. *Dissertation Abstracts*, 1967, *27*, 12A, 4032–4033.

Bereiter, C., Washington, E., Engelmann, S., & Osborn, J. Final Report, OE Contract 6-10-235, Project No. 5-1181: Research and development programs on preschool disadvantaged children. U.S. Department of Health, Education, and Welfare, Office of Education, Bureau of Research, 1969.

Biber, H., Miller, L., & Dyer, J. Feminization in preschool. *Developmental Psychology*, 1972, *7*, 86.

Biddle, S., & Moore, J. The effects of prior conditioning to expectancy statements on persistence and persistence of attention. Paper presented at the annual meeting of the American Educational Research Association, 1973.

Blank, M. *Teaching Learning*. Columbus, Ohio: Charles Merrill, 1973.

Blitz, A., & Smith, T. Personality characteristics and performance in computer-assisted instruction and programmed text. Paper presented at the annual meeting of the American Educational Research Association, 1973.

Blom, G. Sex differences in reading disability. In E. Calkins (Ed.) *Reading forum: A collection of reference papers concerned with reading disability*. NINDS Monograph No. 11, U.S. Department of Health, Education, and Welfare, 1971.

Bloom, B. Learning for mastery. *Evaluation Comment*, 1968, *1*, No. 2.

Bloom, B. An introduction to mastery learning theory. Paper presented at the annual meeting of the American Educational Research Association, 1973.

Bradley, R., & Gaa, J. An investigation of domain specific aspects of locus of control. Unpublished manuscript, The University of North Carolina, 1973.

Branan, J. Negative human interaction. *Journal of Counseling Psychology*, 1972, *19*, 81–82.

Brandt, L. Differential response patterns of adults in a teaching situation as a function of motivation and performance levels of children. Unpublished doctoral dissertation, University of Arizona, 1971.

Brophy, J. Mothers as teachers of their own preschool children: The influence of socioeconomic status and task structure on teaching specificity. *Child Development*, 1970, *41*, 79–94.

Brophy, J. Stability of teacher effectiveness. *American Educational Research Journal*, 1973, *10*, 245–252.

Brophy, J., Evertson, C., Harris, T., & Good, T. Communication of teacher expectations: Fifth grade. Report No. 93, Research and Development Center for Teacher Education, The University of Texas at Austin, 1973.

Brophy, J., & Good, T. Teachers' communication of differential expectations for children's classroom performance: Some behavioral data. *Journal of Educational Psychology*, 1970a, *61*, 365–374.

Brophy, J., & Good, T. Brophy-Good System (Teacher-Child Dyadic Interaction). In A.

Simon and E. Boyer (Eds.), *Mirrors for behavior: An anthology of observation instruments continued, 1970 supplement. Volume A*. Philadelphia: Research for Better Schools, Inc., 1970b.

Brophy, J., & Laosa, L. Effect of a male teacher on the sex typing of kindergarten children. *Proceedings of the 79th Annual Convention of The American Psychological Association*, 1971, 169–170.

Brown, G. *Teacher-pupil interaction as a function of socioeconomic status and ethnic group membership of teachers and pupils*. Unpublished master's thesis, The University of Texas at Austin, 1969.

Brown, W. The influence of student information on the formulation of teacher expectancy. *Dissertation Abstracts*, 1970, *30*, 4822-A.

Burnham, J. *Effects of experimenter's expectancies on children's abilities to learn to swim*. Unpublished master's thesis, Purdue University, 1968.

Burstall, C. *French from eight: A national experiment*. Slough, Great Britain: NFER, 1968.

Byers, P., & Byers, H. Non-verbal communication in the education of children. In C. Cazden, V. John, and D. Hymes (Eds.), *Functions of language in the classroom*. New York: Teachers College Press, 1972.

Cahen, L. An experimental manipulation of the halo effect. Unpublished doctoral dissertation, Stanford University, 1966.

Carbonari, J. An investigation of relationships among instructional mode, teacher needs, and students' personalities. Paper presented at the annual meeting of the American Educational Research Association, 1973.

Carroll, J. A model of school learning. *Teachers College Record*, 1963, *64*, 723–733.

Carter, R. How invalid are marks assigned by teachers? *Journal of Educational Psychology*, 1952, *43*, 218–228.

Carter, R. *Locus of control and teacher's expectancy as related to achievement of young school children*. Unpublished doctoral dissertation, Indiana University, 1969.

Chaikin, A., Sigler, E., & Derlega, V. Non-verbal mediators of teacher expectancy effects. Unpublished manuscript, Old Dominion University, 1972.

Chansky, N. The attitudes students assign to their teacher. *Journal of Educational Psychology*, 1958, *49*, 13–16.

Chase, C. The impact of some obvious variables on essay test scores. *Journal of Educational Measurement*, 1968, *5*, 315–318.

Claiborn, W. Expectancy effects in the classroom: A failure to replicate. *Journal of Educational Psychology*, 1969, *60*, 377–383.

Clapp, R. The relationship of teacher sex to fifth grade boys' achievement gains and attitudes toward school. Unpublished doctoral dissertation, Stanford University, 1967.

Claunch, N. Cognitive and motivational characteristics associated with concrete and abstract levels of conceptual complexity. Unpublished doctoral dissertation, Princeton University, 1964.

Clifford, M., & Walster, E. The effect of physical attractiveness on teacher expectation. Mimeographed research report, The University of Minnesota, 1971.

Coates, B. White adult behavior toward black and white children. *Child Development*, 1972, *43*, 143–154.

Coates, C. Harvey, O., & White, B. Teachers' beliefs, classroom atmosphere, and student behavior: A replication and refinement. Paper presented at the annual meeting of the American Educational Research Association, 1970.

Conn. L., Edwards, C., Rosenthal, R., & Crowne, D. Perception of emotion and response to teachers' expectancy by elementary school children. *Psychological Reports,* 1968, *22,* 27–34.

Cornbleth, C., Davis, O., & Button, C. Teacher-pupil interaction and teacher expectations for pupil achievement in secondary social studies classes. Paper presented at the annual meeting of the American Educational Research Association, 1972.

Cosper, W. An analysis of sex differences in teacher-student interaction as manifest in verbal and nonverbal behavior cues. Unpublished Ed.D. dissertation, The University of Tennessee, 1970.

Covington, M., & Jacoby, K. Work habits, achievement, and course satisfaction as a function of an independence-conformity dimension. Paper presented at the annual meeting of the Western Psychological Association, 1972.

Crandall, V., Katkovsky, W., & Preston, A. Motivational and ability determinants of children's intellectual achievement behaviors. *Child Development,* 1962, *33,* 643–661.

Crawford, R., Elliott, A., & Johanson, M. Evaluation of the SIRS project at Orangethorpe School. Unpublished research, Fullerton, California School District, 1972 (cited in Stanchfield, 1973).

Dahlöff, U. *Ability grouping: Content validity and curriculum process analysis.* New York: Teachers College Press, 1971.

Dalton, W. The relations between classroom interaction and teacher ratings of pupils: An explanation of one means by which a teacher may communicate her expectancies. *Peabody Papers in Human Development,* 1969, *7,* No. 6.

Datta, L., Schaefer, E., & Davis, M. Sex and scholastic aptitude as variables in teachers' ratings of the adjustment and classroom behavior of Negro and other seventh-grade students. *Journal of Educational Psychology,* 1968, *59,* 94–101.

Daum, J. Proxemics in the classroom: Speaker-subject distance and educational performance. Paper presented at the annual meeting of the Southeastern Psychological Association, 1972.

Davidson, H., & Lang, G. Children's perceptions of their teachers' feelings toward them related to self-perception, school achievement, and behavior. *Jounal of Experimental Education,* 1960, *29,* 107–118.

Davis, A., & Dollard, J. *Children of bondage.* Washington, D.C.: American Council on Education, 1940.

Davis, D., & Levine, G. The behavioral manifestations of teachers' expectations. Unpublished manuscript, Hebrew University of Jerusalem, 1970.

Davis, O., & Slobodian, J. Teacher behavior toward boys and girls during first grade reading instruction. *American Educational Research Journal,* 1967, *4,* 261–269.

de Charms, R. The making of pawns in the classroom. Paper presented at the annual meeting of the American Psychological Association, 1970.

de Groat, A., & Thompson, G. A study of the distribution of teacher approval and disapproval among sixth-grade pupils. *Journal of Experimental Education,* 1949, *18,* 57–75.

Delefes, P., & Jackson, B. Teacher-pupil interaction as a function of location in the classroom. *Psychology in the Schools,* 1972, *9,* 119–123.

Della Piana, G., & Gage, N. Pupils' values and the validity of the Minnesota Teacher Attitude Inventory. *Journal of Educational Psychology,* 1955, *46,* 167–178.

Dion, K. Social desirability and the evaluation of a harm-doer. Unpublished doctoral dissertation, University of Minnesota, 1970.

Dion, K., Berscheid, E., & Walster, E. What is beautiful is good. *Journal of Personality and Social Psychology,* 1972, *24,* 285–290.

Douglas, J. *The home and the school*. London: MacGibbon and Kee, 1964.

Dowaliby, F., & Schumer, H. Teacher-centered versus student-centered mode of college classroom instruction as related to manifest anxiety. *Journal of Educational Psychology*, 1973, *64*, 125–132.

Doyle, W., Hancock, G., & Kifer, E. Teachers' perceptions: Do they make a difference? *Journal of the Association for the Study of Perception*, 1972, *7*, Fall, 21–30.

Dreeben, R. School as a work place. In R. Travers (Ed.). *Handbook of Research on Teaching*. (2nd ed.) Chicago: Rand McNally, 1973.

Duel, H. Effect of periodical self-evaluation on student achievement. *Journal of Educational Psychology*, 1958, *49*, 197–199.

Dunkin, M., & Biddle, B. *The study of teaching*. New York: Holt, Rinehart and Winston, 1974.

Dusek, J. Experimenter-bias effects on the simple motor task performance of low- and high-test anxious boys and girls. *Psychological Reports*, 1972, *30*, 107–114.

Dyk, R., & Witkin, H. Family experiences related to the development of differentiation in children. *Child Development*, 1965, *36*, 21–55.

Dykstra, R. Continuation of the coordinating center for first grade reading instruction programs. Final Report, Project No. 6-1651, Office of Education, Bureau of Research, U.S. Department of Health, Education, and Welfare, September, 1967.

Edmiston, R. Do teachers show partiality? *Peabody Journal of Education*, 1943, *20*, 234–238.

Ehman, L. A comparison of three sources of classroom data: Teachers, students, and systematic observation. Paper presented at the annual meeting of the American Educational Research Association, 1970.

Elashoff, J., & Snow, R. *Pygmalion reconsidered*. Worthington, Ohio: Charles A. Jones, 1971.

Emmer, E. The effects of teacher use of student ideas on student verbal initiation. Unpublished doctoral dissertation, University of Michigan, 1967.

Emmer, E., Good, T., & Oakland, T. Effect of feedback expectancy on choice of teaching styles. *Journal of Educational Psychology*, 1971, *62*, 451–455.

Emmer, E., Good, T., & Pilgrim, G. Effects of teacher set. Paper presented at the annual meeting of the American Educational Research Association, 1972.

Entwisle, D. Expectations in mixed racial groups of children. Paper presented at the annual meeting of the American Educational Research Association, 1973.

Entwisle, D., & Webster, M. Raising children's performance expectations. *Social Science Research*, 1972, *1*, 147–158.

Entwistle, N. Personality and academic attainment. *British Journal of Educational Psychology*, 1972, *42*, 137–151.

Etaugh, C., & Harlow, H. School attitudes and performance of elementary school children as related to teacher's sex and behavior. Paper presented at the biennial meeting of the Society for Research in Child Development, 1973.

Evans, J., & Rosenthal, R. Interpersonal self-fulfilling prophecies: Further extrapolations from the laboratory to the classroom. *Proceedings of the 77th Annual Convention of the American Psychological Association*, 1969, *4*(1), 371–372.

Evertson, C., Brophy, J., & Good, T. Communication of teacher expectations: First grade. Report No. 91, Research and Development Center for Teacher Education, The University of Texas at Austin, 1972.

Evertson, C., Brophy, J., & Good, T. Communication of teacher expectations: Second grade. Report No. 92, Research and Development Center for Teacher Education, The University of Texas at Austin, 1973.

Fagot, B., & Patterson, G. An *in vivo* analysis of reinforcing contingencies for sex-role behaviors in the preschool child. *Developmental Psychology*, 1969, *1*, 563–568.

Feitler, F., Wiener, W., & Blumberg, A. The relationship between interpersonal relations and preferred classroom physical settings. Paper presented at the annual meeting of the American Educational Research Association, 1970.

Feldman, R., & Allen, V. Effect of tutee's performance on tutor's attitudes and attribution. *Proceedings of the 80th Annual Convention of the American Psychological Association,* 1972, 519–520.

Feldman, R., & Allen, V. Effects of temporal factors on ability attributions in a tutoring situation. Paper presented at the annual meeting of the American Educational Research Association, 1973.

Felsenthal, H. Sex differences in teacher-pupil interaction in first grade reading instruction. Paper presented at the meeting of the American Educational Research Association, 1970.

Feshbach, N. Variations in teachers' reinforcement style and imitative behavior of children differing in personality characteristics and social backgrounds. CSEIP Technical Report No. 2, The University of California at Los Angeles, 1967.

Feshbach, N. Student teacher preferences for elementary school pupils varying in personality characteristics. *Journal of Educational Psychology*, 1969, *60*, 126–132.

Fiedler, F. The trouble with leadership training is that it doesn't train leaders. *Psychology Today*, 1973, *6* (No. 9), 23–26, 29–30, 92.

Fielder, W., Cohen, R., & Feeney, S. An attempt to replicate the teacher expectancy effect. *Psychological Reports*, 1971, *29*, 1223–1228.

Finn, J. Expectations and the educational environment. *Review of Educational Research*, 1972, *42*, 387–410.

Flanders, N. *Analyzing teaching behavior*. Reading, Massachusetts: Addison-Wesley, 1970.

Flanders, N., & Havumaki, S. The effect of teacher-pupil contacts involving praise on the sociometric choices of students. *Journal of Educational Psychology*, 1960, *51*, 65–68.

Fleming, E., & Anttonen, R. Teacher expectancy or My Fair Lady. *American Educational Research Journal*, 1971, *8*, 241–252.

Fletcher, J., & Atkinson, R. Evaluation of the Stanford CAI program in initial reading. *Journal of Educational Psychology*, 1972, *63*, 597–602.

Flowers, C. Effects of an arbitrary accelerated group placement on the tested academic achievement of educationally disadvantaged students. *Dissertation Abstracts,* 1966, *27*, 991-A.

Flowers, J., & Marston, A. Modification of low self-confidence in elementary school children. *Journal of Educational Research*, 1972, *66*, 30–34.

Fox, D. *Expansion of the more effective school program*. New York: The Center for Urban Education, 1967.

Frank, J. *Persuasion and healing*. New York: Schocken Books, 1963.

Frender, R., Brown, B., & Lambert, W. The role of speech characteristics in scholastic success. *Canadian Journal of Behavioral Science*, 1970, *2*, 299–306.

Friedman, H., & Friedman, P. Frequency and types of teacher reinforcement given to lower- and middle-class students. Paper presented at the annual meeting of the American Educational Research Association, 1973.

Fuller, F. Concerns of teachers: A developmental conceptualization. *American Educational Research Journal*, 1969, *6*, 207–226.

Gabbert, B. The influence of pupil socio-economic status on teacher behavior. Unpublished doctoral dissertation, The University of Texas at Austin, 1973.

Gage, N., Runkel, J., & Chatterjee, B. Equilibrium theory and behavior change: An experiment in feedback from pupils to teachers. Bureau of Educational Research, Urbana, Illinois, 1960.

Gagné, E., & Biddle, W. The cue value of adult expectancy. Paper presented at the annual meeting of the American Educational Research Association, 1973.

Garner, C. Survey of teachers' marks. *School and Community*, 1935, *21*, 116–117.

Garner, J., & Bing, M. Teacher-pupil contacts: An empirical typology. *Research in Education,* 1973a, in press.

Garner, J., & Bing, M. The elusiveness of Pygmalion and differences in teacher-pupil contacts. *Interchange,* 1973b, *4* (No. 1), 34–42.

Gates, A. Sex differences in reading ability. *Elementary School Journal*, 1961, *61*, 431–434.

Getzels, J., & Jackson, P. *Creativity and Intelligence.* New York: John Wiley & Sons, 1962.

Glasser, W. *Schools without failure.* New York: Harper & Row, 1969.

Glick, O. Some social-emotional consequences of early inadequate acquisition of reading skills. *Journal of Educational Psychology*, 1972, *63*, 253–257.

Goldberg, M., Passow, A., & Justman, J. *The effects of ability grouping.* New York: Teachers College Press, 1966.

Goldenberg, I. Social class differences in teacher attitudes toward children. *Child Development*, 1971, *42*, 1637–1640.

Goldsmith, J., & Fry, E. The test of a high expectancy prediction on reading achievements and IQ of students in grade 10 (or, Pygmalion in puberty). 1970 research report summarized in Elashoff and Snow, 1971.

Good, T. Which pupils do teachers call on? *Elementary School Journal*, 1970, *70*, 190–198.

Good, T. Stability of teacher attitudes in secondary classrooms: Some behavioral data. Technical Report No. 63, Center for Research in Social Behavior, University of Missouri at Columbia, 1972.

Good, T., & Brophy, J. Teacher-child dyadic interactions: A new method of classroom observation. *Journal of School Psychology*, 1970, *8*, 131–138.

Good, T., & Brophy, J. Analyzing classroom interaction: A more powerful alternative. *Educational Technology*, 1971a, *11*, 36–41.

Good, T., & Brophy, J. Questioned equality for grade one boys and girls. *The Reading Teacher*, 1971b, *25*, 247–252.

Good, T., & Brophy, J. Behavioral expression of teacher attitudes. *Journal of Educational Psychology*, 1972a, *63*, 617–624.

Good, T., & Brophy, J. Changing teacher & student behavior: An empirical investigation. Technical Report No. 58, Center for Research in Social Behavior, University of Missouri at Columbia, 1972b.

Good, T., & Brophy, J. *Looking in classrooms.* New York: Harper & Row, 1973.

Good, T., & Dembo, M. Teacher expectations: Self-report data. *School Review*, 1973, *81*, 247–253.

Good, T., & Grouws, D. Reaction of male and female teacher trainees to descriptions of elementary school pupils. Technical Report No. 62, Center for Research in Social Behavior, University of Missouri at Columbia, 1972.

Good, T., & Grouws, D. *Multiple criteria of teacher effectiveness.* NIE project FD 3-2834, 1973 (in progress).

Good, T., & Limbacher, P. Stability of student teachers' attitudes toward students. Technical Report No. 84, Center for Research in Social Behavior, University of Missouri at Columbia, 1973.

Good, T., Schmidt, L., Peck, R., & Williams, D. Listening to teachers. Report Series No. 34, Research and Development Center for Teacher Education, The University of Texas at Austin, 1969.

Good, T., Sikes, J., & Brophy, J. Effects of teacher sex, student sex, and student achievement on classroom interaction. Technical Report No. 61, Center for Research in Social Behavior, University of Missouri at Columbia, 1972.

Goodacre, E. *Teachers and their pupils' home background.* London: NFER, 1967.

Goodwin, W., & Sanders, J. An exploratory study of the effect of selected variables upon teacher expectation of pupil success. Paper presented at the annual meeting of the American Educational Research Association, 1969.

Gordon, E. Taking into account musical aptitude difference among beginning instrumental students. *American Educational Research Journal,* 1970, *7,* 41–53.

Graf, R., & Riddell, J. Sex differences in problem-solving as a function of problem context. *Journal of Educational Research,* 1972, *65,* 451–452.

Greeley Public Schools. *Greeley's all-boy program: C.N. Jackson Elementary School.* Greeley, Colorado: Greeley Public Schools, Department of Instruction, 1969.

Greenberg, S., & Peck, L. An experimental curriculum designed to modify children's sex role perceptions and aspiration levels. Paper presented at the annual meeting of the American Educational Research Association, 1973.

Gregersen, G., & Travers, R. A study of the child's concept of the teacher. *Journal of Educational Research,* 1968, *61,* 324–327.

Griffin, J. Influence strategies: theory and research. A study of teacher behavior. Unpublished doctoral dissertation, The University of Missouri at Columbia, 1972.

Grimes, J., & Allinsmith, W. Compulsivity, anxiety, and school achievement. *Merrill-Palmer Quarterly,* 1961, *7,* 247–271.

Gronlund, N. The accuracy of teachers' judgments concerning the sociometric status of sixth-grade pupils. *Sociometry,* 1950, *13,* 197–225, 329–357.

Gurin, G., & Gurin, P. Expectancy theory in the study of poverty. *Journal of Social Issues,* 1970, *26,* 83–104.

Guskin, J. The social perception of language variations: Black dialect and expectations of ability. Paper presented at the annual meeting of the American Educational Research Association, 1970.

Guskin, S. Role perception in teaching and learning. Reprint 11.4, *Viewpoints* (Bulletin of the School of Education, Indiana University), 1971, *47,* No. 4.

Hadley, S. A school mark—fact or fancy? *Educational Administration and Supervision,* 1954, *40,* 305–312.

Halpin, G., & Goldenberg, R. Relationships between measures of creativity and pupil control ideology. Paper presented at the annual meeting of the American Educational Research Association, 1973.

Hamachek, D. Effects of early school failure on self-image development and implications for school counselors. Paper presented at the annual meeting of the American Educational Research Association, 1972.

Hamachek, D. Self-concept theory and research: Implications for school counselors. Paper presented at the annual meeting of the American Educational Research Association, 1973.

Harvey, O., Hunt, D., & Schroder, H. *Conceptual systems and personality organization.* New York: John Wiley & Sons, 1961.

Harvey, O., Prather, M., White, B. & Hoffmeister J. Teachers' beliefs, classroom atmosphere, and student behavior. *American Educational Research Journal,* 1968, *5*, 151–166.

Harvey, O., White, B., Prather, M., Alter, R., & Hoffmeister, J. Teachers' belief systems and preschool atmospheres. *Journal of Educational Psychology,* 1966, *57*, 373–381.

Hawkes, T. Teacher expectations and friendship patterns in the elementary classroom. In M. Silberman (Ed.), *The experience of schooling.* New York: Holt, Rinehart and Winston, 1971.

Heapy, N., & Siess, T. Behavioral consequences of impression formation: Effects of teachers' impressions upon essay evaluations. Paper presented at the annual meeting of the Eastern Psychological Association, 1970.

Heil, L., Powell, M., & Feifer, I. *Characteristics of teacher behavior related to the achievement of children in several elementary grades.* Washington: HEW, Office of Education, Cooperative Research Branch, 1960.

Helton, G. Teacher attitudinal response to selected characteristics of elementary school students. Unpublished doctoral dissertation, University of Texas at Austin, 1972.

Henry, J. Attitude organization in elementary school classrooms. *American Journal of Orthopsychiatry,* 1957, *27*, 117–133.

Herrell, J. Galatea in the classroom: Student expectations affect teacher behavior. Paper presented at the annual meeting of the American Psychological Association, 1971.

Hersh, J. Effects of referral information on testers. *Journal of Consulting and Clinical Psychology,* 1971, *37*, 116–122.

Hess, R., Shipman, V., Brophy, J., & Bear, R. (in collaboration with A. Adelberger). *The cognitive environments of urban preschool children: Follow-up phase.* Chicago: Graduate School of Education, University of Chicago, 1969 (mimeo final report).

Hoehn, A. A study of social status differentiation in the classroom behavior of 19 third grade teachers. *Journal of Social Psychology,* 1954, *39*, 269–292.

Horn, E. *Distribution of opportunity for participation among the various pupils in the classroom recitations.* New York: Teachers College, Columbia University, 1914.

Hoyt, K. A study of the effects of teacher knowledge of pupil characteristics on pupil achievement and attitudes towards classwork. *Journal of Educational Psychology,* 1955, *46*, 302–310.

Huck, S., & Bounds, W. Essay grades: An interaction between graders' handwriting clarity and the neatness of examination papers. *American Educational Research Journal,* 1972, *9*, 279–283.

Hudgins, B. *The instructional process.* New York: Rand McNally, 1971.

Hughes, D. An experimental investigation of the effects of pupil responding and teacher reacting on pupil achievement. *American Educational Research Journal,* 1973, *10*, 21–37.

Hunt, D. *Matching models in education: The coordination of teaching methods with student characteristics.* Toronto: Ontario Institute for Studies in Education, Monograph Series No. 10, 1971.

Hunt, D., & Hardt, R. *Characterization of 1966 summer Upward Bound programs.* Syracuse: Youth Development Center, Syracuse University, 1967.

Husén, T. (Ed.) *International study of achievement in mathematics: A comparison of twelve countries* (2 volumes). Stockholm: Almqvist and Wiksell, 1967.

Husén, T., & Svennson, N. Pedagogic milieu and development of intellectual skills. *School Review*, 1960, *68*, 36–51.

Jackson, P. Teacher-pupil communication in the elementary classroom: An observational study. Paper presented at the annual meeting of the American Educational Research Association, 1965.

Jackson, P. *Life in classrooms.* New York: Holt, Rinehart and Winston, 1968.

Jackson, P. After apple-picking. *Harvard Educational Review*, 1973, *43*, 51–60.

Jackson, P., & Lahaderne, H. Inequalities of teacher-pupil contacts. *Psychology in the Schools*, 1967, *4*, 204–211.

Jackson, P., Silberman, M., & Wolfson, B. Signs of personal involvement in teachers' descriptions of their students. *Journal of Educational Psychology*, 1969, *60*, 22–27.

Jacobs, J., & De Graaf, C. Expectancy and race: Their influences upon the scoring of individual intelligence tests. Paper presented at the annual meetings of the American Educational Research Association, 1973.

Jacobs, J., & Richard, W. Teacher expectancies: Their effect on peer acceptance. Paper presented at the annual meeting of the American Educational Research Association, 1970.

James, N. Personal preference for method as a factor in learning. *Journal of Educational Psychology*, 1962, *53*, 43–47.

Jansen, M., Jensen, P., & Mylov, P. Teacher characteristics and other factors affecting classroom interaction and teaching behaviour. *International Review of Education*, 1972, *18*, 529–540.

Jecker, J., Maccoby, N., Breitrose, H., & Rose, E. Teacher accuracy in assessing cognitive visual feedback from students. *Journal of Applied Psychology*, 1964, *48*, 393–397.

Jenkins, B. Teachers' views of particular students and their behavior in the classroom. Unpublished doctoral dissertation, The University of Chicago, 1972.

Jenkins, J., & Deno, S. Influence of student behavior on teachers' self-evaluation. *Journal of Educational Psychology*, 1969, *60*, 439–442.

Jensen, A. How much can we boost IQ and scholastic achievement? *Harvard Educational Review*, 1969, *39*, 1–123.

Jersild, A., Goldman, B., Jersild, C., & Loftus, J. Studies of elementary school classes in action: Pupil participation and aspects of pupil–teacher relationships. *Journal of Experimental Education*, 1941, *10*, 119–137.

Jeter, J., & Davis, O. Elementary school teachers' differential classroom interaction with children as a function of differential expectations of pupil achievements. Paper presented at the annual meeting of the American Educational Research Association, 1973.

Johnson, D. An investigation of sex differences in reading in four English-speaking nations. Technical Report No. 209, Research and Development Center for Cognitive Learning, The University of Wisconsin, 1972.

Johnson, D. *The social psychology of education.* New York: Holt, Rinehart and Winston, 1970.

Johnson, R. Subject performance as affected by experimenter expectancy, sex of experimenter, and verbal reinforcement. *Canadian Journal of Behavioral Science*, 1970, *2*, 60–66.

Johnson, T., Feigenbaum, R., & Weiby, M. Some determinants and consequences of the teacher's perception of causation. *Journal of Educational Psychology*, 1964, *55*, 237–246.

Jones, V. The influence of teacher-student introversion, achievement, and similarity on teacher-student dyadic classroom interactions. Unpublished doctoral dissertation, University of Texas at Austin, 1971.

José, J., & Cody, J. Teacher-pupil interaction as it relates to attempted changes in teacher expectancy of academic ability and achievement. *American Educational Research Journal*, 1971, *8*, 39–49.

Joyce, C., & Hudson, L. Student style and teacher style: An experimental study. *British Journal of Medical Education*, 1968, *2*, 28–32.

Kagan, J. The child's sex role classification of school objects. *Child Development*, 1964, *35*, 1051–1056.

Kagan, J. Personality and intellectual development in the school age child. In I. Janis (Ed.), *Personality: Dynamics, development, and assessment*. New York: Harcourt Brace Jovanovich, 1969.

Kaplan, L. The annoyances of elementary school teachers. *Journal of Educational Research*, 1952, *45*, 649–665.

Katz, L. Developmental stages of preschool teachers. *Elementary School Journal*, 1972, *73*, 50–54.

Katz, M. Attitudinal modernity, classroom power and status characteristics: An investigation. Paper presented at the annual meeting of the American Educational Research Association, 1973.

Kelley, H. The warm–cold variable in first impressions of people. *Journal of Personality*, 1950, *18*, 431–439.

Kellogg, R. A direct approach to sex-role identification of school-related objects. *Psychological Reports*, 1969, *24*, 839–841.

Kelly, E. A study of consistent discrepancies between instructor grades and term-end examination grades. *Journal of Educational Psychology*, 1958, *49*, 328–334.

Kernkamp, E., & Price, E. Coeducation may be a no-no for the six year old boy. *Phi Delta Kappan*, 1972, *53*, 662–663.

Kester, S., & Letchworth, G. Communication of teacher expectations and their effects on achievement and attitudes of secondary school students. *The Journal of Educational Research*, 1972, *66*, 51–55.

King, A. Managerial relations with disadvantaged work groups: Supervisory expectations of the underprivileged worker. Unpublished doctoral dissertation, Texas Tech University, 1970.

King, A. Self-fulfilling prophecies in training the hard core: Supervisors' expectations and the underprivileged worker's performance. *Social Science Quarterly*, 1971, *52*, 369–378.

Klein, S. Student influence on teacher behavior. *American Educational Research Journal*, 1971, *8*, 403–421.

Kleinfeld, J. Instructional style and the intellectual performance of Indian and Eskimo students. Final Report, Project No. 1-J-027, Office of Education, U.S. Department of Health, Education, and Welfare, 1972.

Konski, V. An investigation into differences between boys and girls in selected reading readiness areas and in reading achievement. Unpublished doctoral dissertation, University of Missouri, 1951.

Kounin, J. *Discipline and group management in classrooms*. New York: Holt, Rinehart and Winston, 1970.

Kozol, J. *Death at an early age*. Boston: Houghton Mifflin, 1967.

Kranz, P., & Tyo, A. Do teachers' perception of pupils affect their behavior toward those pupils? Unpublished manuscript, Millersville State College, 1973.

Kranz, P., Weber, W., & Fishell, K. The relationships between teacher perception of pupils and teacher behavior toward those pupils. Paper presented at the annual meeting of the American Educational Research Association, 1970.

Kremer, B. The adjective check list as an indicator of teachers' stereotypes of students. Unpublished doctoral dissertation, Michigan State University, 1965.

Lahaderne, H., & Cohen, S. Freedom and fairness: A comparison of male and female teachers in elementary classrooms. Paper presented at the annual meeting of the American Educational Research Association, 1972.

Lahaderne, H., & Jackson, P. Withdrawal in the classroom: A note on some educational correlates of social desirability among school children. *Journal of Educational Psychology*, 1970, *61*, 97–101.

Lambert, W. Unpublished data, 1968. (cited in Blom, 1971).

Lanzetta, J., & Hannah, T. Reinforcing behavior of "naive" trainers. *Journal of Personality and Social Psychology*, 1969, *11*, 245–252.

Larrabee, L., & Kleinsasser, L. The effect of experimenter bias on WISC performance. Unpublished manuscript, Psychological Associates, St. Louis, 1967.

Leacock, E. *Teaching and learning in city schools*. New York: Basic Books, 1969.

Lehman, H., & Witty, P. Sex differences in reference to reading books, just for fun. *Education*, 1928, *48*, 602–617.

Leipold, L. Students do have favorite teachers. *The Clearing House*, 1959, *34*, 240–241.

Lesser, G. Matching instruction to student characteristics. In G. Lesser (Ed), *Psychology and educational practice*. Glenview, Illinois: Scott, Foresman and Company, 1971.

Levitin, T., & Chananie, J. Responses of female primary school teachers to sex-typed behaviors in male and female children. *Child Development*, 1972, *43*, 1309–1316.

Lewin, K., Lippitt, R., & White, R. Patterns of aggressive behavior in experimentally created "social climates." *Journal of Social Psychology*, 1939, *10*, 271–299.

Lightfoot, S. An ethnographic study of the status structure of the classroom. Unpublished doctoral dissertation, Harvard University, 1972.

Lindzey, G., & Byrne, D. Measurement of social choice and interpersonal attractiveness. In G. Lindzey and E. Aronson (Eds.), *Handbook of social psychology*. (2nd ed.) Volume II. Reading, Massachusetts: Addison-Wesley, 1968.

Lippitt, R., & Gold, M. Classroom social structure as a mental health problem. *Journal of Social Issues*, 1959, *15*, 40–49.

Long, B. & Henderson, E. Teacher judgments of classroom behavior of Negro and White school beginners. Paper presented at the annual meeting of the American Educational Research Association, 1970.

Long, B., & Henderson, E. The effects of pupils' race, class, test scores, and classroom behavior on the academic expectancies of southern and nonsouthern white teachers. Paper presented at the annual meeting of the American Educational Research Association, 1972.

Lortie, D. Observations on teaching as work. In R. Travers (Ed.), *Handbook of Research on Teaching*, (2nd ed.) Chicago: Rand McNally, 1973.

Lotzoff, E. Reinforcement value as related to decision time. *Journal of Psychology*, 1956, *41*, 427–435.

Lundgren, U. *Frame factors and the teaching process: A contribution to curriculum theory and theory on teaching.* Stockholm: Almqvist and Wiksell, 1972.

Lyles, T. Grouping by sex. *The National Elementary Principal*, 1966, *46*, No. 2, 38–41.

Maccoby, E. *The development of sex differences.* Stanford, California: Stanford University Press, 1966.

Mackler, B. Grouping in the ghetto. *Education and Urban Society*, 1969, *2*, 80–96.

Marlowe, D., & Gergen, K. Personality and social interaction. In G. Lindzey and E. Aronson (Eds.), *Handbook of social psychology*, (2nd ed.) Volume III. Reading, Massachusetts: Addison-Wesley, 1969.

Marquart, D. The pattern of punishment and its relation to abnormal fixation in adult human subjects. *Journal of General Psychology*. 1948, *39*, 107–144.

Martin, R. Student sex and behavior as determinants of the type and frequency of teacher-student contacts. *Journal of School Psychology*, 1972, *10*, 339–347.

Mason, E. Teachers' observations and expectations of boys and girls as influenced by biased psychological reports and knowledge of the effects of bias. *Journal of Educational Psychology*, 1973, *65*, 238–243.

Mayhew, D. An attribution theory approach to teacher expectancy effects: the manipulation of teacher attributions of student and self causality for success and failure. Unpublished doctoral dissertation, The University of California at Los Angeles, 1972.

McCandless, B., Roberts, A., & Starnes, T. Teachers' marks, achievement test scores, and aptitude relations with respect to social class, race, and sex. *Journal of Educational Psychology*, 1972, *63*, 153–159.

McCracken, J. Sex typing of reading by boys attending all male classes. *Developmental Psychology*, 1973, *8*, 148.

McDonald, C. The influence of pupil liking of teacher, pupil perception of being liked, and pupil socio-economic status on classroom behavior. Unpublished doctoral dissertation, University of Texas at Austin, 1972.

McFarland, W. Are girls really smarter? *Elementary School Journal*, 1969, *70*, (October) 14–19.

McKeachie, W. Students, groups, and teaching methods. *The American Psychologist*, 1958, *13*, 580–584.

McKeachie, W., & Lin, Y. Sex differences in student responses to college teachers: Teacher warmth and teacher sex. *American Educational Research Journal*, 1971, *8*, 221–226.

McKeachie, W., Lin, Y., & Mann, W. Student ratings of teacher effectiveness: Validity studies. *American Educational Research Journal*, 1971, *8*, 435–445.

McNeil, J. Programmed instruction versus usual classroom procedures in teaching boys to read. *American Educational Research Journal*, 1964, *1*, 113–119.

McNeil, J. *Toward accountable teachers: Their appraisal and improvement.* New York: Holt, Rinehart and Winston, 1971.

Means, G., Means, R., Castleman, J., & Elsom, B. Verbal participation as a function of the presence of prior information concerning aptitude. *California Journal of Educational Research*, 1971, *22*, 58–63.

Means, R., & Means, G. Achievement as a function of the presence of prior information concerning aptitude. *Journal of Educational Psychology*, 1971, *62*, 185–187.

Medinnus, G. An examination of several correlates of sociometric status in a first grade group. *Journal of Genetic Psychology*, 1962, *101*, 3–13.

Medinnus, G., & Unruh, R. Teacher expectations and verbal communication. Paper presented at the annual meeting of the Western Psychological Association, 1971.

Medley, D. The language of teacher behavior. In R. Burkhart (Ed.). *The assessment revolution: New viewpoints for teacher evaluation.* Buffalo: New York State Education Department and Buffalo State University College, 1969.

Meeker, M. Individualized curriculum based on intelligence patterns. In R. Coop and K. White (Eds.). *Psychological Concepts in the Classroom.* New York: Harper & Row, 1973.

Meichenbaum, D. The nature and modification of impulsive children: Training impulsive children to talk to themselves. Waterloo, Ontario: Research report No. 23, University of Waterloo, Department of Psychology, 1971.

Meichenbaum, D., Bowers, K., & Ross, R. A behavioral analysis of teacher expectancy effect. *Journal of Personality and Social Psychology,* 1969, *13,* 306–316.

Meichenbaum, D., & Smart, I. Use of direct expectancy to modify academic performance and attitudes of college students. *Journal of Counseling Psychology,* 1971, *18,* 531–535.

Mendoza, S., Good, T., & Brophy, J. Who talks in junior high classrooms? Report Series No. 68, Research and Development Center for Teacher Education, The University of Texas at Austin, 1972.

Merton, R. The self-fulfilling prophecy. *Antioch Review,* 1948, *8,* 193–210.

Meyer, W., & Lindstrom, D. *The distribution of teacher approval and disapproval of Head Start children.* U.S. Office of Economic Opportunity, Contract No. OEO-4120, 1969.

Meyer, W., & Thompson, G. Sex differences in the distribution of teacher approval and disapproval among sixth-grade children. *Journal of Educational Psychology,* 1956, *47,* 385–396.

Middleman, R. An experimental field study of the impact of nonverbal communication of affect on children from two socio-economic backgrounds. Paper presented at the annual meeting of the American Educational Research Association, 1972.

Miller, C., McLaughlin, J., Haddon, J., & Chansky, N. Socio-economic class and teacher bias. *Psychological Reports,* 1968, *23,* 806.

Milton, G. Five studies of the relation between sex role identification and achievement in problem solving. Technical Report No. 3, Department of Psychology, Yale University, 1958.

Moore, J., Gagné, E., & Hauck, W. Conditions moderating the self-fulfilling prophecy phenomenon. Paper presented at the annual meeting of the American Educational Research Association, 1973.

Moore, J., Means, V., & Gagné, E. Expectancy statements in meaningful classroom learning. Paper presented at the annual meeting of the American Educational Research Association, 1973.

Morrison, A., & McIntyre, D. *Teachers and teaching.* Baltimore: Penguin Books, 1969.

Murphy, P., & Brown, M. Conceptual systems and teaching styles. *American Educational Research Journal,* 1970, *7,* 529–540.

Murray, H., Herling, G., & Staebler, B. The effects of locus of control and pattern of performance on teacher's evaluation of a student. Paper presented at the annual convention of the American Psychological Association, 1972.

Naremore, R. Teacher differences in attitudes toward children's speech characteristics. Paper presented at the annual meeting of the American Educational Research Association, 1970.

Ojemann, R., & Wilkinson, F. The effect on pupil growth of an increase in teacher's understanding of pupil behavior. *Journal of Experimental Education,* 1939, *8,* 143–147.

Opdyke, J., & Williams, R. The effects of expectancy bias on perceptual motor learning in retardates. Unpublished manuscript, University of Southern Illinois, 1972.

Oppenlander, L. The relative influence of the group of pupils and of the teacher as determinants of classroom interaction. Paper presented at the annual meeting of the American Educational Research Association, 1969.

Ostfeld, B., & Katz, P. The effect of threat severity in children of varying socioeconomic levels. *Developmental Psychology*, 1969, *1*, 205–210.

Oswald, R., & Broadbent, F. Conceptual level as a determinant of teacher behavior and attitudes in a non-structured type learning activity. Paper presented at the annual meeting of the American Educational Research Association, 1972.

Page, S. Social interaction and experimenter effects in the verbal conditioning experiment. *Canadian Journal of Psychology*, 1971, *25*, 463–475.

Palardy, J. What teachers believe—what children achieve. *Elementary School Journal*, 1969, *69*, 370–374.

Panda, K., & Guskin, S. Effect of social reinforcement, locus of control, and cognitive style on concept learning among retarded children. Annual Report, Center for Educational Research and Development for Handicapped Children, Indiana University, 1970.

Peck, R. A cross-national comparison of sex and socio-economic differences in aptitude and achievement. Paper presented at the annual meeting of the American Educational Research Association, 1971.

Peck, R., & Tucker, J. Research on teacher education. In R. Travers (Ed.), *Handbook of research on teaching*. (2nd ed.). New York: Rand McNally, 1973.

Pellegrini, R., & Hicks, R. Prophecy effects and tutorial instruction for the disadvantaged child. *American Educational Research Journal*, 1972, *9*, 413–419.

Peterson, J. Effects of sex of E and sex of S in the first and fifth grade children's paired-associate learning. *The Journal of Educational Research*, 1972, *66*, 81–84.

Phillips, M., & Sinclair, R. Conceptual systems and educational environment: Relationships between teacher conceptual systems, student conceptual systems, and classroom environment as perceived by fifth- and sixth-grade students. Paper presented at the annual meeting of the American Educational Research Association, 1973.

Pidgeon, D. *Expectation and pupil performance*. Slough, Great Britain: NFER, 1970.

Pitt, C. An experimental study of the effects of teachers' knowledge or incorrect knowledge of pupil I.Q.'s on teachers' attitudes and practices and pupils' attitudes and achievement. *Dissertation Abstracts*, 1956, *16*, 2387–2388.

Poggio, J. An alternative to ability grouping: Personality grouping. Paper presented at the annual meeting of the American Educational Research Association, 1973.

Pohl, R., & Pervin, L. Academic performance as a function of task requirements and cognitive style. *Psychological Reports*, 1968, *22*, 1017–1020.

Portuges, S., & Feshbach, N. The influence of sex and socioethnic factors upon imitation of teachers by elementary schoolchildren. *Child Development*, 1972, *43*, 981–989.

Power, C. The effects of communication patterns on student sociometric status, attitudes, and achievement in science. Unpublished doctoral dissertation, University of Queensland, 1971.

Preston, R. Reading achievement of German and American children. *School and Society*, 1962, *90*, 350–354.

Price, E., & Rosemier, R. Some cognitive and affective outcomes of same-sex versus coeducational grouping in first grade. *Journal of Experimental Education*, 1972, *40*, 70–77.

Putnins, B. Teacher behavior and awareness of classroom social structure. Unpublished doctoral dissertation, Indiana State University, 1970.

Quirk, T. An experimental investigation of the teacher's attribution of the locus of causality of student performance. *Dissertation Abstracts,* 1967/1968, *28,* 2565-A.

Rexford, G., Willower, D., & Lynch, P. Teachers' pupil control ideology and classroom verbal behavior. *Journal of Experimental Education,* 1972, *40,* No. 4, 78–82.

Ring, A. First-grade boys will be boys. *The Instructor,* 1970, *80,* (December) 51.

Rist, R. Student social class and teacher expectations: The self-fulfilling prophecy in ghetto education. *Harvard Educational Review,* 1970, *40,* 411–451.

Rosenfeld, H., & Zander, A. The influence of teachers on aspirations of students. *Journal of Educational Psychology,* 1961, *52,* 1–11.

Rosenshine, B. Enthusiastic teaching: A research review. *School Review,* 1970, *78,* 499–514.

Rosenshine, B. *Teaching behaviours and student achievement.* London: NFER, 1971.

Rosenshine, B., & Furst, N. Research on teacher performance criteria. In B. Smith (Ed.). *Research in teacher education: a symposium.* Englewood Cliffs, New Jersey: Prentice-Hall, 1971.

Rosenthal, R., & Jacobson, L. *Pygmalion in the classroom: Teacher expectation and pupils' intellectual development.* New York: Holt, Rinehart and Winston, 1968.

Rosenthal, R., & Rubin, D. Appendix C: Pygmalion reaffirmed. In J. Elashoff and R. Snow. *Pygmalion reconsidered.* Belmont, California: Wadsworth Publishing Co., 1971.

Rothbart, M., Dalfen, S., & Barrett, R. Effects of teacher's expectancy on student-teacher interaction. *Journal of Educational Psychology,* 1971, *62,* 49–54.

Rotter, J. Generalized expectancies for internal versus external control of reinforcement. *Psychological Monographs,* 1966, *80,* (Whole No. 609).

Rowe, M. Science, silence, and sanctions. *Science and Children,* 1969, *6,* 11–13.

Rowe, M. Wait-time and rewards as instructional variables: Their influence on language, logic, and fate control. Paper presented at the annual meeting of the National Association for Research in Science Teaching, 1972.

Rubin, L. A study on teaching style. Paper presented at the annual meeting of the American Educational Research Association, 1971.

Rubovits, P., & Maehr, M. Pygmalion analyzed: Toward an explanation of the Rosenthal-Jacobson findings. *Journal of Personality and Social Psychology,* 1971, *19,* 197–203.

Rubovits, P., & Maehr, M. Pygmalion black and white. *Journal of Personality and Social Psychology,* 1973, *25,* 210–218.

Sarason, S., et al. *Anxiety in elementary school children: A report of research.* New York: John Wiley & Sons, 1960.

Sarbin, T., & Allen, V. Increasing participation in a natural group setting: A preliminary report. *Psychological Record,* 1968, *18,* 1–7.

Schmuck, R. Some relationships of peer liking patterns in the classroom to pupil attitudes and achievements. *School Review,* 1963, *71,* 337–359.

Schrank, W. The labeling effect of ability grouping. *Journal of Educational Research,* 1968, *62,* 51–52.

Schrank, W. A further study of the labeling effects of ability grouping. *Journal of Educational Research,* 1970, *63,* 358–360.

Schultz, C., & Dangel, T. The effects of recitation on the retention of two personality types. *American Educational Research Journal,* 1972, *9,* 421–430.

Schwebel, A., & Cherlin, D. Physical and social distancing in teacher-pupil relationships. *Journal of Educational Psychology,* 1972, *63,* 543–550.

Sears, P. *The effect of classroom conditions on the strength of achievement motive and work output of elementary school children.* Washington: HEW Cooperative Research Project No. OE873, 1963.

Sears, P., & Hilgard, E. The teacher's role in the motivation of the learner. In *Theories of learning and instruction.* Sixty-third Yearbook of the National Society for the Study of Education, Part I, 1964.

Seaver, W. Effects of naturally induced expectancies on the academic performances of pupils in primary grades. Unpublished doctoral dissertation, The University of Illinois, 1971.

Securro, S., & Walls, R. Strategies for increasing self-initiated verbal interaction. Paper presented at the annual meeting of the American Educational Research Association, 1972.

Seligman, C., Tucker, G., & Lambert, W. The effects of speech style and other attributes on teachers' attitudes toward pupils. *Language in Society,* 1972, *1,* 131–142.

Serbin, L., O'Leary, K., Kent, R., and Tonick, I. A comparison of teacher response to the preacademic and problem behavior of boys and girls. *Child Development,* 1973, *44,* 796–804.

Sexton, P. *The feminized male: classrooms, white collars and the decline of manliness.* New York: Random House, 1969.

Shinedling, M., & Pedersen, D. Effects of sex of teacher and student on children's gain in quantitative and verbal performance. *The Journal of Psychology,* 1970, *76,* 79–84.

Shore, A. Confirmation of expectancy and changes in teachers' evaluations of student behaviors. *Dissertation Abtsracts,* 1969, *30,* 1878–1879-A

Sikes, J. Differential behavior of male and female teachers with male and female students. Unpublished doctoral dissertation, The University of Texas at Austin, 1971.

Silberman, M. Behavioral expression of teachers' attitudes toward elementary school students. *Journal of Educational Psychology,* 1969, *60,* 402–407.

Silberman, M. Teachers' attitudes and actions towards their students. In M. Silberman (Ed.), *The experience of schooling.* New York: Holt, Rinehart and Winston, 1971.

Simon, A., & Boyer, E. (Eds.) *Mirrors for behavior: An anthology of classroom observation instruments.* Philadelphia: Research for Better Schools, Inc., 1967.

Simon, J., & Feather, N. Causal attributions for success and failure at university examinations. *Journal of Educational Psychology,* 1973, *64,* 46–56.

Simon, W. Expectancy effects in the scoring of vocabulary items: A study of scorer bias. *Journal of Educational Measurement.* 1969, *6,* 159–164.

Smith, D. Fit teaching methods to personality structure. *High School Journal,* 1955, *39,* 167–171.

Smith, D. A study of the relationship of teacher sex to fifth grade boys' sex preference, general self concept, and scholastic achievement in science and mathematics. Unpublished Ed.D. dissertation, The University of Miami, 1970.

Smith, M. Interpersonal relationships in the classroom based on the expected socio-economic status of sixth grade boys. *The Teachers College Journal,* 1965, *36,* 200–206.

Snow, R. Unfinished Pygmalion. *Contemporary Psychology,* 1969, *14,* 197–199.

Solomon, D., & Oberlander, M. Locus of control and education. In R. Coop and K. White (Eds.), *Psychological Concepts in the Classroom.* New York: Harper & Row, 1973.

Spaulding, R. *Achievement, creativity, and self-concept correlates of teacher-pupil transactions in elementary schools.* Cooperative Research Project No. 1352, U.S. Department of Health, Education, and Welfare, Office of Education, 1963.

Spector, P. The communication of expectancies: The interaction of reinforcement and expectancy instructions. Unpublished manuscript, Washington University of St. Louis, 1973.

Sperry, L. Learning performance and individual differences: Perspective. In Sperry, L. (Ed.), *Learning performance and individual differences.* Glenview, Illinois: Scott, Foresman and Company, 1972.

Sperry, L. (Ed.) *Learning performance and individual differences.* Glenview, Illinois: Scott, Foresman and Company, 1972.

St. John, C. The maladjustment of boys in certain elementary grades. *Educational Administration and Supervision,* 1932, *18,* 659–672.

St. John, N. Thirty-six teachers: Their characteristics, and outcomes for black and white pupils. *American Educational Research Journal,* 1971, *8,* 635–648.

Stanchfield, J. Differences in learning patterns of boys and girls. Paper presented at the meeting of the International Reading Association, 1969.

Stanchfield, J. *Sex differences in learning to read.* Bloomington, Indiana: Phi Delta Kappa Educational Foundation, 1973.

Stasz, C., Weinberg, S., & McDonald, F. The influence of sex of student and sex of teacher on students' achievement and evaluation of the teacher. Paper presented at the annual meeting of the American Educational Research Association, 1973.

Stein, A. The effects of sex-role standards for achievement and sex-role preference on three determinants of achievement motivation. *Developmental Psychology,* 1971, *4,* 219–231.

Stein, A., Pohly, S., & Mueller, E. Sex typing of achievement areas as a determinant of children's motivation and effort. Paper presented at the meeting of the Society for Research in Child Development, 1969.

Stein, A., & Smithells, J. Age and sex differences in children's sex-role standards about achievement. *Developmental Psychology,* 1969, *1,* 252–259.

Stephens, J. *The process of schooling: A psychological examination.* New York: Holt, Rinehart and Winston, 1967.

Strickler, R., & Phillips, C. Kindergarten success story. *The Instructor,* 1970, *80,* (December) 50–51.

Stroud, J., & Lindquist, E. Sex differences in achievement in the elementary and secondary schools. *Journal of Educational Psychology,* 1942, *33,* 657–667.

Sweely, H. The effect of the male elementary teacher on children's self-concepts. Paper presented at the annual meeting of the American Educational Research Association, 1970.

Tagatz, G. Grouping by sex at the first and second grade. *Journal of Educational Research,* 1966, *59,* 415–418.

Taylor, C. The expectations of Pygmalion's creators. *Educational Leadership,* 1970, *28,* 161–164.

Taylor, M. Intercorrelations among three methods of estimating student attention. Report Series No. 39, Stanford Research and Development Center, 1968.

Taylor, P., Christie, T., & Platts, C. An exploratory study of science teachers' perceptions of effective teaching. *Educational Review,* 1970, *23,* 19–32.

Thelen, H. Matching teachers and pupils. *National Education Association Journal,* 1967, *56*(4), 18–20.

Thorndike, R. Review of Pygmalion in the classroom. *American Educational Research Journal,* 1968, *5,* 708–711.

Thrash, S., & Hapkiewicz, W. Student characteristics associated with success in a mastery learning strategy. Paper presented at the annual meeting of the American Educational Research Association, 1973.

Tilton, J. An experimental effort to change the achievement test profile. *Journal of Experimental Education*, 1947, *15*, 318–322.

Tobias, S. Preference for instructional method and achievement. Paper presented at the annual meeting of the Eastern Psychological Association, 1972.

Tomlinson, P., & Hunt, D. The differential effectiveness of three teaching strategies for students of high and low conceptual levels. Paper presented at the annual meeting of the American Educational Research Association, 1970.

Tuckman, B. Study of the interactive effects of teaching style and student personality. *Proceedings of the 77th annual convention, American Psychological Association*, 1969.

Tuckman, B., & Bierman, M. Beyond Pygmalion: Galatea in the schools. Paper presented at the annual meeting of the American Educational Research Association, 1971.

Tuckman, B., Cochran, D., & Travers, E. Evaluating the open classroom. Paper presented at the annual meeting of the American Educational Research Association, 1973.

Tuckman, B., McCall, K., & Hyman, R. The modification of teacher behavior: Effects of dissonance and coded feedback. *American Educational Research Journal*, 1969, *6*, 607–619.

Tuckman, B., & Oliver, W. Effectiveness of feedback to teachers as a function of source. *Journal of Educational Psychology*, 1968, *59*, 297–301.

Turnure, J., & Samuels, S. Attention and reading achievement in first grade boys and girls. Research Report No. 43, Research, Development and Demonstration Center in Education of Handicapped Children, The University of Minnesota, 1972.

Tyler, B. Expectancy for eventual success as a factor in problem solving behavior. *Journal of Educational Psychology*, 1958, *49*, 166–172.

Tyler, R. Investing in better schools. In K. Gordon (Ed.), *Agenda for the nation*. Garden City, New Jersey: Doubleday, 1969.

Tyo, A., & Kranz, P. A study of the verbal behavior patterns of teachers in interaction with migrant and non-migrant pupils. Unpublished manuscript, Millersville State College, 1973.

Veldman, D. Adjective self-description. Research Methodology Monograph No. 11, Research & Development Center for Teacher Education, The University of Texas at Austin, 1970.

Veldman, D. Scale structure of "Your School Days." Preliminary manuscript, Project Prime, Bureau for the Education of the Handicapped, USOE, 1973.

Veldman, D., & Peck, R. The influence of teacher and pupil sex on pupil evaluations of student teachers. *Journal of Teacher Education*, 1964, *15*, 393–396.

Waetjen, W. Is learning sexless? *Education Digest*, 1962, *28*, 12–14.

Walberg, H. Physical and psychological distance in the classroom. *School Review*, 1969, *77*, 64–70.

Walberg, H., Welch, W., & Rothman, A. Teacher heterosexuality and student learning. *Psychology in the Schools*, 1969, *6*, 258–266.

Wartenberg-Ekren, U. The effect of experimenter knowledge of a subject's scholastic standing on the performance of a reasoning task. Unpublished master's thesis, Marquette University, 1962 (cited in Rosenthal and Jacobson, 1968).

Welch, W., & Walberg, H. A national experiment in curriculum evaluation. *American Educational Research Journal*, 1972, *9*, 373–383.

Williams, D., Schmidt, L., Good, T., & Peck, R. Consultation: Helping schools to cope. Mimeographed report, Research and Development Center for Teacher Education, The University of Texas at Austin, 1970.

Williams, F., Whitehead, J., & Miller, L. Relations between language attitudes and teacher expectancy. *American Educational Research Journal*, 1972, *9*, 263–277.

Williamson, R. *An investigation of the sex of the teacher as an influence on the learning abilities of kindergarten children.* Unpublished master's thesis, The University of Texas at Austin, 1970.

Willis, B. The influence of teacher expectation on teachers' classroom interaction with selected children. *Dissertation Abstracts*, 1970, *30*, 5072-A.

Willis, S. *Formation of teachers' expectations of students' academic performance.* Unpublished doctoral dissertation, The University of Texas at Austin, 1972.

Willis, S., & Brophy, J. The origins of teachers' attitudes towards young children. *Journal of Educational Psychology*, 1974, in press.

Wilson, J. *The effects of academic feedback on teachers and pupils in the primary school.* Unpublished master's thesis, University of Edinburgh, 1969.

Wisenthal, M. Unpublished studies, 1968. (cited in Blom, 1971).

Wispé, L. Evaluating section teaching methods in the introductory course. *Journal of Educational Research*, 1951, *45*, 161–186.

Withall, J. An objective measurement of a teacher's classroom interactions. *Journal of Educational Psychology*, 1956, *47*, 203–212.

Wolfson, B., & Nash, S. Perceptions of decision-making in elementary-school classrooms. *Elementary School Journal*, 1968, *69*, 89–93.

Yamamoto, K. A further analysis of the role of creative thinking in high school achievement. *Journal of Psychology*, 1964, *58*, 277–283.

Yando, R., & Kagan, J. The effect of teacher tempo on the child. *Child Development*, 1968, *39*, 27–34.

Yarrow, M., Waxler, C., & Scott, P. Child effects on adult behavior. *Developmental Psychology*, 1971, *5*, 300–311.

Ycas, M., & Pascal, C. Convergent, divergent, and esthetic ability and bias in college students: Their relation to personality and preference for major subject and instructional method. Paper presented at the annual meeting of the American Educational Research Association, 1973.

Yee, A. Do cooperating teachers influence the attitudes of student teachers? *Journal of Educational Psychology*, 1969, *60*, 327–332.

Yee, A. Interpersonal attitudes of teachers and advantaged and disadvantaged pupils. *Journal of Human Resources*, 1968, *3*, 327–345.

Zajonc, R., & Brickman, P. Expectancy and feedback as independent factors in task performance. *Journal of Personality and Social Psychology*, 1969, *11*, 148–156.

Zussman, D., & Pascal, C. The interaction of divergence and convergence of students and teachers with personality and instructional variables affecting educational outcomes. Paper presented at the annual meeting of the American Educational Research Association, 1973.